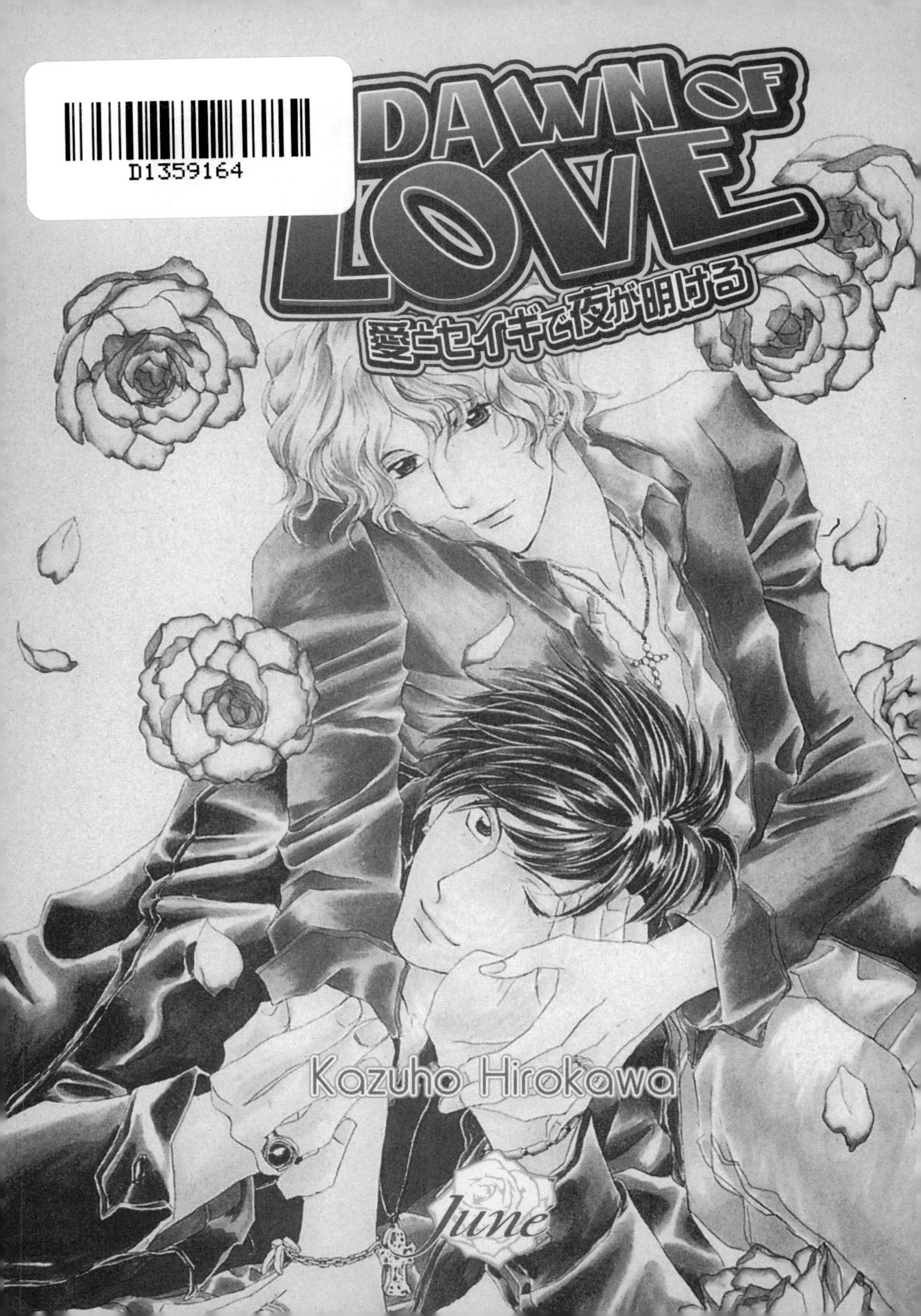
DAWN OF LOVE
愛とセイギで夜が明ける
Kazuho Hirokawa
June

THE DAWN OF LOVE
愛とセイギで夜が明ける

Translation	Sachiko Sato
Editing	Daryl Kuxhouse
Lettering	Ed Brisson
Graphic Design	Daryl Kuxhouse / Michelle Mauk
Editor in Chief	Fred Lui
Publisher	Hikaru Sasahara

English Edition Published by
DIGITAL MANGA PUBLISHING
A division of DIGITAL MANGA, Inc.
1487 W 178th Street, Suite 300
Gardena, CA 90248

www.dmpbooks.com

First Edition: November 2008
ISBN-10: 1-56970-583-6
ISBN-13: 978-1-56970-583-4

1 3 5 7 9 10 8 6 4 2

Printed in Canada

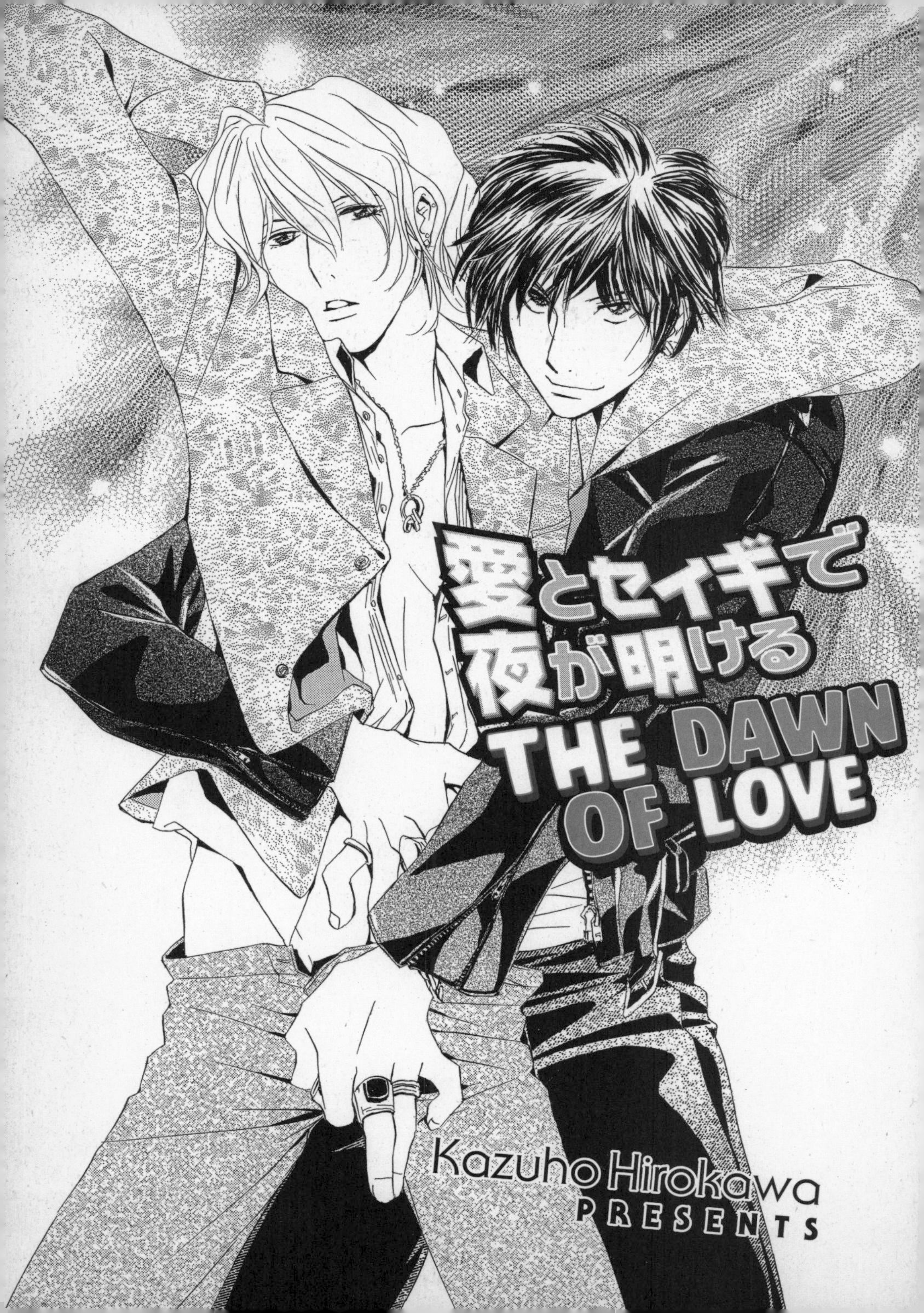
愛とセイギで夜が明ける
THE DAWN OF LOVE
Kazuho Hirokawa
PRESENTS

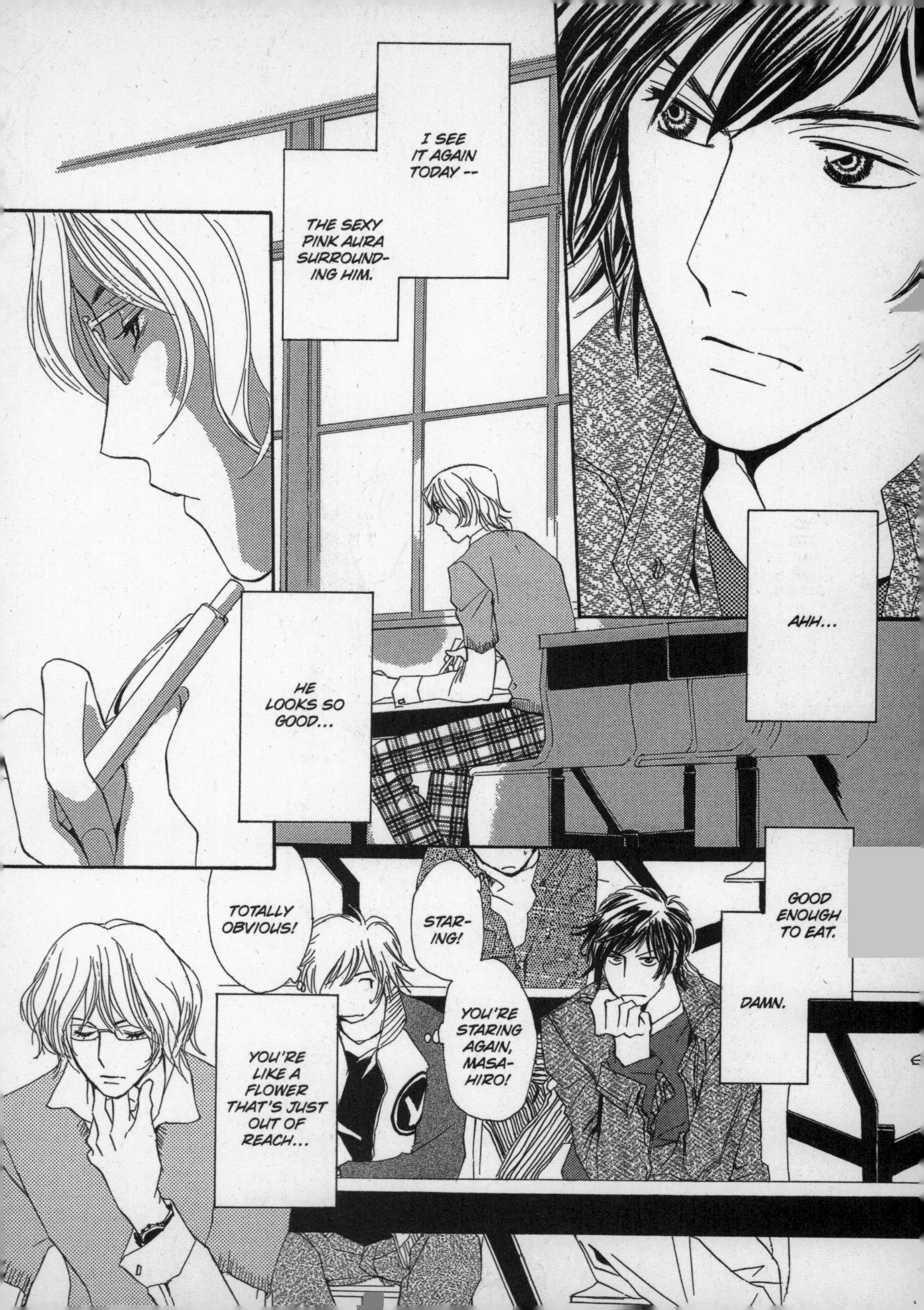
I SEE IT AGAIN TODAY --
THE SEXY PINK AURA SURROUND-ING HIM.
AHH...
HE LOOKS SO GOOD...
GOOD ENOUGH TO EAT.
DAMN.
STAR-ING!
YOU'RE STARING AGAIN, MASA-HIRO!
TOTALLY OBVIOUS!
YOU'RE LIKE A FLOWER THAT'S JUST OUT OF REACH...

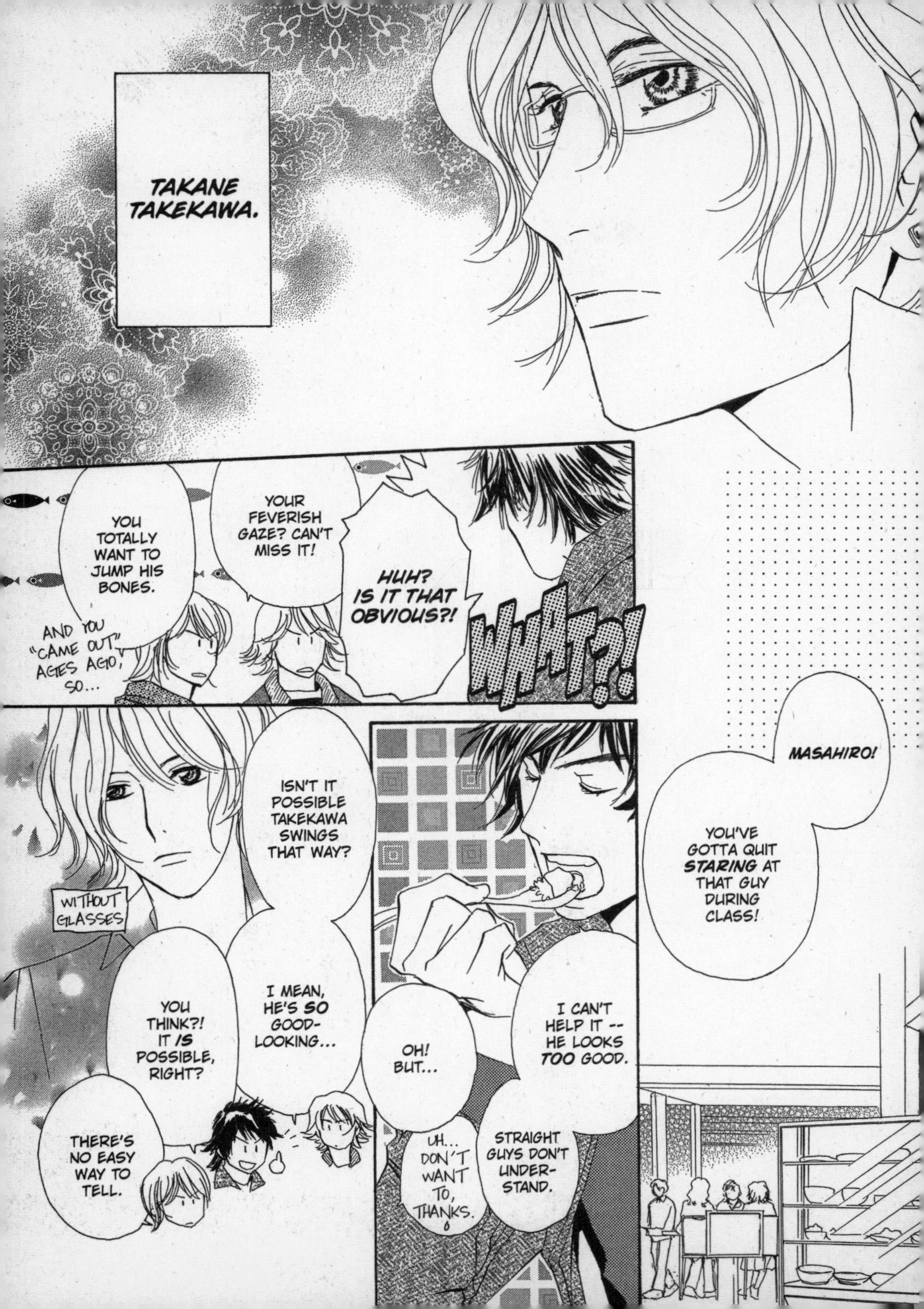

TAKANE TAKEKAWA.
MASAHIRO!
YOU'VE GOTTA QUIT STARING AT THAT GUY DURING CLASS!
WHAT?!
HUH? IS IT THAT OBVIOUS?!
YOUR FEVERISH GAZE? CAN'T MISS IT!
YOU TOTALLY WANT TO JUMP HIS BONES.
AND YOU "CAME OUT" AGES AGO, SO...
I CAN'T HELP IT -- HE LOOKS TOO GOOD.
STRAIGHT GUYS DON'T UNDER-STAND.
ISN'T IT POSSIBLE TAKEKAWA SWINGS THAT WAY?
WITHOUT GLASSES
I MEAN, HE'S SO GOOD-LOOKING...
YOU THINK?! IT IS POSSIBLE, RIGHT?
OH! BUT...
UH... DON'T WANT TO, THANKS.
THERE'S NO EASY WAY TO TELL.

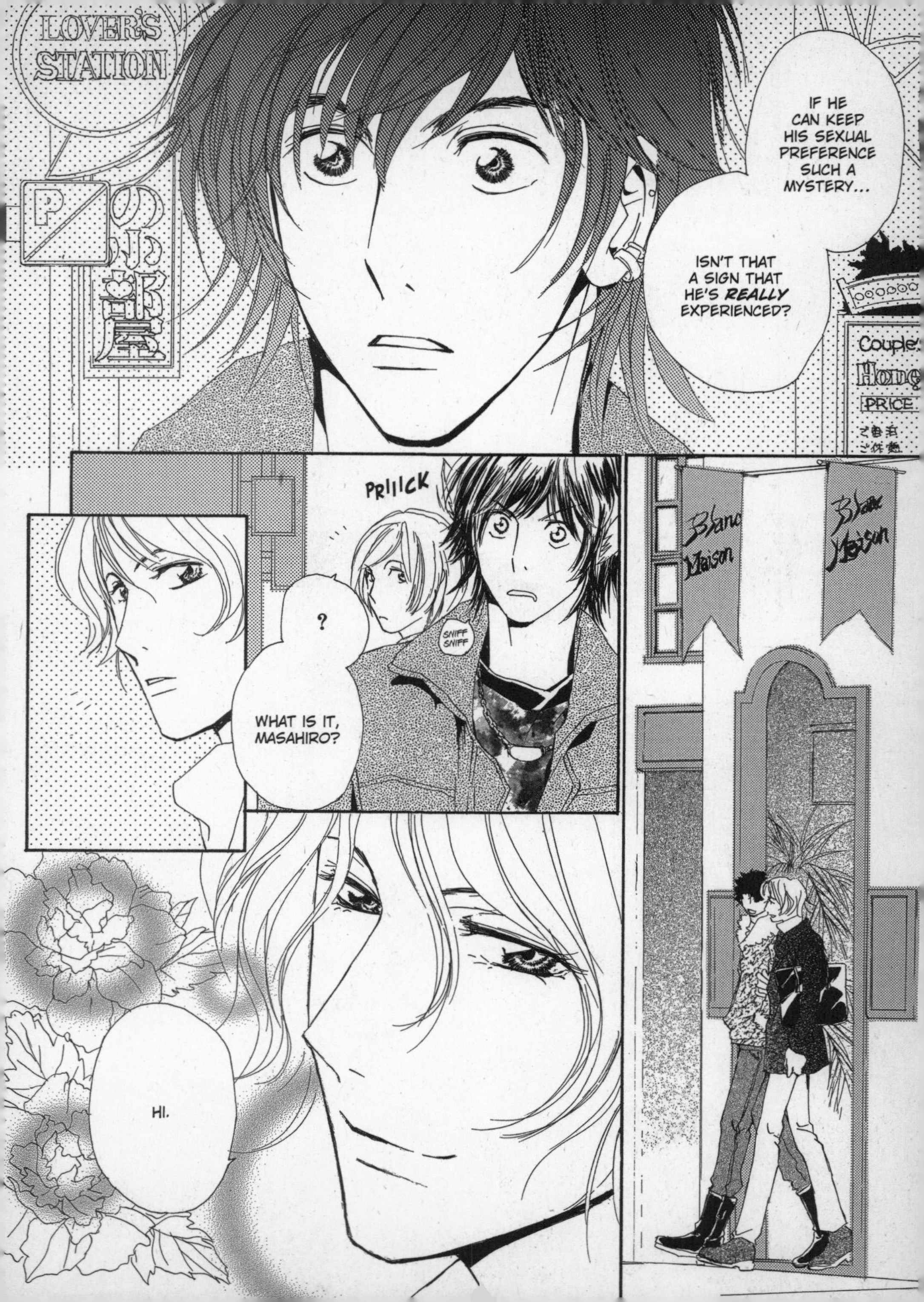

LOVER'S STATION
IF HE CAN KEEP HIS SEXUAL PREFERENCE SUCH A MYSTERY...
ISN'T THAT A SIGN THAT HE'S ***REALLY*** EXPERIENCED?
PRICE
Blanc Maison
Blanc Maison
PRIIICK
?
SNIFF SNIFF
WHAT IS IT, MASAHIRO?
HI.

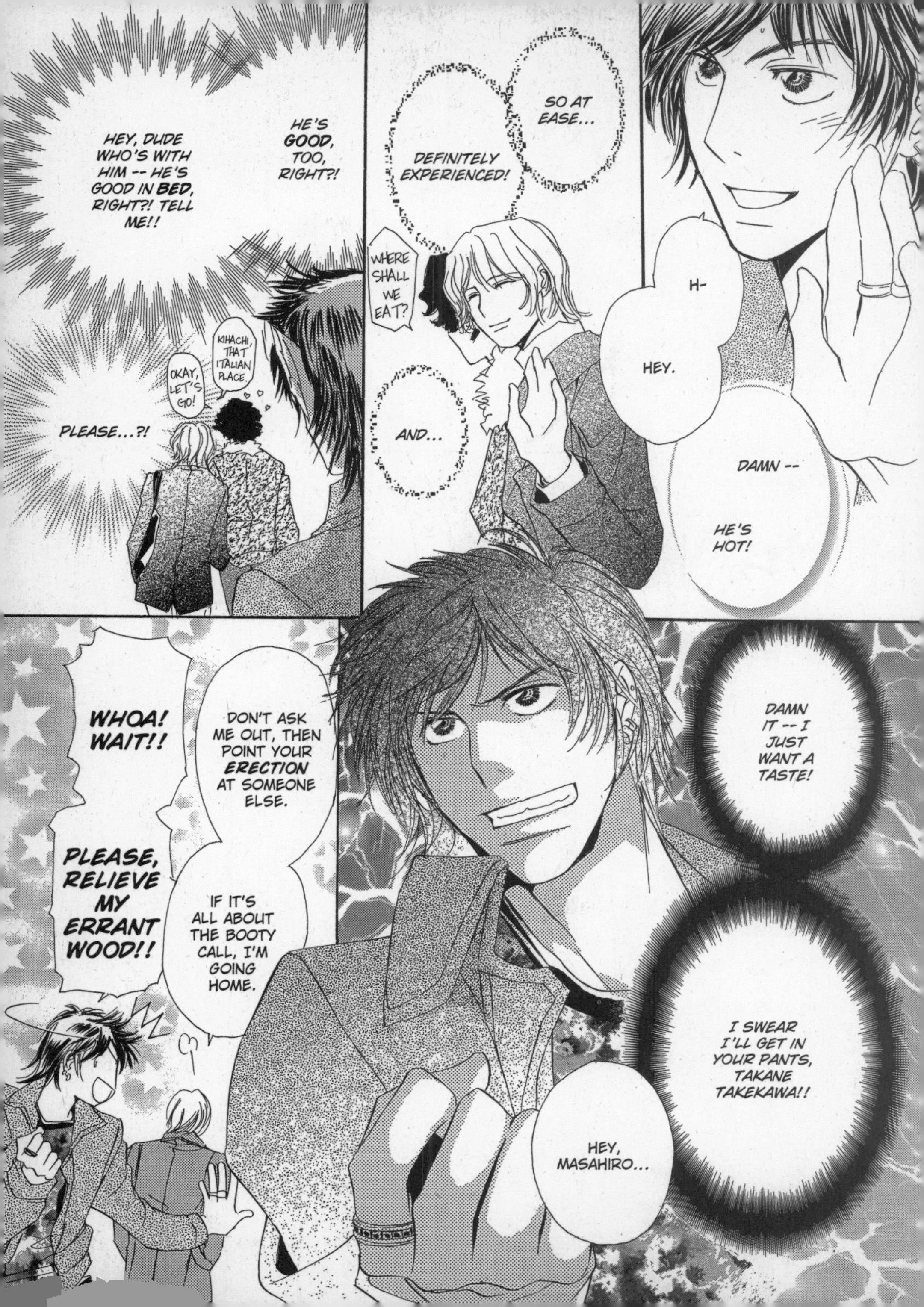
H-
HEY.
DAMN --
HE'S HOT!
SO AT EASE...
DEFINITELY EXPERIENCED!
WHERE SHALL WE EAT?
AND...
HE'S GOOD, TOO, RIGHT?!
HEY, DUDE WHO'S WITH HIM -- HE'S GOOD IN BED, RIGHT?! TELL ME!!
KIHACHI, THAT ITALIAN PLACE.
OKAY, LET'S GO!
PLEASE...?!
DAMN IT -- I JUST WANT A TASTE!
I SWEAR I'LL GET IN YOUR PANTS, TAKANE TAKEKAWA!!
HEY, MASAHIRO...
DON'T ASK ME OUT, THEN POINT YOUR ERECTION AT SOMEONE ELSE.
IF IT'S ALL ABOUT THE BOOTY CALL, I'M GOING HOME.
WHOA! WAIT!!
PLEASE, RELIEVE MY ERRANT WOOD!!

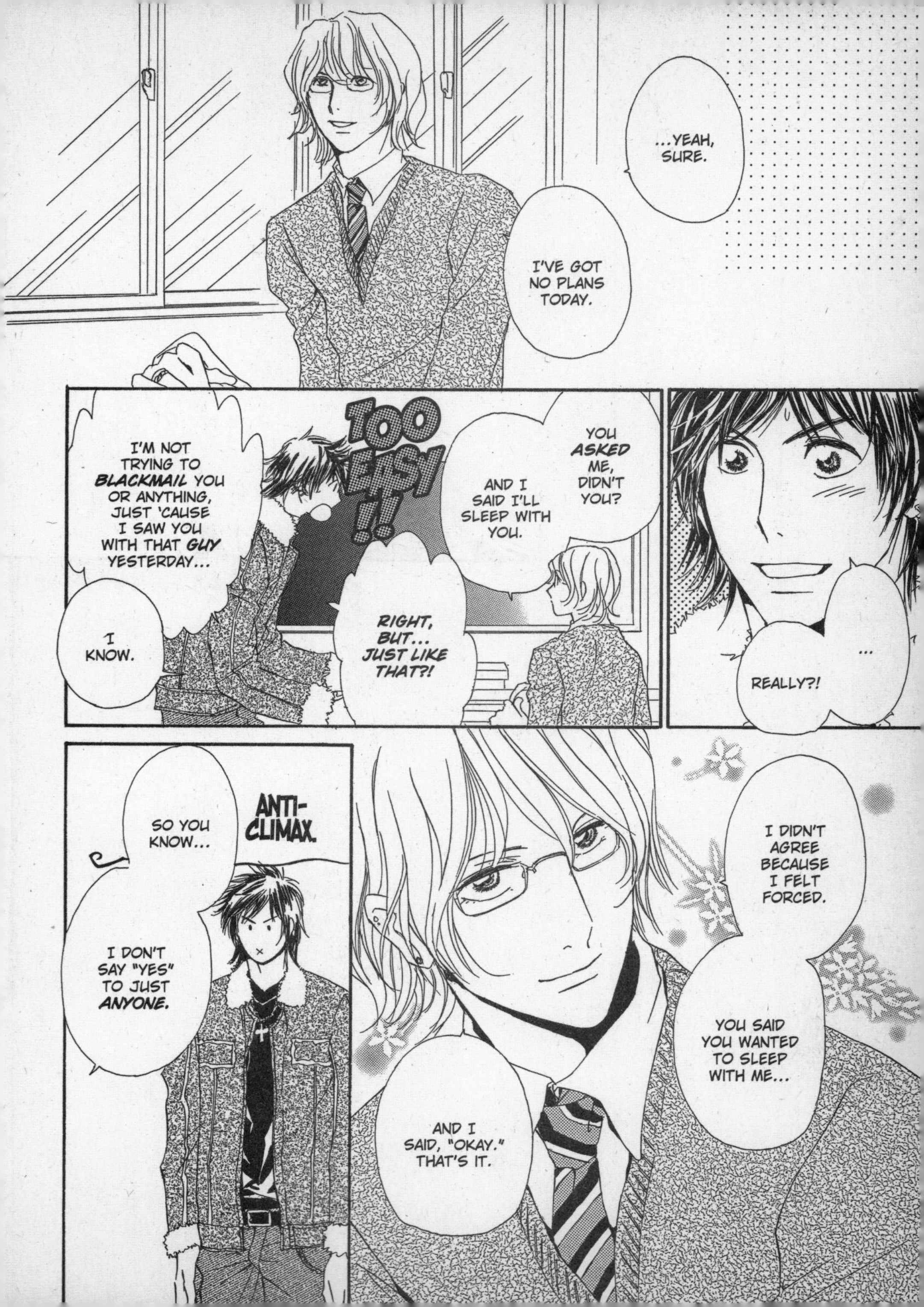
...YEAH, SURE.
I'VE GOT NO PLANS TODAY.
...
REALLY?!
YOU ASKED ME, DIDN'T YOU?
AND I SAID I'LL SLEEP WITH YOU.
TOO EASY!!
RIGHT, BUT... JUST LIKE THAT?!
I'M NOT TRYING TO BLACKMAIL YOU OR ANYTHING, JUST 'CAUSE I SAW YOU WITH THAT GUY YESTERDAY...
I KNOW.
I DIDN'T AGREE BECAUSE I FELT FORCED.
YOU SAID YOU WANTED TO SLEEP WITH ME...
AND I SAID, "OKAY." THAT'S IT.
ANTI-CLIMAX.
SO YOU KNOW...
I DON'T SAY "YES" TO JUST ANYONE.

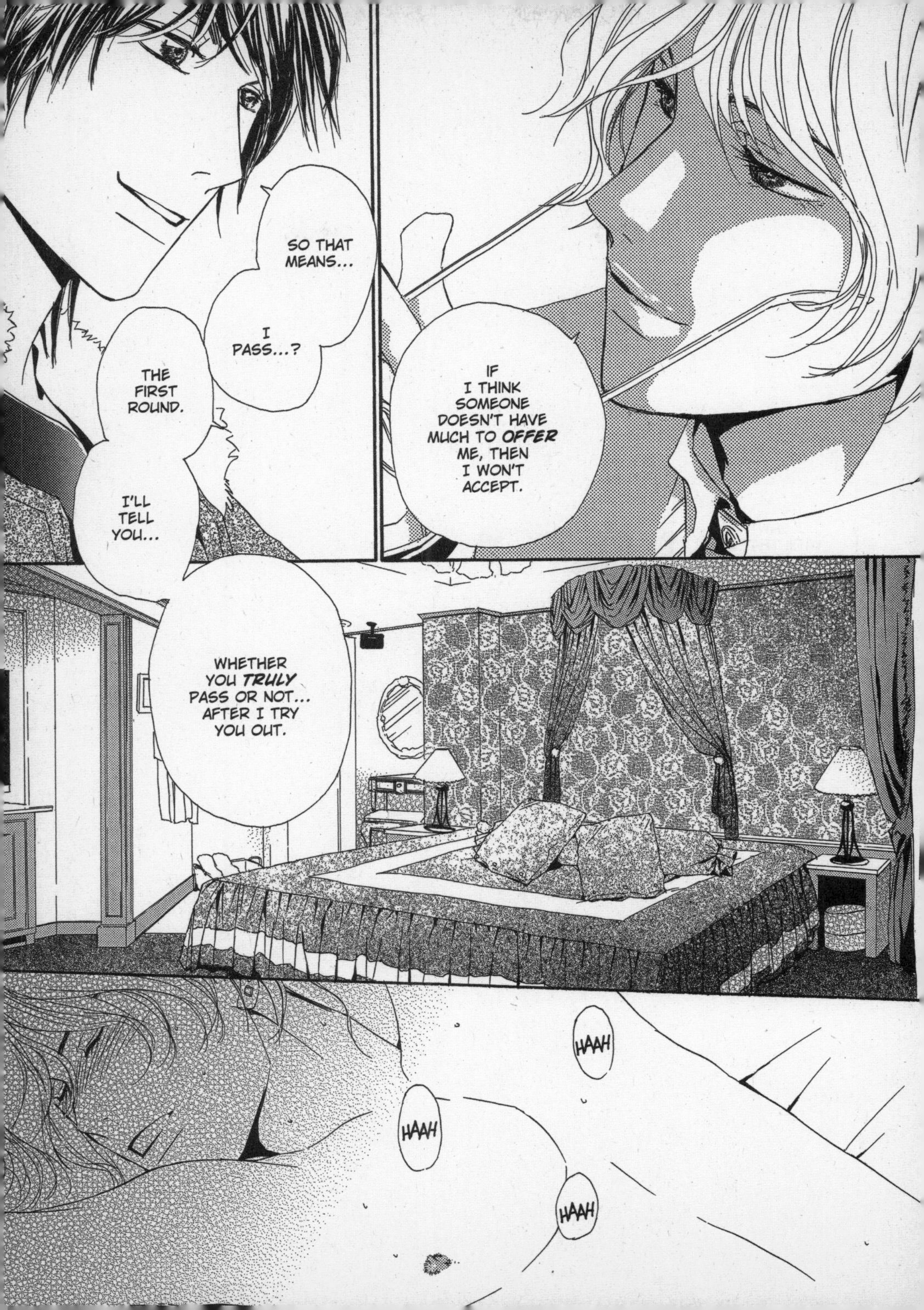
IF I THINK SOMEONE DOESN'T HAVE MUCH TO *OFFER* ME, THEN I WON'T ACCEPT.
SO THAT MEANS...
I PASS...?
THE FIRST ROUND.
I'LL TELL YOU...
WHETHER YOU *TRULY* PASS OR NOT... AFTER I TRY YOU OUT.
HAAH
HAAH
HAAH

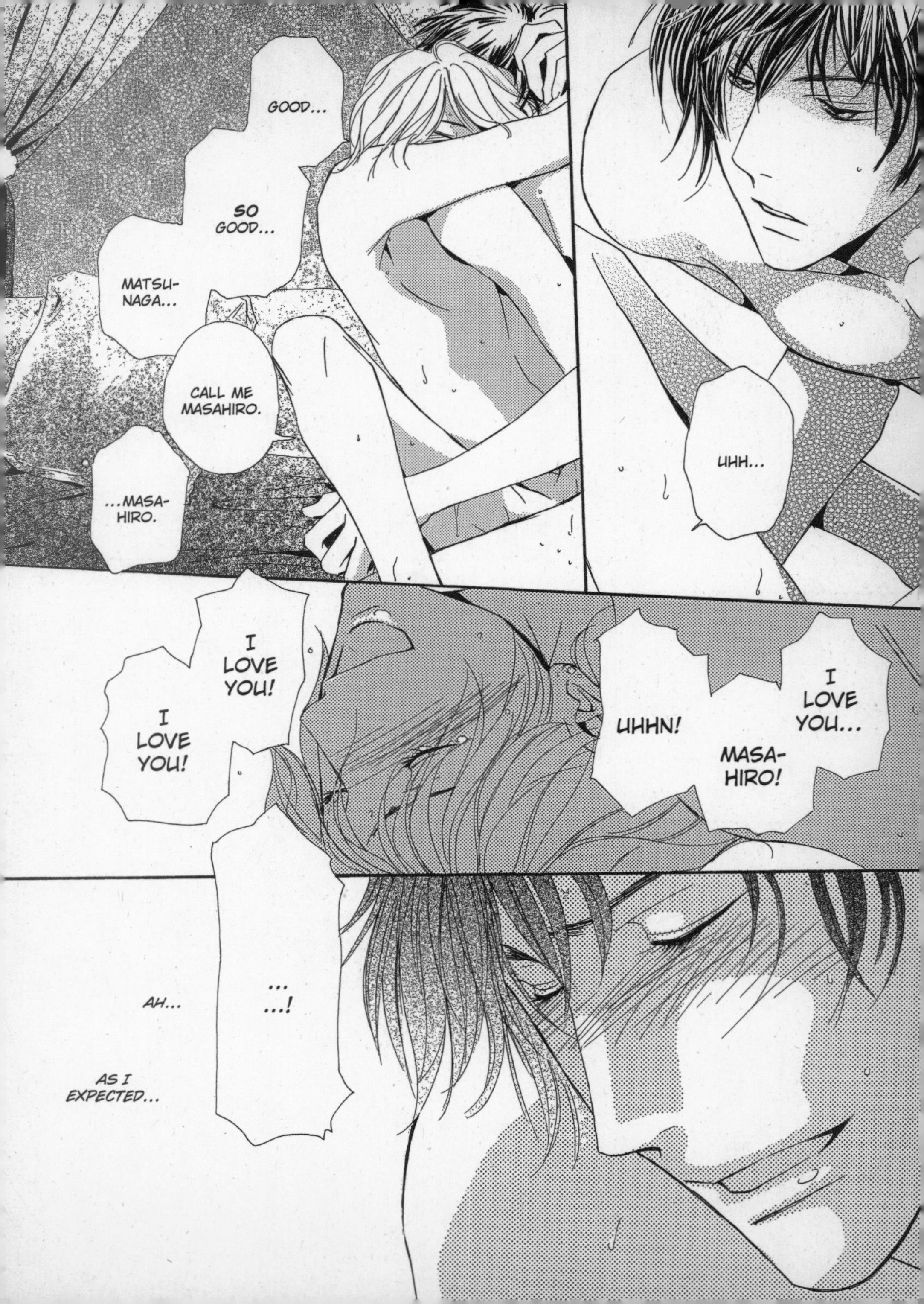
UHH...
GOOD...
SO GOOD...
MATSU-NAGA...
CALL ME MASAHIRO.
...MASA-HIRO.
I LOVE YOU...
MASA-HIRO!
UHHN!
I LOVE YOU!
I LOVE YOU!
... ...!
AH...
AS I EXPECTED...

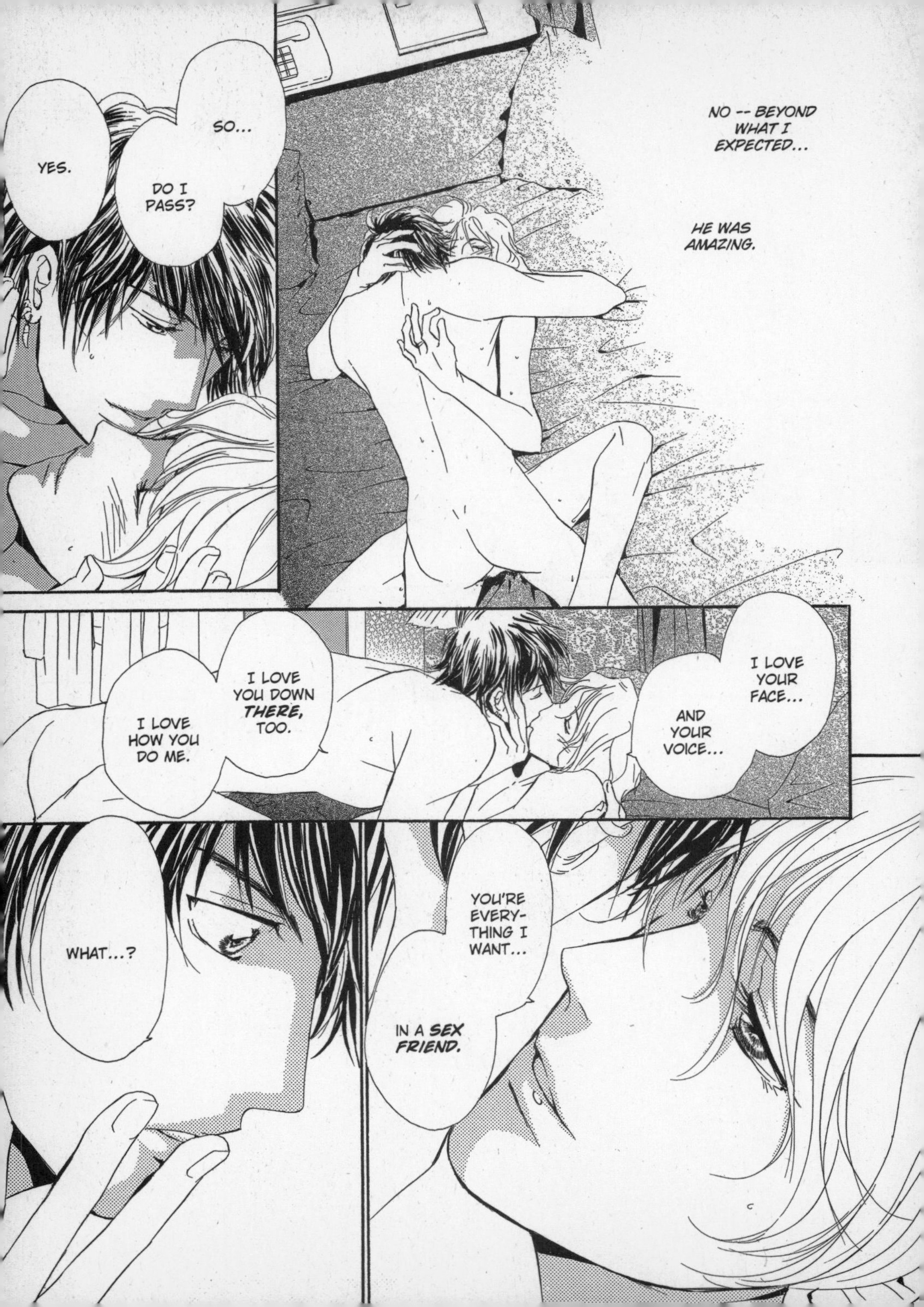
NO -- BEYOND WHAT I EXPECTED...
HE WAS AMAZING.
SO...
DO I PASS?
YES.
I LOVE YOUR FACE...
AND YOUR VOICE...
I LOVE YOU DOWN ***THERE,*** TOO.
I LOVE HOW YOU DO ME.
YOU'RE EVERY-THING I WANT...
IN A ***SEX FRIEND.***
WHAT...?

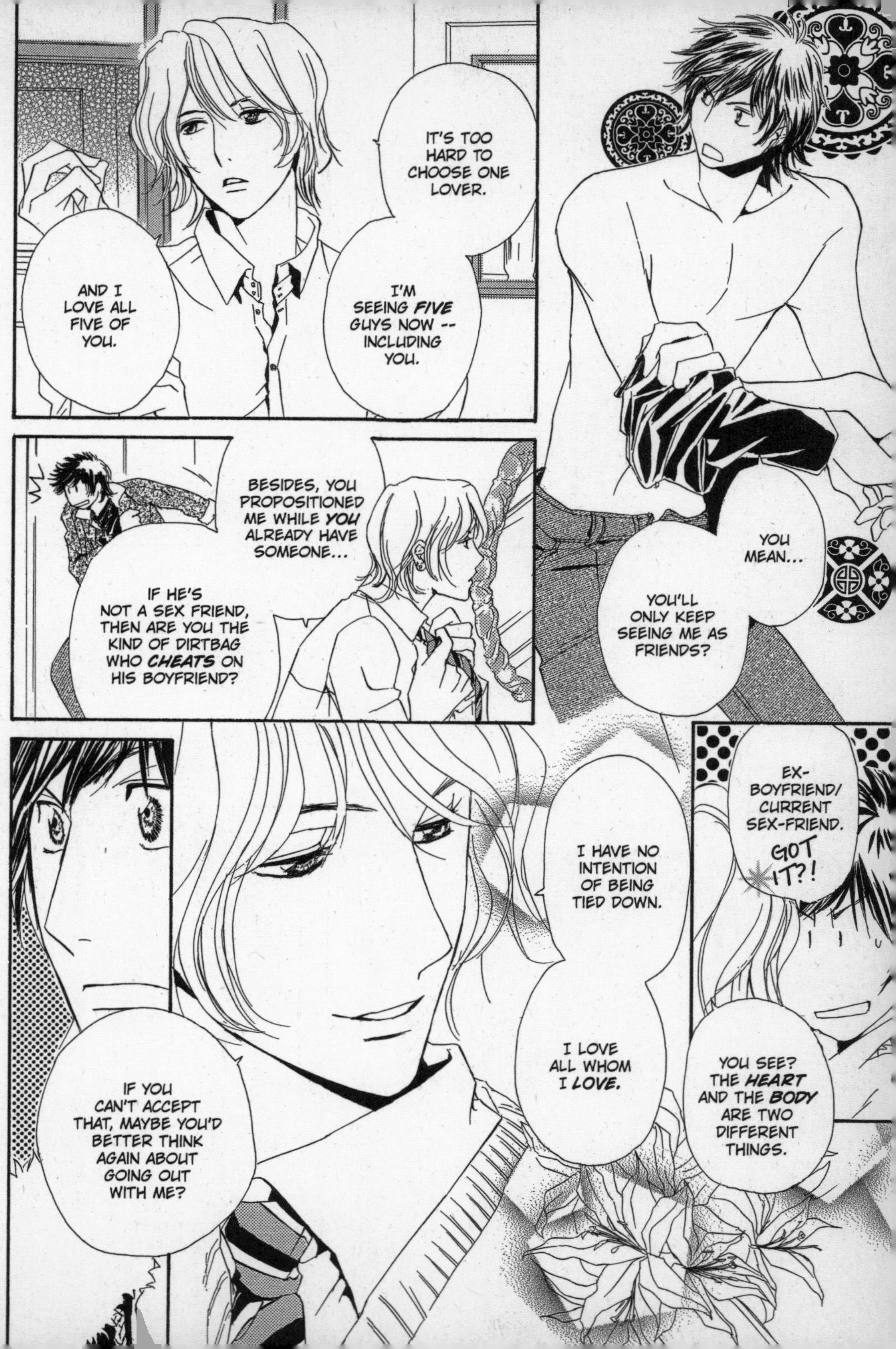
YOU MEAN...
YOU'LL ONLY KEEP SEEING ME AS FRIENDS?
IT'S TOO HARD TO CHOOSE ONE LOVER.
I'M SEEING *FIVE* GUYS NOW -- INCLUDING YOU.
AND I LOVE ALL FIVE OF YOU.
BESIDES, YOU PROPOSITIONED ME WHILE *YOU* ALREADY HAVE SOMEONE...
IF HE'S NOT A SEX FRIEND, THEN ARE YOU THE KIND OF DIRTBAG WHO *CHEATS* ON HIS BOYFRIEND?
EX-BOYFRIEND/ CURRENT SEX-FRIEND. GOT IT?!
YOU SEE? THE *HEART* AND THE *BODY* ARE TWO DIFFERENT THINGS.
I HAVE NO INTENTION OF BEING TIED DOWN.
I LOVE ALL WHOM I *LOVE.*
IF YOU CAN'T ACCEPT THAT, MAYBE YOU'D BETTER THINK AGAIN ABOUT GOING OUT WITH ME?

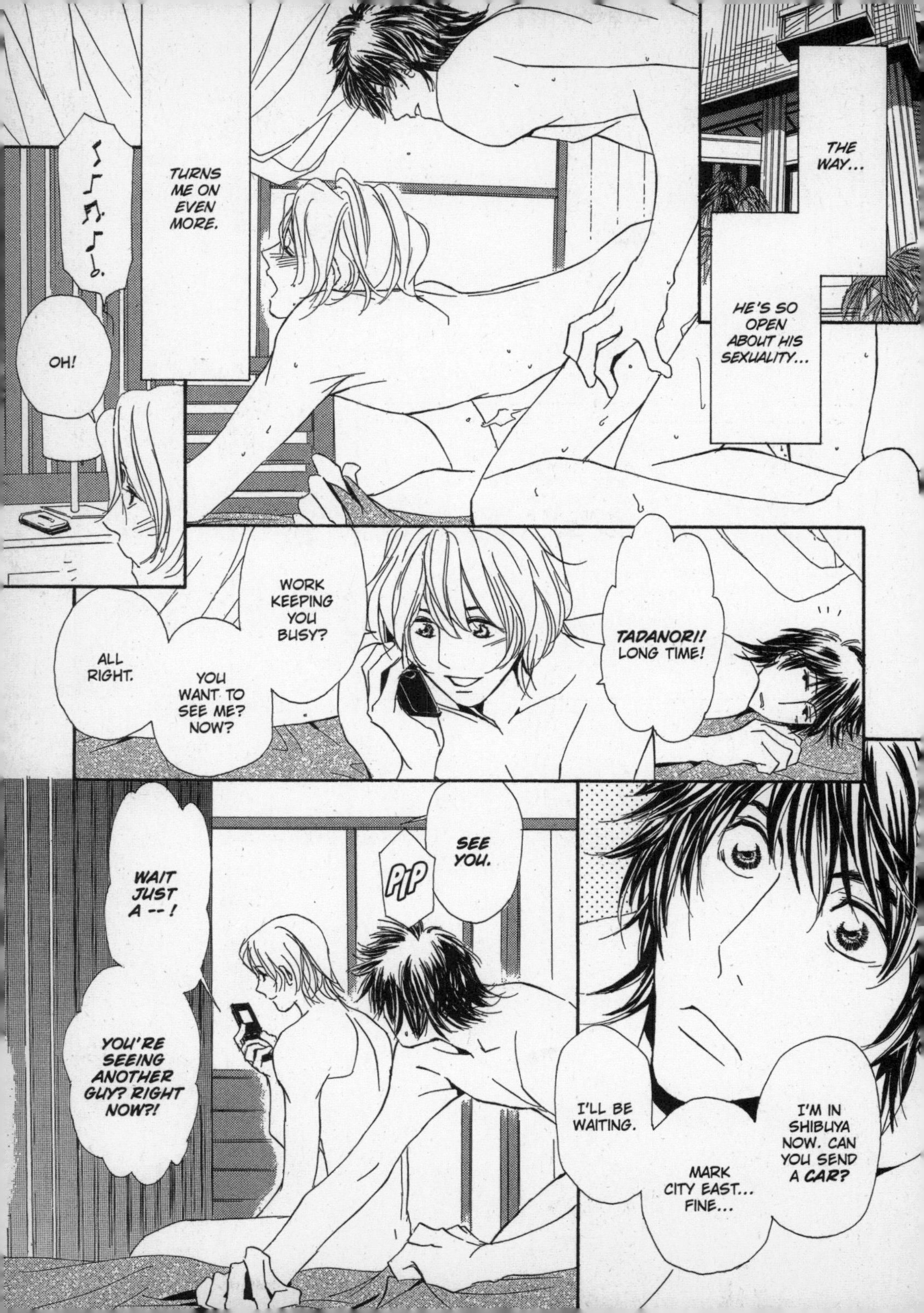
THE WAY...
HE'S SO OPEN ABOUT HIS SEXUALITY...
TURNS ME ON EVEN MORE.
OH!
TADANORI! LONG TIME!
WORK KEEPING YOU BUSY?
YOU WANT TO SEE ME? NOW?
ALL RIGHT.
I'M IN SHIBUYA NOW. CAN YOU SEND A CAR?
MARK CITY EAST... FINE...
I'LL BE WAITING.
SEE YOU.
PIP
WAIT JUST A --!
YOU'RE SEEING ANOTHER GUY? RIGHT NOW?!

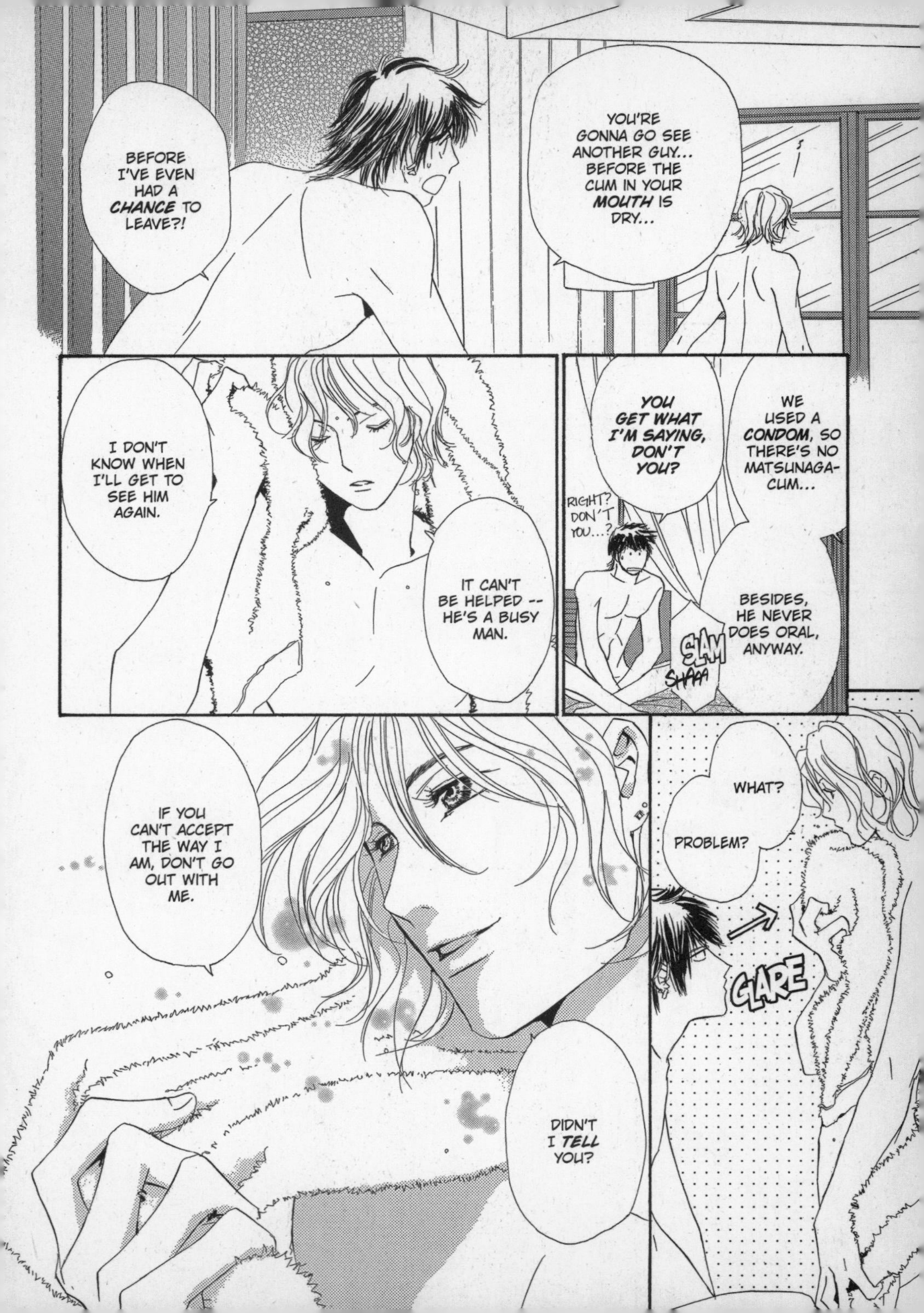
YOU'RE GONNA GO SEE ANOTHER GUY... BEFORE THE CUM IN YOUR MOUTH IS DRY...
BEFORE I'VE EVEN HAD A CHANCE TO LEAVE?!
WE USED A CONDOM, SO THERE'S NO MATSUNAGA-CUM...
YOU GET WHAT I'M SAYING, DON'T YOU?
RIGHT? DON'T YOU...?
BESIDES, HE NEVER DOES ORAL, ANYWAY.
SLAM
SHAAA
I DON'T KNOW WHEN I'LL GET TO SEE HIM AGAIN.
IT CAN'T BE HELPED -- HE'S A BUSY MAN.
WHAT?
PROBLEM?
GLARE
IF YOU CAN'T ACCEPT THE WAY I AM, DON'T GO OUT WITH ME.
DIDN'T I TELL YOU?

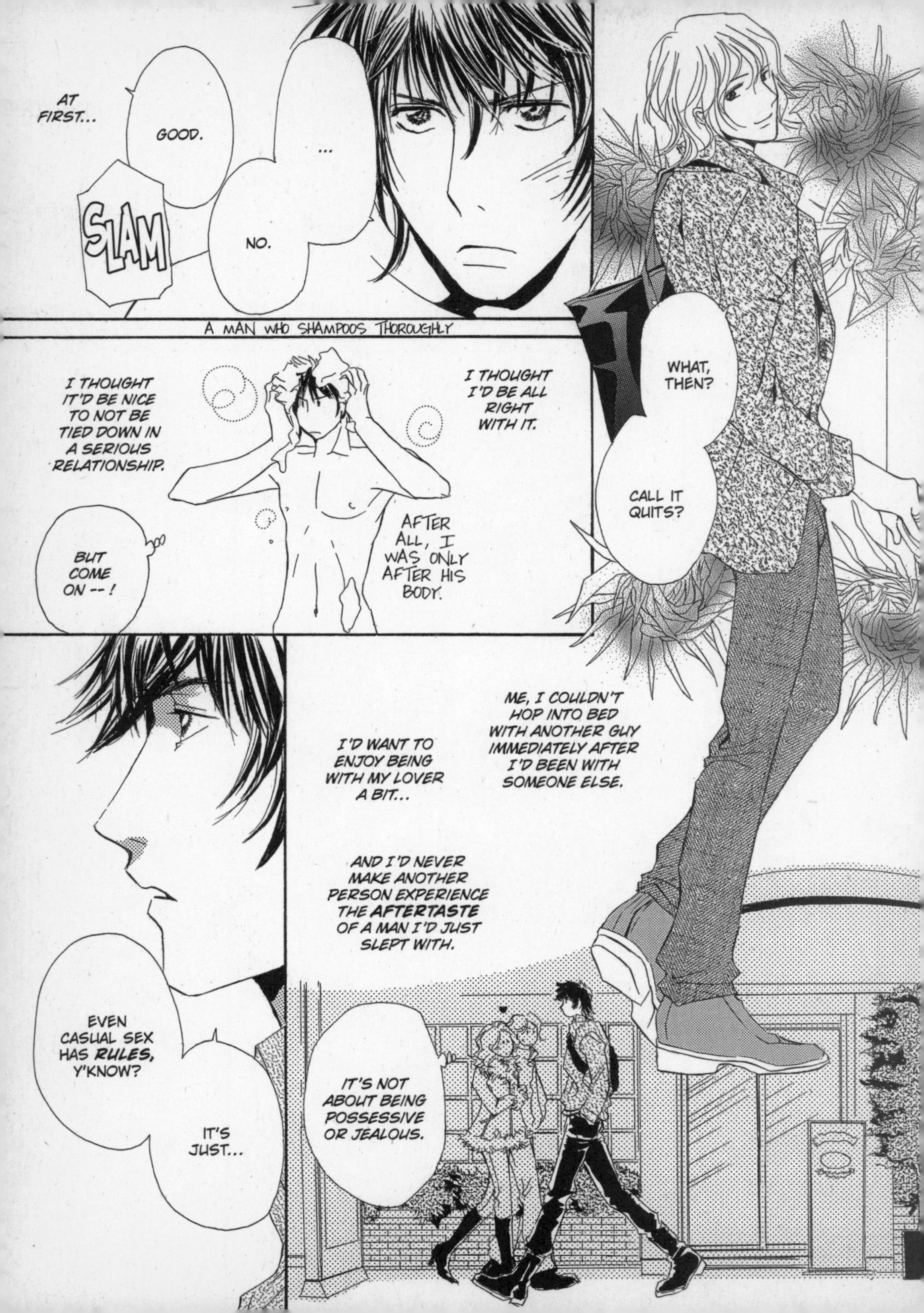
WHAT, THEN?
CALL IT QUITS?
...
NO.
GOOD.
SLAM
AT FIRST...
A MAN WHO SHAMPOOS THOROUGHLY
I THOUGHT I'D BE ALL RIGHT WITH IT.
I THOUGHT IT'D BE NICE TO NOT BE TIED DOWN IN A SERIOUS RELATIONSHIP.
AFTER ALL, I WAS ONLY AFTER HIS BODY.
BUT COME ON -- !
ME, I COULDN'T HOP INTO BED WITH ANOTHER GUY IMMEDIATELY AFTER I'D BEEN WITH SOMEONE ELSE.
I'D WANT TO ENJOY BEING WITH MY LOVER A BIT...
AND I'D NEVER MAKE ANOTHER PERSON EXPERIENCE THE AFTERTASTE OF A MAN I'D JUST SLEPT WITH.
IT'S NOT ABOUT BEING POSSESSIVE OR JEALOUS.
EVEN CASUAL SEX HAS RULES, Y'KNOW?
IT'S JUST...

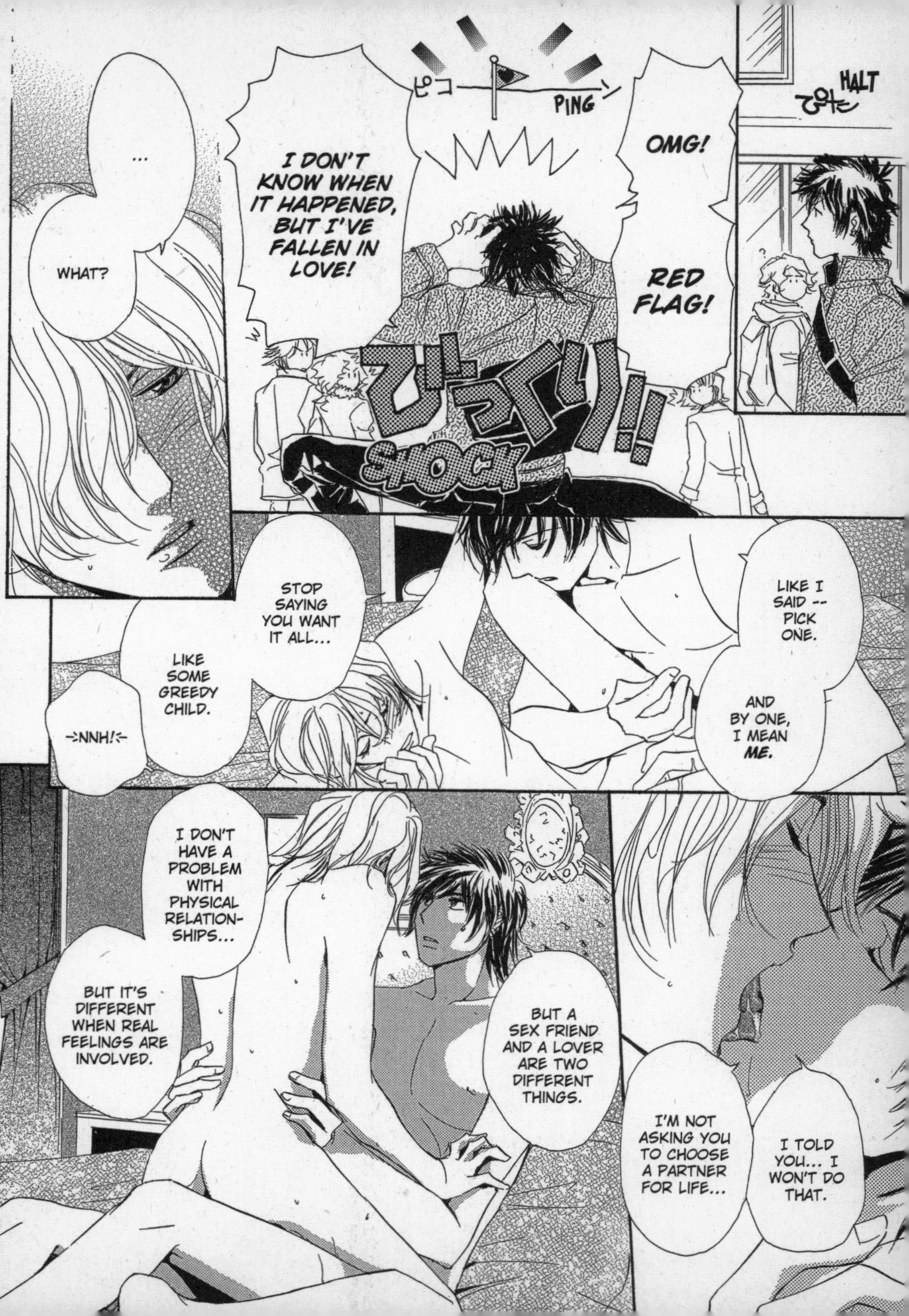
HALT
ぴた
ピコーン
PING
OMG!
RED FLAG!
I DON'T KNOW WHEN IT HAPPENED, BUT I'VE FALLEN IN LOVE!
びっくり!!
SHOCK
...
WHAT?
LIKE I SAID -- PICK ONE.
AND BY ONE, I MEAN *ME*.
STOP SAYING YOU WANT IT ALL...
LIKE SOME GREEDY CHILD.
–NNH!–
I TOLD YOU... I WON'T DO THAT.
I'M NOT ASKING YOU TO CHOOSE A PARTNER FOR LIFE...
I DON'T HAVE A PROBLEM WITH PHYSICAL RELATION-SHIPS...
BUT IT'S DIFFERENT WHEN REAL FEELINGS ARE INVOLVED.
BUT A SEX FRIEND AND A LOVER ARE TWO DIFFERENT THINGS.

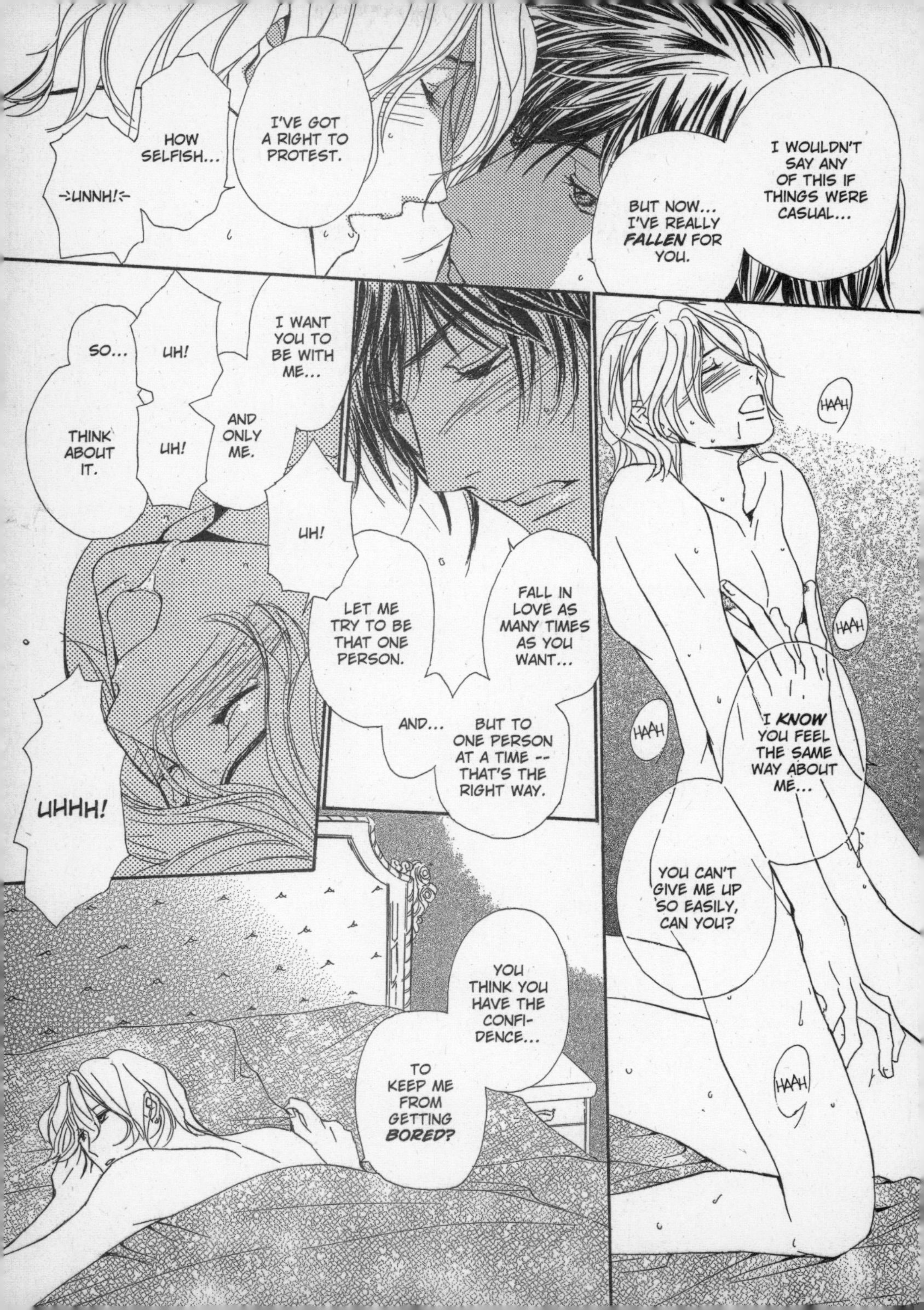
I WOULDN'T SAY ANY OF THIS IF THINGS WERE CASUAL...
BUT NOW... I'VE REALLY *FALLEN* FOR YOU.
I'VE GOT A RIGHT TO PROTEST.
HOW SELFISH...
-UNNH!-
HAAH
HAAH
I *KNOW* YOU FEEL THE SAME WAY ABOUT ME...
HAAH
YOU CAN'T GIVE ME UP SO EASILY, CAN YOU?
HAAH
I WANT YOU TO BE WITH ME...
AND ONLY ME.
UH!
FALL IN LOVE AS MANY TIMES AS YOU WANT...
BUT TO ONE PERSON AT A TIME -- THAT'S THE RIGHT WAY.
LET ME TRY TO BE THAT ONE PERSON.
AND...
UH!
UH!
SO...
THINK ABOUT IT.
UHHH!
YOU THINK YOU HAVE THE CONFI-DENCE...
TO KEEP ME FROM GETTING *BORED?*

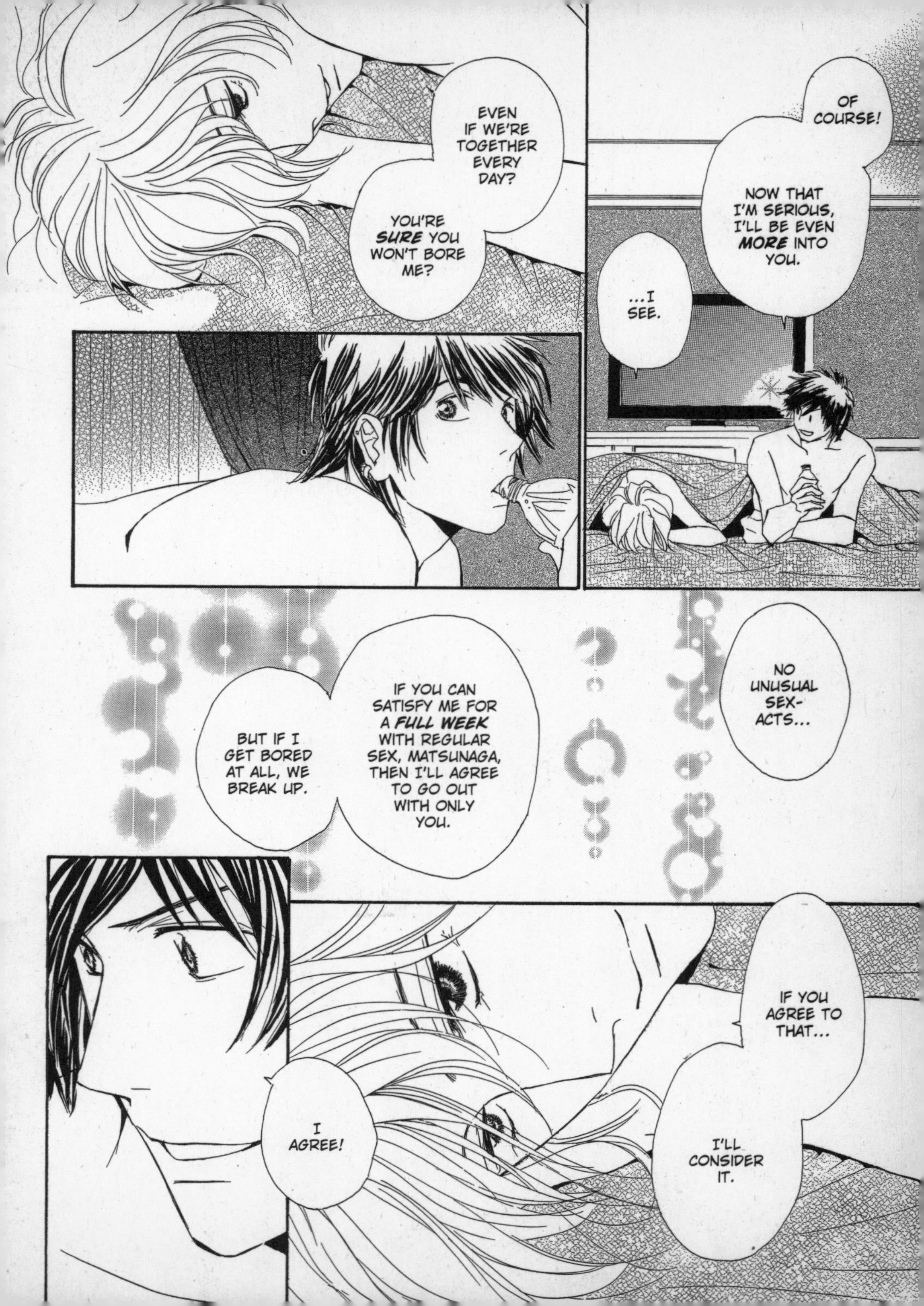
OF COURSE!
NOW THAT I'M SERIOUS, I'LL BE EVEN MORE INTO YOU.
...I SEE.
EVEN IF WE'RE TOGETHER EVERY DAY?
YOU'RE SURE YOU WON'T BORE ME?
NO UNUSUAL SEX-ACTS...
IF YOU CAN SATISFY ME FOR A FULL WEEK WITH REGULAR SEX, MATSUNAGA, THEN I'LL AGREE TO GO OUT WITH ONLY YOU.
BUT IF I GET BORED AT ALL, WE BREAK UP.
IF YOU AGREE TO THAT...
I'LL CONSIDER IT.
I AGREE!

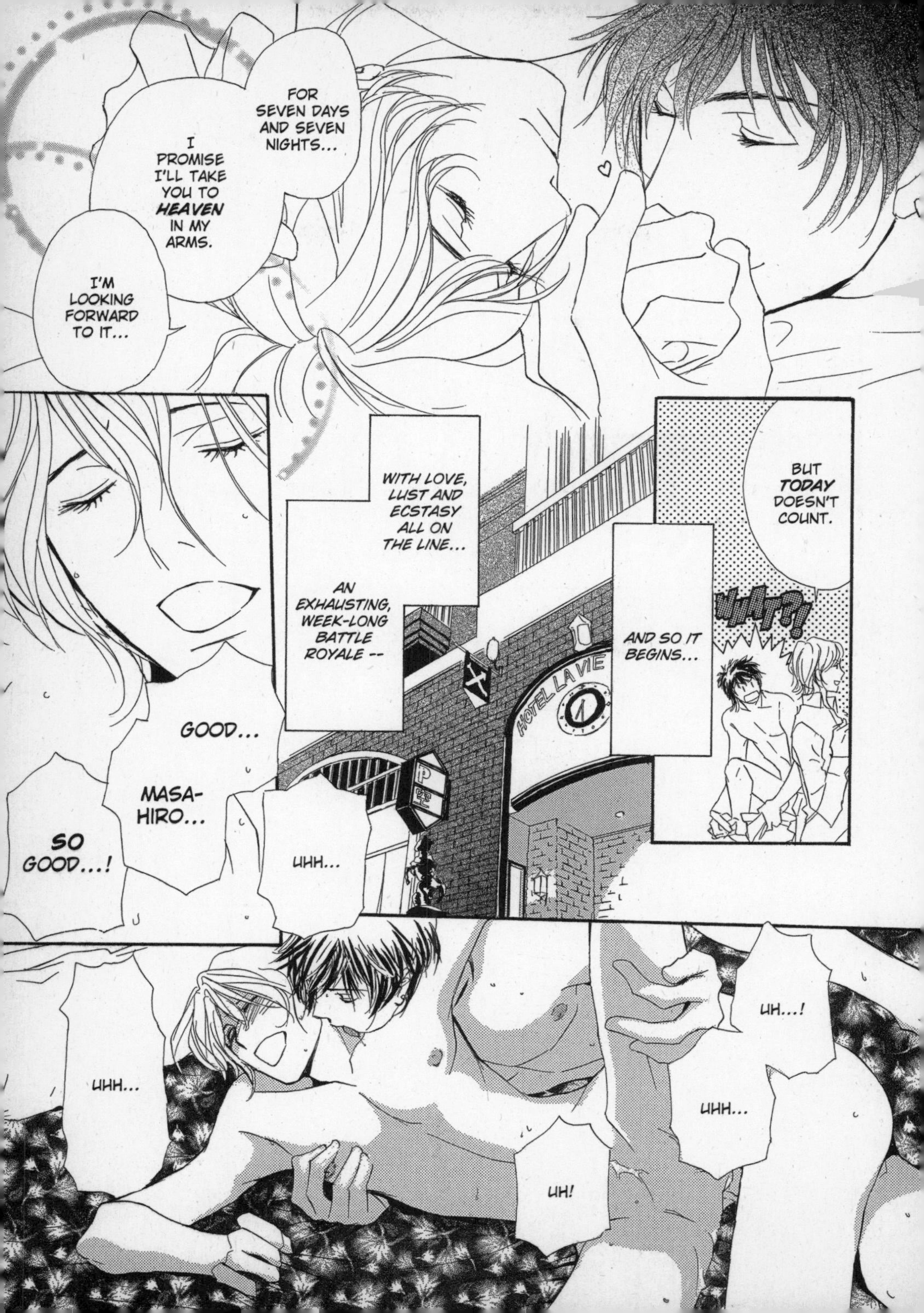
FOR SEVEN DAYS AND SEVEN NIGHTS...
I PROMISE I'LL TAKE YOU TO ***HEAVEN*** IN MY ARMS.
I'M LOOKING FORWARD TO IT...
BUT ***TODAY*** DOESN'T COUNT.
WHAT?!
AND SO IT BEGINS...
WITH LOVE, LUST AND ECSTASY ALL ON THE LINE...
AN EXHAUSTING, WEEK-LONG BATTLE ROYALE --
HOTEL LA VIE
GOOD...
MASA-HIRO...
SO GOOD...!
UHH...
UH...!
UHH...
UH!
UHH...

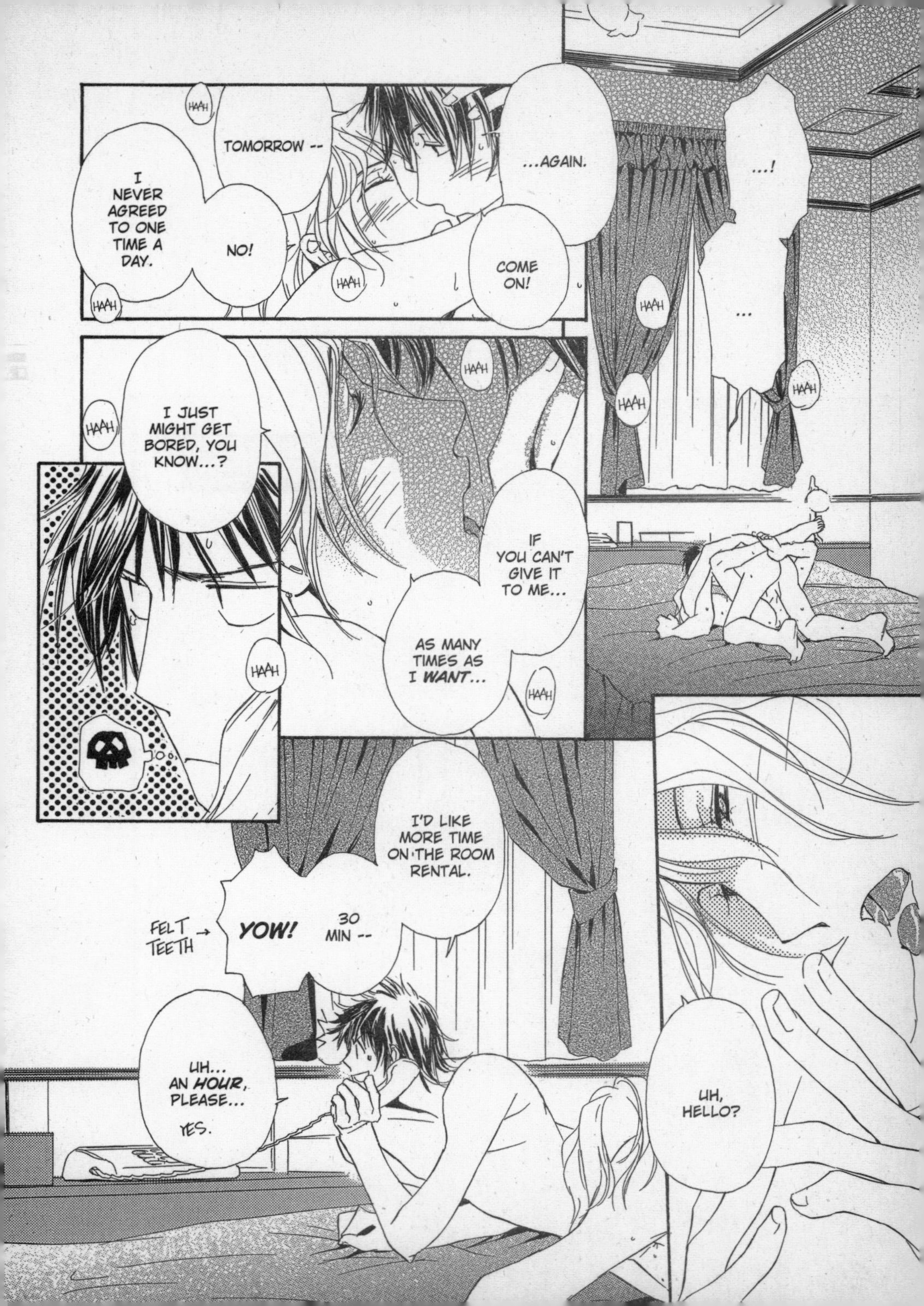
...!
...
HAAH
HAAH
HAAH
...AGAIN.
COME ON!
HAAH
TOMORROW --
NO!
I NEVER AGREED TO ONE TIME A DAY.
HAAH
HAAH
I JUST MIGHT GET BORED, YOU KNOW...?
HAAH
HAAH
IF YOU CAN'T GIVE IT TO ME...
AS MANY TIMES AS I WANT...
HAAH
HAAH
UH, HELLO?
I'D LIKE MORE TIME ON THE ROOM RENTAL.
30 MIN --
YOW!
FELT → TEETH
UH... AN HOUR, PLEASE...
YES.

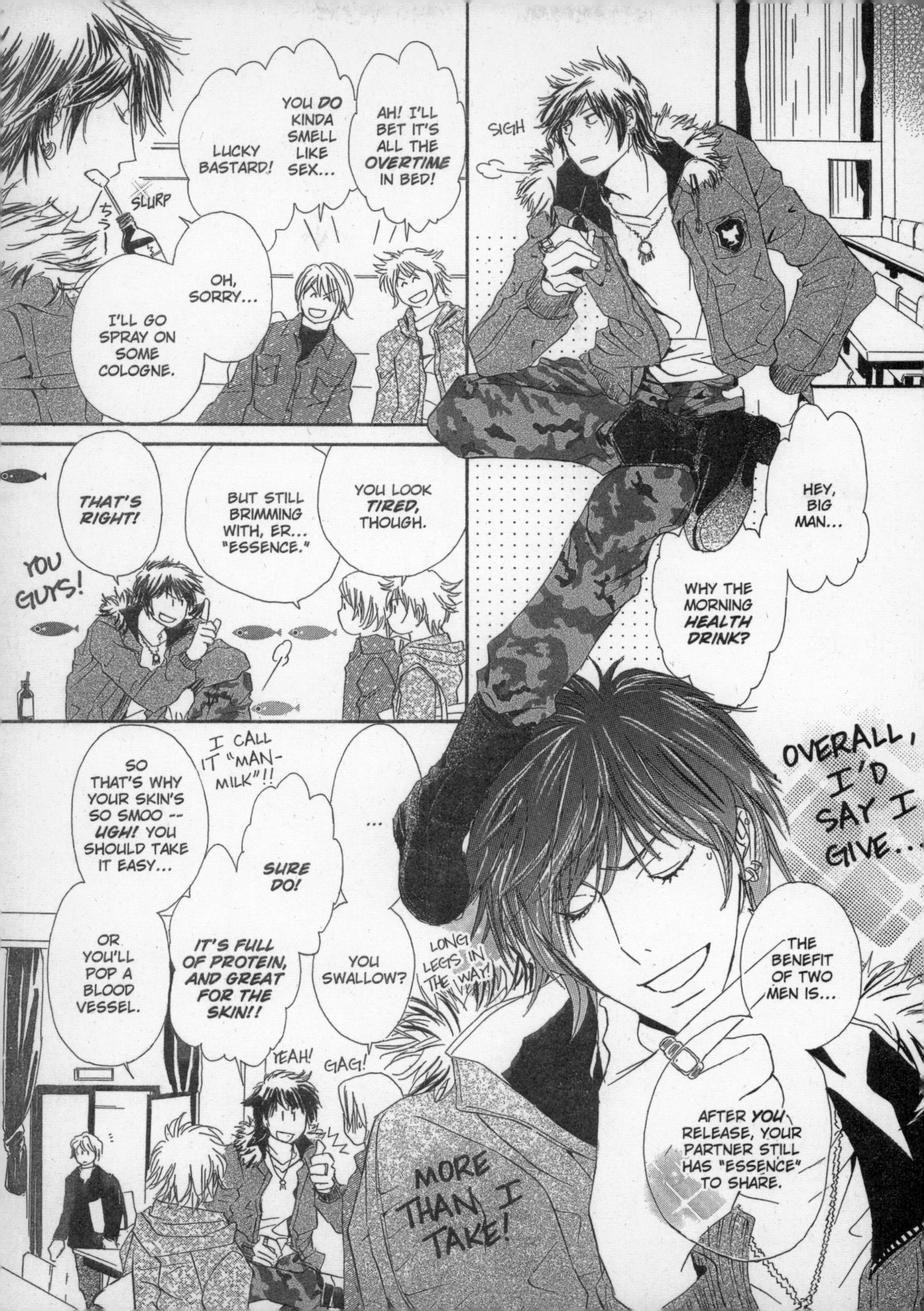
SIGH
HEY, BIG MAN...
WHY THE MORNING HEALTH DRINK?
AH! I'LL BET IT'S ALL THE OVERTIME IN BED!
YOU DO KINDA SMELL LIKE SEX...
LUCKY BASTARD!
SLURP
OH, SORRY...
I'LL GO SPRAY ON SOME COLOGNE.
YOU LOOK TIRED, THOUGH.
BUT STILL BRIMMING WITH, ER... "ESSENCE."
THAT'S RIGHT!
YOU GUYS!
THE BENEFIT OF TWO MEN IS...
AFTER YOU RELEASE, YOUR PARTNER STILL HAS "ESSENCE" TO SHARE.
OVERALL, I'D SAY I GIVE...
MORE THAN I TAKE!
LONG LEGS IN THE WAY!
...
YOU SWALLOW?
SURE DO!
I CALL IT "MAN-MILK"!!
IT'S FULL OF PROTEIN, AND GREAT FOR THE SKIN!!
SO THAT'S WHY YOUR SKIN'S SO SMOO -- UGH! YOU SHOULD TAKE IT EASY...
OR YOU'LL POP A BLOOD VESSEL.
YEAH!
GAG!

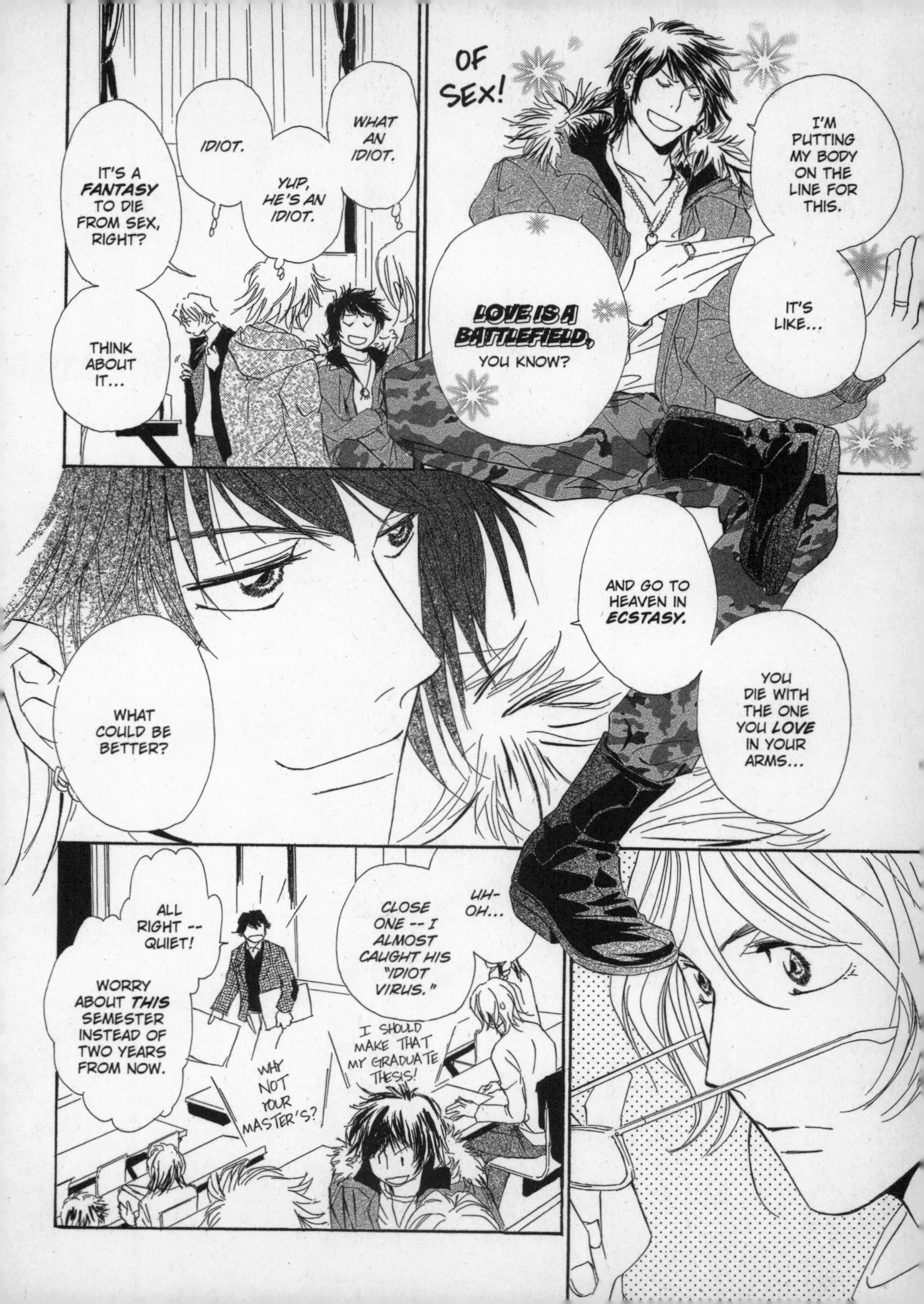
OF SEX!
I'M PUTTING MY BODY ON THE LINE FOR THIS.
IT'S LIKE...
LOVE IS A BATTLEFIELD, YOU KNOW?
WHAT AN IDIOT.
YUP, HE'S AN IDIOT.
IDIOT.
IT'S A FANTASY TO DIE FROM SEX, RIGHT?
THINK ABOUT IT...
YOU DIE WITH THE ONE YOU LOVE IN YOUR ARMS...
AND GO TO HEAVEN IN ECSTASY.
WHAT COULD BE BETTER?
UH-OH...
CLOSE ONE -- I ALMOST CAUGHT HIS "IDIOT VIRUS."
ALL RIGHT -- QUIET!
WORRY ABOUT THIS SEMESTER INSTEAD OF TWO YEARS FROM NOW.
I SHOULD MAKE THAT MY GRADUATE THESIS!
WHY NOT YOUR MASTER'S?

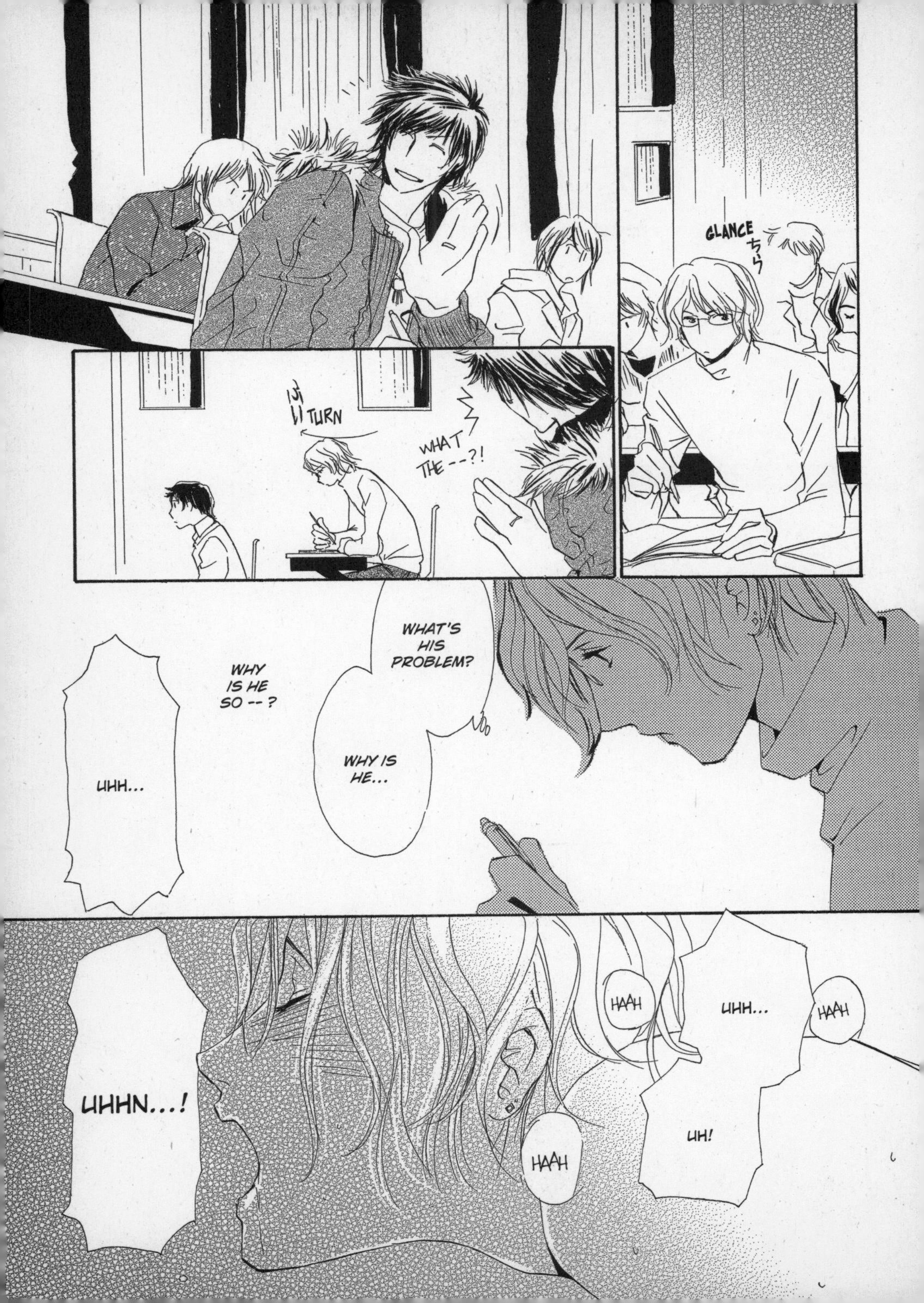
GLANCE ちら
TURN
WHAT THE --?!
WHAT'S HIS PROBLEM?
WHY IS HE SO --?
WHY IS HE...
UHH...
HAAH
UHH...
HAAH
UH!
HAAH
UHHN...!

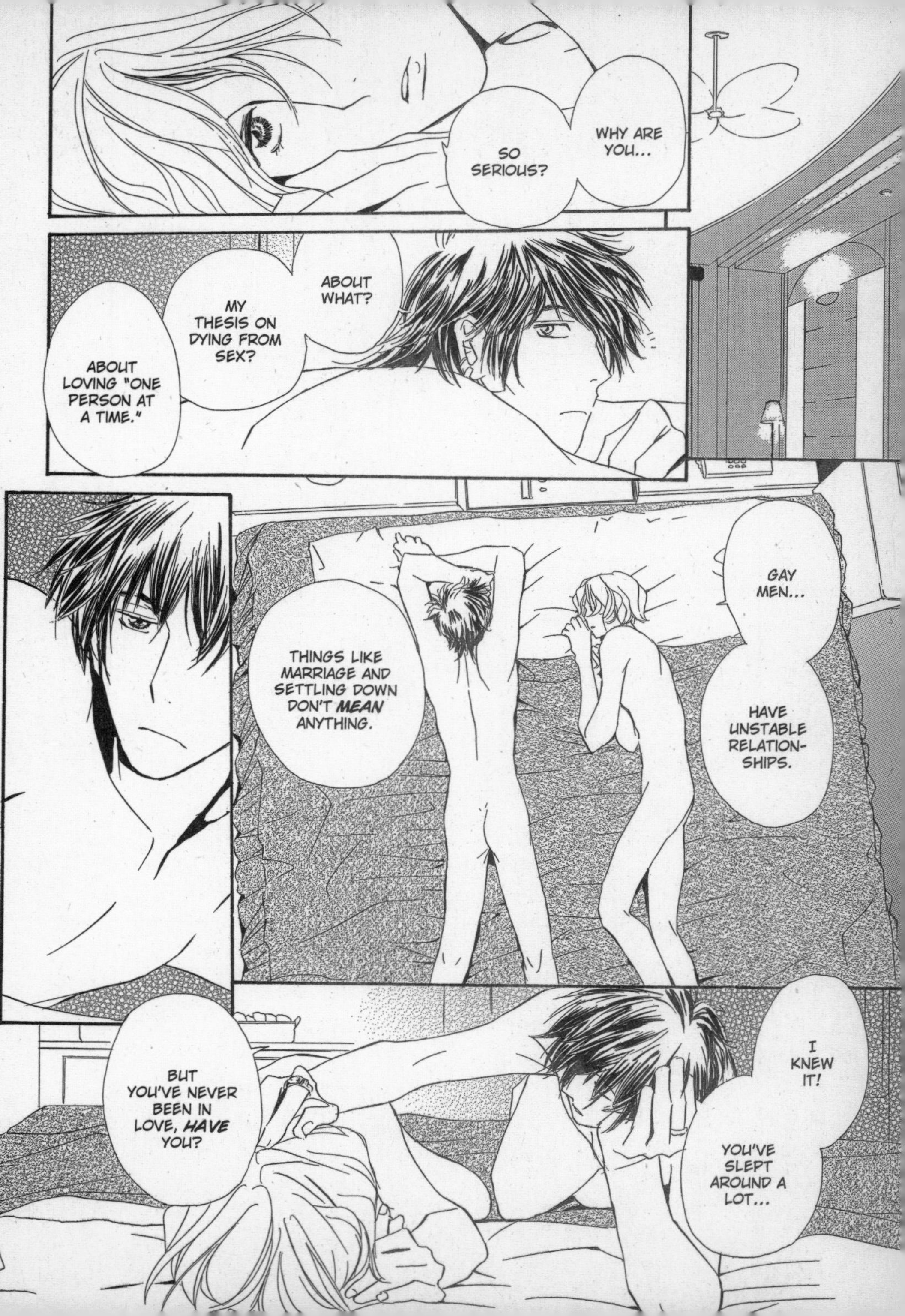
WHY ARE YOU...
SO SERIOUS?
ABOUT WHAT?
MY THESIS ON DYING FROM SEX?
ABOUT LOVING "ONE PERSON AT A TIME."
GAY MEN...
HAVE UNSTABLE RELATION-SHIPS.
THINGS LIKE MARRIAGE AND SETTLING DOWN DON'T *MEAN* ANYTHING.
I KNEW IT!
YOU'VE SLEPT AROUND A LOT...
BUT YOU'VE NEVER BEEN IN LOVE, *HAVE* YOU?

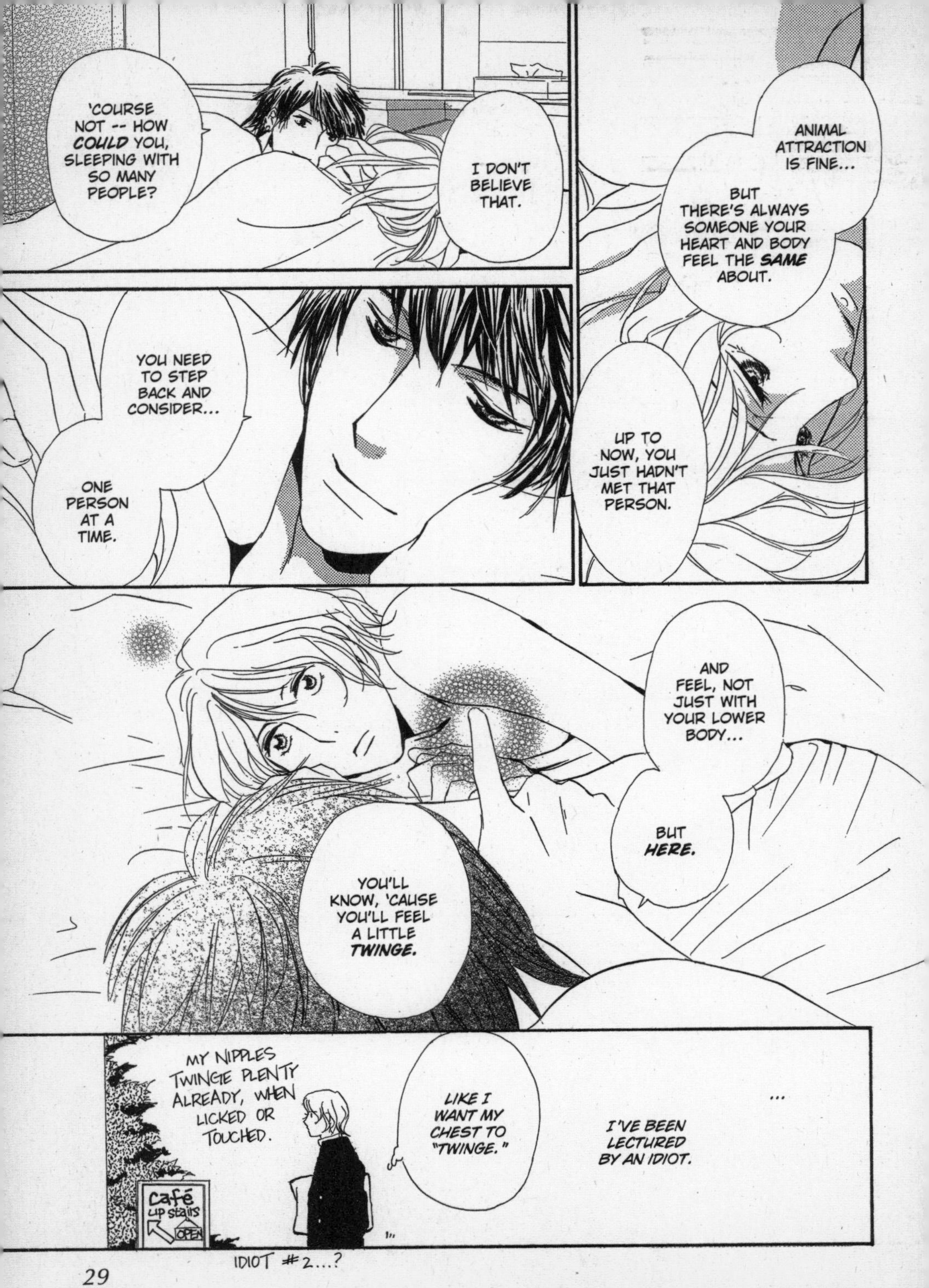
ANIMAL ATTRACTION IS FINE...
BUT THERE'S ALWAYS SOMEONE YOUR HEART AND BODY FEEL THE **SAME** ABOUT.
UP TO NOW, YOU JUST HADN'T MET THAT PERSON.
I DON'T BELIEVE THAT.
'COURSE NOT -- HOW **COULD** YOU, SLEEPING WITH SO MANY PEOPLE?
YOU NEED TO STEP BACK AND CONSIDER...
ONE PERSON AT A TIME.
AND FEEL, NOT JUST WITH YOUR LOWER BODY...
BUT **HERE.**
YOU'LL KNOW, 'CAUSE YOU'LL FEEL A LITTLE ***TWINGE.***
...
I'VE BEEN LECTURED BY AN IDIOT.
LIKE I WANT MY CHEST TO "TWINGE."
MY NIPPLES TWINGE PLENTY ALREADY, WHEN LICKED OR TOUCHED.
Café up stairs
OPEN
IDIOT #2...?

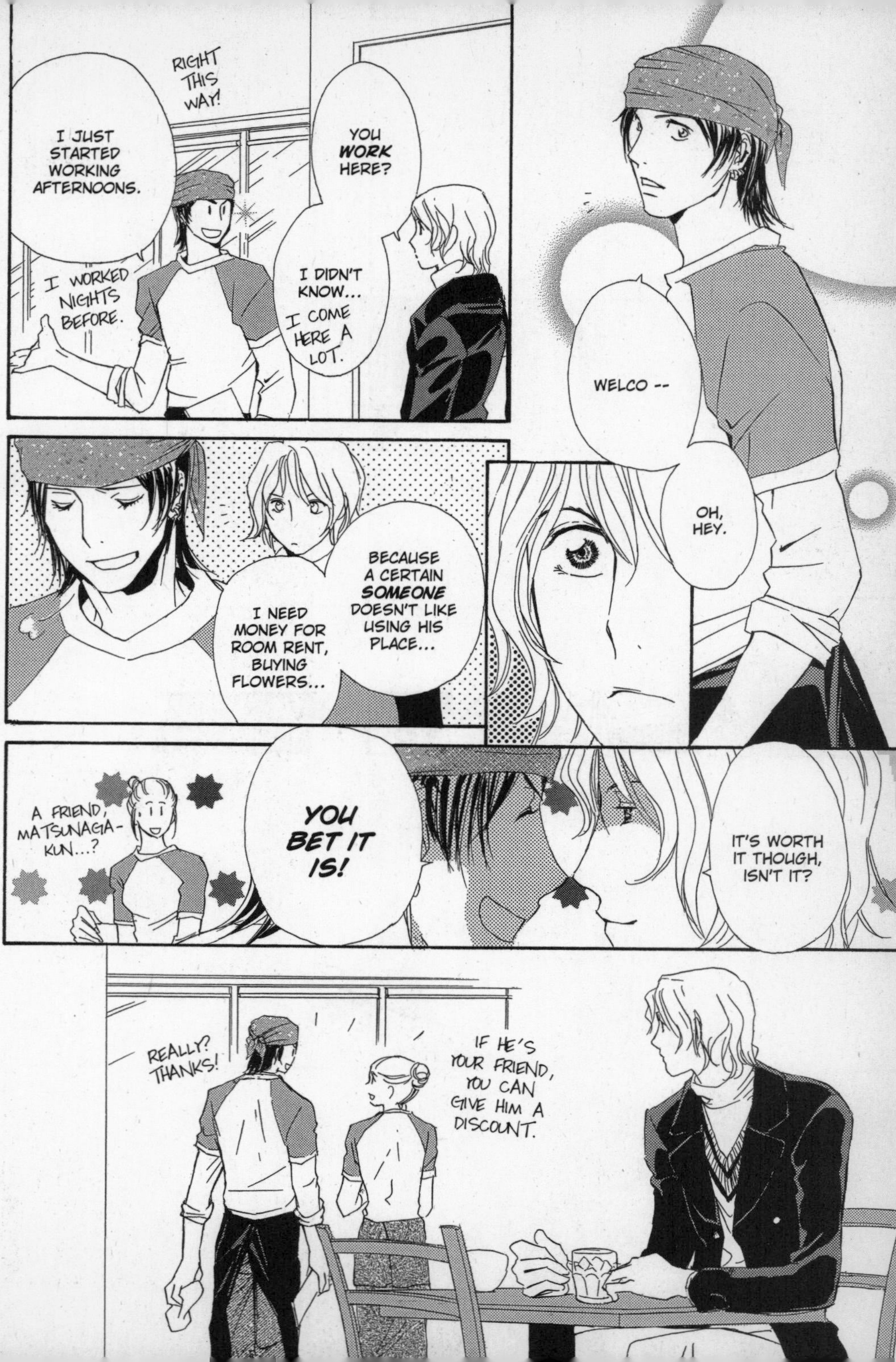
WELCO --
OH, HEY.
YOU WORK HERE?
RIGHT THIS WAY!
I JUST STARTED WORKING AFTERNOONS.
I DIDN'T KNOW... I COME HERE A LOT.
I WORKED NIGHTS BEFORE.
BECAUSE A CERTAIN SOMEONE DOESN'T LIKE USING HIS PLACE...
I NEED MONEY FOR ROOM RENT, BUYING FLOWERS...
IT'S WORTH IT THOUGH, ISN'T IT?
YOU BET IT IS!
A FRIEND, MATSUNAGA-KUN...?
IF HE'S YOUR FRIEND, YOU CAN GIVE HIM A DISCOUNT.
REALLY? THANKS!

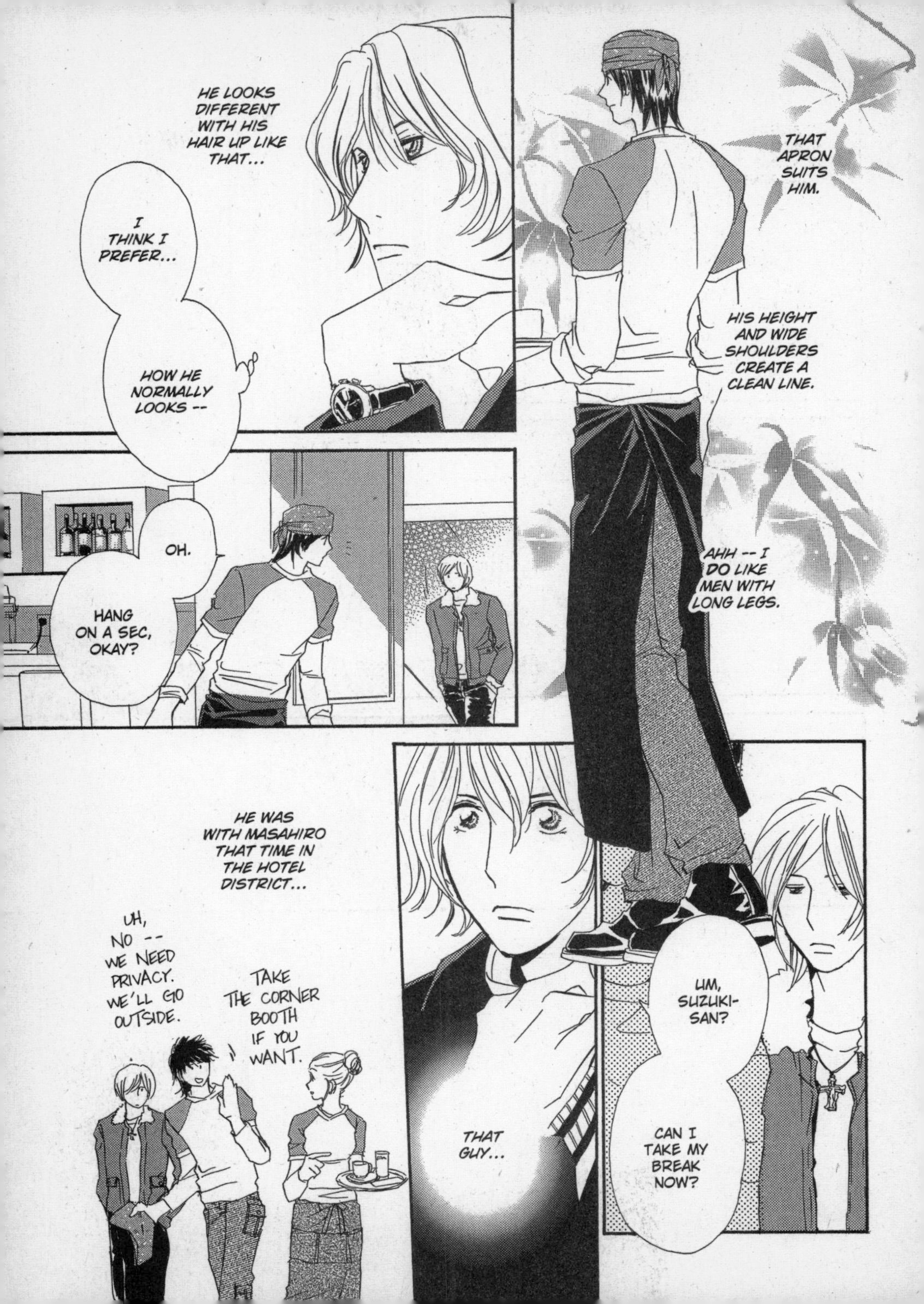
THAT APRON SUITS HIM.
HIS HEIGHT AND WIDE SHOULDERS CREATE A CLEAN LINE.
AHH -- I DO LIKE MEN WITH LONG LEGS.
HE LOOKS DIFFERENT WITH HIS HAIR UP LIKE THAT...
I THINK I PREFER...
HOW HE NORMALLY LOOKS --
OH.
HANG ON A SEC, OKAY?
UM, SUZUKI-SAN?
CAN I TAKE MY BREAK NOW?
THAT GUY...
HE WAS WITH MASAHIRO THAT TIME IN THE HOTEL DISTRICT...
TAKE THE CORNER BOOTH IF YOU WANT.
UH, NO -- WE NEED PRIVACY. WE'LL GO OUTSIDE.

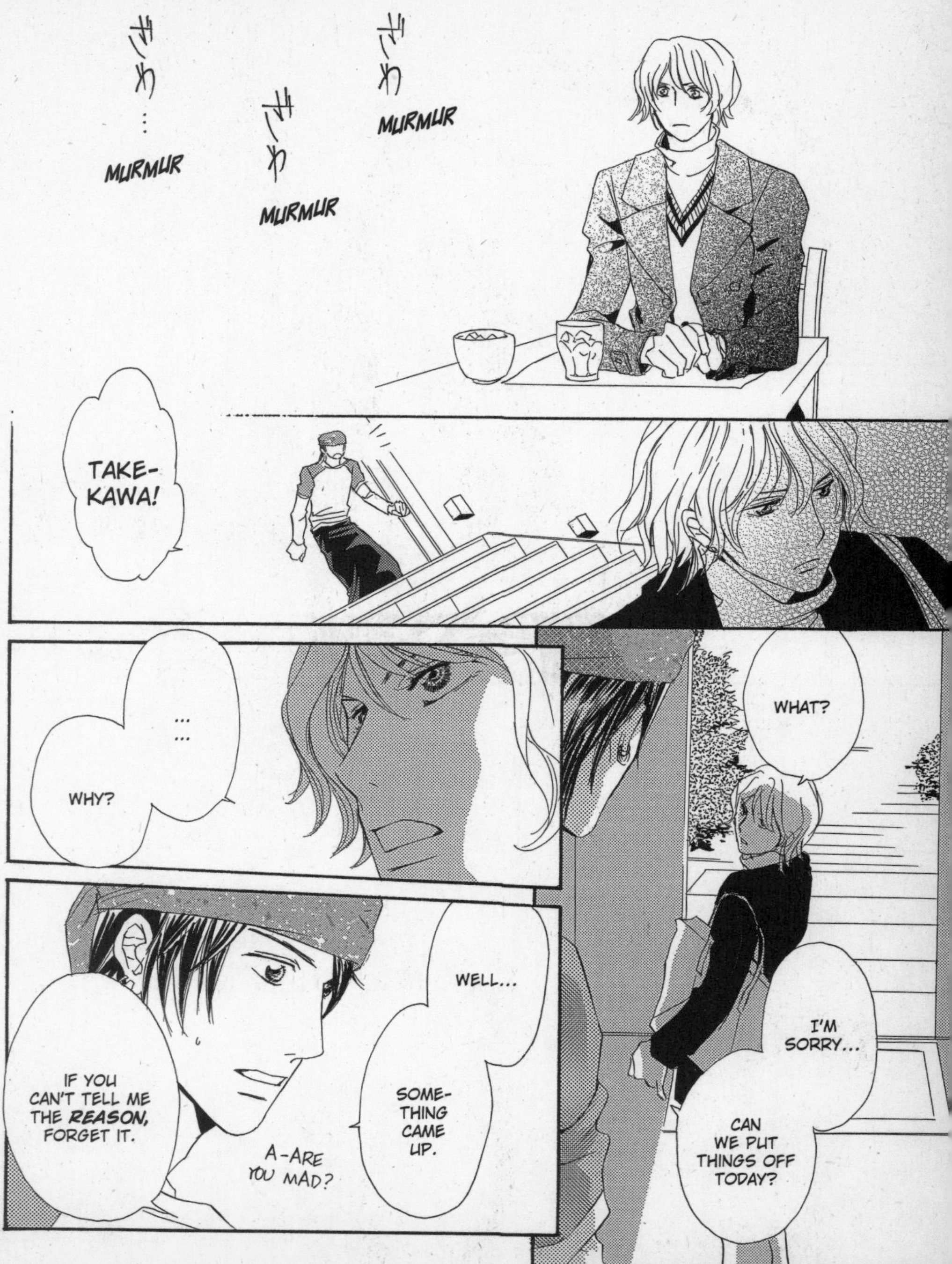
ざわ
MURMUR
ざわ
MURMUR
ざわ…
MURMUR
TAKE-KAWA!
WHAT?
I'M SORRY...
CAN WE PUT THINGS OFF TODAY?
...
...
WHY?
WELL...
SOME-THING CAME UP.
A-ARE YOU MAD?
IF YOU CAN'T TELL ME THE ***REASON,*** FORGET IT.

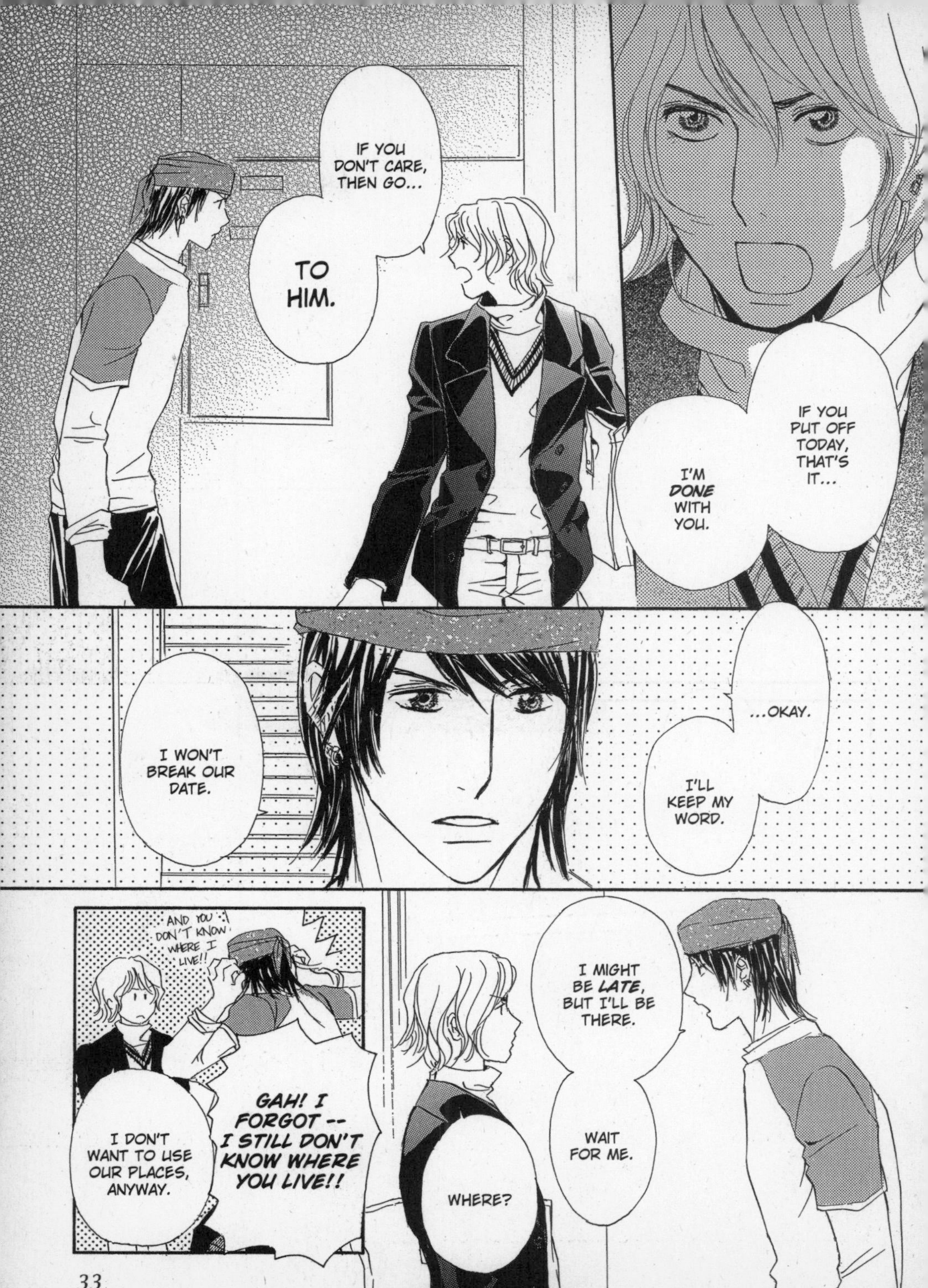
IF YOU PUT OFF TODAY, THAT'S IT...
I'M *DONE* WITH YOU.
IF YOU DON'T CARE, THEN GO...
TO HIM.
...OKAY.
I'LL KEEP MY WORD.
I WON'T BREAK OUR DATE.
I MIGHT BE *LATE*, BUT I'LL BE THERE.
WAIT FOR ME.
WHERE?
GAH! I FORGOT -- I STILL DON'T KNOW WHERE YOU LIVE!!
AND YOU DON'T KNOW WHERE I LIVE!!
I DON'T WANT TO USE OUR PLACES, ANYWAY.

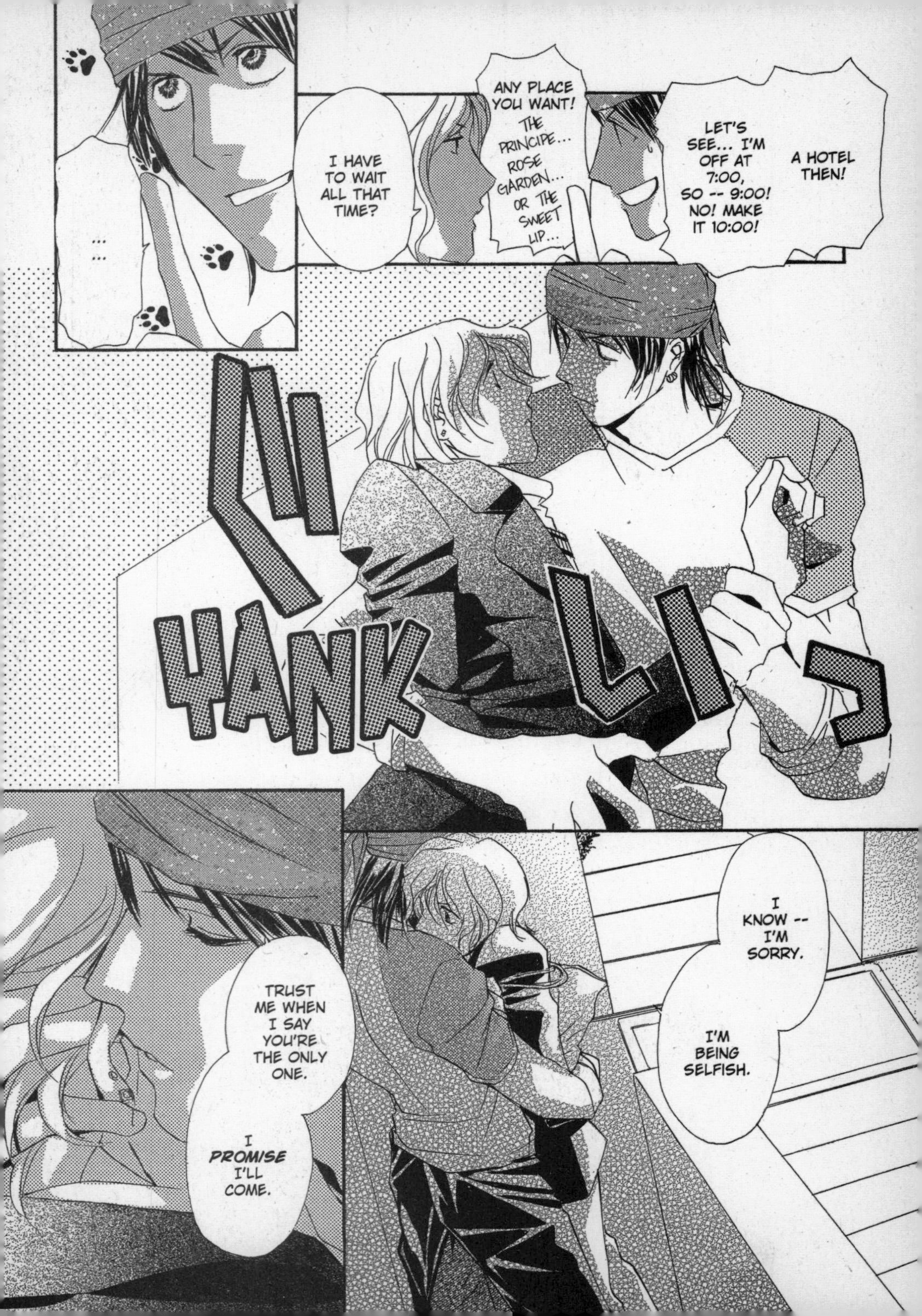
A HOTEL THEN!
LET'S SEE... I'M OFF AT 7:00, SO -- 9:00! NO! MAKE IT 10:00!
ANY PLACE YOU WANT! THE PRINCIPE... ROSE GARDEN... OR THE SWEET LIP...
I HAVE TO WAIT ALL THAT TIME?
... ...
YANK
I KNOW -- I'M SORRY.
I'M BEING SELFISH.
TRUST ME WHEN I SAY YOU'RE THE ONLY ONE.
I *PROMISE* I'LL COME.

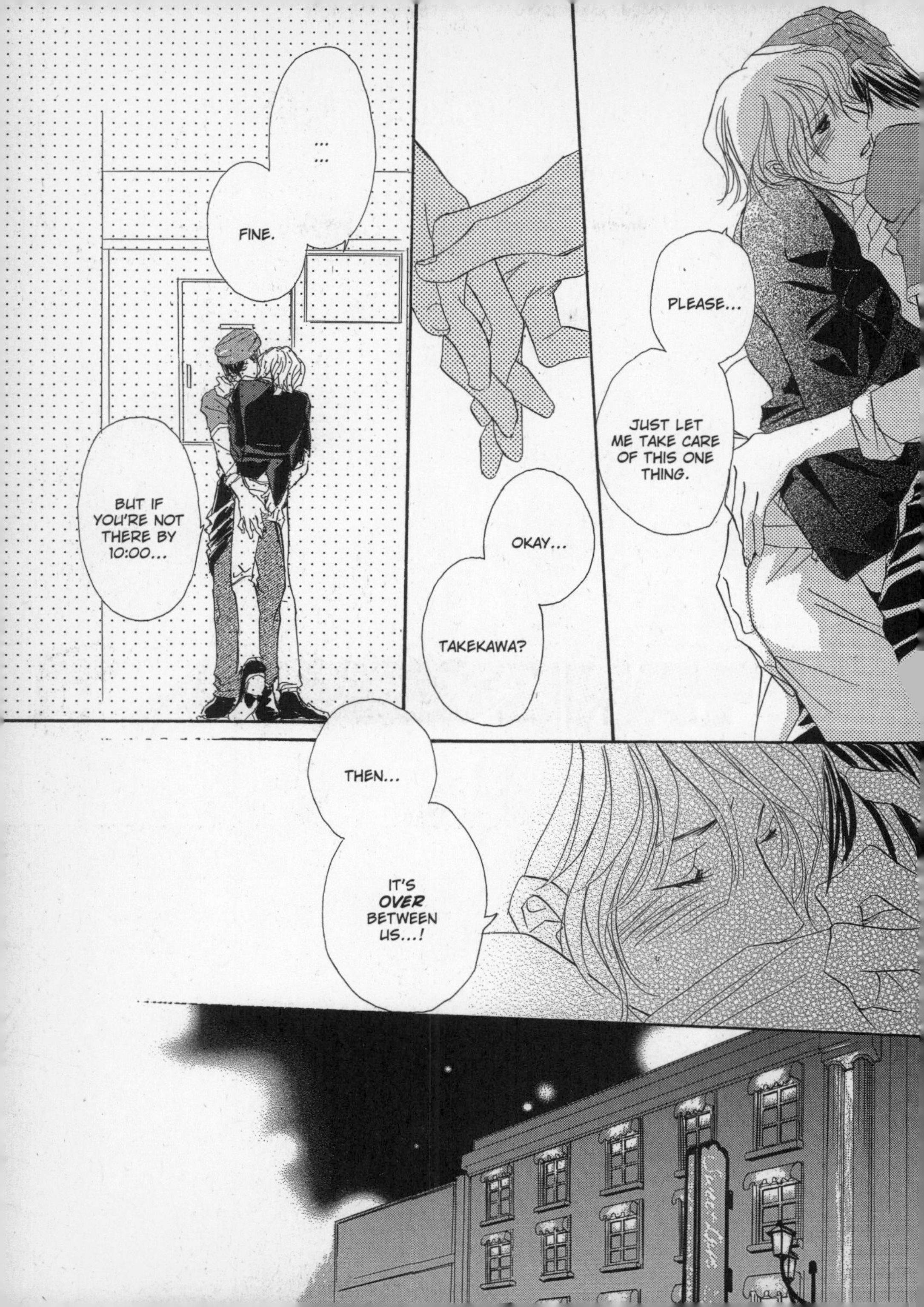
PLEASE...
JUST LET ME TAKE CARE OF THIS ONE THING.
OKAY...
TAKEKAWA?
... ...
FINE.
BUT IF YOU'RE NOT THERE BY 10:00...
THEN...
IT'S **OVER** BETWEEN US...!

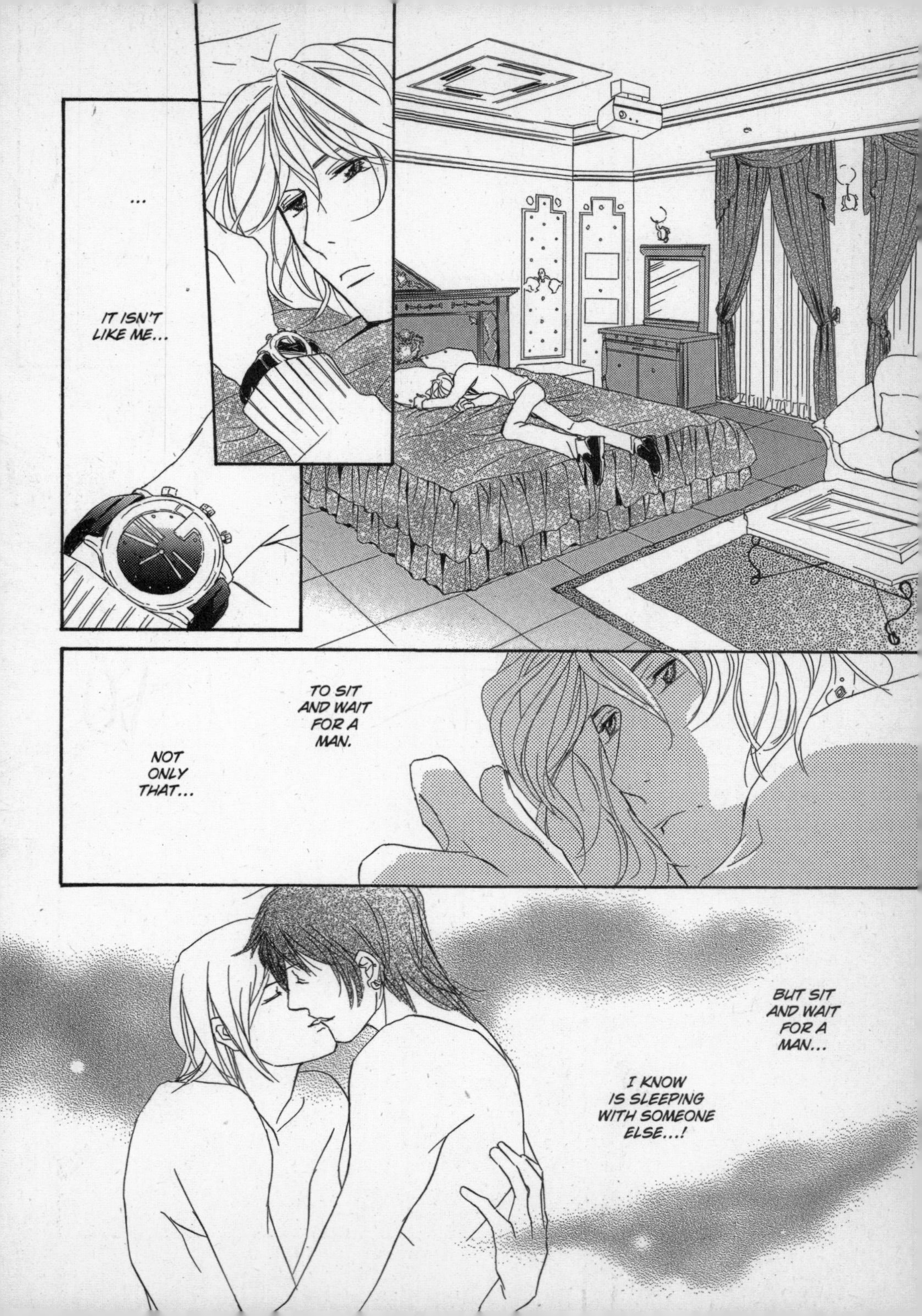
...
IT ISN'T LIKE ME...
TO SIT AND WAIT FOR A MAN.
NOT ONLY THAT...
BUT SIT AND WAIT FOR A MAN...
I KNOW IS SLEEPING WITH SOMEONE ELSE...!

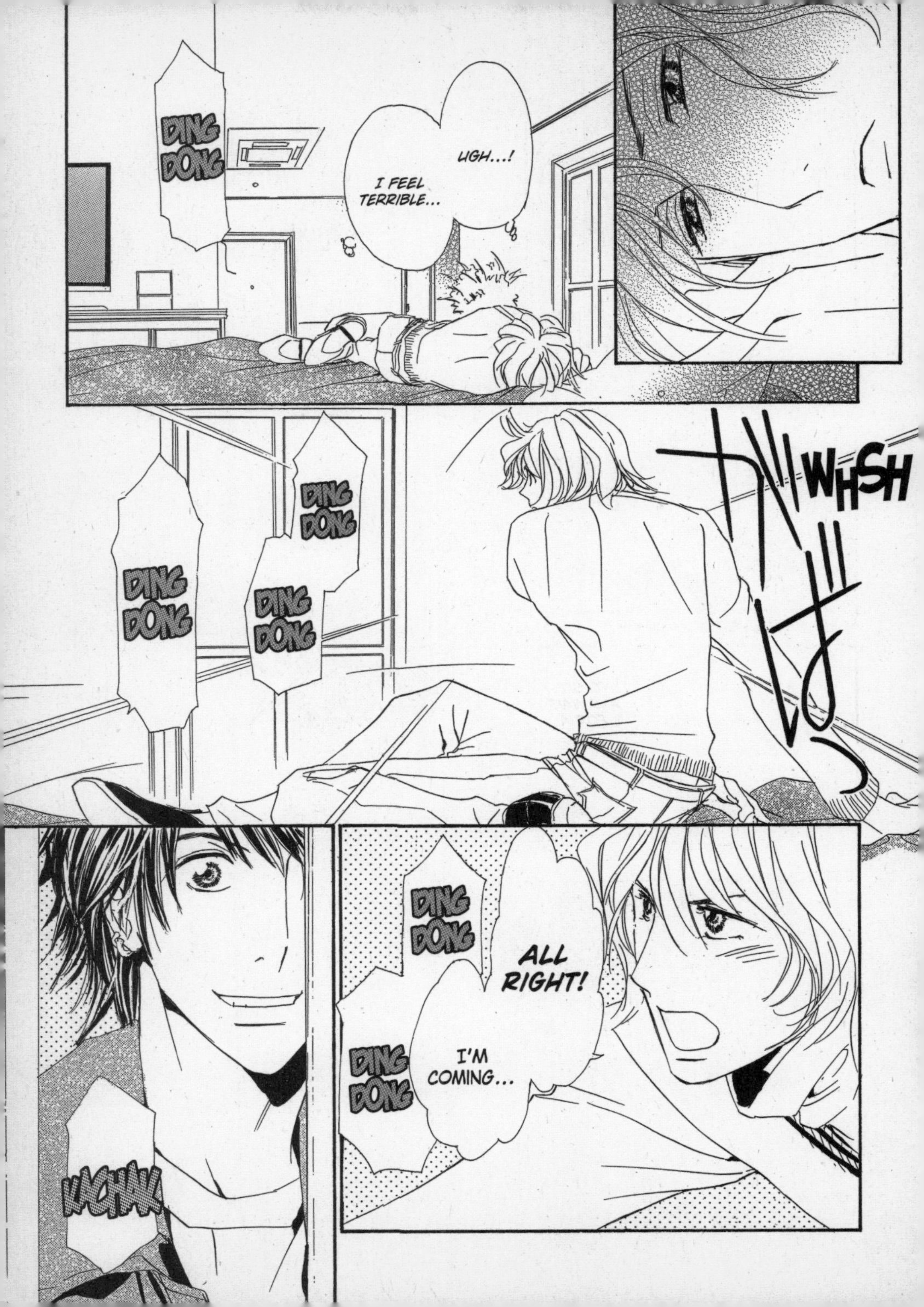
UGH...!
I FEEL TERRIBLE...
DING DONG
WHSH
DING DONG
DING DONG
DING DONG
ALL RIGHT!
DING DONG
I'M COMING...
DING DONG
KACHAK

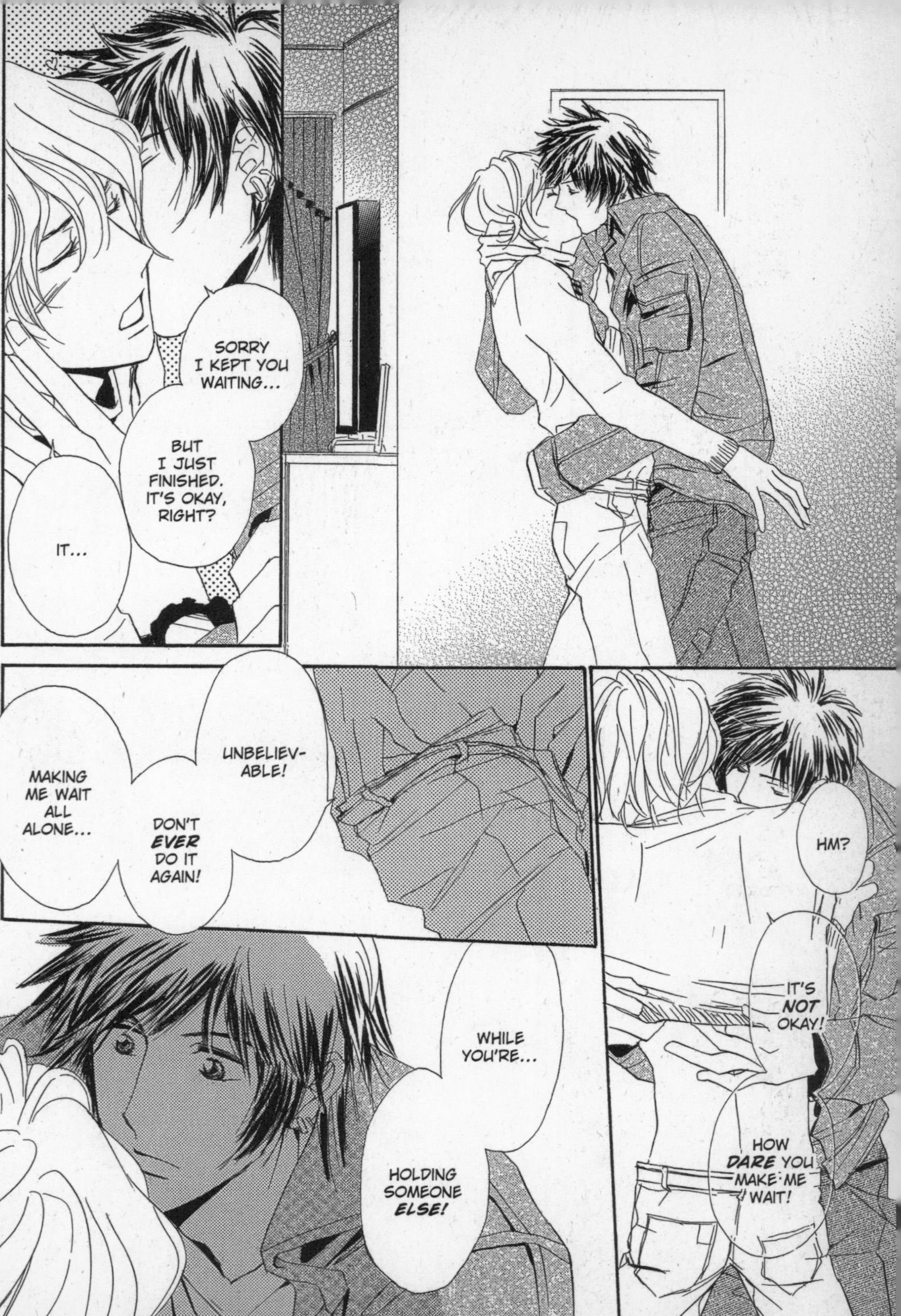
SORRY I KEPT YOU WAITING...
BUT I JUST FINISHED. IT'S OKAY, RIGHT?
IT...
HM?
IT'S *NOT* OKAY!
HOW *DARE* YOU MAKE ME WAIT!
UNBELIEVABLE!
MAKING ME WAIT ALL ALONE...
DON'T *EVER* DO IT AGAIN!
WHILE YOU'RE...
HOLDING SOMEONE *ELSE!*

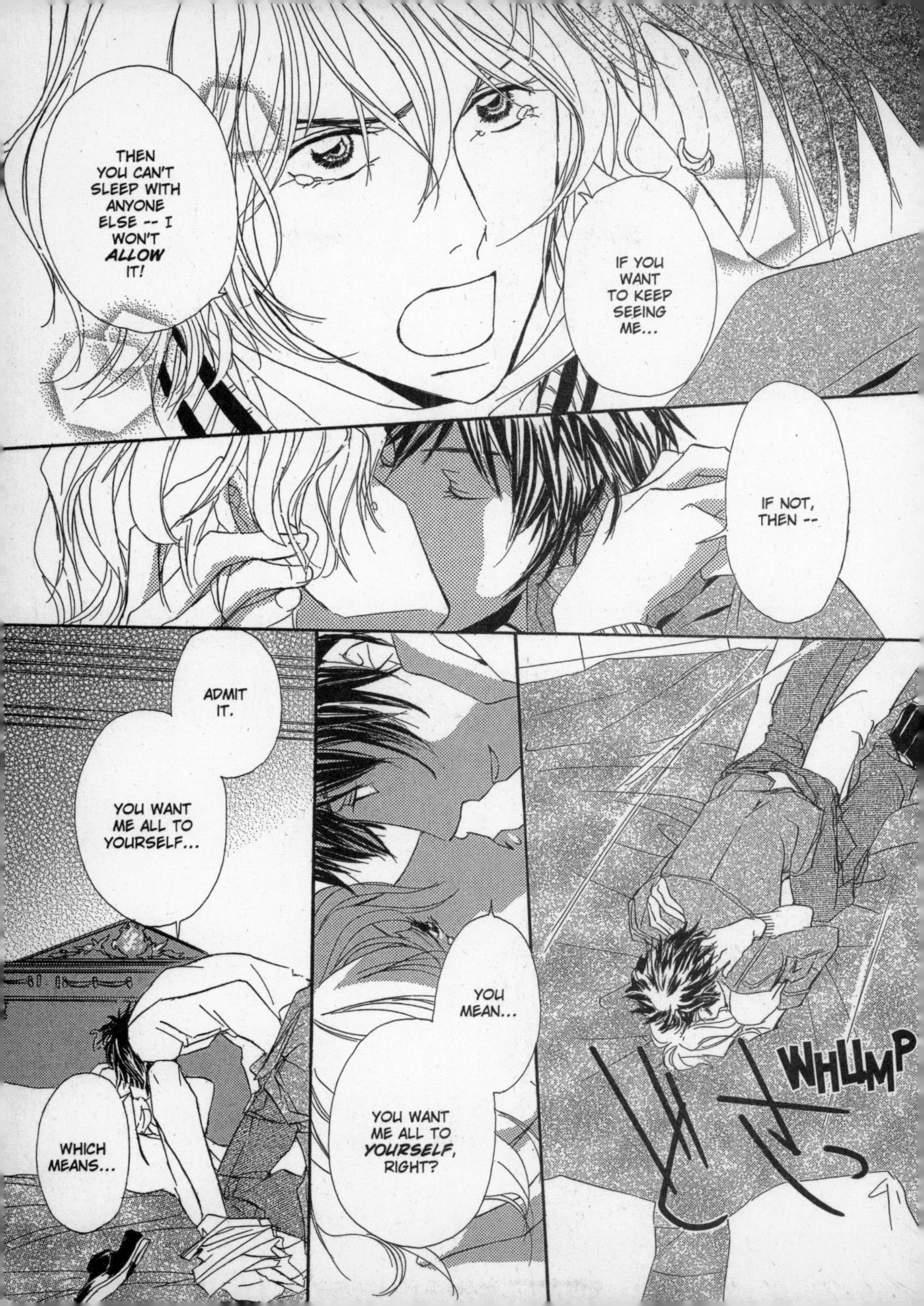
IF YOU WANT TO KEEP SEEING ME...
THEN YOU CAN'T SLEEP WITH ANYONE ELSE -- I WON'T **ALLOW** IT!
IF NOT, THEN --
WHUMP
YOU MEAN...
YOU WANT ME ALL TO ***YOURSELF***, RIGHT?
ADMIT IT.
YOU WANT ME ALL TO YOURSELF...
WHICH MEANS...

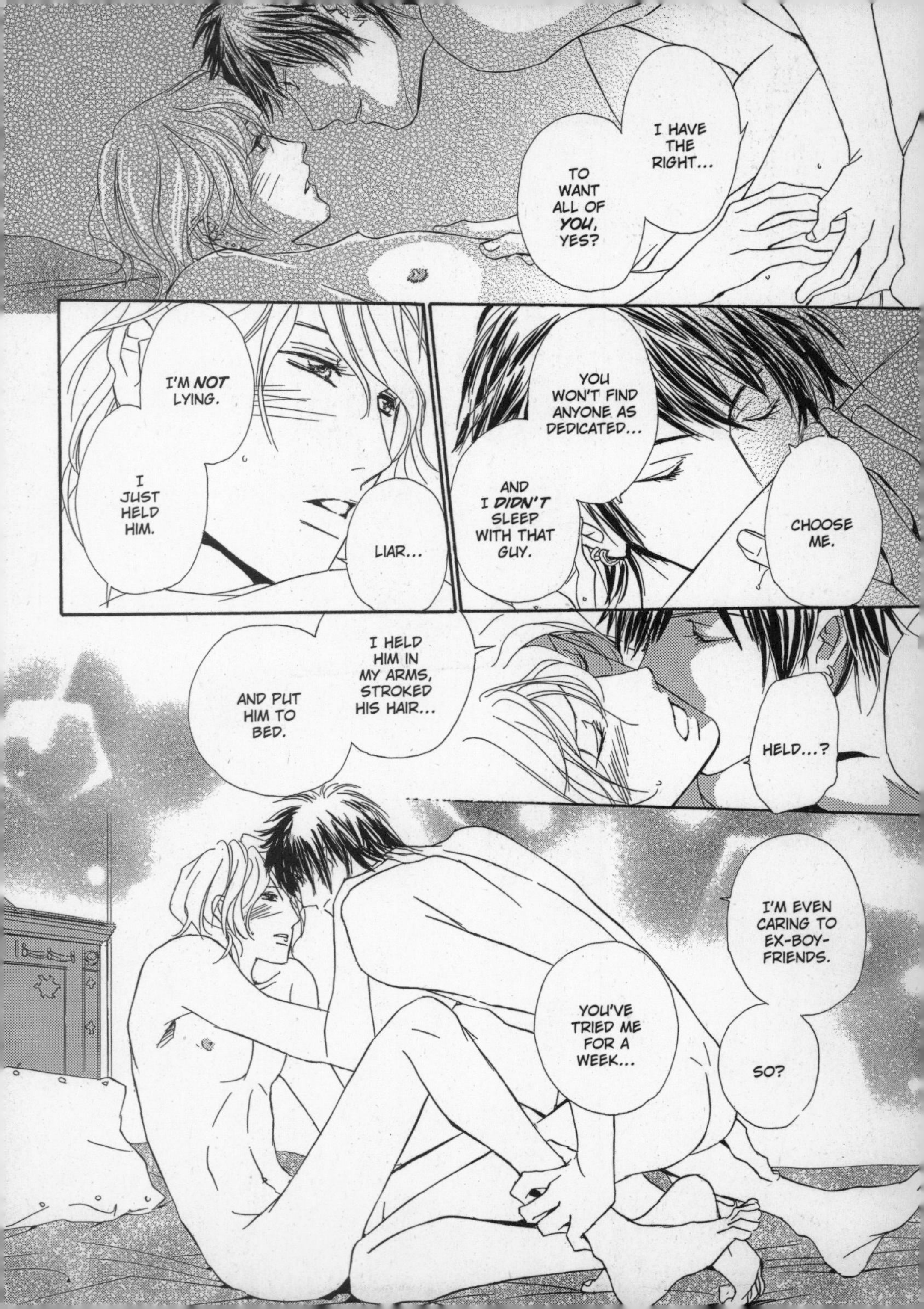
I HAVE THE RIGHT...
TO WANT ALL OF YOU, YES?
YOU WON'T FIND ANYONE AS DEDICATED...
CHOOSE ME.
AND I DIDN'T SLEEP WITH THAT GUY.
LIAR...
I'M NOT LYING.
I JUST HELD HIM.
HELD...?
I HELD HIM IN MY ARMS, STROKED HIS HAIR...
AND PUT HIM TO BED.
I'M EVEN CARING TO EX-BOY-FRIENDS.
SO?
YOU'VE TRIED ME FOR A WEEK...

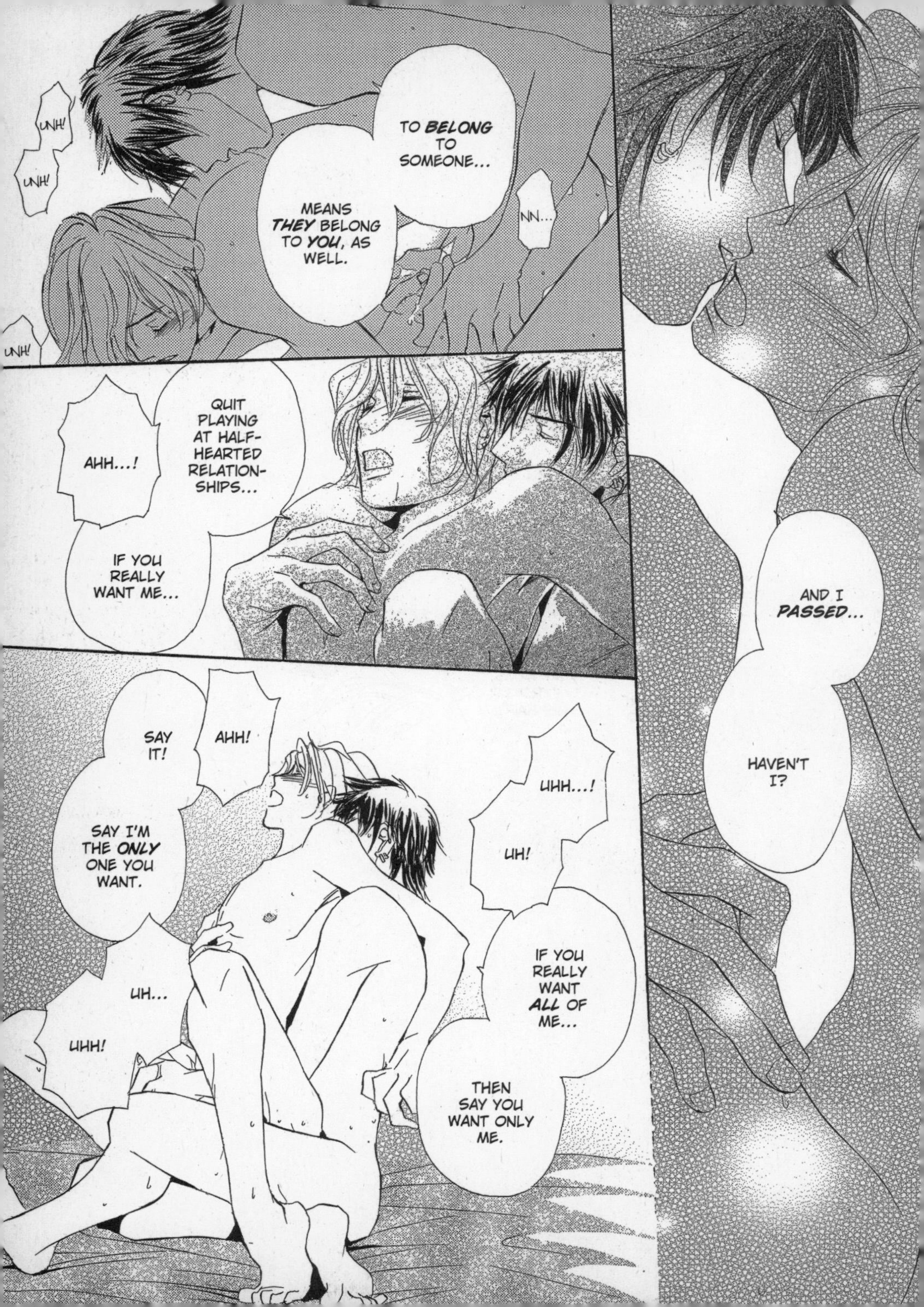
AND I PASSED...
HAVEN'T I?
NN...
TO BELONG TO SOMEONE...
MEANS THEY BELONG TO YOU, AS WELL.
UNH!
UNH!
UNH!
QUIT PLAYING AT HALF-HEARTED RELATIONSHIPS...
AHH...!
IF YOU REALLY WANT ME...
UHH...!
UH!
IF YOU REALLY WANT ALL OF ME...
THEN SAY YOU WANT ONLY ME.
AHH!
SAY IT!
SAY I'M THE ONLY ONE YOU WANT.
UH...
UHH!

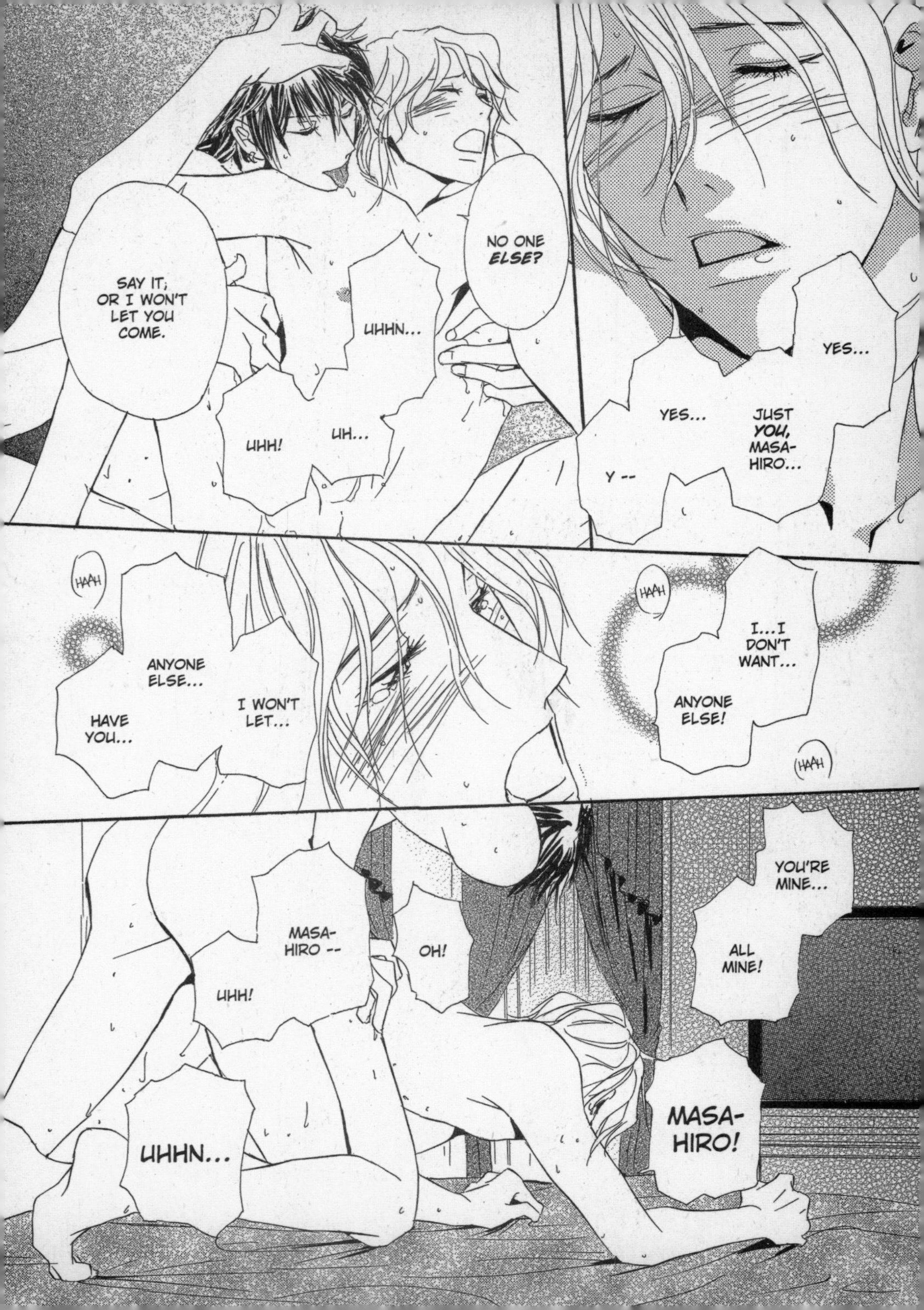
YES...
JUST YOU, MASA-HIRO...
YES...
Y --
NO ONE ELSE?
SAY IT, OR I WON'T LET YOU COME.
UHHN...
UH...
UHH!
HAAH
I...I DON'T WANT...
ANYONE ELSE!
HAAH
HAAH
I WON'T LET...
ANYONE ELSE...
HAVE YOU...
YOU'RE MINE...
ALL MINE!
MASA-HIRO!
OH!
MASA-HIRO --
UHH!
UHHN...

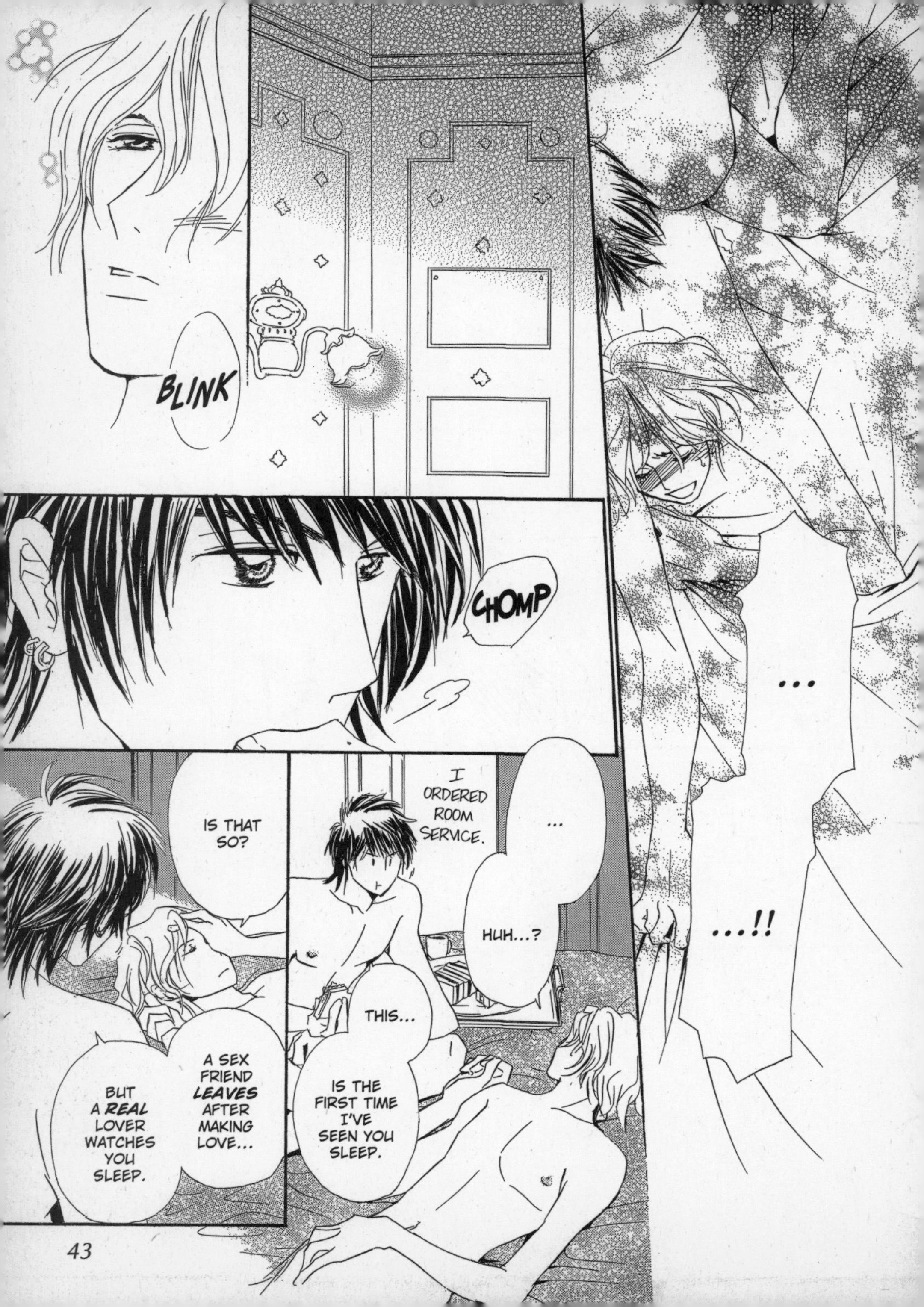
...
...!!
BLINK
CHOMP
I ORDERED ROOM SERVICE.
...
HUH...?
THIS...
IS THE FIRST TIME I'VE SEEN YOU SLEEP.
IS THAT SO?
A SEX FRIEND *LEAVES* AFTER MAKING LOVE...
BUT A *REAL* LOVER WATCHES YOU SLEEP.

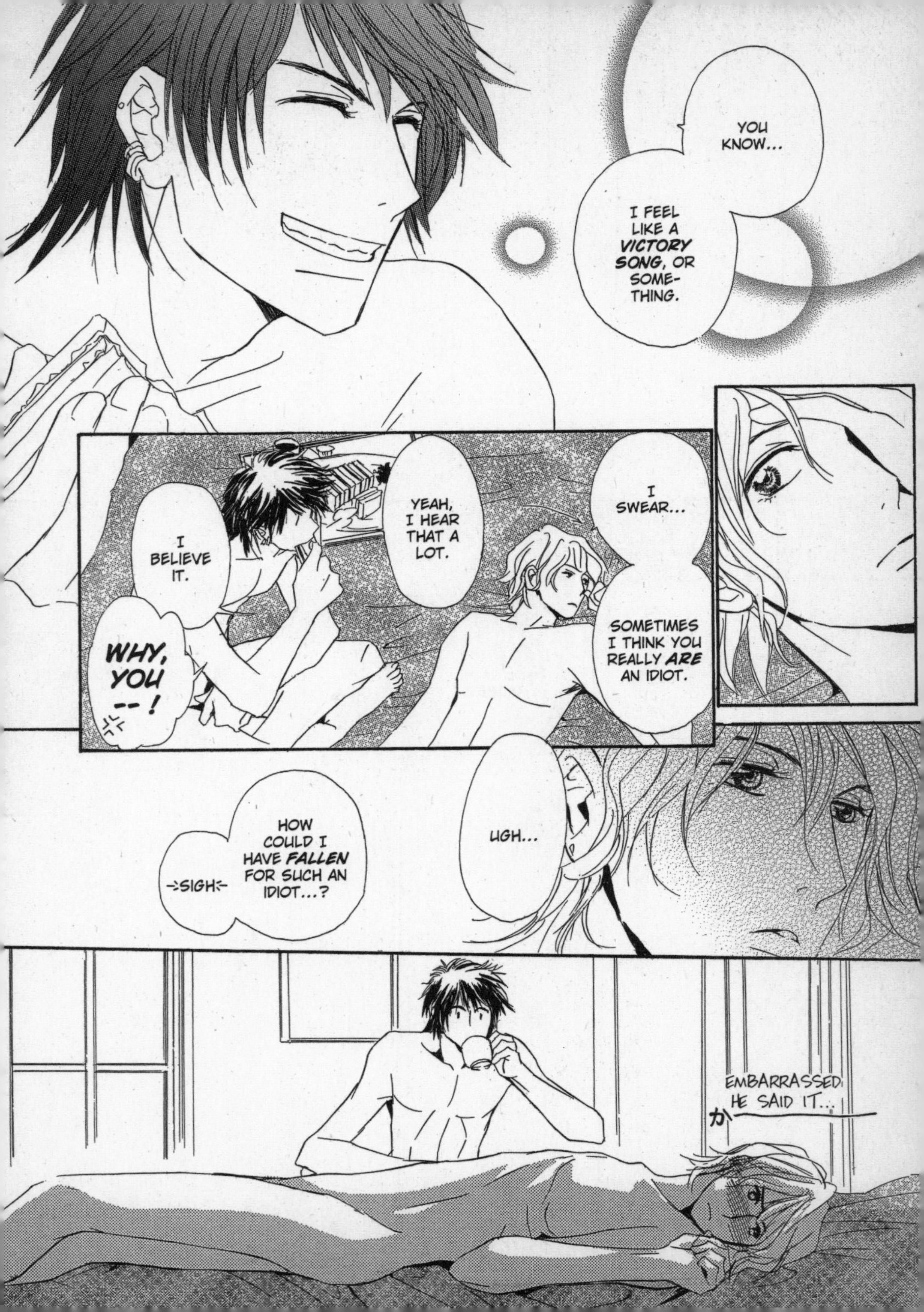
YOU KNOW...
I FEEL LIKE A VICTORY SONG, OR SOME-THING.
I SWEAR...
SOMETIMES I THINK YOU REALLY ARE AN IDIOT.
YEAH, I HEAR THAT A LOT.
I BELIEVE IT.
WHY, YOU--!
UGH...
HOW COULD I HAVE FALLEN FOR SUCH AN IDIOT...?
-SIGH-
EMBARRASSED HE SAID IT...
か

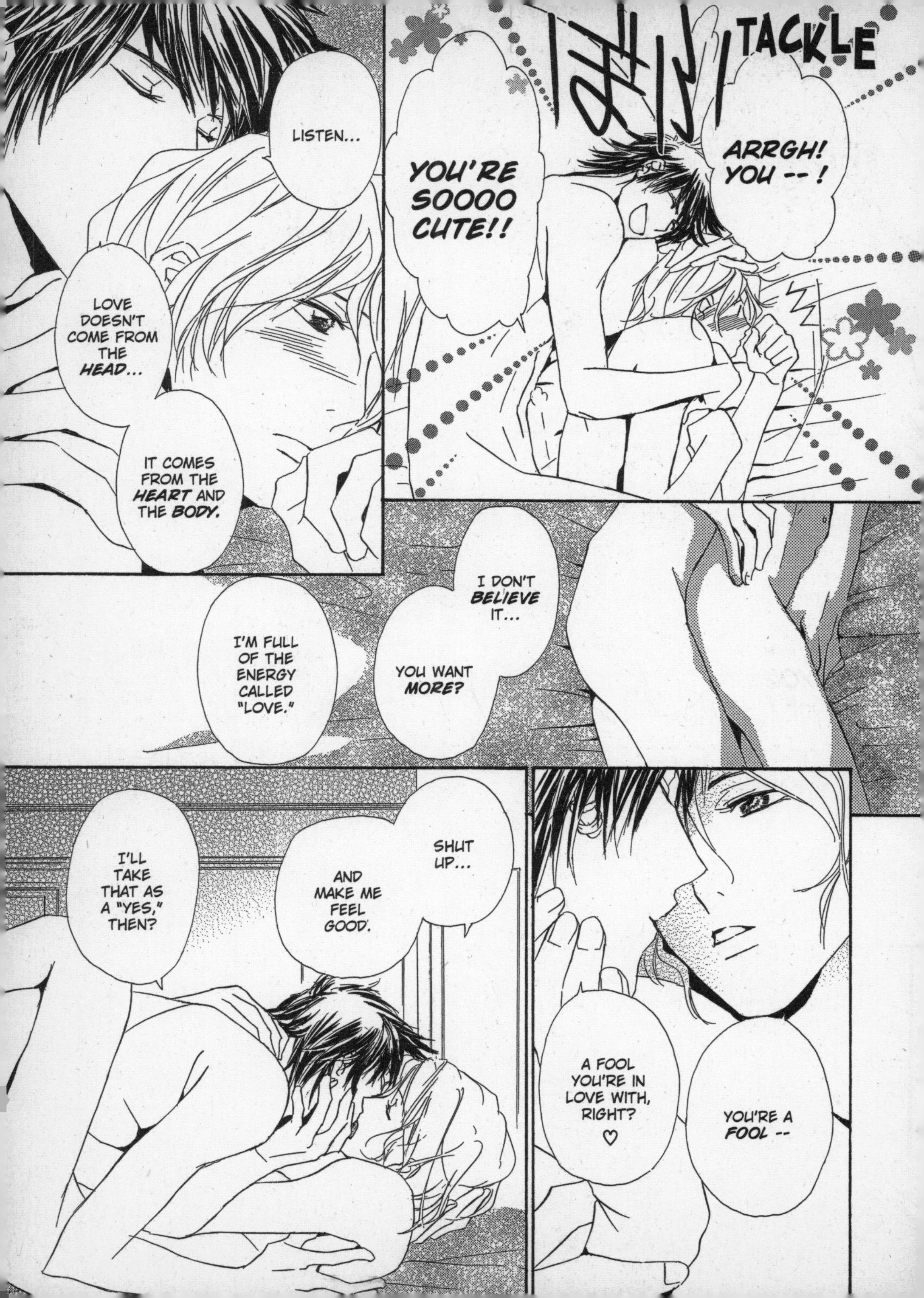
TACKLE
ARRGH! YOU -- !
YOU'RE SOOOO CUTE!!
LISTEN...
LOVE DOESN'T COME FROM THE HEAD...
IT COMES FROM THE HEART AND THE BODY.
I DON'T BELIEVE IT...
YOU WANT MORE?
I'M FULL OF THE ENERGY CALLED "LOVE."
YOU'RE A FOOL --
A FOOL YOU'RE IN LOVE WITH, RIGHT? ♡
SHUT UP...
AND MAKE ME FEEL GOOD.
I'LL TAKE THAT AS A "YES," THEN?

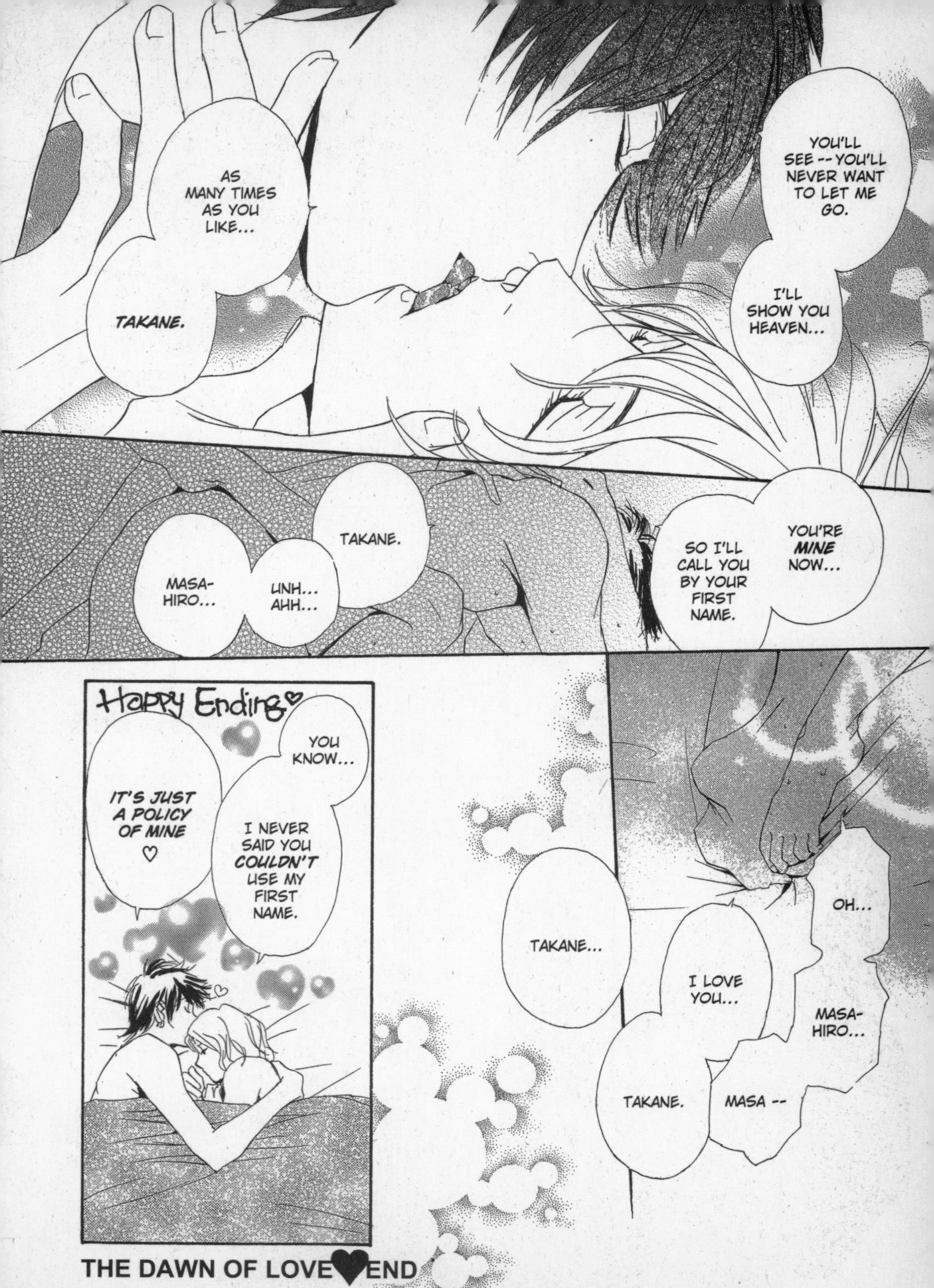
YOU'LL SEE--YOU'LL NEVER WANT TO LET ME GO.
I'LL SHOW YOU HEAVEN...
AS MANY TIMES AS YOU LIKE...
TAKANE.
YOU'RE *MINE* NOW...
SO I'LL CALL YOU BY YOUR FIRST NAME.
TAKANE.
UNH... AHH...
MASA-HIRO...
OH...
MASA-HIRO...
I LOVE YOU...
TAKANE...
MASA --
TAKANE.
Happy Ending♡
YOU KNOW...
I NEVER SAID YOU *COULDN'T* USE MY FIRST NAME.
IT'S JUST A POLICY OF MINE ♡

THE DAWN OF LOVE♥END

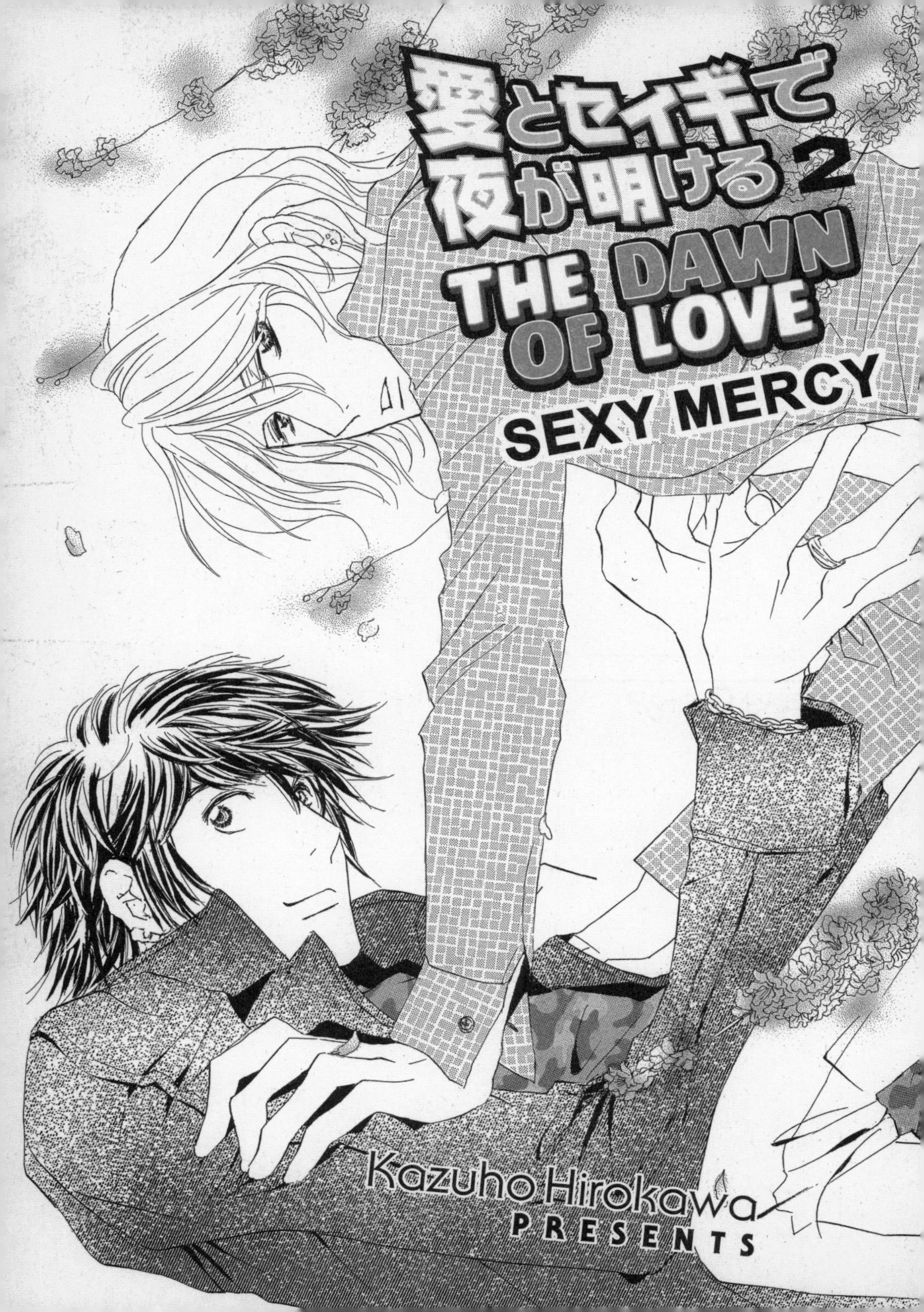
愛とセィギで夜が明ける 2
THE DAWN OF LOVE
SEXY MERCY
Kazuho Hirokawa PRESENTS

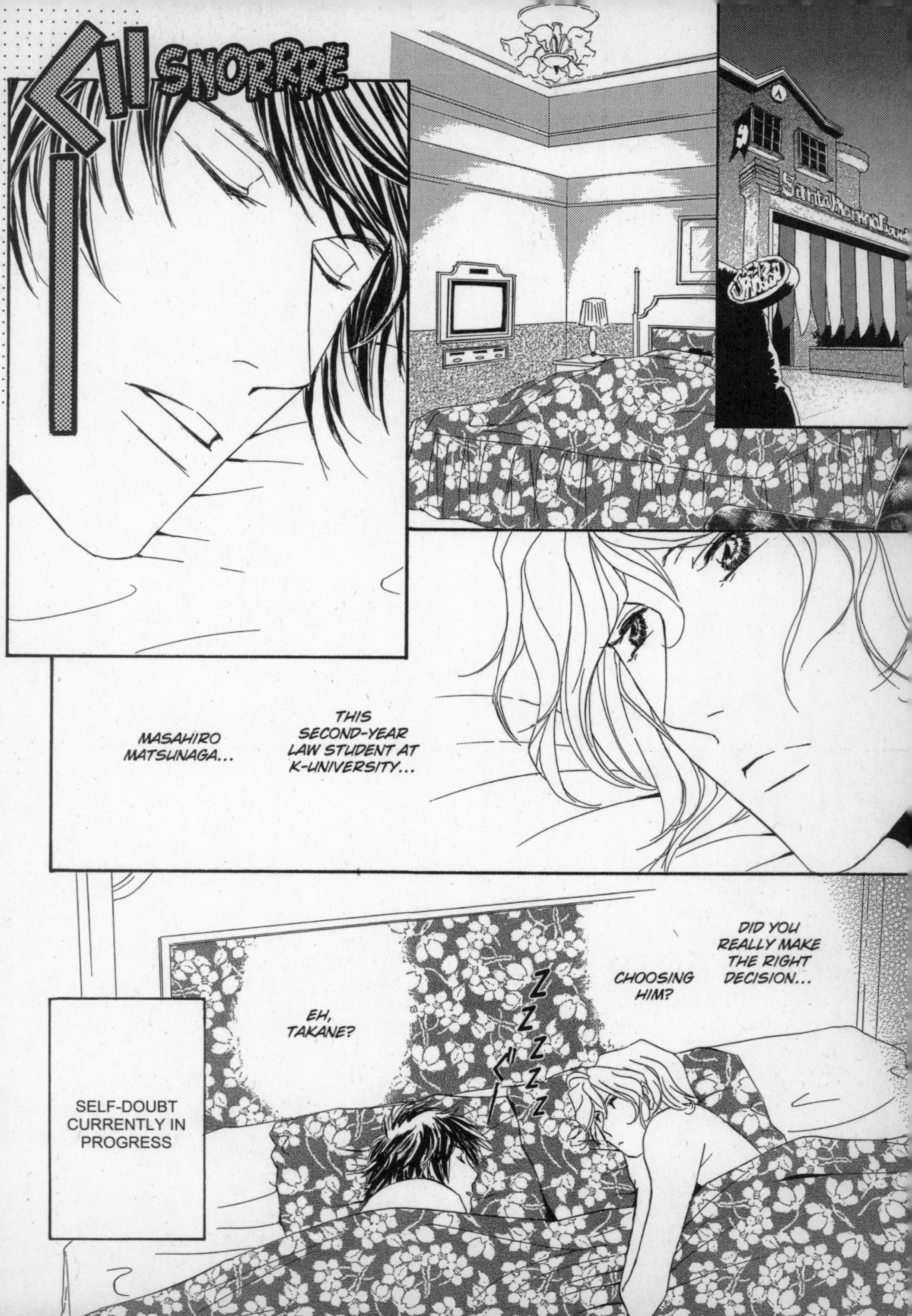
SNORRRE
THIS SECOND-YEAR LAW STUDENT AT K-UNIVERSITY...
MASAHIRO MATSUNAGA...
DID YOU REALLY MAKE THE RIGHT DECISION...
CHOOSING HIM?
EH, TAKANE?
ZZZZZ
SELF-DOUBT CURRENTLY IN PROGRESS

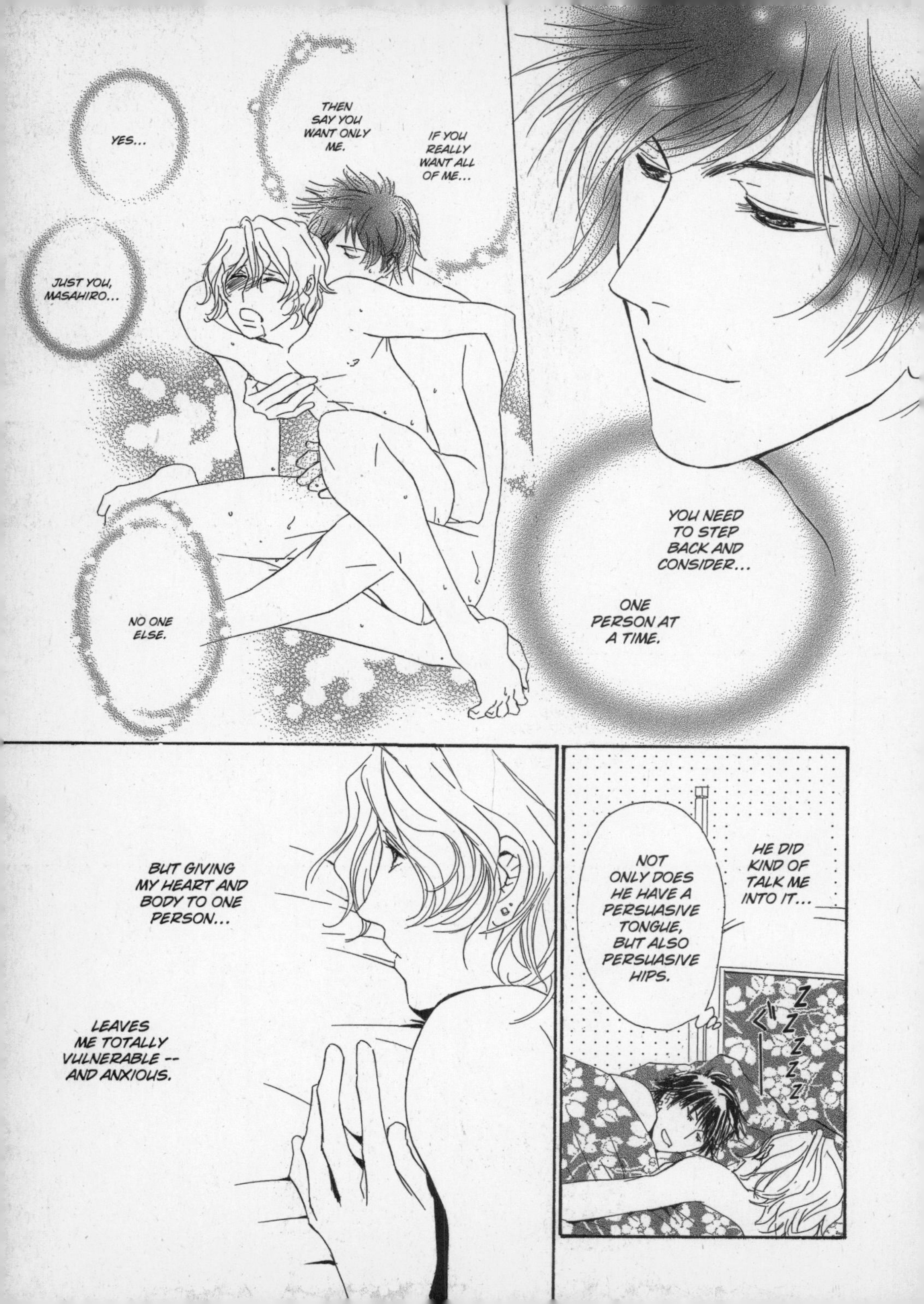
YOU NEED TO STEP BACK AND CONSIDER...
ONE PERSON AT A TIME.
IF YOU REALLY WANT ALL OF ME...
THEN SAY YOU WANT ONLY ME.
YES...
JUST YOU, MASAHIRO...
NO ONE ELSE.
HE DID KIND OF TALK ME INTO IT...
NOT ONLY DOES HE HAVE A PERSUASIVE TONGUE, BUT ALSO PERSUASIVE HIPS.
ZZZZZ
BUT GIVING MY HEART AND BODY TO ONE PERSON...
LEAVES ME TOTALLY VULNERABLE -- AND ANXIOUS.

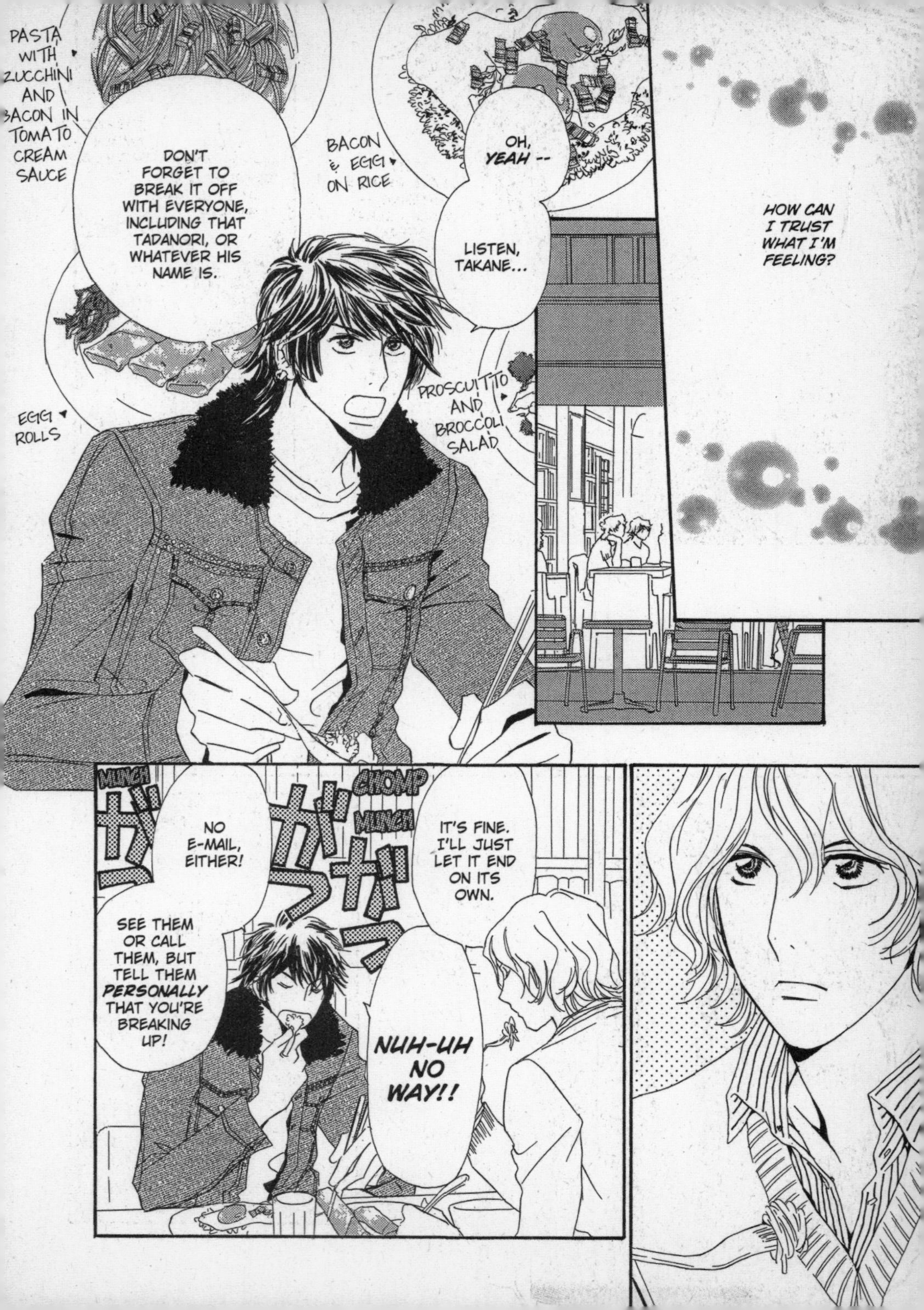

HOW CAN I TRUST WHAT I'M FEELING?
OH, YEAH --
LISTEN, TAKANE...
BACON & EGG ON RICE
PROSCUITTO AND BROCCOLI SALAD
DON'T FORGET TO BREAK IT OFF WITH EVERYONE, INCLUDING THAT TADANORI, OR WHATEVER HIS NAME IS.
PASTA WITH ZUCCHINI AND BACON IN TOMATO CREAM SAUCE
EGG ROLLS
CHOMP
MUNCH
IT'S FINE. I'LL JUST LET IT END ON ITS OWN.
NUH-UH NO WAY!!
MUNCH
NO E-MAIL, EITHER!
SEE THEM OR CALL THEM, BUT TELL THEM PERSONALLY THAT YOU'RE BREAKING UP!

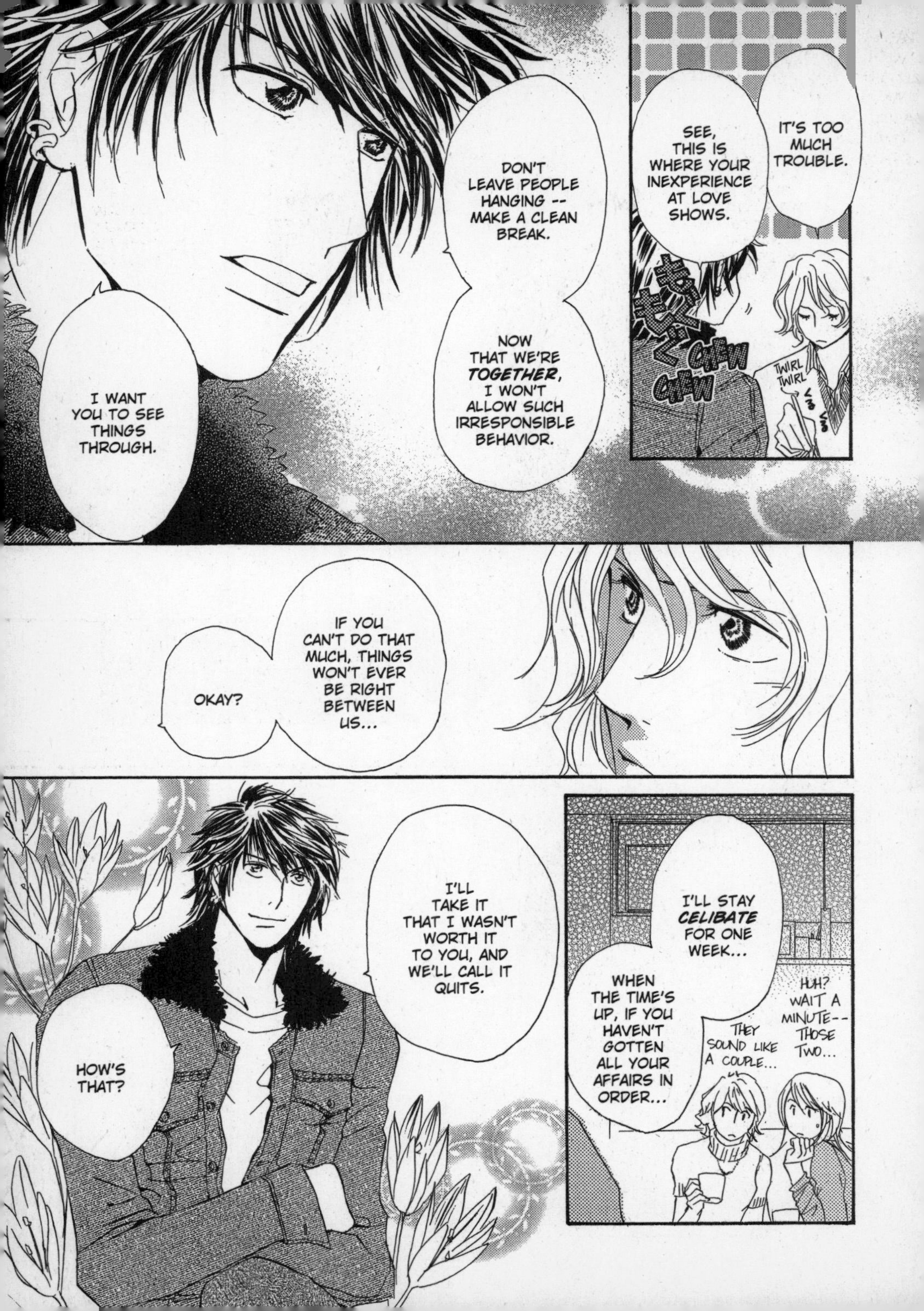
IT'S TOO MUCH TROUBLE.
SEE, THIS IS WHERE YOUR INEXPERIENCE AT LOVE SHOWS.
CHEW CHEW
TWIRL TWIRL
DON'T LEAVE PEOPLE HANGING -- MAKE A CLEAN BREAK.
NOW THAT WE'RE *TOGETHER*, I WON'T ALLOW SUCH IRRESPONSIBLE BEHAVIOR.
I WANT YOU TO SEE THINGS THROUGH.
IF YOU CAN'T DO THAT MUCH, THINGS WON'T EVER BE RIGHT BETWEEN US...
OKAY?
I'LL STAY *CELIBATE* FOR ONE WEEK...
WHEN THE TIME'S UP, IF YOU HAVEN'T GOTTEN ALL YOUR AFFAIRS IN ORDER...
HUH? WAIT A MINUTE-- THOSE TWO...
THEY SOUND LIKE A COUPLE...
I'LL TAKE IT THAT I WASN'T WORTH IT TO YOU, AND WE'LL CALL IT QUITS.
HOW'S THAT?

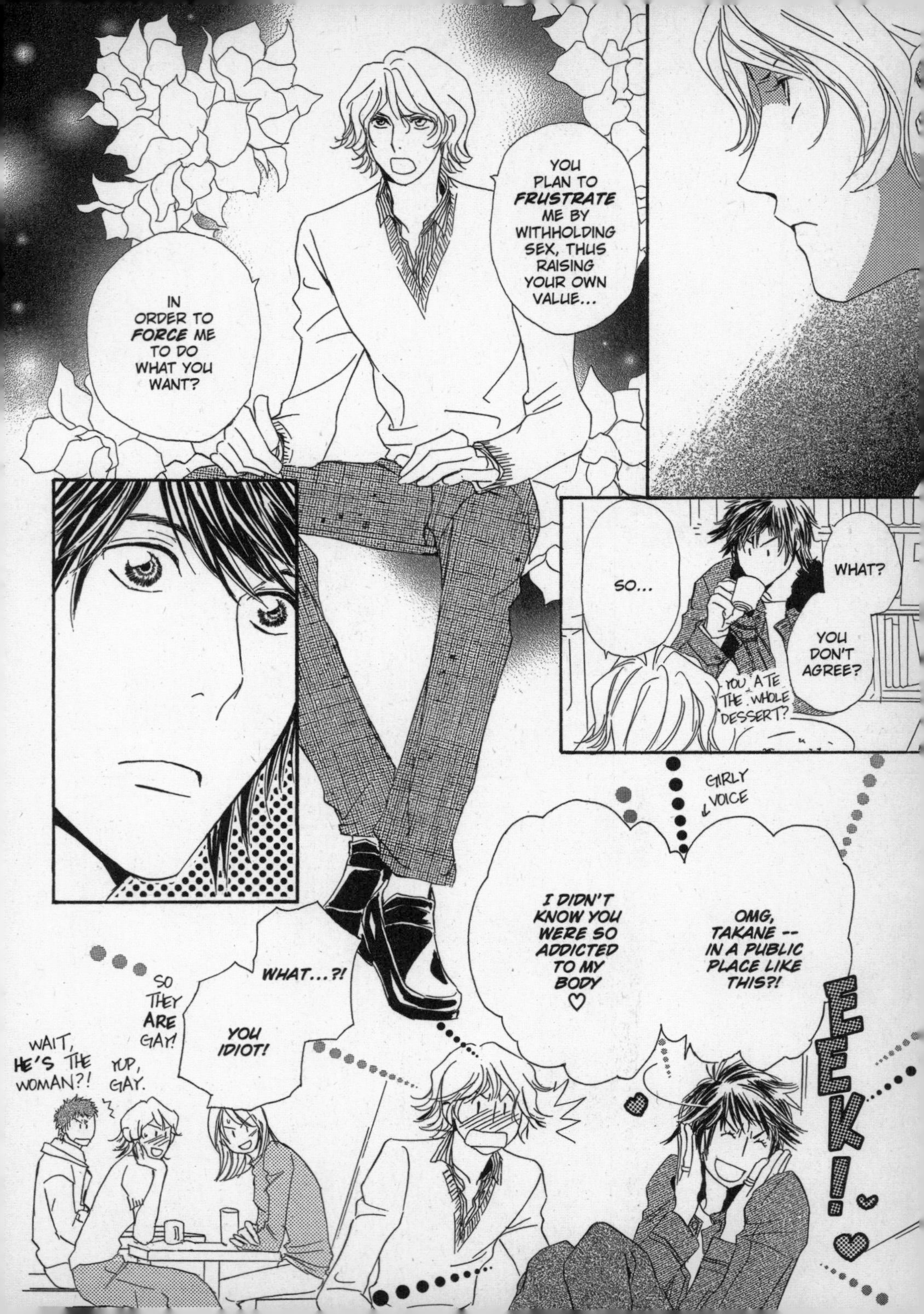
YOU PLAN TO FRUSTRATE ME BY WITHHOLDING SEX, THUS RAISING YOUR OWN VALUE...
IN ORDER TO FORCE ME TO DO WHAT YOU WANT?
WHAT?
YOU DON'T AGREE?
SO...
YOU ATE THE WHOLE DESSERT?
GIRLY VOICE
OMG, TAKANE -- IN A PUBLIC PLACE LIKE THIS?!
I DIDN'T KNOW YOU WERE SO ADDICTED TO MY BODY ♡
EEK!
WHAT...?!
YOU IDIOT!
SO THEY ARE GAY!
YUP, GAY.
WAIT, HE'S THE WOMAN?!

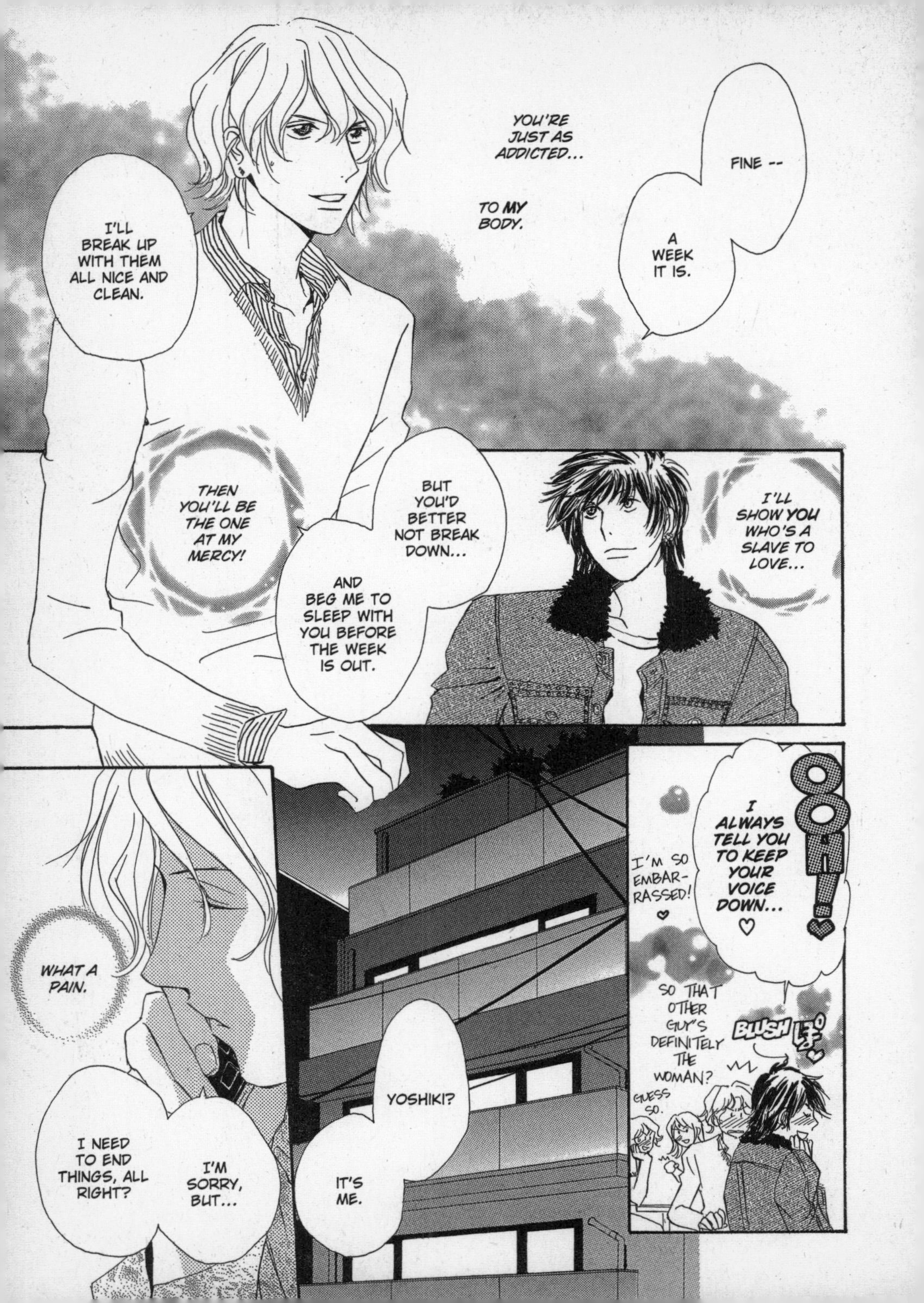
FINE --
A WEEK IT IS.
YOU'RE JUST AS ADDICTED...
TO MY BODY.
I'LL BREAK UP WITH THEM ALL NICE AND CLEAN.
I'LL SHOW YOU WHO'S A SLAVE TO LOVE...
BUT YOU'D BETTER NOT BREAK DOWN...
AND BEG ME TO SLEEP WITH YOU BEFORE THE WEEK IS OUT.
THEN YOU'LL BE THE ONE AT MY MERCY!
OOH!
I ALWAYS TELL YOU TO KEEP YOUR VOICE DOWN... ♡
I'M SO EMBARRASSED! ♡
BLUSH ぽ
SO THAT OTHER GUY'S DEFINITELY THE WOMAN?
GUESS SO.
YOSHIKI?
IT'S ME.
I'M SORRY, BUT...
I NEED TO END THINGS, ALL RIGHT?
WHAT A PAIN.

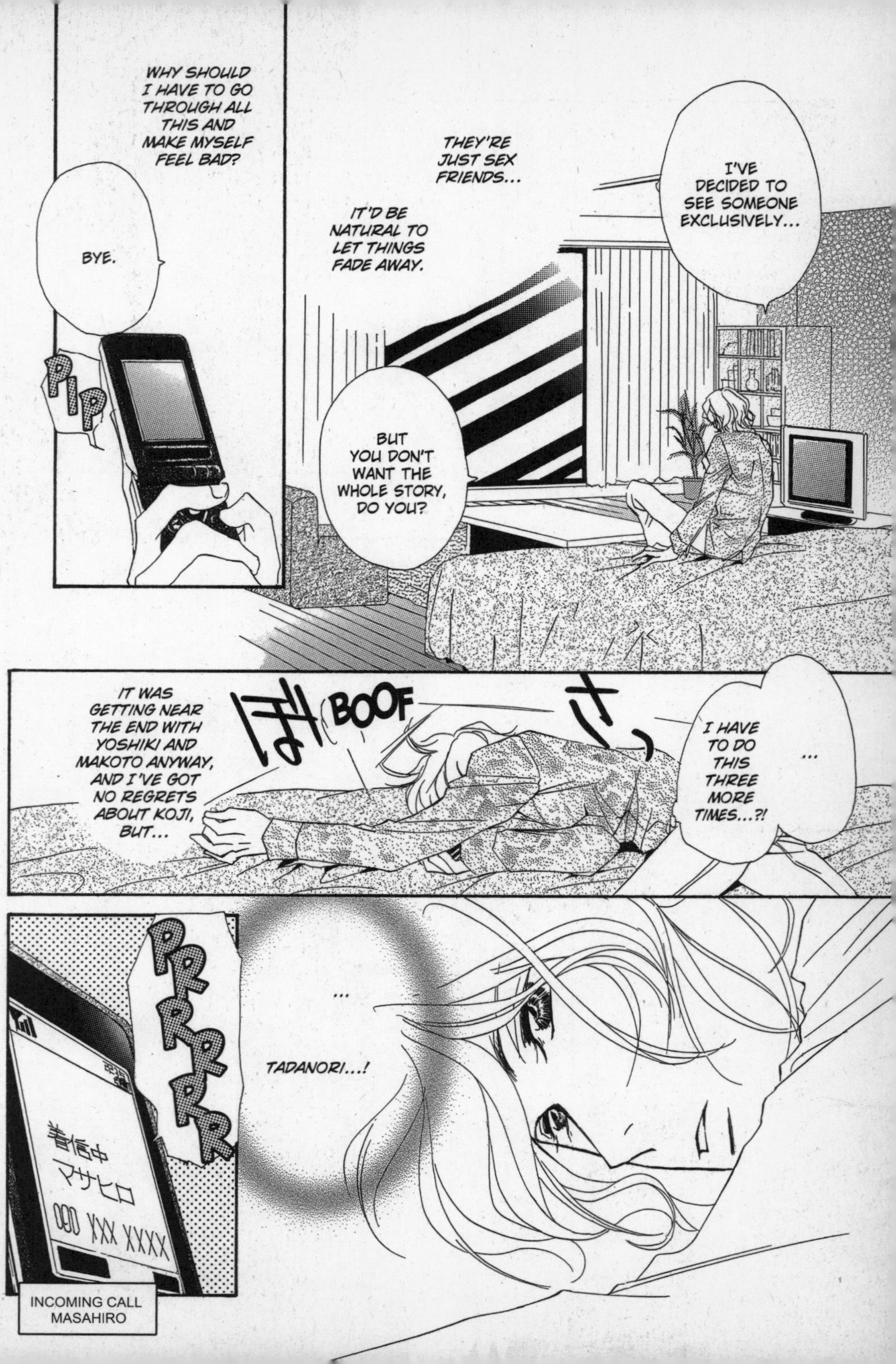
I'VE DECIDED TO SEE SOMEONE EXCLUSIVELY...
THEY'RE JUST SEX FRIENDS...
IT'D BE NATURAL TO LET THINGS FADE AWAY.
BUT YOU DON'T WANT THE WHOLE STORY, DO YOU?
WHY SHOULD I HAVE TO GO THROUGH ALL THIS AND MAKE MYSELF FEEL BAD?
BYE.
PIP
I HAVE TO DO THIS THREE MORE TIMES...?!
...
BOOF
IT WAS GETTING NEAR THE END WITH YOSHIKI AND MAKOTO ANYWAY, AND I'VE GOT NO REGRETS ABOUT KOJI, BUT...
...
TADANORI...!
PRRRRR
着信中
マサヒロ
090 XXX XXXX
INCOMING CALL MASAHIRO

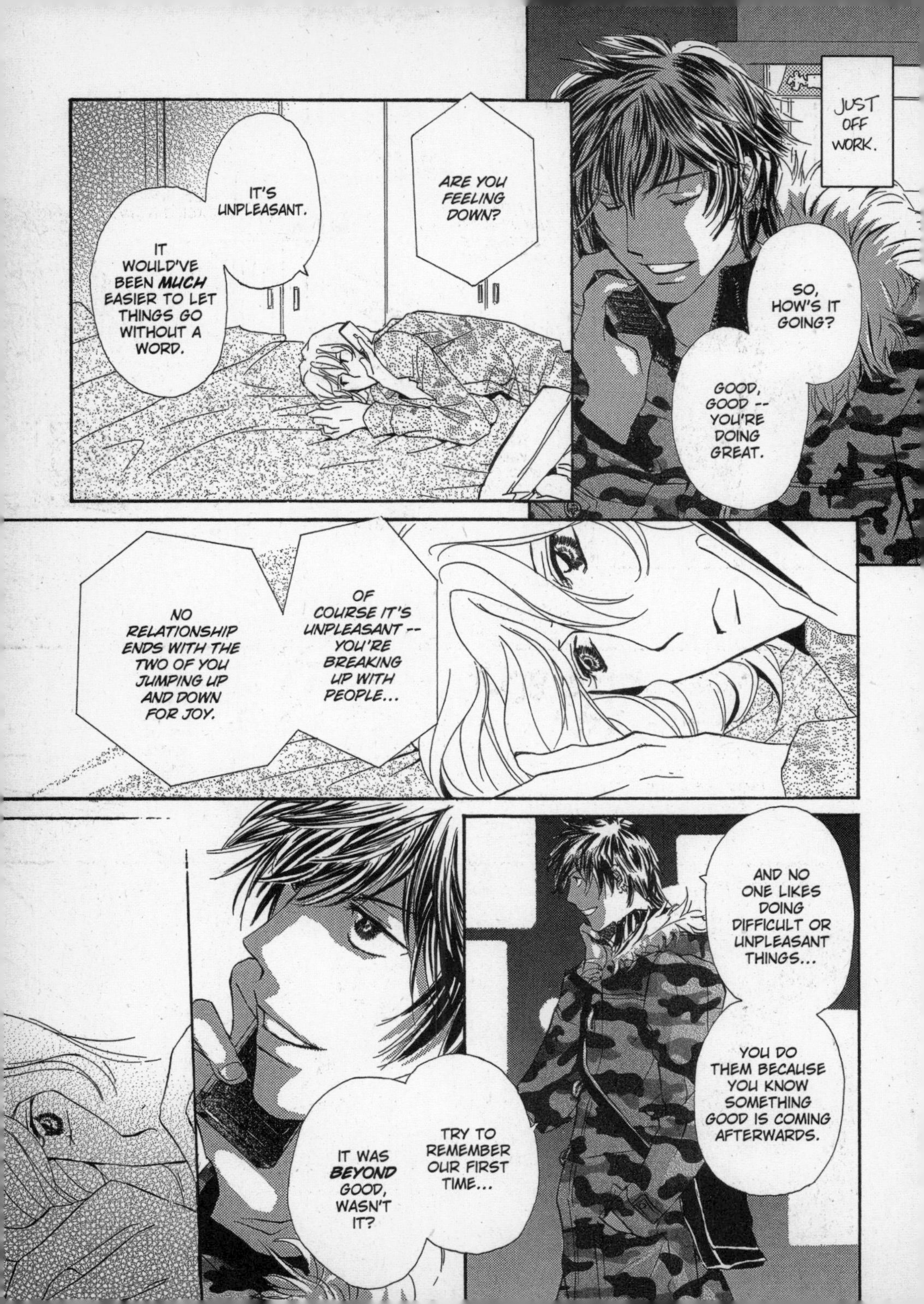
JUST OFF WORK.
SO, HOW'S IT GOING?
GOOD, GOOD -- YOU'RE DOING GREAT.
ARE YOU FEELING DOWN?
IT'S UNPLEASANT.
IT WOULD'VE BEEN MUCH EASIER TO LET THINGS GO WITHOUT A WORD.
OF COURSE IT'S UNPLEASANT -- YOU'RE BREAKING UP WITH PEOPLE...
NO RELATIONSHIP ENDS WITH THE TWO OF YOU JUMPING UP AND DOWN FOR JOY.
AND NO ONE LIKES DOING DIFFICULT OR UNPLEASANT THINGS...
YOU DO THEM BECAUSE YOU KNOW SOMETHING GOOD IS COMING AFTERWARDS.
TRY TO REMEMBER OUR FIRST TIME...
IT WAS BEYOND GOOD, WASN'T IT?

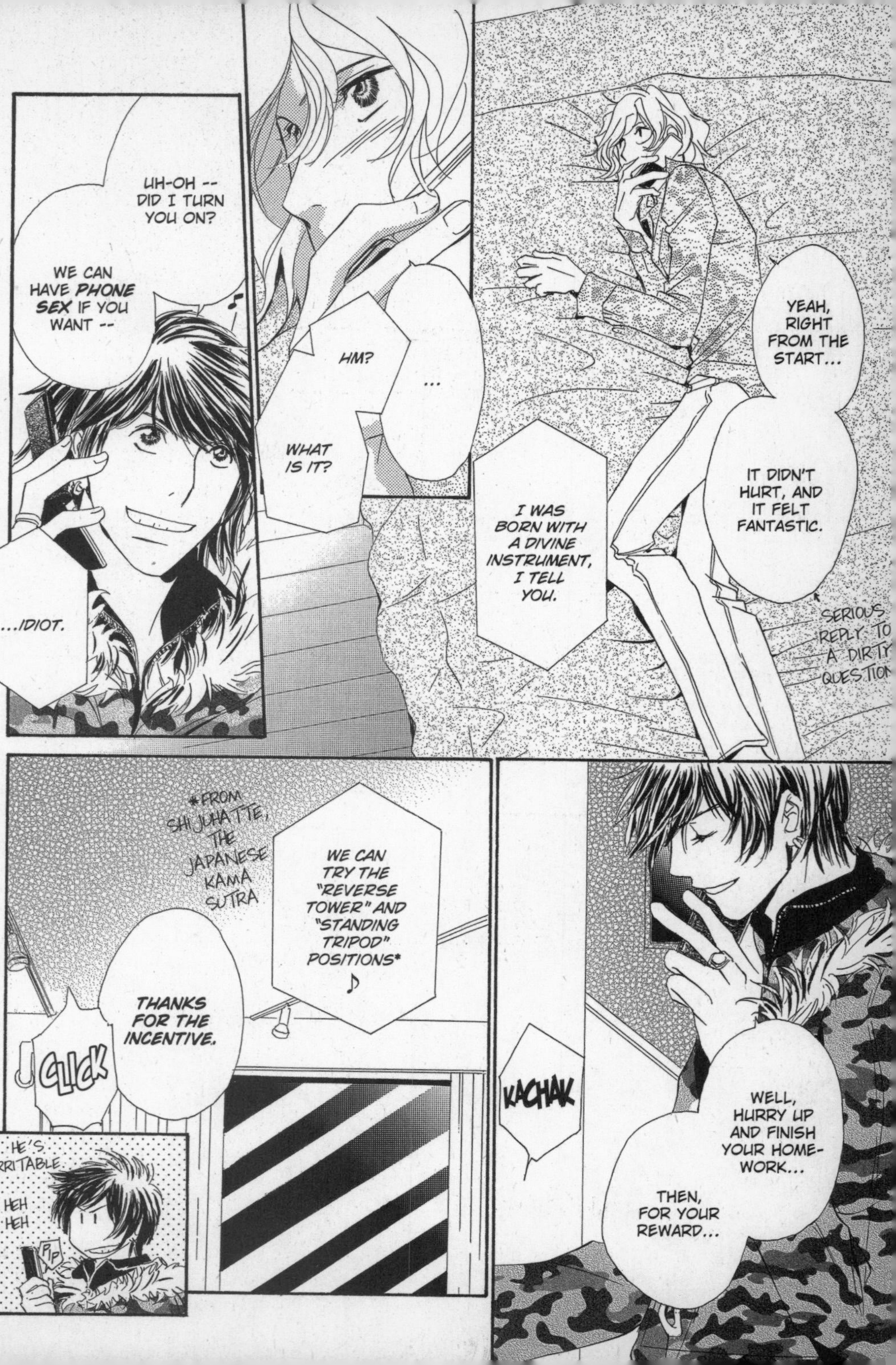
YEAH, RIGHT FROM THE START...
IT DIDN'T HURT, AND IT FELT FANTASTIC.
I WAS BORN WITH A DIVINE INSTRUMENT, I TELL YOU.
SERIOUS REPLY TO A DIRTY QUESTION
...
HM?
WHAT IS IT?
UH-OH -- DID I TURN YOU ON?
WE CAN HAVE PHONE SEX IF YOU WANT --
...IDIOT.
WELL, HURRY UP AND FINISH YOUR HOME-WORK...
THEN, FOR YOUR REWARD...
KACHAK
WE CAN TRY THE "REVERSE TOWER" AND "STANDING TRIPOD" POSITIONS* ♪
*FROM SHIJUHATTE, THE JAPANESE KAMA SUTRA
THANKS FOR THE INCENTIVE.
CLICK
HE'S IRRITABLE.
HEH HEH
PIP

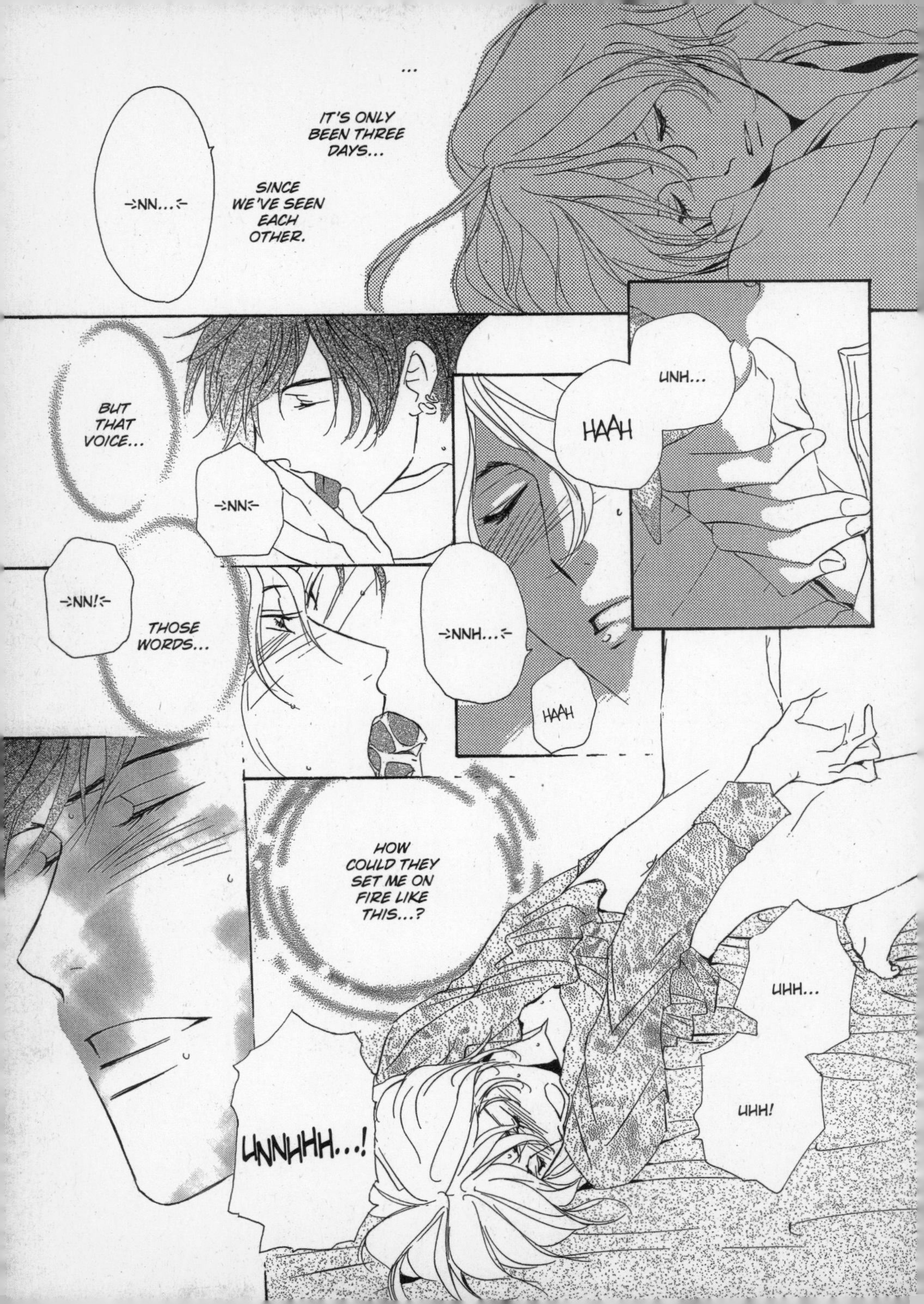
...
IT'S ONLY BEEN THREE DAYS...
SINCE WE'VE SEEN EACH OTHER.
NN...
UNH...
HAAH
NNH...
HAAH
BUT THAT VOICE...
NN
NN!
THOSE WORDS...
UHH...
UHH!
HOW COULD THEY SET ME ON FIRE LIKE THIS...?
UNNHHH...!

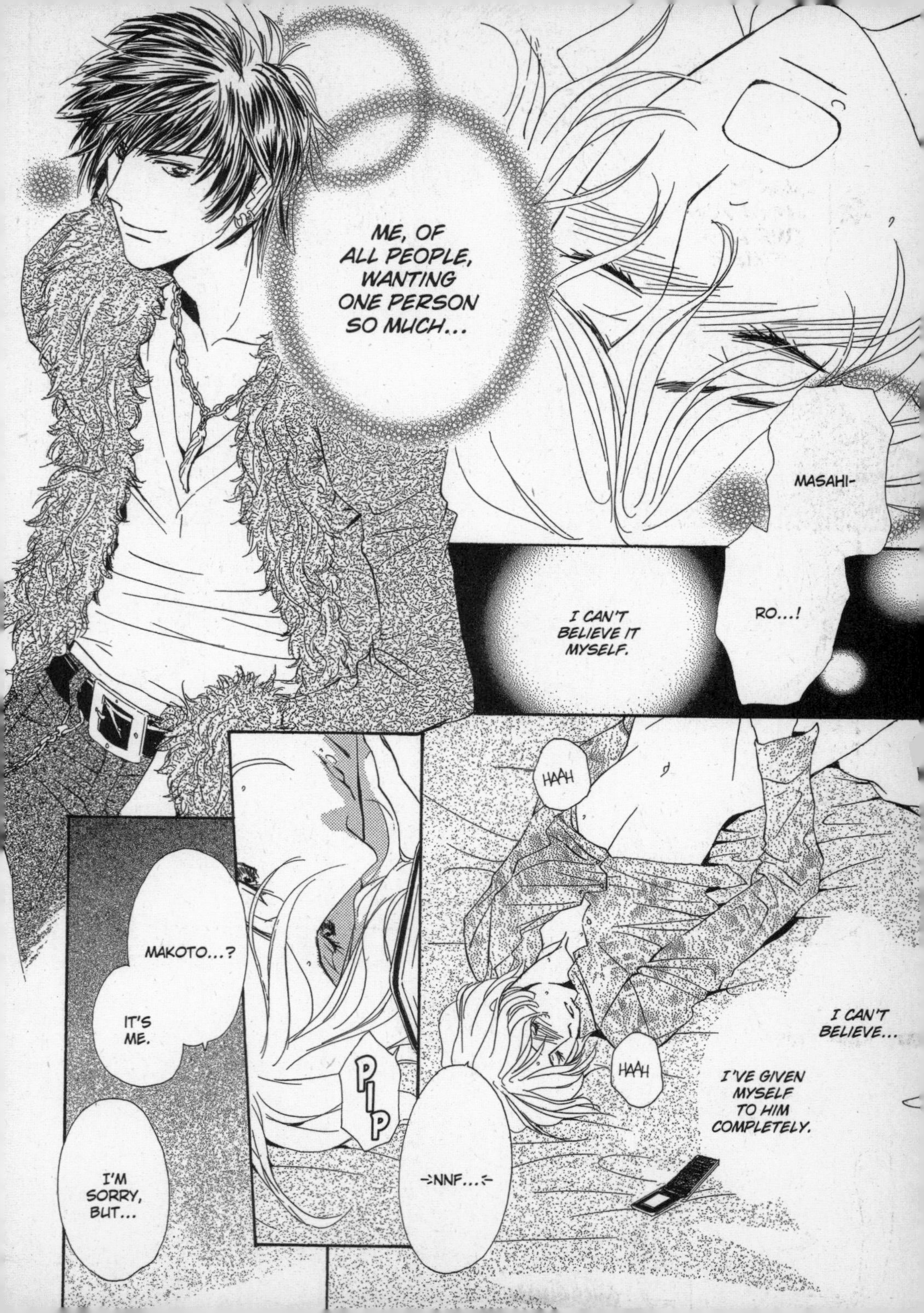

MASAHI-
RO...!
I CAN'T BELIEVE IT MYSELF.
ME, OF ALL PEOPLE, WANTING ONE PERSON SO MUCH...
I CAN'T BELIEVE...
I'VE GIVEN MYSELF TO HIM COMPLETELY.
HAAH
HAAH
-NNF...-
PIP
MAKOTO...?
IT'S ME.
I'M SORRY, BUT...

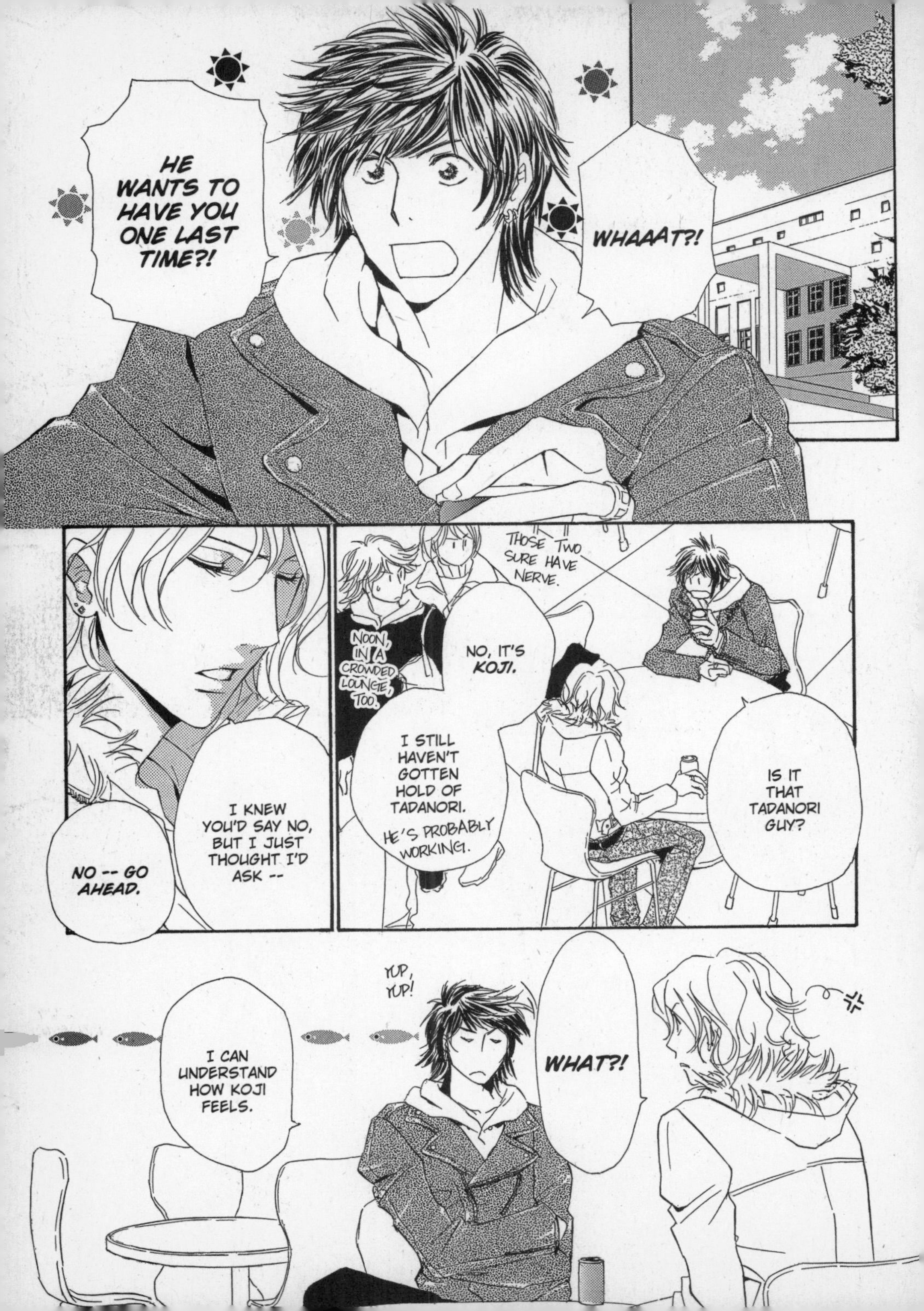
WHAAAT?!
HE WANTS TO HAVE YOU ONE LAST TIME?!
THOSE TWO SURE HAVE NERVE.
IS IT THAT TADANORI GUY?
NO, IT'S KOJI.
I STILL HAVEN'T GOTTEN HOLD OF TADANORI.
HE'S PROBABLY WORKING.
NOON, IN A CROWDED LOUNGE, TOO.
I KNEW YOU'D SAY NO, BUT I JUST THOUGHT I'D ASK --
NO -- GO AHEAD.
YUP, YUP!
WHAT?!
I CAN UNDERSTAND HOW KOJI FEELS.

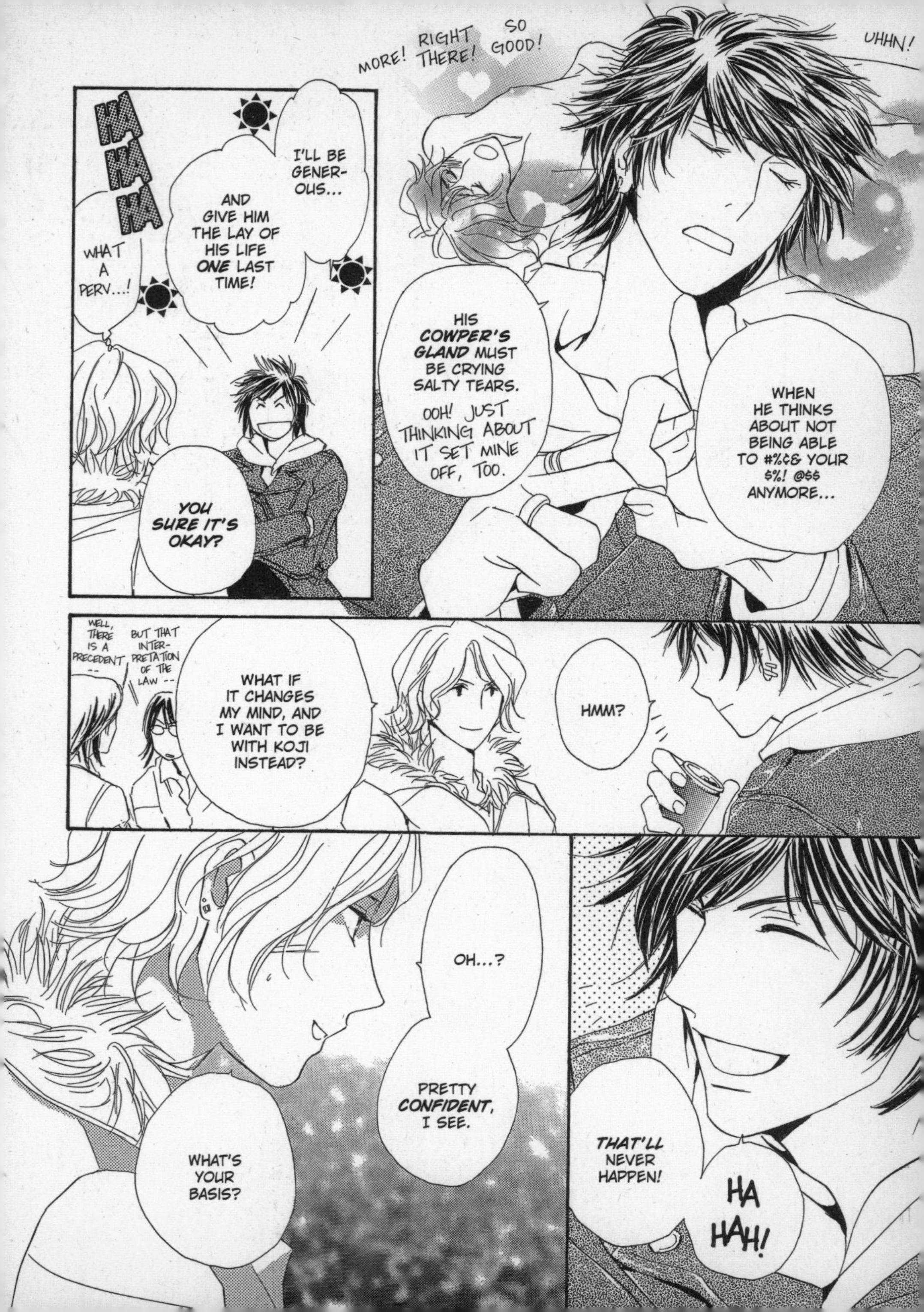
UHHN!
MORE! RIGHT THERE! SO GOOD!
WHEN HE THINKS ABOUT NOT BEING ABLE TO #%¢& YOUR $%! @$$ ANYMORE...
HIS COWPER'S GLAND MUST BE CRYING SALTY TEARS.
OOH! JUST THINKING ABOUT IT SET MINE OFF, TOO.
I'LL BE GENER-OUS...
AND GIVE HIM THE LAY OF HIS LIFE ONE LAST TIME!
HA HA HA
WHAT A PERV...!
YOU SURE IT'S OKAY?
HMM?
WHAT IF IT CHANGES MY MIND, AND I WANT TO BE WITH KOJI INSTEAD?
BUT THAT INTER-PRETATION OF THE LAW --
WELL, THERE IS A PRECEDENT --
THAT'LL NEVER HAPPEN!
HA HAH!
OH...?
PRETTY CONFIDENT, I SEE.
WHAT'S YOUR BASIS?

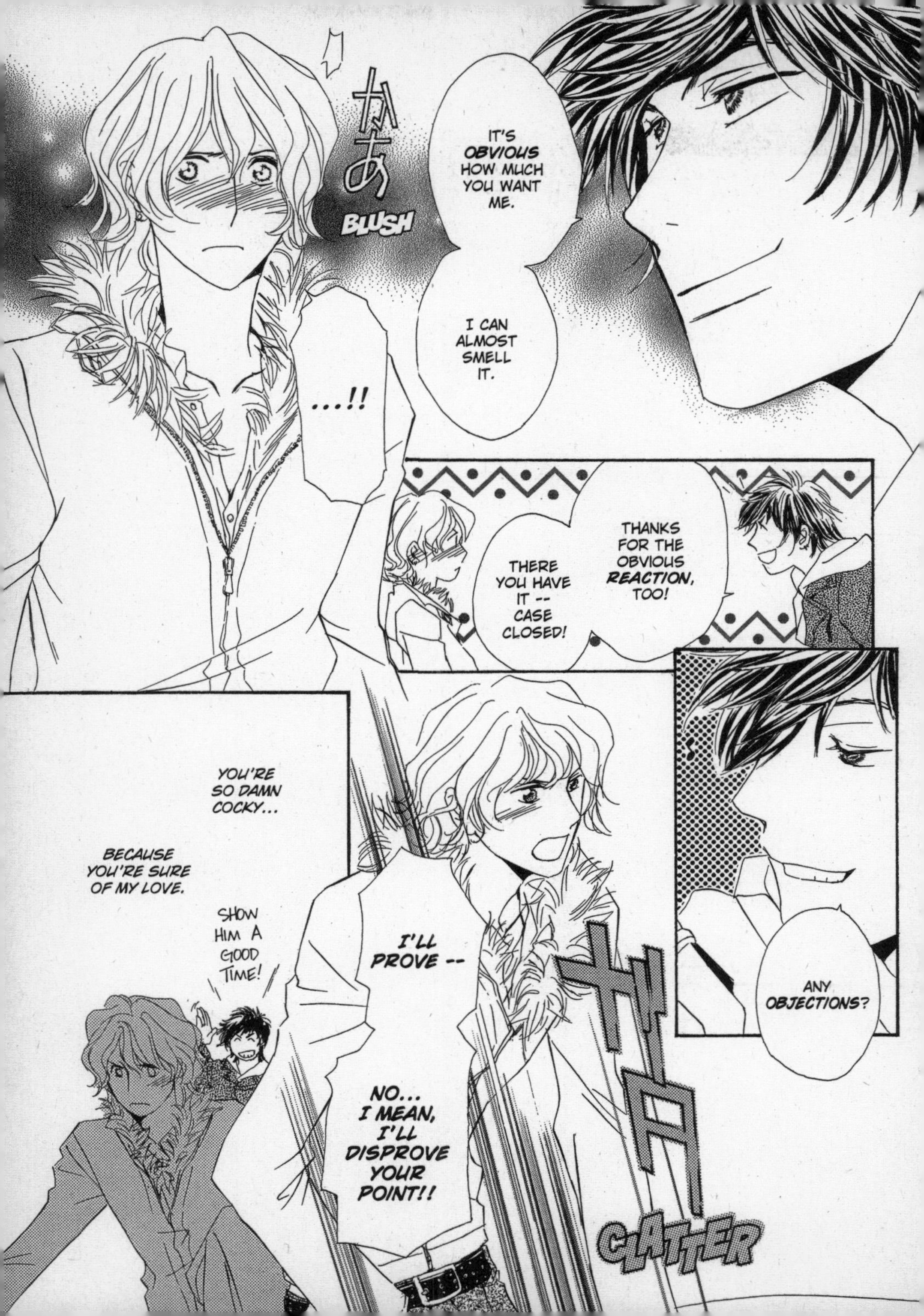
IT'S OBVIOUS HOW MUCH YOU WANT ME.
I CAN ALMOST SMELL IT.
かあ
BLUSH
...!!
THANKS FOR THE OBVIOUS REACTION, TOO!
THERE YOU HAVE IT -- CASE CLOSED!
ANY OBJECTIONS?
YOU'RE SO DAMN COCKY...
BECAUSE YOU'RE SURE OF MY LOVE.
SHOW HIM A GOOD TIME!
I'LL PROVE --
NO... I MEAN, I'LL DISPROVE YOUR POINT!!
ガタ
CLATTER

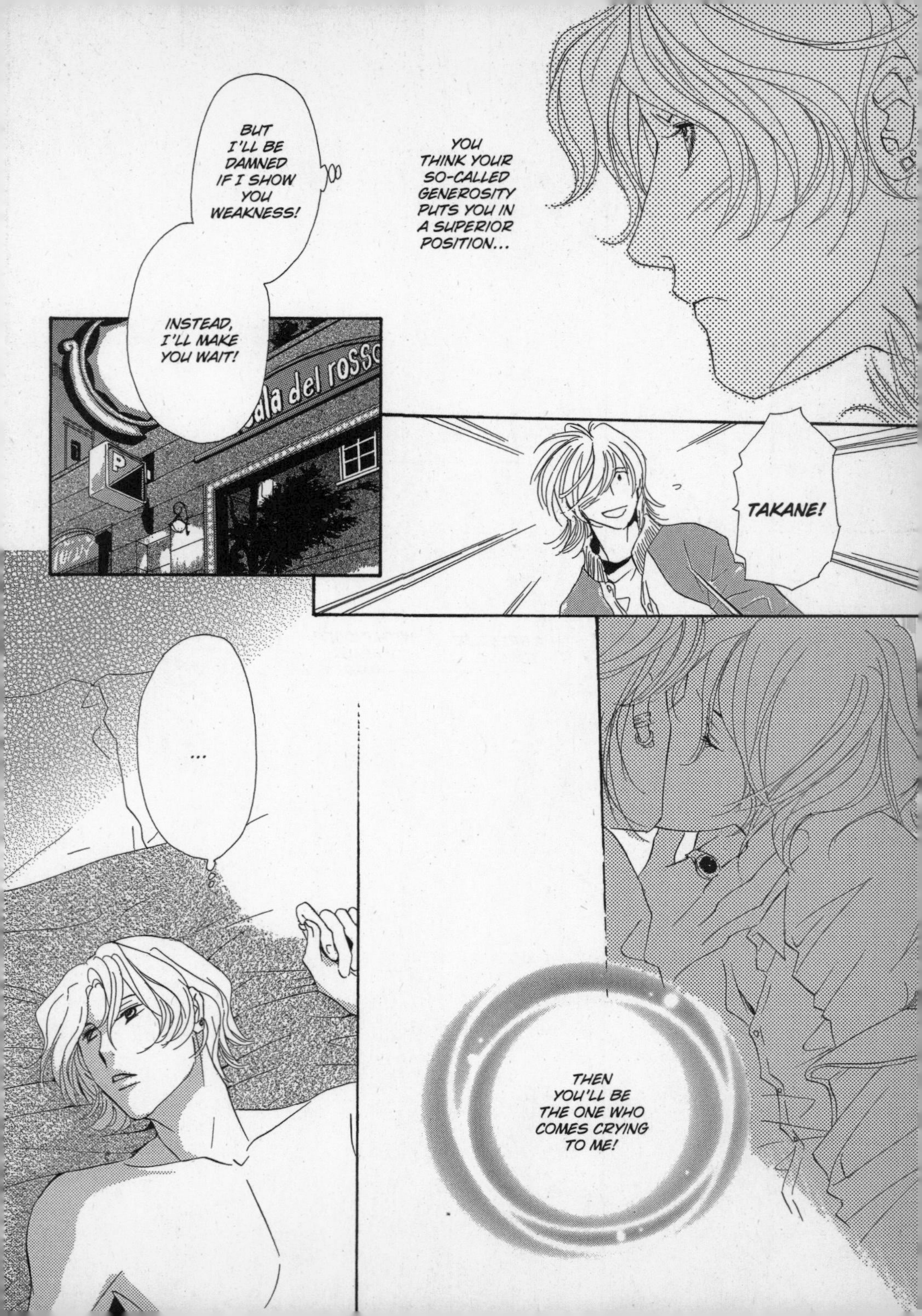
YOU THINK YOUR SO-CALLED GENEROSITY PUTS YOU IN A SUPERIOR POSITION...
BUT I'LL BE DAMNED IF I SHOW YOU WEAKNESS!
INSTEAD, I'LL MAKE YOU WAIT!
TAKANE!
THEN YOU'LL BE THE ONE WHO COMES CRYING TO ME!
...

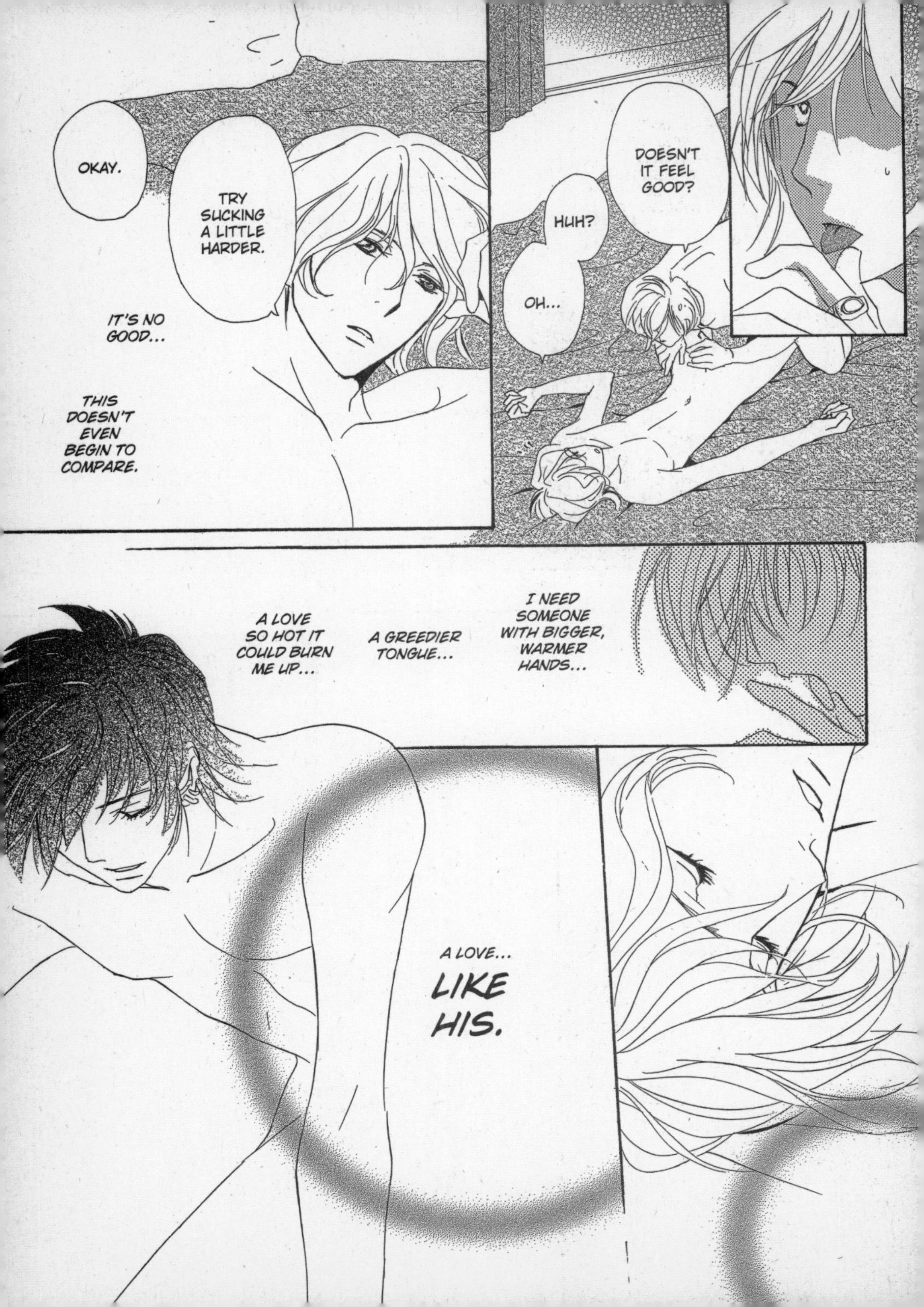
DOESN'T IT FEEL GOOD?
HUH?
OH...
TRY SUCKING A LITTLE HARDER.
OKAY.
IT'S NO GOOD...
THIS DOESN'T EVEN BEGIN TO COMPARE.
I NEED SOMEONE WITH BIGGER, WARMER HANDS...
A GREEDIER TONGUE...
A LOVE SO HOT IT COULD BURN ME UP...
A LOVE...
LIKE HIS.

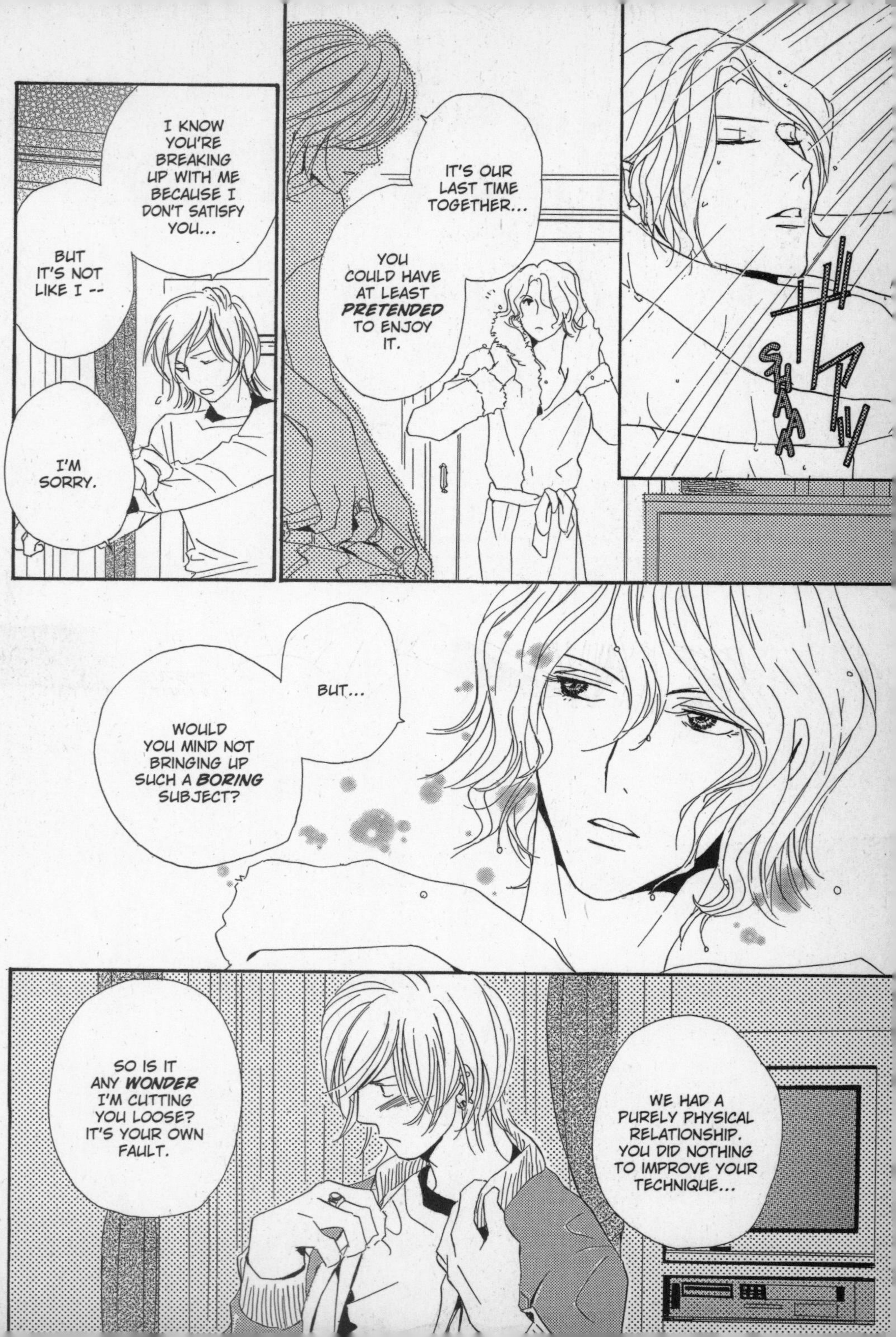
SHAAA
IT'S OUR LAST TIME TOGETHER...
YOU COULD HAVE AT LEAST PRETENDED TO ENJOY IT.
I KNOW YOU'RE BREAKING UP WITH ME BECAUSE I DON'T SATISFY YOU...
BUT IT'S NOT LIKE I --
I'M SORRY.
BUT...
WOULD YOU MIND NOT BRINGING UP SUCH A BORING SUBJECT?
WE HAD A PURELY PHYSICAL RELATIONSHIP. YOU DID NOTHING TO IMPROVE YOUR TECHNIQUE...
SO IS IT ANY WONDER I'M CUTTING YOU LOOSE? IT'S YOUR OWN FAULT.

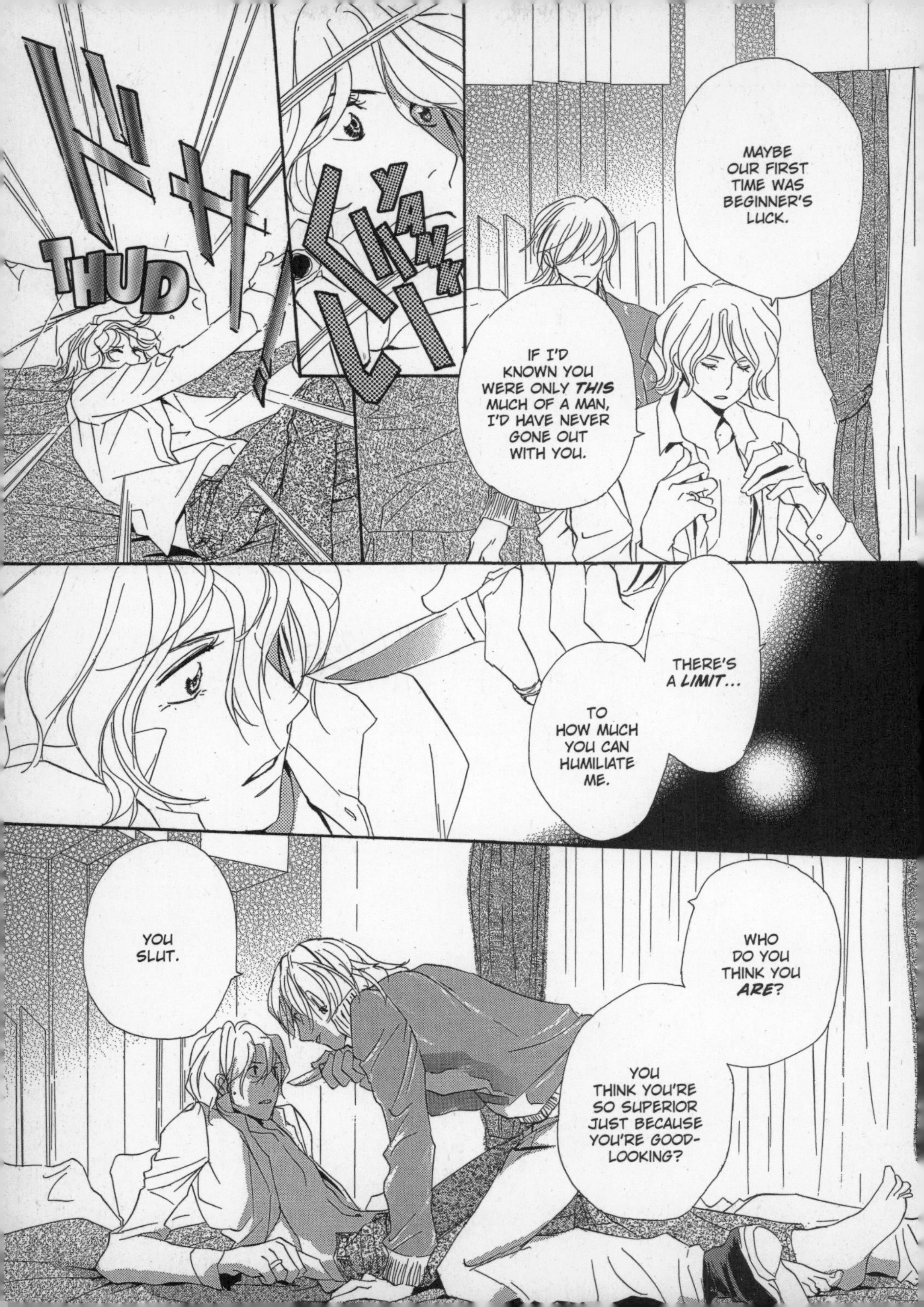
MAYBE OUR FIRST TIME WAS BEGINNER'S LUCK.
IF I'D KNOWN YOU WERE ONLY *THIS* MUCH OF A MAN, I'D HAVE NEVER GONE OUT WITH YOU.
YANK
THUD
THERE'S A *LIMIT*...
TO HOW MUCH YOU CAN HUMILIATE ME.
WHO DO YOU THINK YOU *ARE*?
YOU THINK YOU'RE SO SUPERIOR JUST BECAUSE YOU'RE GOOD-LOOKING?
YOU SLUT.

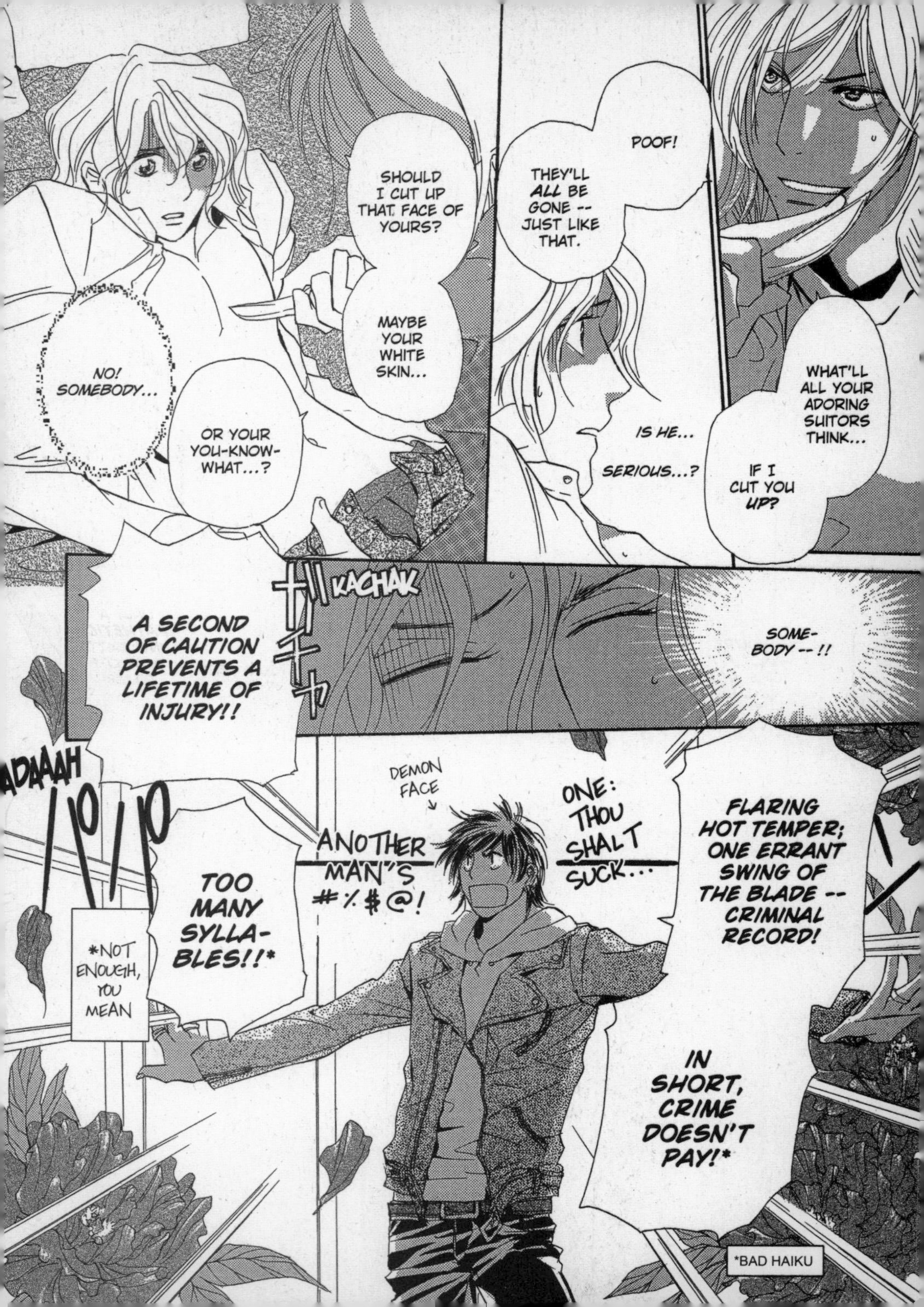
WHAT'LL ALL YOUR ADORING SUITORS THINK...
IF I CUT YOU UP?
POOF!
THEY'LL ALL BE GONE -- JUST LIKE THAT.
IS HE...
SERIOUS...?
SHOULD I CUT UP THAT FACE OF YOURS?
MAYBE YOUR WHITE SKIN...
OR YOUR YOU-KNOW-WHAT...?
NO! SOMEBODY...
SOME-BODY --!!
KACHAK
A SECOND OF CAUTION PREVENTS A LIFETIME OF INJURY!!
FLARING HOT TEMPER; ONE ERRANT SWING OF THE BLADE -- CRIMINAL RECORD!
IN SHORT, CRIME DOESN'T PAY!*
ONE: THOU SHALT SUCK...
DEMON FACE
ANOTHER MAN'S #%$@!
TOO MANY SYLLA-BLES!!*
*NOT ENOUGH, YOU MEAN
ADAAAH
*BAD HAIKU

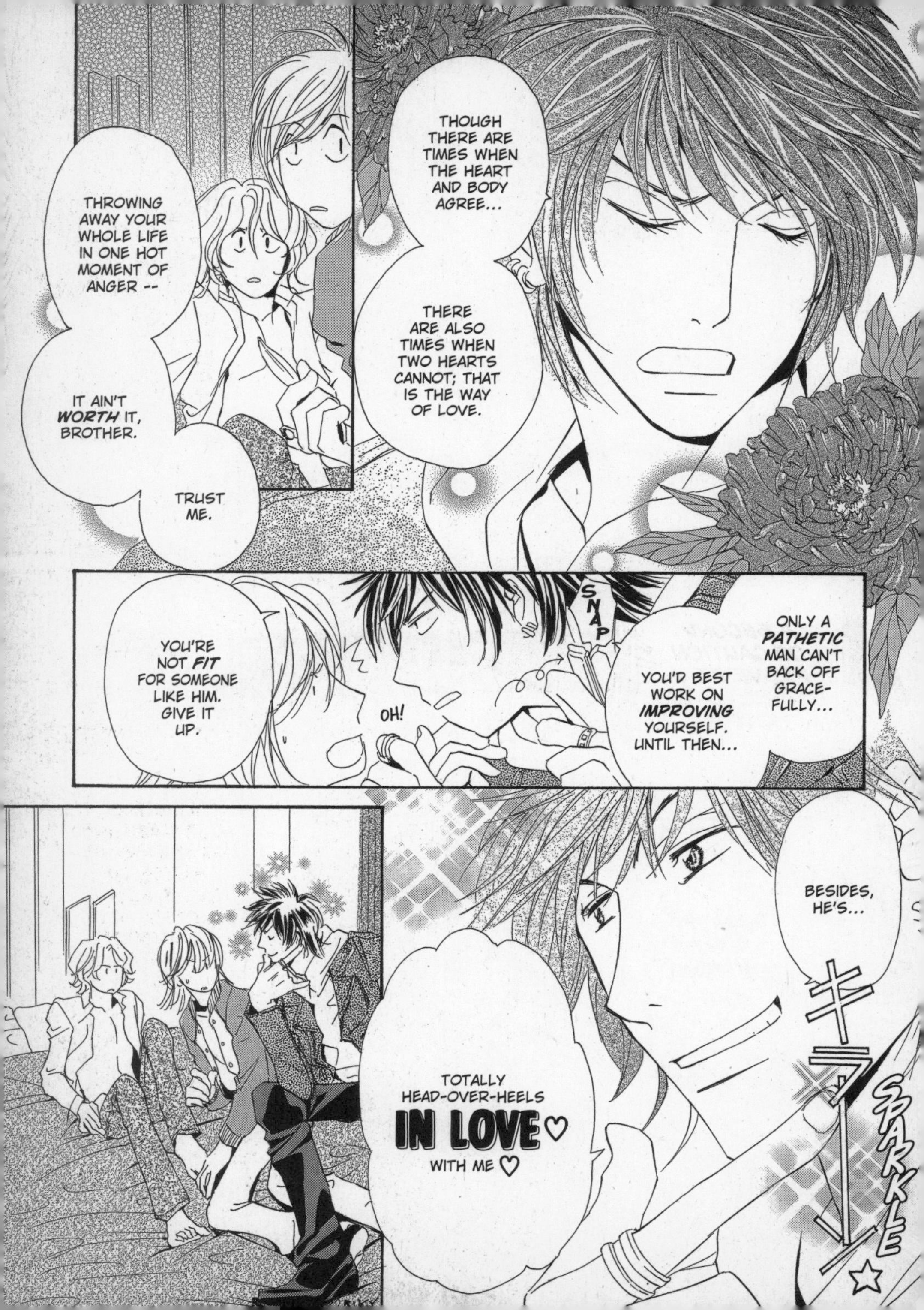
THOUGH THERE ARE TIMES WHEN THE HEART AND BODY AGREE...
THERE ARE ALSO TIMES WHEN TWO HEARTS CANNOT; THAT IS THE WAY OF LOVE.
THROWING AWAY YOUR WHOLE LIFE IN ONE HOT MOMENT OF ANGER --
IT AIN'T *WORTH* IT, BROTHER.
TRUST ME.
ONLY A *PATHETIC* MAN CAN'T BACK OFF GRACE-FULLY...
YOU'D BEST WORK ON *IMPROVING* YOURSELF. UNTIL THEN...
SNAP
OH!
YOU'RE NOT *FIT* FOR SOMEONE LIKE HIM. GIVE IT UP.
BESIDES, HE'S...
キラーン
SPARKLE ☆
TOTALLY HEAD-OVER-HEELS **IN LOVE** ♡ WITH ME ♡

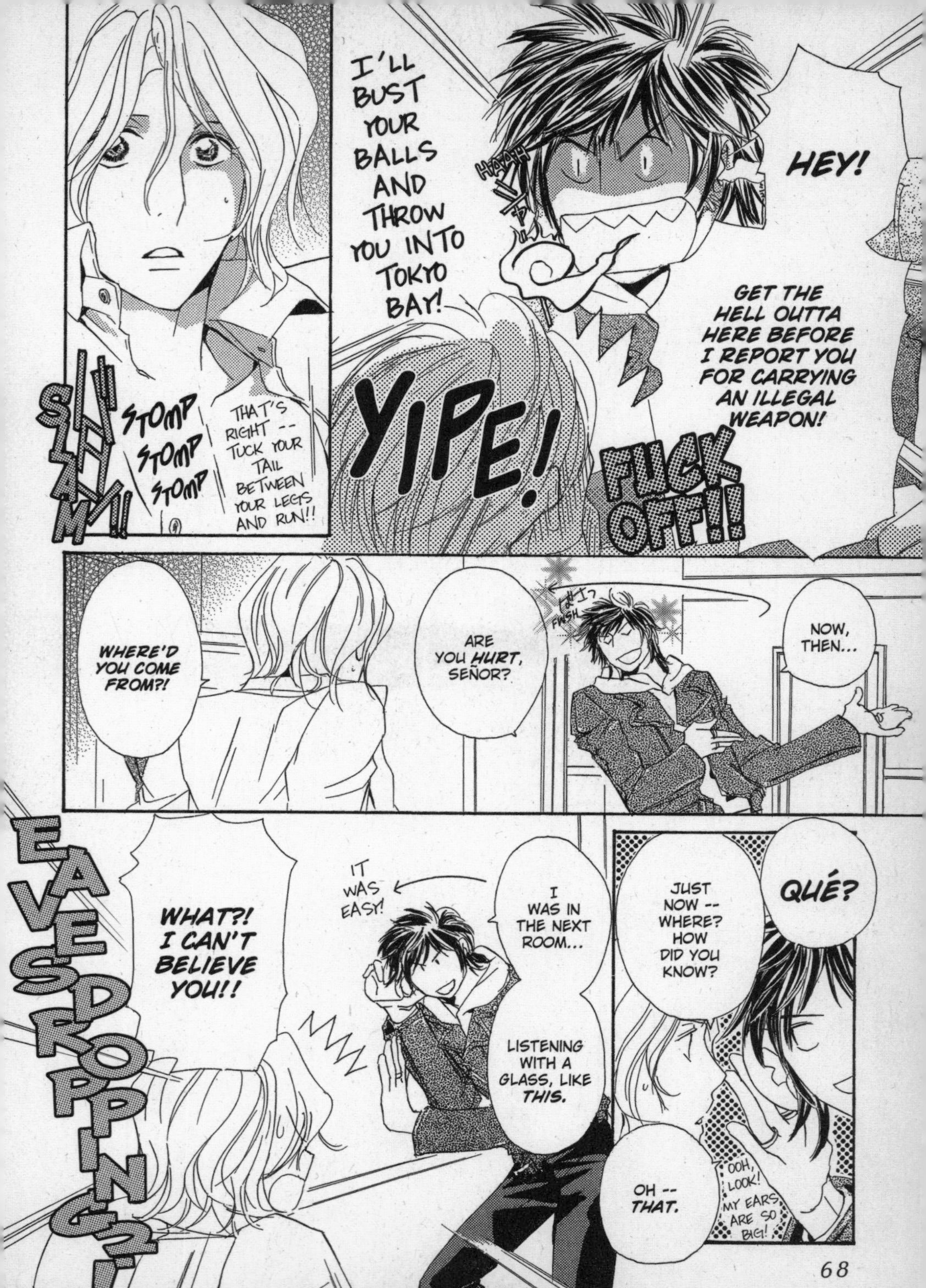
HEY!
I'LL BUST YOUR BALLS AND THROW YOU INTO TOKYO BAY!
GET THE HELL OUTTA HERE BEFORE I REPORT YOU FOR CARRYING AN ILLEGAL WEAPON!
FUCK OFF!!
YIPE!
THAT'S RIGHT -- TUCK YOUR TAIL BETWEEN YOUR LEGS AND RUN!!
STOMP STOMP STOMP
SLAM!!
NOW, THEN...
FWSH
ARE YOU HURT, SEÑOR?
WHERE'D YOU COME FROM?!
QUÉ?
JUST NOW -- WHERE? HOW DID YOU KNOW?
I WAS IN THE NEXT ROOM...
IT WAS EASY!
LISTENING WITH A GLASS, LIKE THIS.
OH -- THAT.
OOH, LOOK! MY EARS ARE SO BIG!
WHAT?! I CAN'T BELIEVE YOU!!
EAVESDROPPING?!

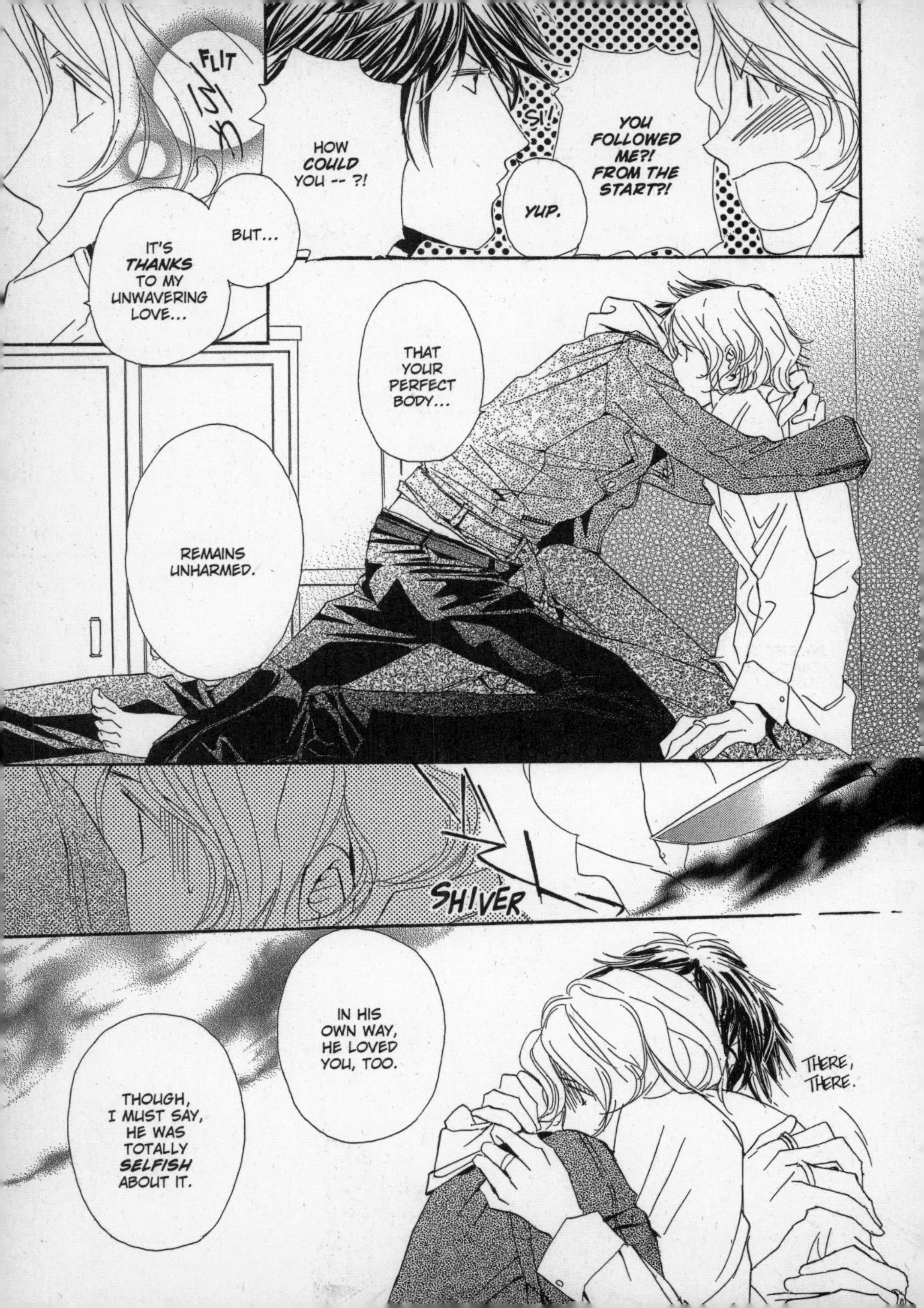
YOU FOLLOWED ME?! FROM THE START?!
SI!
YUP.
HOW COULD YOU -- ?!
FLIT
BUT...
IT'S THANKS TO MY UNWAVERING LOVE...
THAT YOUR PERFECT BODY...
REMAINS UNHARMED.
SHIVER
THERE, THERE.
IN HIS OWN WAY, HE LOVED YOU, TOO.
THOUGH, I MUST SAY, HE WAS TOTALLY SELFISH ABOUT IT.

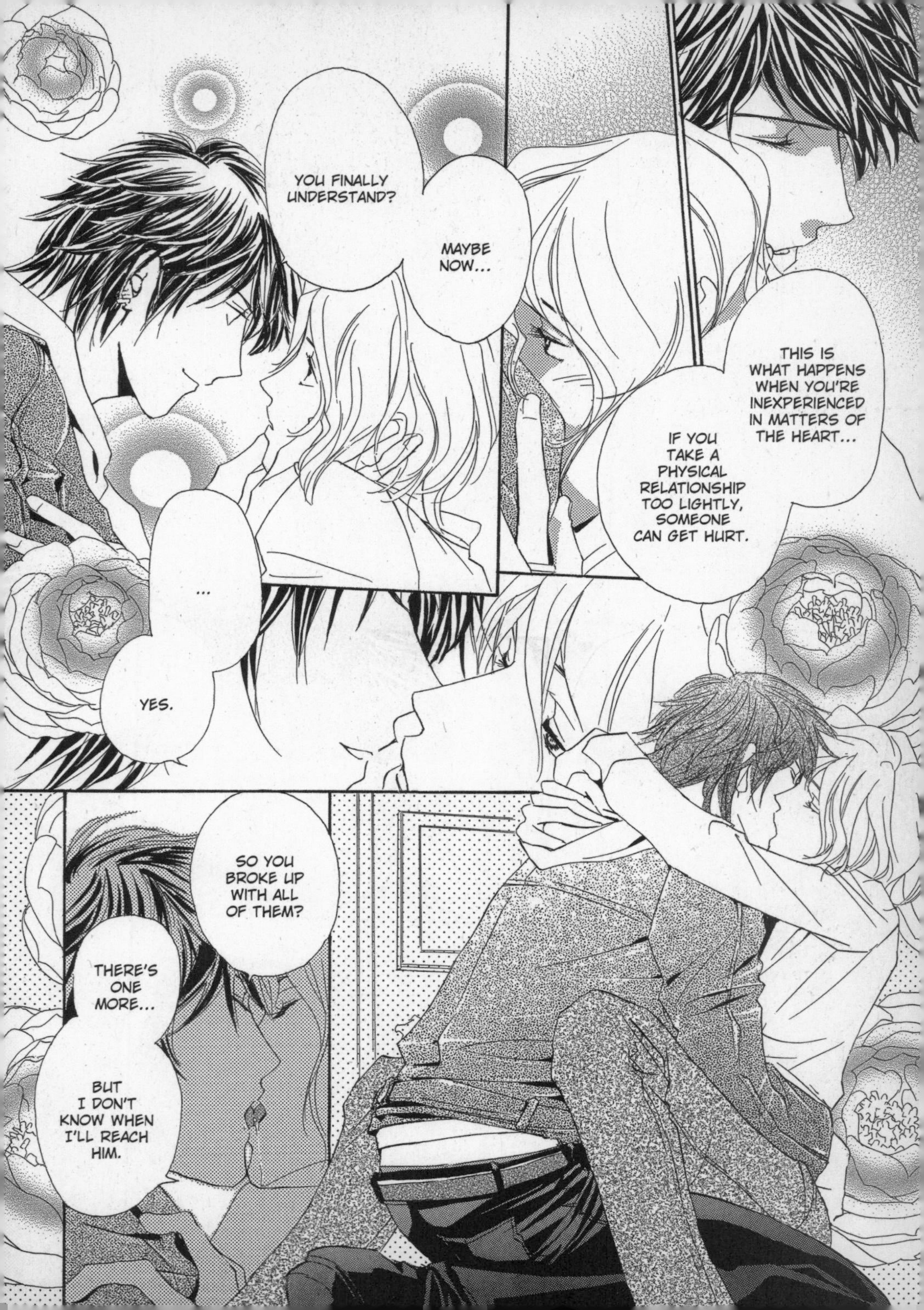
THIS IS WHAT HAPPENS WHEN YOU'RE INEXPERIENCED IN MATTERS OF THE HEART...
IF YOU TAKE A PHYSICAL RELATIONSHIP TOO LIGHTLY, SOMEONE CAN GET HURT.
YOU FINALLY UNDERSTAND?
MAYBE NOW...
...
YES.
SO YOU BROKE UP WITH ALL OF THEM?
THERE'S ONE MORE...
BUT I DON'T KNOW WHEN I'LL REACH HIM.

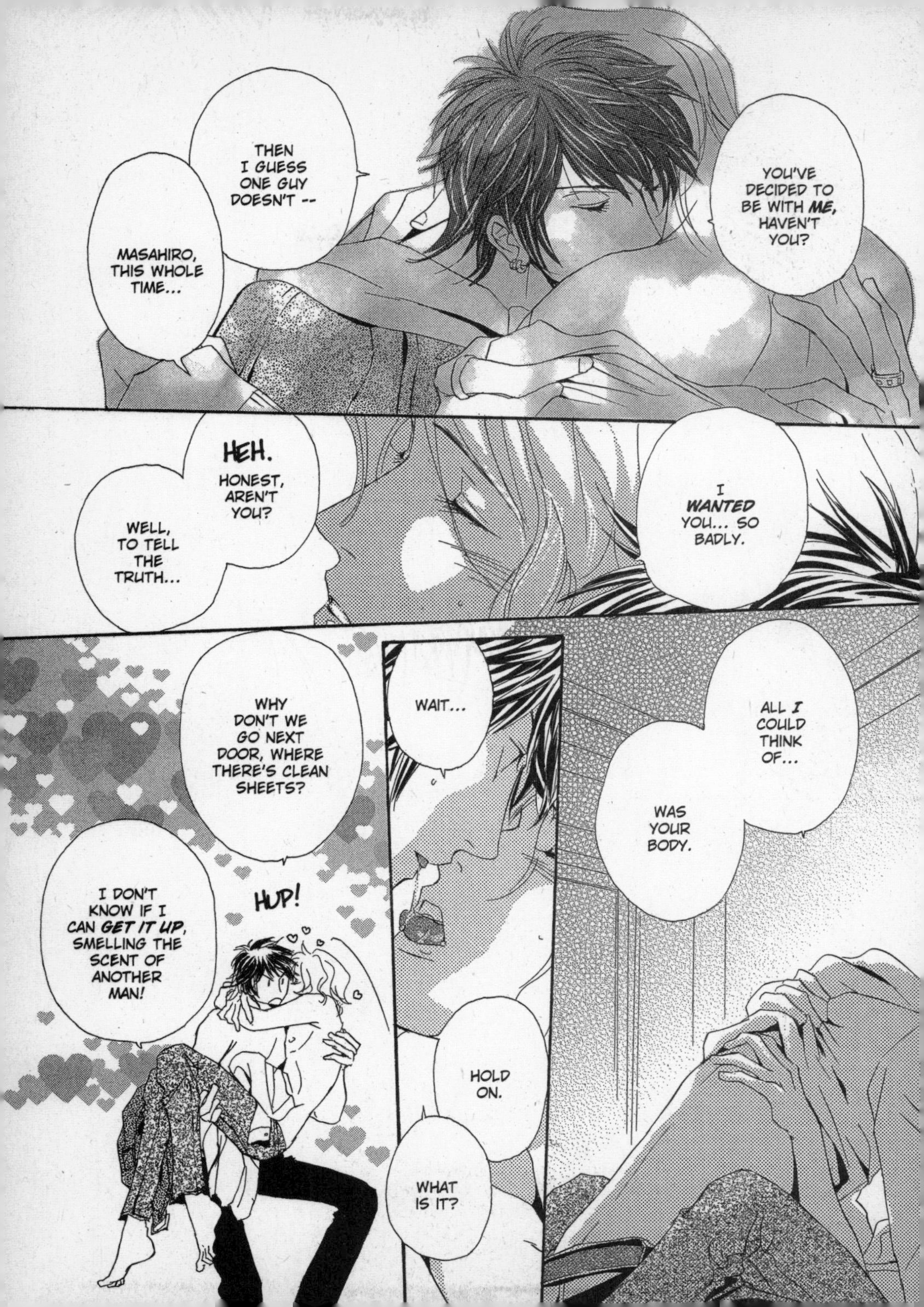
YOU'VE DECIDED TO BE WITH **ME,** HAVEN'T YOU?
THEN I GUESS ONE GUY DOESN'T --
MASAHIRO, THIS WHOLE TIME...
I **WANTED** YOU... SO BADLY.
HEH. HONEST, AREN'T YOU?
WELL, TO TELL THE TRUTH...
ALL **I** COULD THINK OF...
WAS YOUR BODY.
WAIT...
HOLD ON.
WHAT IS IT?
WHY DON'T WE GO NEXT DOOR, WHERE THERE'S CLEAN SHEETS?
HUP!
I DON'T KNOW IF I CAN **GET IT UP,** SMELLING THE SCENT OF ANOTHER MAN!

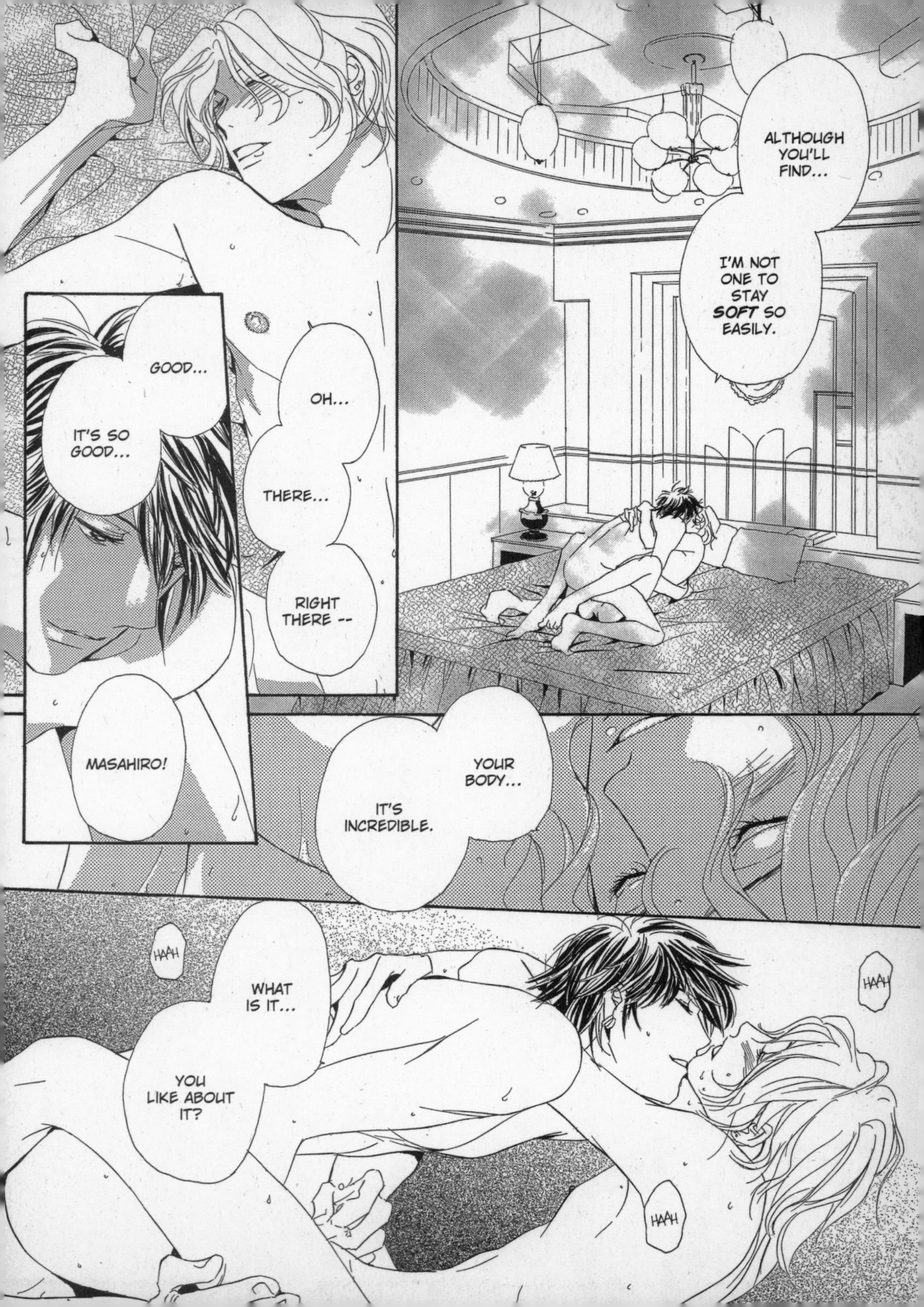

ALTHOUGH YOU'LL FIND...
I'M NOT ONE TO STAY **SOFT** SO EASILY.
OH... THERE... RIGHT THERE --
GOOD... IT'S SO GOOD...
MASAHIRO!
YOUR BODY... IT'S INCREDIBLE.
HAAH
WHAT IS IT... YOU LIKE ABOUT IT?
HAAH
HAAH

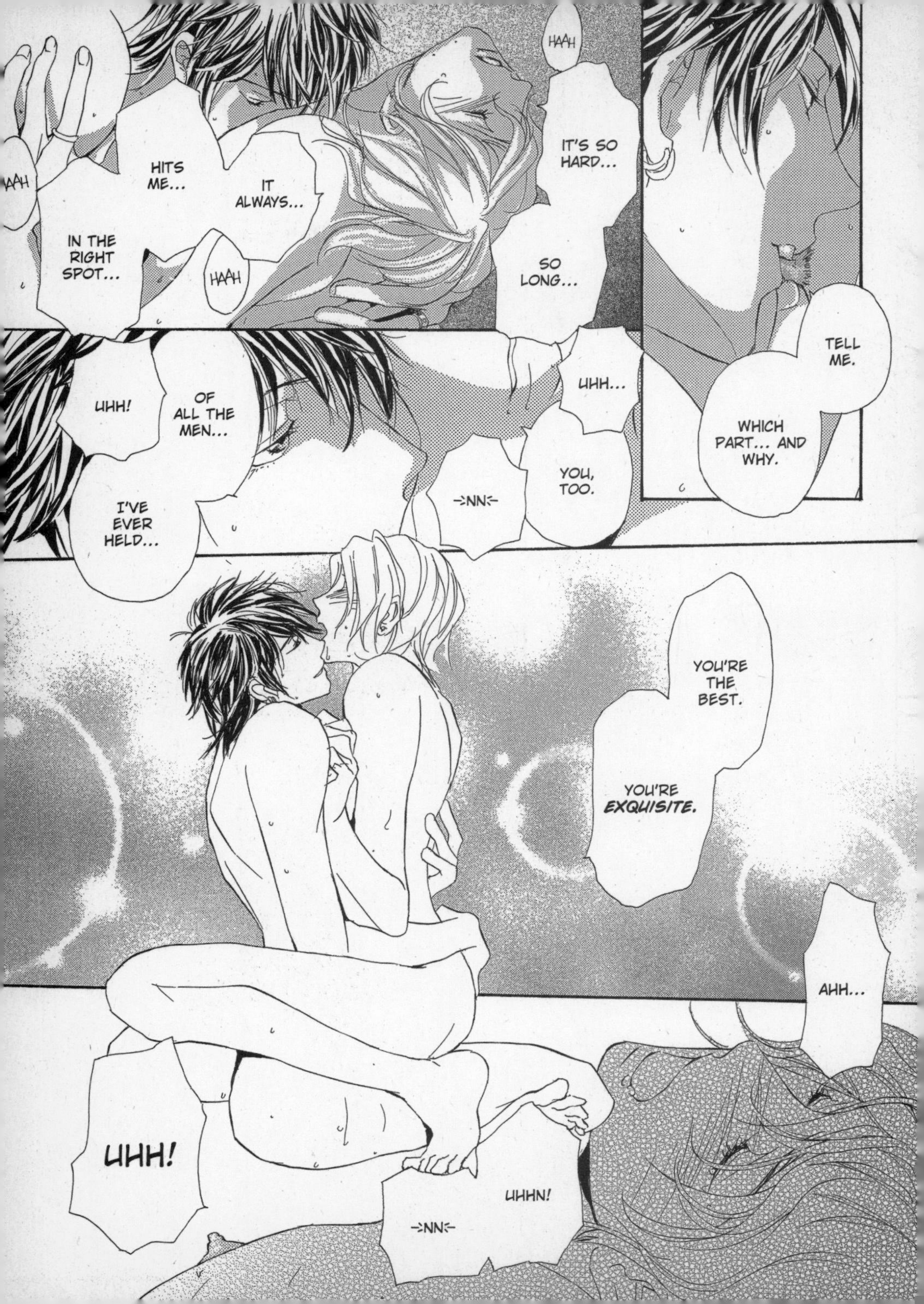

TELL ME.
WHICH PART... AND WHY.
HAAH
IT'S SO HARD...
SO LONG...
IT ALWAYS...
HITS ME...
HAAH
IN THE RIGHT SPOT...
HAAH
UHH...
YOU, TOO.
-NN-
OF ALL THE MEN...
UHH!
I'VE EVER HELD...
YOU'RE THE BEST.
YOU'RE ***EXQUISITE.***
AHH...
UHHN!
-NN-
UHH!

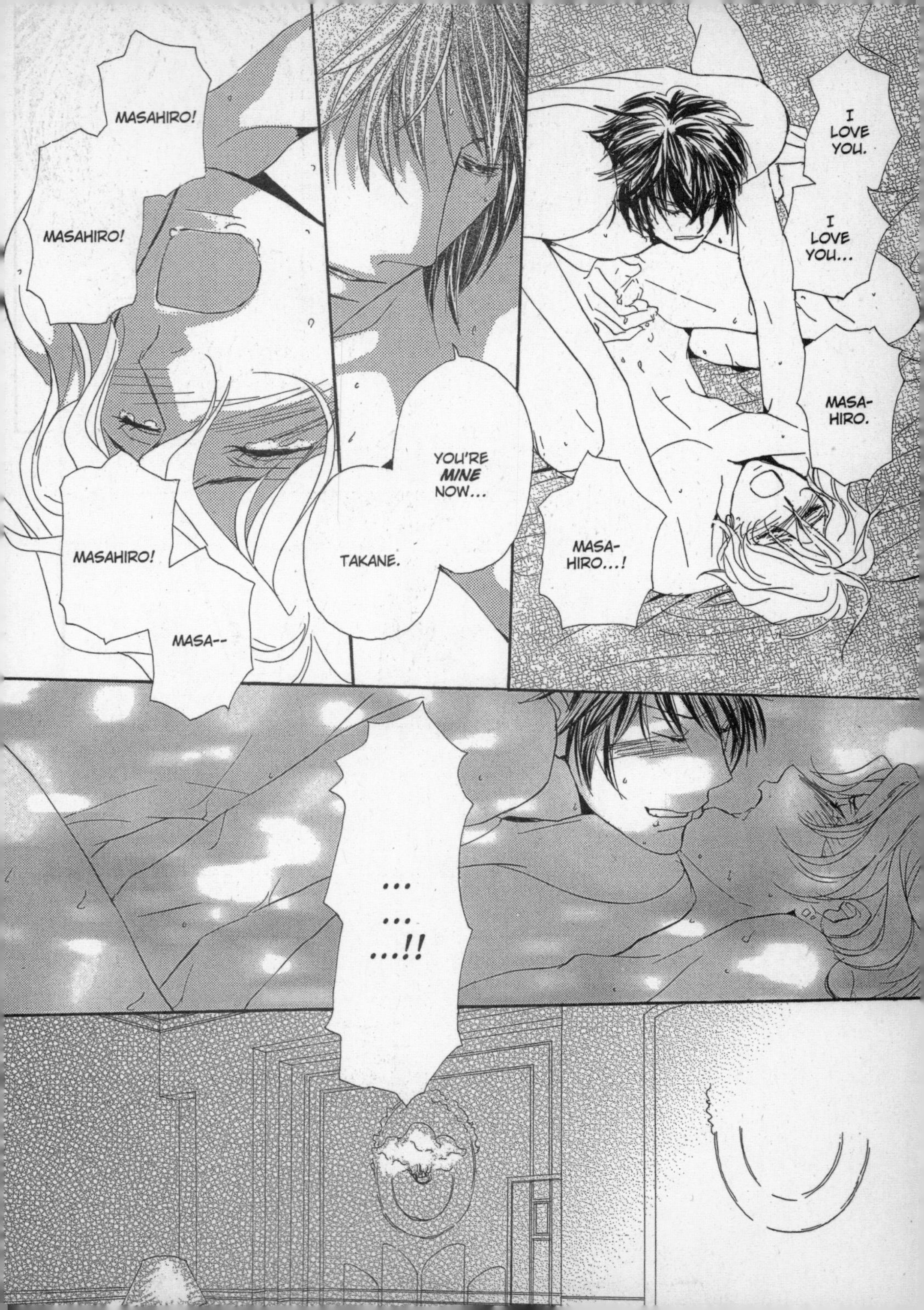
I LOVE YOU.
I LOVE YOU...
MASA-HIRO.
MASA-HIRO...!
YOU'RE *MINE* NOW...
TAKANE.
MASAHIRO!
MASAHIRO!
MASAHIRO!
MASA--
... ...!!

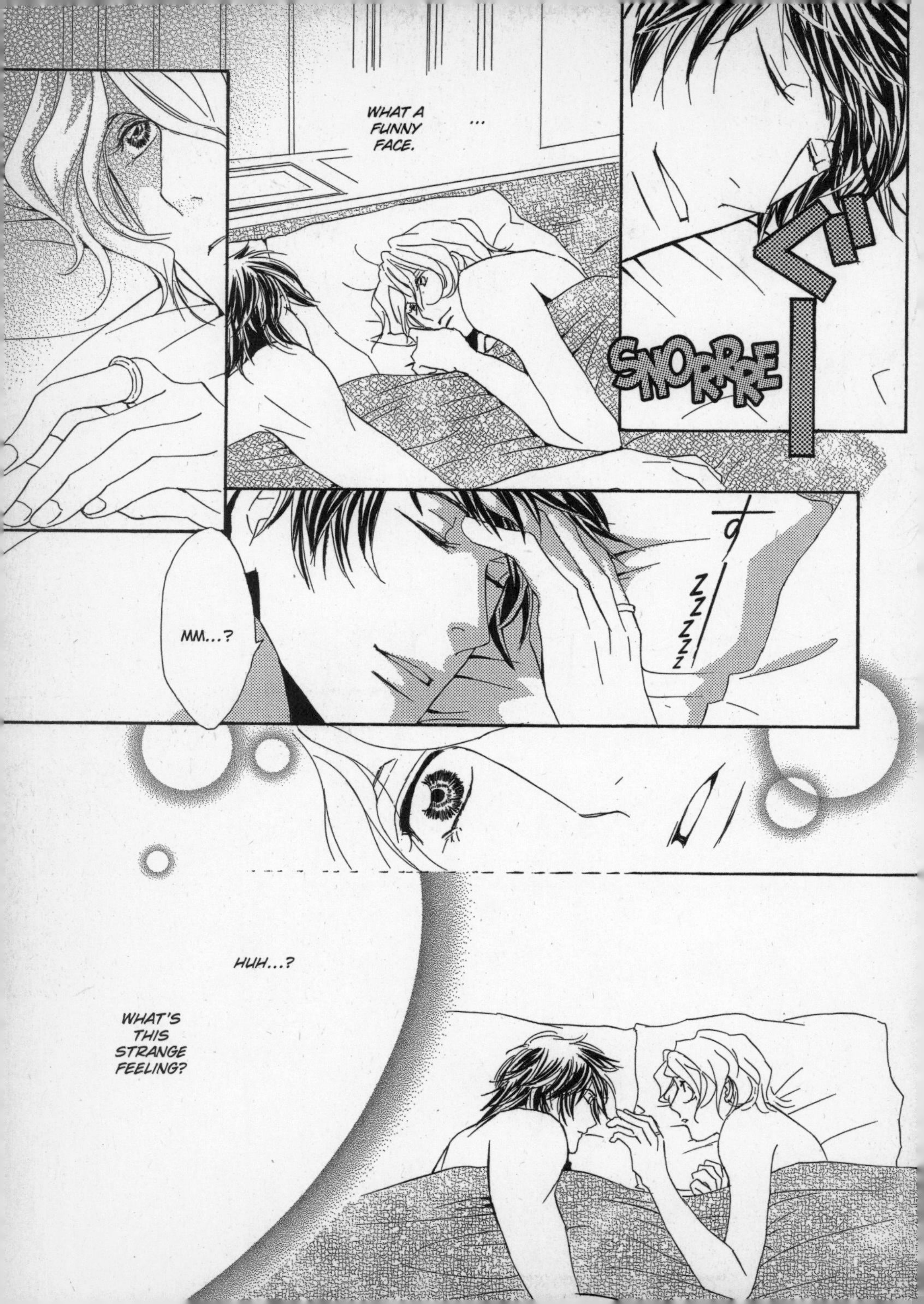
SNORRRE
...
WHAT A FUNNY FACE.
ZZZZZZ
MM...?
HUH...?
WHAT'S THIS STRANGE FEELING?

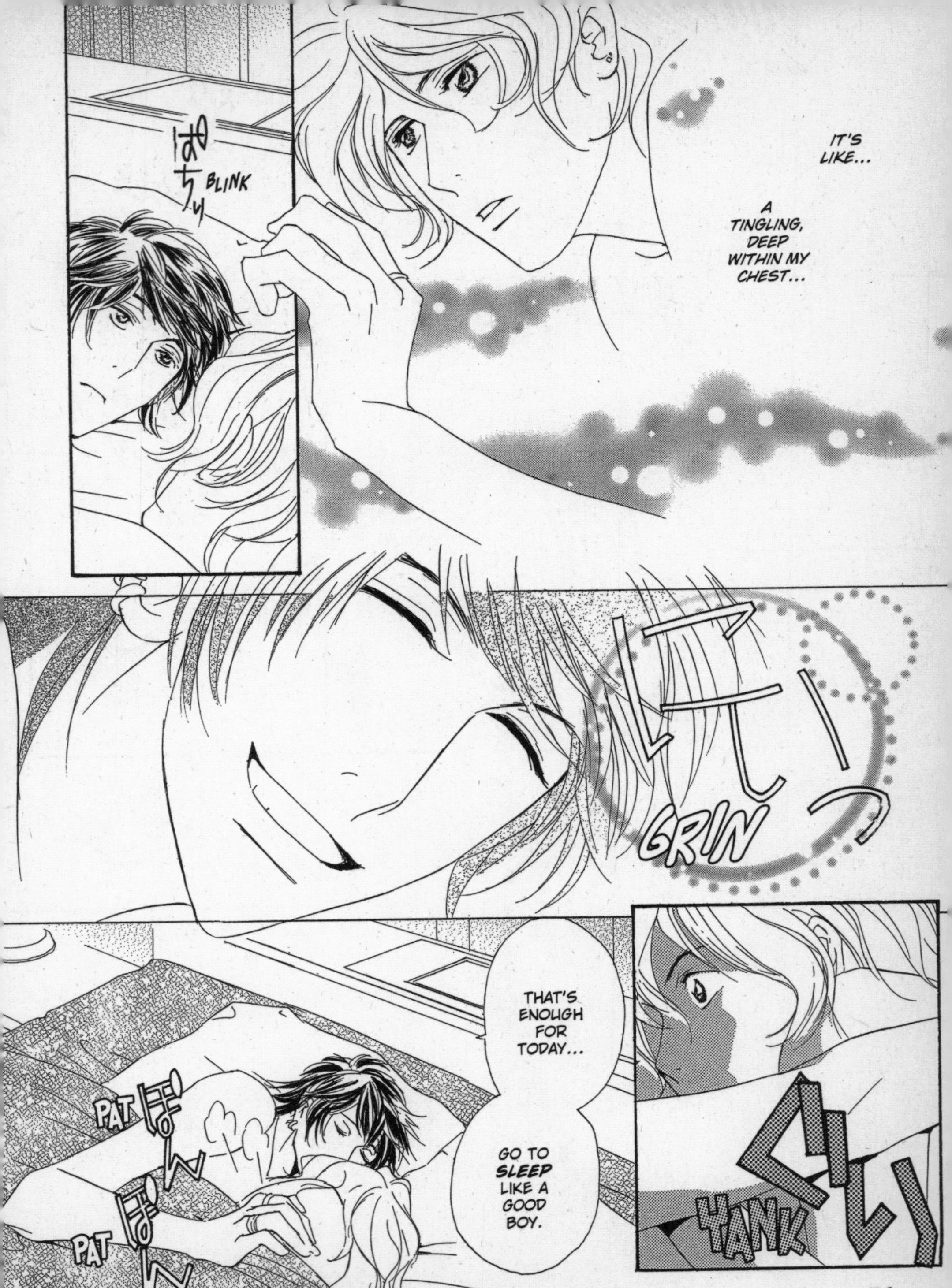
IT'S LIKE...
A TINGLING, DEEP WITHIN MY CHEST...
ぱちり
BLINK
にこーっ
GRIN
ぐいっ
YANK
THAT'S ENOUGH FOR TODAY...
GO TO SLEEP LIKE A GOOD BOY.
PAT
ぽん
ぽん
PAT

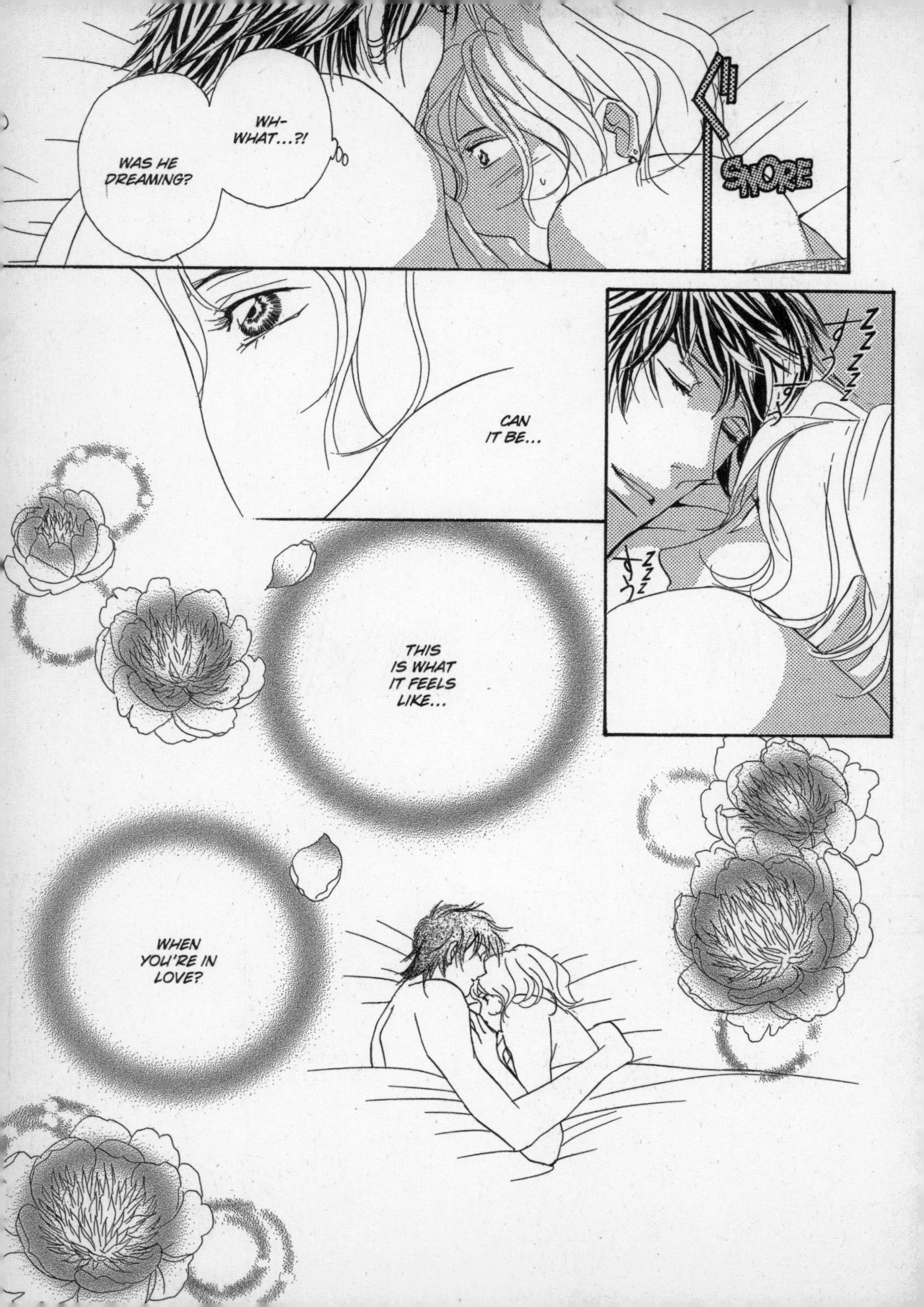
SNORE
WH- WHAT...?!
WAS HE DREAMING?
CAN IT BE...
THIS IS WHAT IT FEELS LIKE...
WHEN YOU'RE IN LOVE?

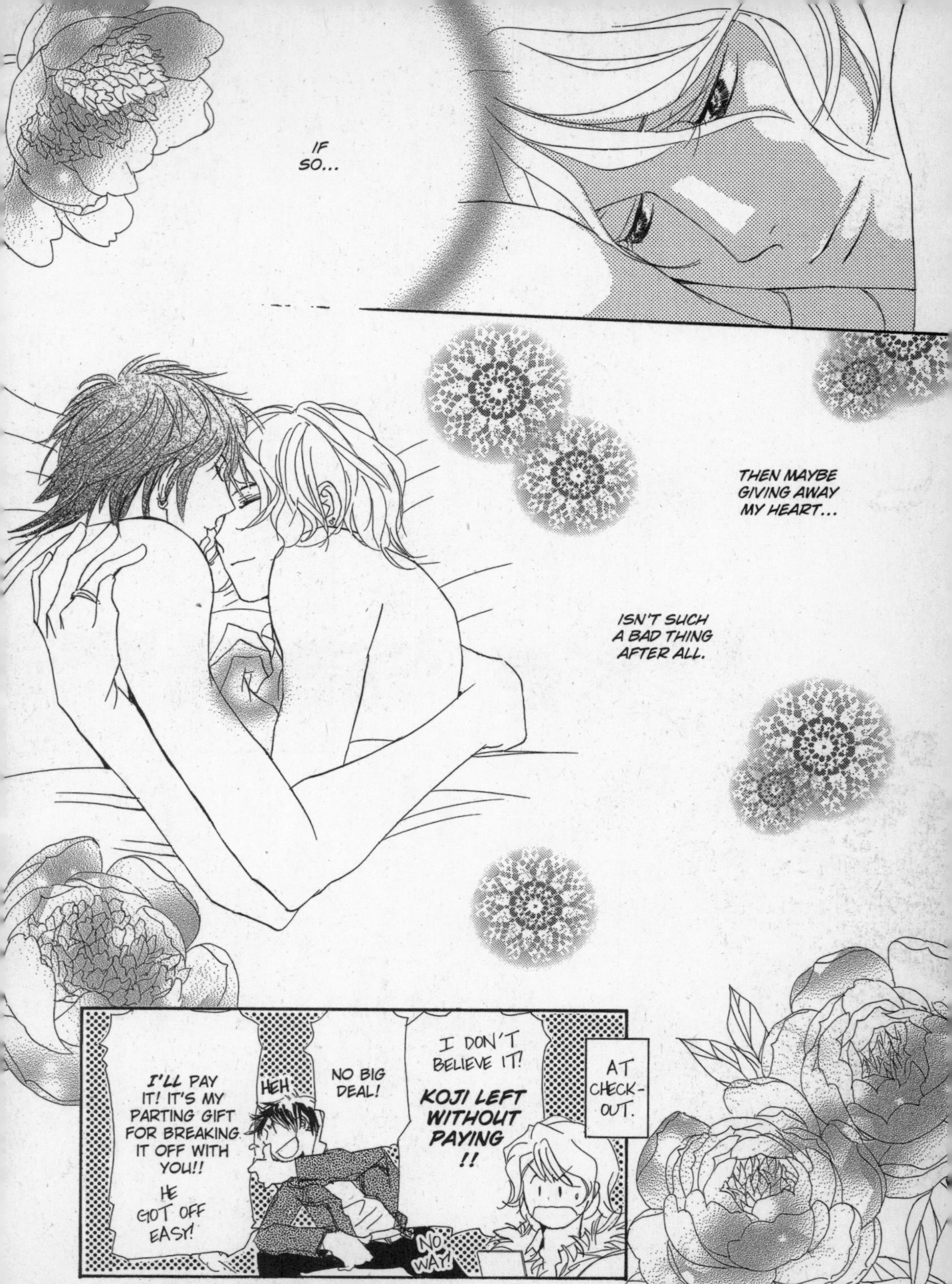
IF SO...
THEN MAYBE GIVING AWAY MY HEART...
ISN'T SUCH A BAD THING AFTER ALL.
AT CHECK-OUT.
I DON'T BELIEVE IT!
KOJI LEFT WITHOUT PAYING !!
NO WAY!
NO BIG DEAL!
HEH
I'LL PAY IT! IT'S MY PARTING GIFT FOR BREAKING IT OFF WITH YOU!!
HE GOT OFF EASY!

THE DAWN OF LOVE 2 END

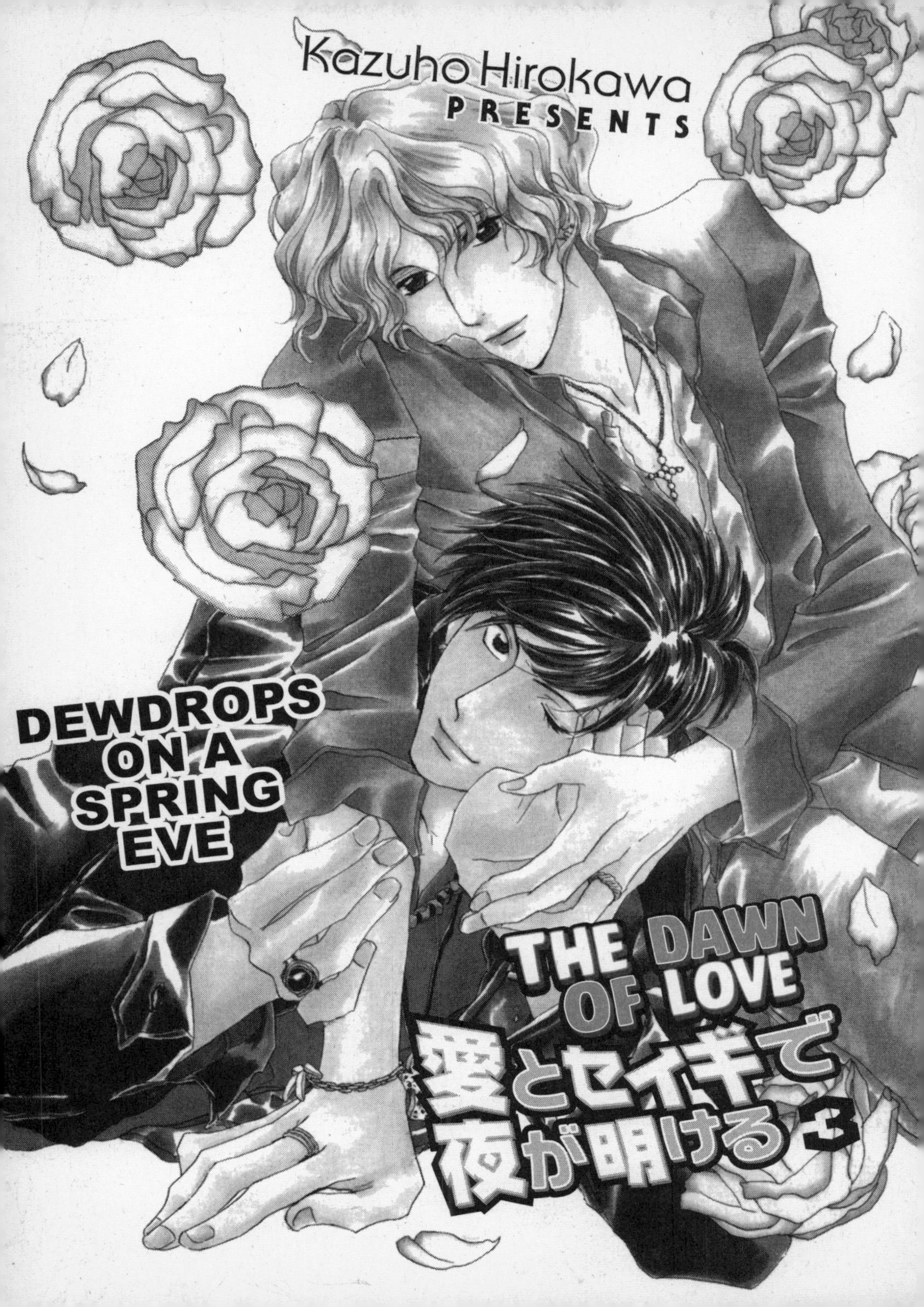
Kazuho Hirokawa
PRESENTS
DEWDROPS ON A SPRING EVE
THE DAWN OF LOVE
愛とセイギで夜が明ける 3

Free Talk

• SOME MORE CHATTER •

• BGM •

#1: SUEDE AND THE TEARS, FRANZ FERDINAND'S 1ST.

#2: ON HEAVY ROTATION WAS THE DARKNESS, FRANZ FERDINAND'S 2ND, JET, KAISER CHIEFS, THE ORDINARY BOYS. LATER ON, VAN HALEN'S 1984. IT WAS RIGHT AROUND THE TIME OF THE 2006 WINTER OLYMPICS. I'LL PROBABLY NEVER FORGET THE SPARKLING BEAUTY OF SHIZUKA ARAKAWA SKATING TO TURANDOT FOR THE REST OF MY LIFE.

#3: FOR THE SCENES WITH MASAHIRO, CAPTAIN SENSIBLE'S "BEST OF" ALBUM, DURAN DURAN'S RIO (MY FAVORITE ALBUM) AND "BEST OF", JELLYFISH'S 2ND, JASON FALKNER'S 1ST AND 2ND. FOR TAKANE'S SCENES, THE FIVE COCTEAU TWINS' ALBUMS AFTER TREASURE. ALSO, MY BLOODY VALENTINE.

#4: REPEATING THE SAME SELECTIONS AS #2 AND #3, ADDING FIVE 2-CD SETS OF PET SHOP BOYS - ACTUALLY, VERY, BILINGUAL, POPART (A BEST OF), FUNDAMENTAL. THE SONG "3-CD "SHAMELESS," ON THE BONUS SET CD OF VERY, I SELECT AS MY OWN PERSONAL ANTHEM.

A FLOWER AWAITS SUMMER: IT WAS SO LONG AGO, I DON'T REMEMBER... I VAGUELY RECALL LISTENING TO BRIAN AND MATTHEW JAY... PROBABLY SOME PREFAB, AS WELL...

• DOUJINSHI NOTICE •

FOR SUMMER AND WINTER COMIKET, INTEX OSAKA, AND J GARDEN, I PLAN TO PARTICIPATE WITH "SWEET HAKKA." FOR DETAILS, PLEASE SEE THE HOME PAGE FOR "MYAAKO NO OTAKARA (MYAAKO'S TREASURE)". TRY A SEARCH UNDER "KAZUHO HIROKAWA."

TO ALL MY REGULAR READERS, HELLO AGAIN.

TO THOSE OF YOU READING FOR THE FIRST TIME, NICE TO MEET YOU.

SORRY TO SUDDENLY POP UP IN THE MIDDLE LIKE THIS. I'M KAZUHO HIROKAWA. COMING EXACTLY ONE YEAR AFTER LOVE BLOSSOM, THIS SECOND MANGA OF MINE JUST WRAPPED UP ITS LIMITED SERIES MAGAZINE RUN THE OTHER DAY. IT'S THANKS TO ALL YOUR SUPPORT. THANK YOU VERY MUCH!!

#1: MY EDITOR REQUESTED THAT THE STORY FEATURE THREE THINGS: ①: YOUNG MEN; ②: SEX FRIENDS; ③: SEX SCENES. NUMBER TWO GAVE ME A BIT OF TROUBLE AT FIRST, BUT AS THE CHARACTERS OF TAKANE & MASAHIRO (IN THAT ORDER) DEVELOPED, THEY TOOK ON A LIFE OF THEIR OWN. UNBELIEVABLY, THEY SPEND 45% OF THE TIME NAKED! THE STORY STILL MANAGES TO PROGRESS SOMEHOW, THANKS TO THESE TWO CHARACTERS, THE LOVE HOTEL GUIDE BOOK I OBTAINED SEVERAL YEARS AGO, AND MY PHOTO-ILLUSTRATED MANUAL OF SEXUAL POSITIONS, THE SHIJUHATTE (IT FEATURES WOMEN, SO THE PHOTOS ARE PRETTY).

BY THE WAY, UPON SEEING THE TITLE PAGE FOR THIS STORY, EIGHT OR NINE OUT OF TEN PEOPLE SAY, "IS HE... GRABBING HIM DOWN THERE?" BUT I SWEAR... HE'S ONLY PULLING DOWN THE ZIPPER... OR THAT'S HOW IT WAS SUPPOSED TO LOOK... REALLY...!!

#2: AS THE STORY PROGRESSES, MASAHIRO'S IDIOCY SEEMS TO INCREASE... AND FRANKLY, YOU CAN TELL TAKANE'S CAUGHT THE IDIOT VIRUS AS WELL. WHAT? I HAVE, TOO, YOU SAY?! (HA HA). THESE CHARACTERS ARE VERY FUN AND EASY TO DRAW, BUT IF I GO TOO FAR, I MIGHT LOSE SOME OF YOU READERS... A-ARE YOU GUYS OKAY WITH IT SO FAR...?!

#3: I DIDN'T MAKE IT OBVIOUS, BUT IN THE STORY THEY GRADUATE FROM SECOND-YEAR TO THIRD-YEAR STUDENTS. THAT'S JUST BECAUSE I GOT TIRED OF DRAWING WINTER CLOTHES AND WANTED TO DRAW THEM IN SPRING FASHIONS (WHAT?!). ABOUT TADANORI: I RECEIVE TWO DISTINCT, CONFLICTING OPINIONS OF, "I HATE HIM!" AND "HE MIGHT EVEN BE COOLER THAN MASAHIRO" FROM READERS... BUT THAT WAS EXACTLY MY INTENTION! (HEH HEH). IT'S FUN DRAWING MEANIES -- EVEN BETTER WHEN THEY'RE THE MATURE, SOPHISTICATED, BESPECTACLED TYPE!

#4: IT'S EVEN MORE FUN TO SEE SAID MEANY DEFEATED!! PERHAPS THIS MAKES ME A NATURAL-BORN SADIST...? (WHAAAT?! LOL). WHEN I'M DRAWING A CHARACTER LIKE TADANORI, I HAVE TO BE VERY AWARE OF WHAT I'M DOING... SO WHEN THE SCENE CAME WHERE MASAHIRO FINALLY APPEARS, QUITE FRANKLY, I WAS RELIEVED (HA HA). THE TWINS REVELATION WAS BECAUSE... WELL, I HAVE A THING FOR TWINS... AND FOR THE CHIBI VERSION OF MASAHIRO, TOO (HA HA). I WISH I COULD'VE DRAWN A TWO-SHOT OF HIM WITH A CHIBI TAKANE...

A FLOWER AWAITS SUMMER: EVEN THOUGH THE ARTIST AND THE MATERIALS THE ARTIST USED ARE EXACTLY THE SAME, LOOK AT THE DIFFERENCE... WHY?! WHY ARE THE LINES SO THICK, ME OF THREE YEARS AGO?! AND IT'S SO ROUGH-LOOKING! AND NANAO'S SO DEPRESSING! THESE ARE THE THINGS I CRIED AS I REWORKED THE ORIGINAL ART FOR THIS MANGA. AT THE TIME, I WAS STILL VERY GREEN (HA HA) AND THIS STORY BRINGS BACK A LOT OF MEMORIES. I ACTUALLY LIKE THE CHARACTER KENSHO QUITE A BIT.

AS ALWAYS, THE MORE I DRAW, THE MORE I'M FORCED TO ACKNOWLEDGE HOW INADEQUATE I STILL AM -- BUT I'LL KEEP WORKING HARD SO THAT I MAY IMPROVE. YOUR CONTINUED SUPPORT WOULD MAKE ME VERY HAPPY!

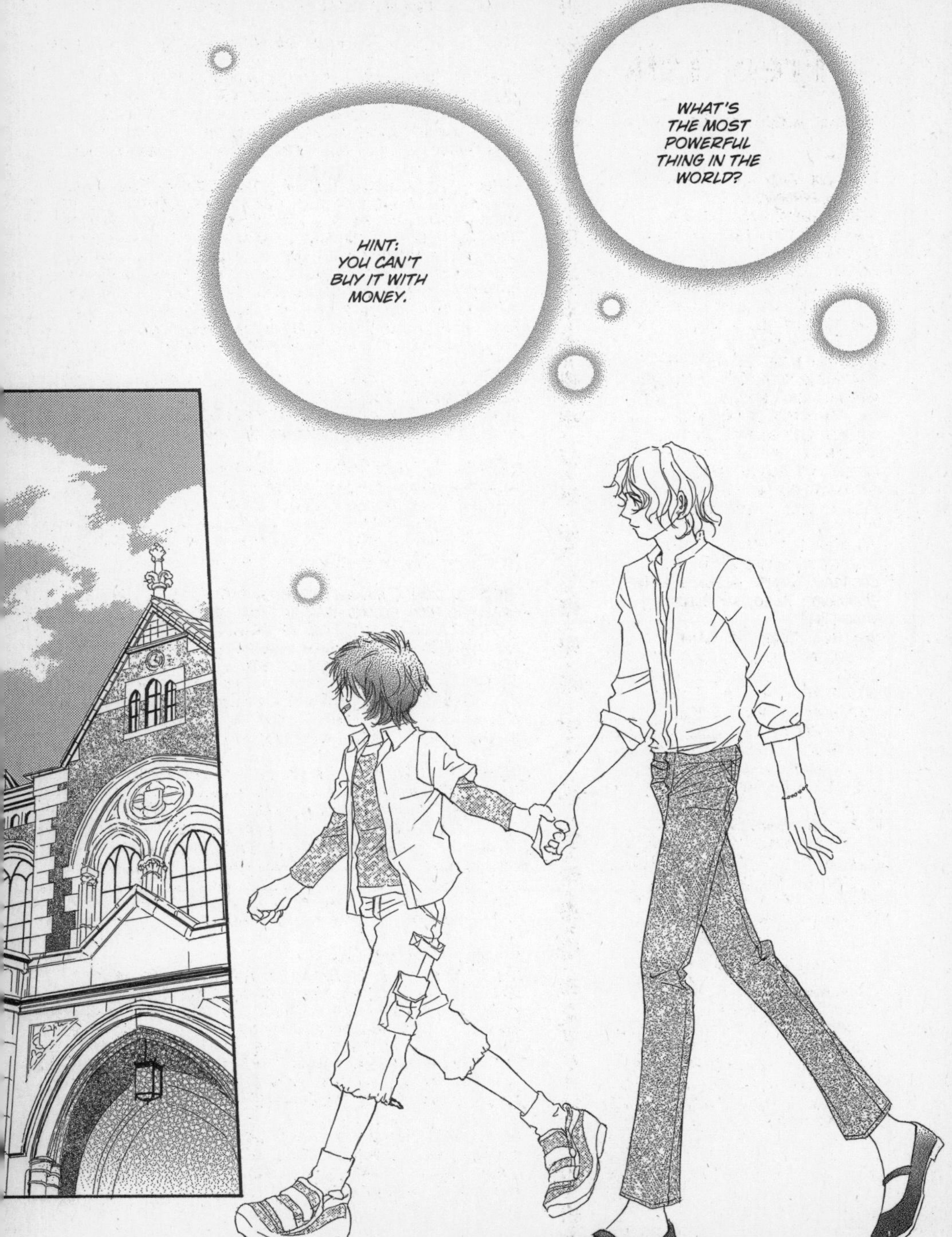
WHAT'S THE MOST POWERFUL THING IN THE WORLD?
HINT: YOU CAN'T BUY IT WITH MONEY.

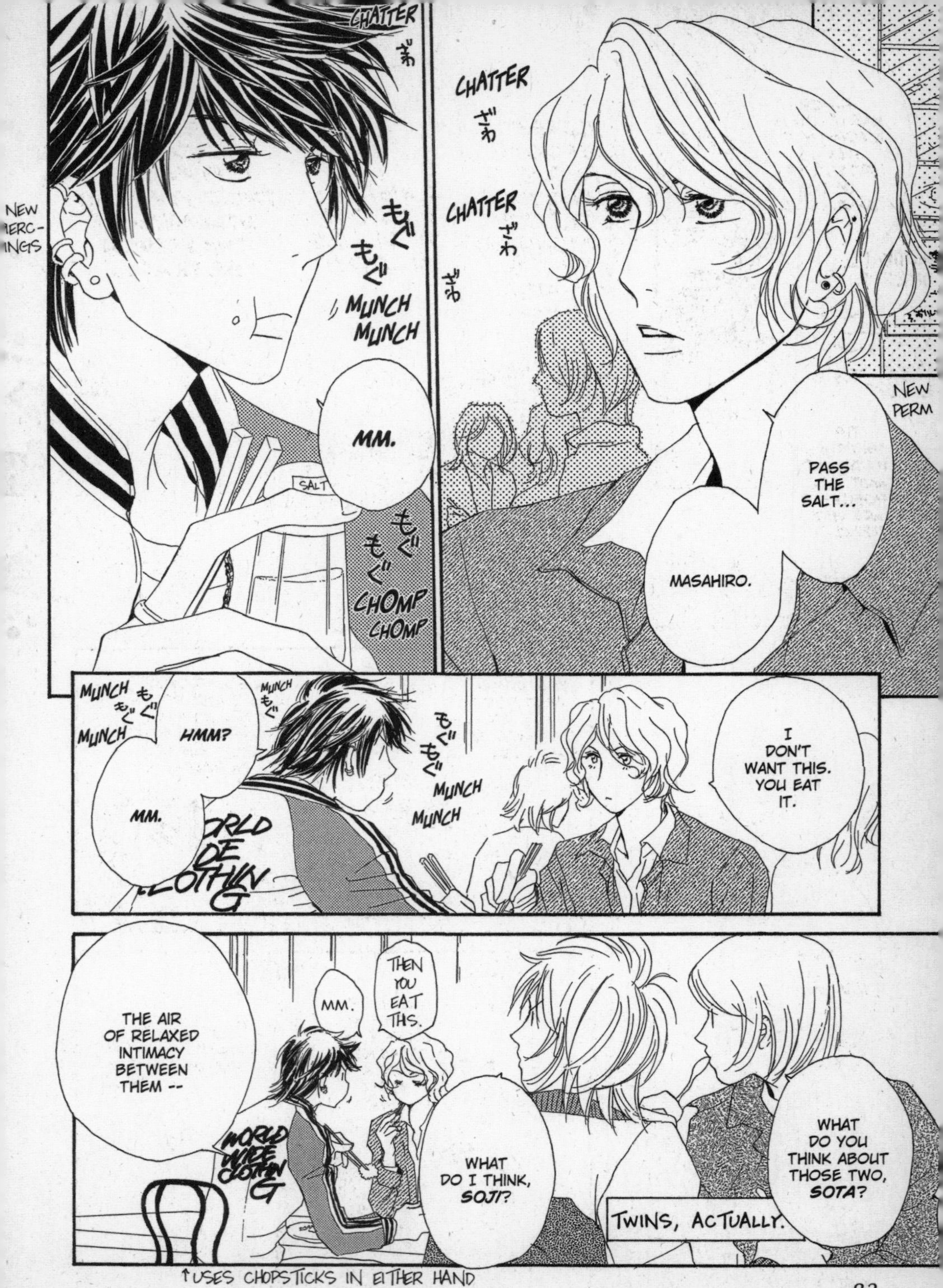
CHATTER
ざわ
CHATTER
ざわ
ざわ
NEW PERM
PASS THE SALT...
MASAHIRO.
CHATTER
ざわ
もぐ もぐ
MUNCH MUNCH
MM.
SALT
もぐ もぐ
CHOMP CHOMP
NEW
I DON'T WANT THIS. YOU EAT IT.
もぐ もぐ
MUNCH MUNCH
MUNCH もぐ
HMM?
MUNCH もぐ もぐ MUNCH
MM.
WHAT DO YOU THINK ABOUT THOSE TWO, SOTA?
TWINS, ACTUALLY.
WHAT DO I THINK, SOJI?
THEN YOU EAT THIS.
MM.
THE AIR OF RELAXED INTIMACY BETWEEN THEM --
WORLD WIDE CLOTHING
↑USES CHOPSTICKS IN EITHER HAND

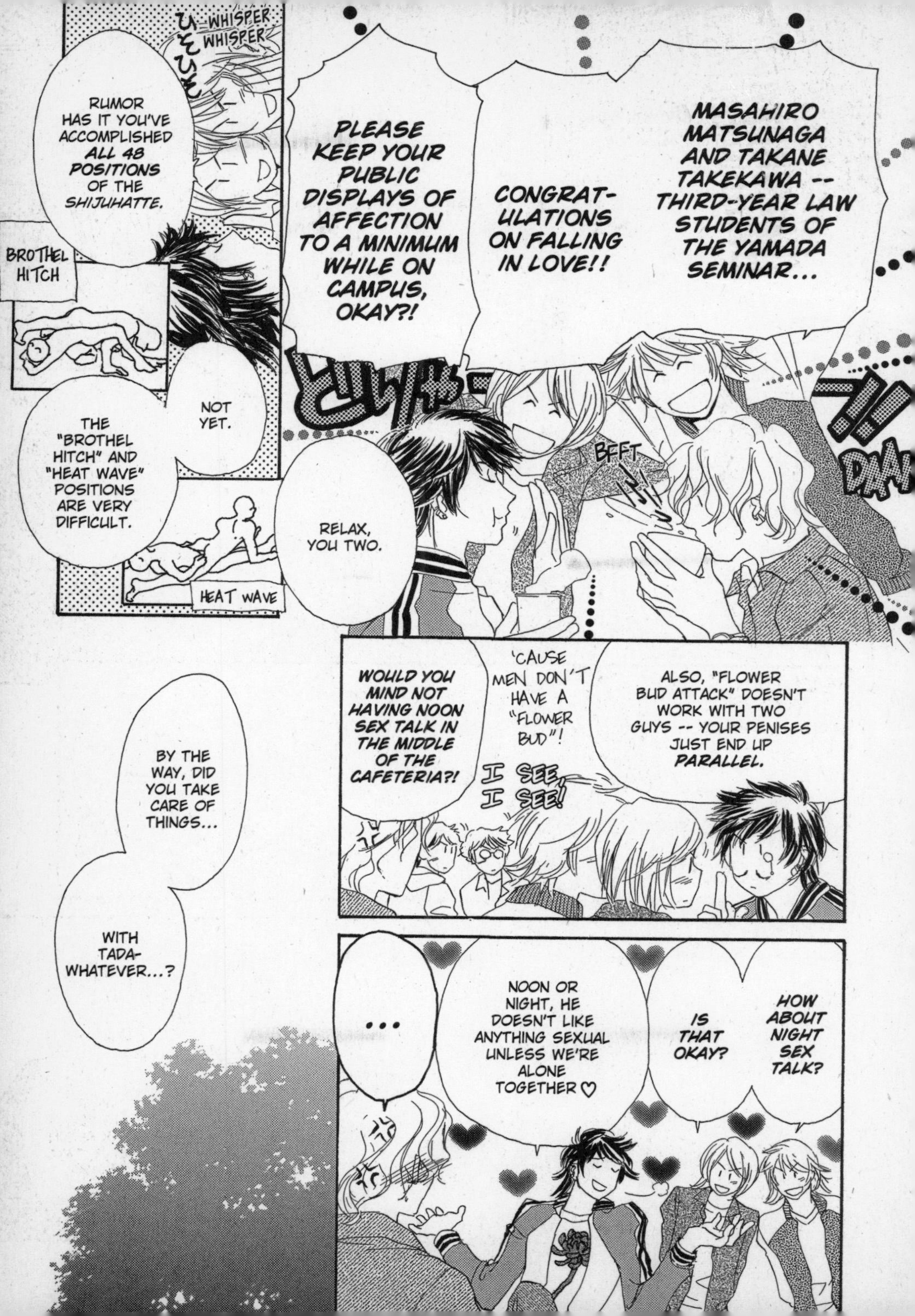
MASAHIRO MATSUNAGA AND TAKANE TAKEKAWA -- THIRD-YEAR LAW STUDENTS OF THE YAMADA SEMINAR...
CONGRATULATIONS ON FALLING IN LOVE!!
PLEASE KEEP YOUR PUBLIC DISPLAYS OF AFFECTION TO A MINIMUM WHILE ON CAMPUS, OKAY?!
?!
BFFT
RELAX, YOU TWO.
ひそひそ
WHISPER WHISPER
RUMOR HAS IT YOU'VE ACCOMPLISHED **ALL 48 POSITIONS** OF THE SHIJUHATTE.
BROTHEL HITCH
NOT YET.
THE "BROTHEL HITCH" AND "HEAT WAVE" POSITIONS ARE VERY DIFFICULT.
HEAT WAVE
ALSO, "FLOWER BUD ATTACK" DOESN'T WORK WITH TWO GUYS -- YOUR PENISES JUST END UP **PARALLEL.**
'CAUSE MEN DON'T HAVE A "FLOWER BUD"!
I SEE, I SEE!
WOULD YOU MIND NOT HAVING NOON SEX TALK IN THE MIDDLE OF THE CAFETERIA?!
HOW ABOUT NIGHT SEX TALK?
IS THAT OKAY?
NOON OR NIGHT, HE DOESN'T LIKE ANYTHING SEXUAL UNLESS WE'RE ALONE TOGETHER ♡
...
BY THE WAY, DID YOU TAKE CARE OF THINGS...
WITH TADA-WHATEVER...?

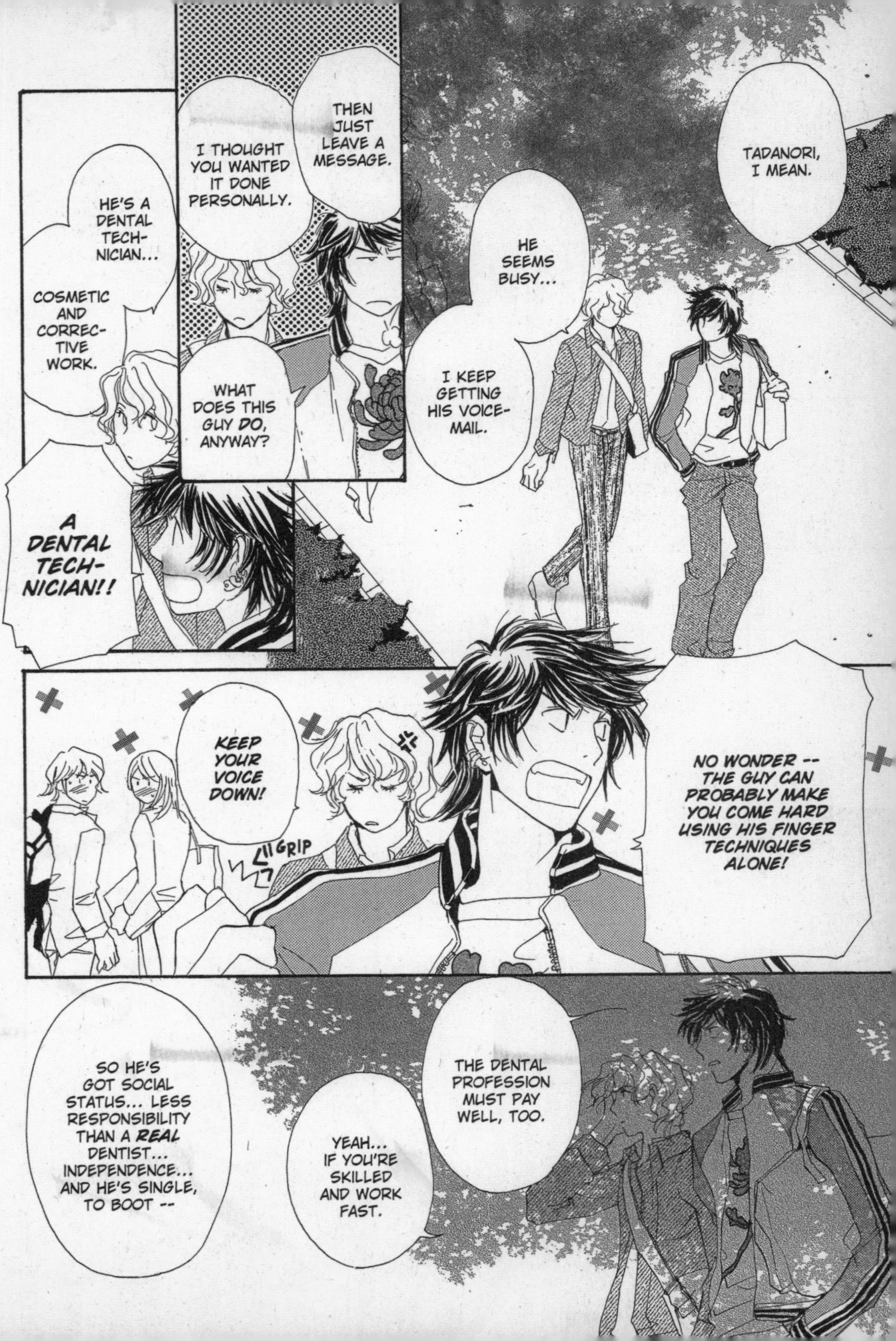
TADANORI, I MEAN.
HE SEEMS BUSY...
I KEEP GETTING HIS VOICE-MAIL.
THEN JUST LEAVE A MESSAGE.
I THOUGHT YOU WANTED IT DONE PERSONALLY.
WHAT DOES THIS GUY *DO*, ANYWAY?
HE'S A DENTAL TECHNICIAN...
COSMETIC AND CORRECTIVE WORK.
A DENTAL TECHNICIAN!!
NO WONDER -- THE GUY CAN PROBABLY MAKE YOU COME HARD USING HIS FINGER TECHNIQUES ALONE!
KEEP YOUR VOICE DOWN!
GRIP
THE DENTAL PROFESSION MUST PAY WELL, TOO.
YEAH... IF YOU'RE SKILLED AND WORK FAST.
SO HE'S GOT SOCIAL STATUS... LESS RESPONSIBILITY THAN A *REAL* DENTIST... INDEPENDENCE... AND HE'S SINGLE, TO BOOT --

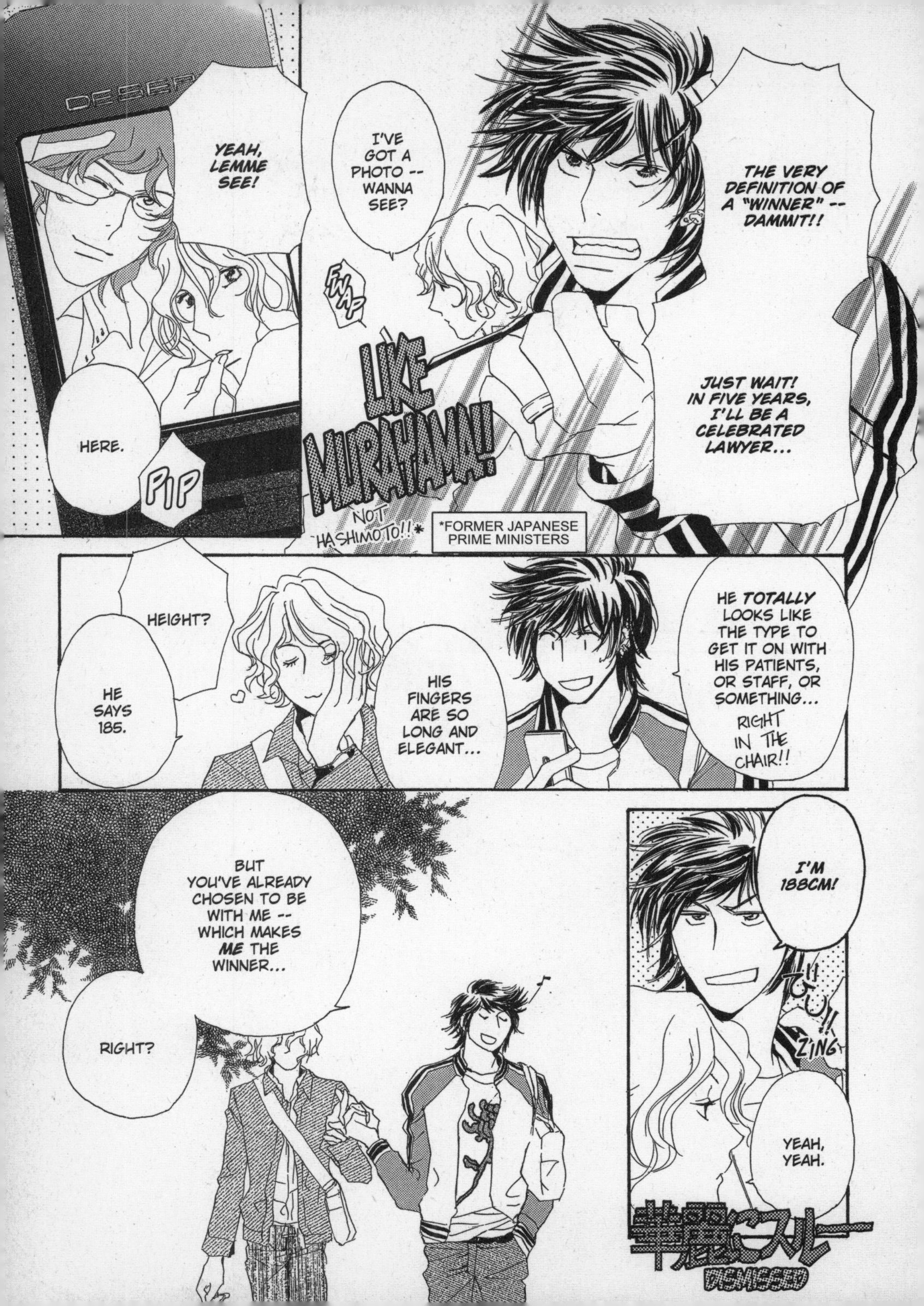
THE VERY DEFINITION OF A "WINNER" -- DAMMIT!!
JUST WAIT! IN FIVE YEARS, I'LL BE A CELEBRATED LAWYER...
LIKE MURAYAMA!!
NOT HASHIMOTO!!*
*FORMER JAPANESE PRIME MINISTERS
FWAP
I'VE GOT A PHOTO -- WANNA SEE?
YEAH, LEMME SEE!
HERE.
PIP
HE *TOTALLY* LOOKS LIKE THE TYPE TO GET IT ON WITH HIS PATIENTS, OR STAFF, OR SOMETHING...
RIGHT IN THE CHAIR!!
HIS FINGERS ARE SO LONG AND ELEGANT...
HEIGHT?
HE SAYS 185.
I'M 188CM!
ZING
YEAH, YEAH.
BUT YOU'VE ALREADY CHOSEN TO BE WITH ME -- WHICH MAKES *ME* THE WINNER...
RIGHT?
華麗にスルー
DISMISSED

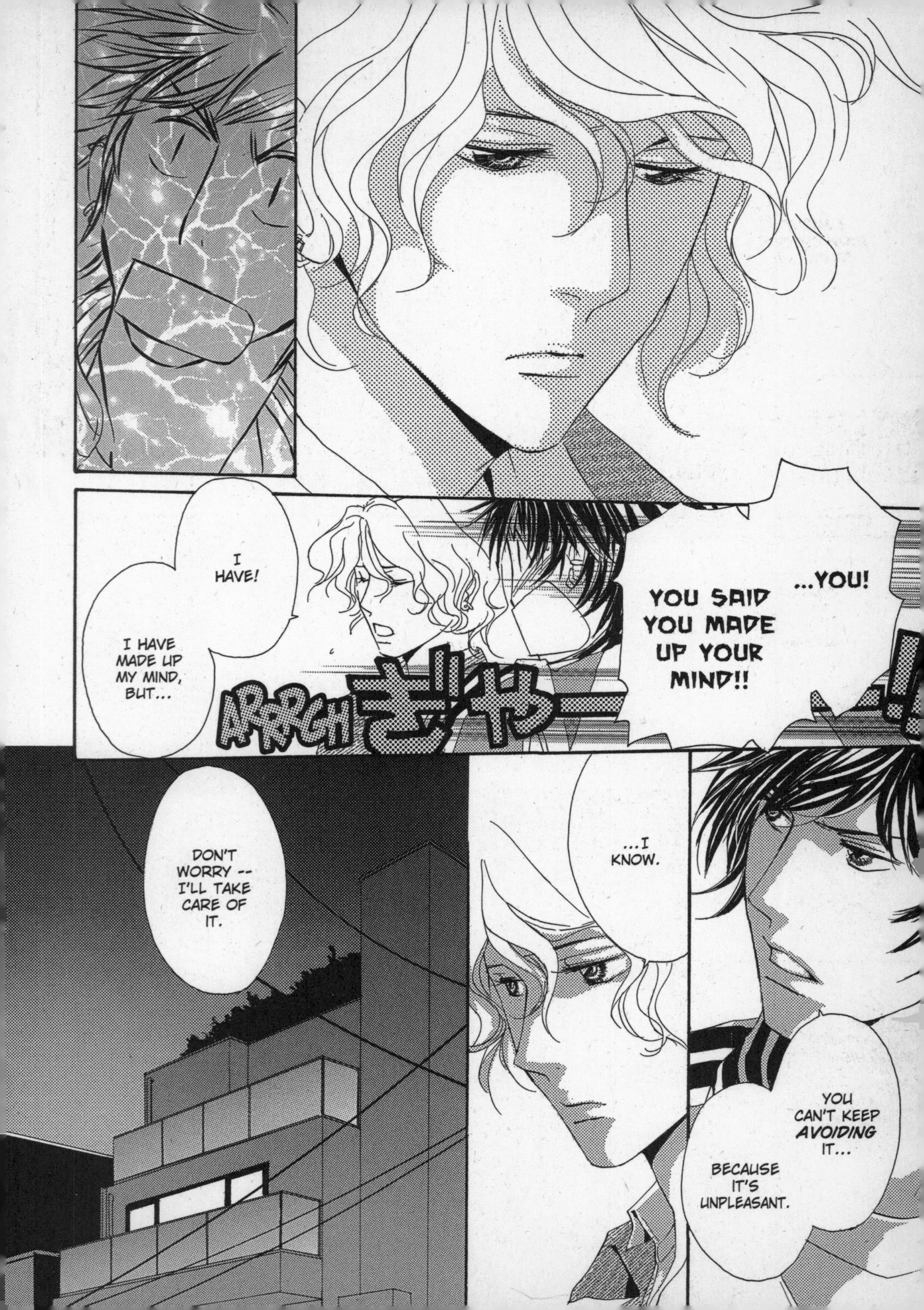
...YOU!
YOU SAID YOU MADE UP YOUR MIND!!
ARRRGH キャー
I HAVE!
I HAVE MADE UP MY MIND, BUT...
YOU CAN'T KEEP *AVOIDING* IT...
BECAUSE IT'S UNPLEASANT.
...I KNOW.
DON'T WORRY -- I'LL TAKE CARE OF IT.

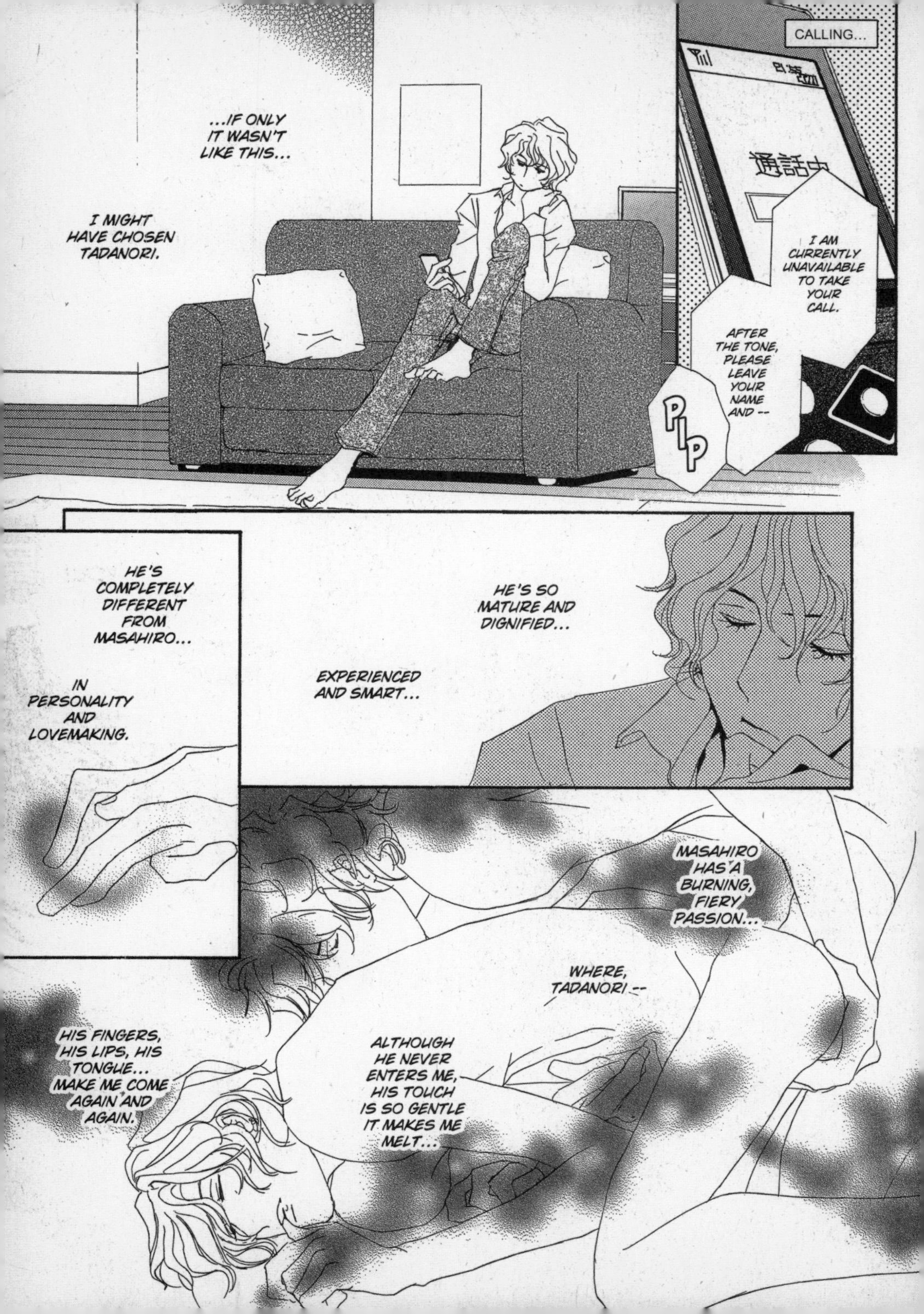
CALLING...
通話中
I AM CURRENTLY UNAVAILABLE TO TAKE YOUR CALL.
AFTER THE TONE, PLEASE LEAVE YOUR NAME AND --
PIP
...IF ONLY IT WASN'T LIKE THIS...
I MIGHT HAVE CHOSEN TADANORI.
HE'S SO MATURE AND DIGNIFIED...
EXPERIENCED AND SMART...
HE'S COMPLETELY DIFFERENT FROM MASAHIRO...
IN PERSONALITY AND LOVEMAKING.
MASAHIRO HAS A BURNING, FIERY PASSION...
WHERE, TADANORI --
ALTHOUGH HE NEVER ENTERS ME, HIS TOUCH IS SO GENTLE IT MAKES ME MELT...
HIS FINGERS, HIS LIPS, HIS TONGUE... MAKE ME COME AGAIN AND AGAIN.

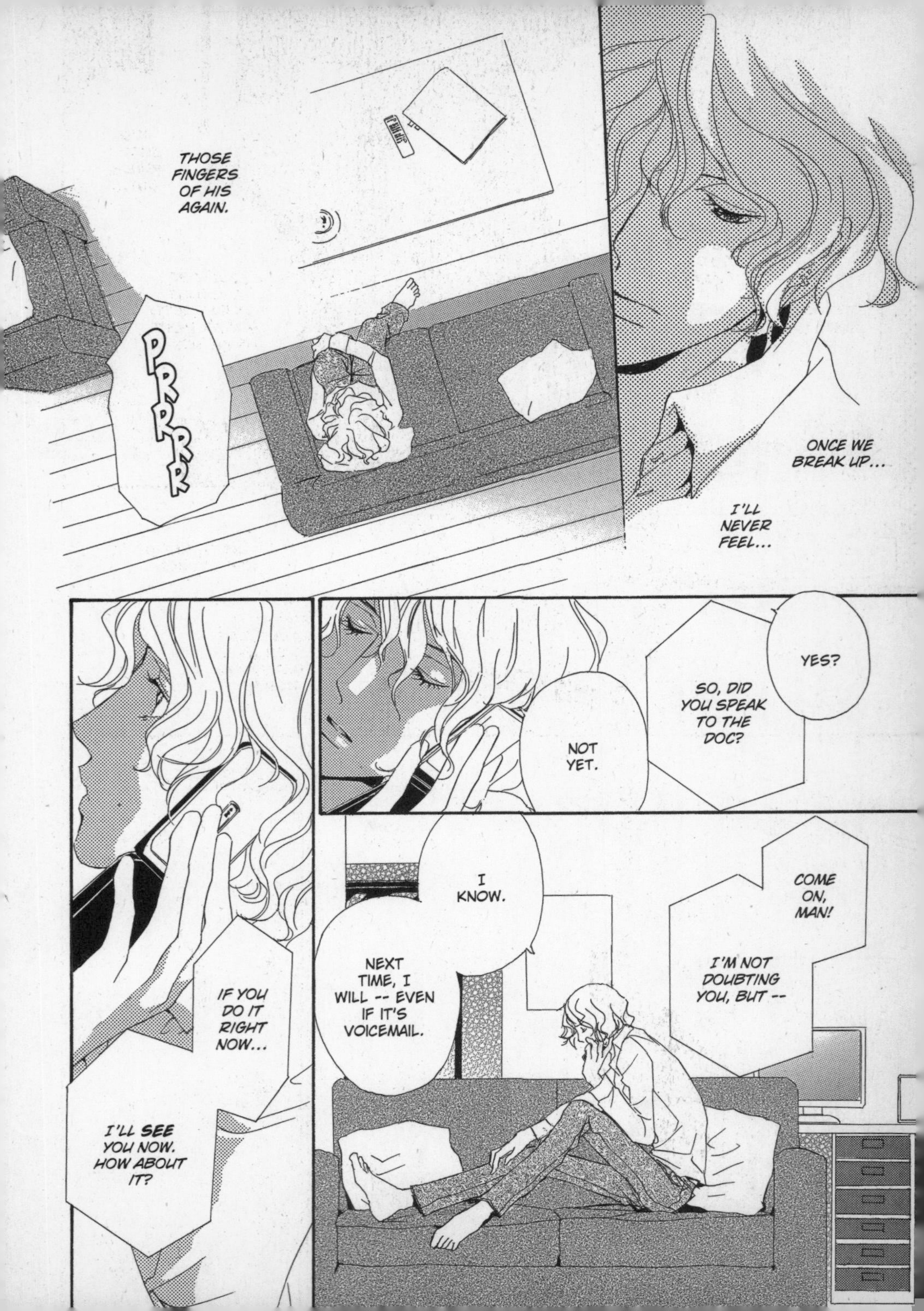

ONCE WE BREAK UP...
I'LL NEVER FEEL...
THOSE FINGERS OF HIS AGAIN.
PRRRR
YES?
SO, DID YOU SPEAK TO THE DOC?
NOT YET.
COME ON, MAN!
I'M NOT DOUBTING YOU, BUT --
I KNOW.
NEXT TIME, I WILL -- EVEN IF IT'S VOICEMAIL.
IF YOU DO IT RIGHT NOW...
I'LL SEE YOU NOW. HOW ABOUT IT?

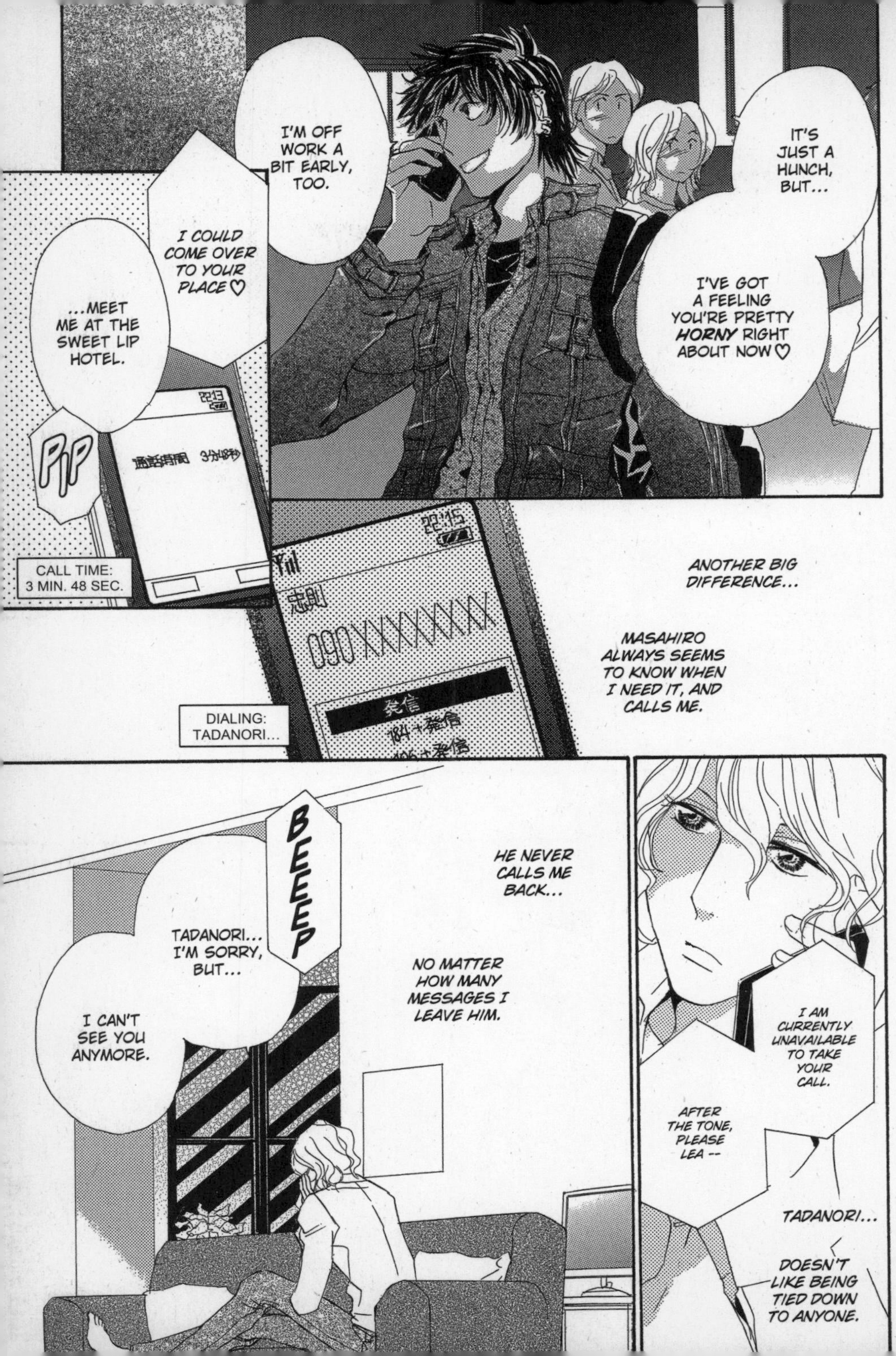
IT'S JUST A HUNCH, BUT...
I'VE GOT A FEELING YOU'RE PRETTY **HORNY** RIGHT ABOUT NOW♡
I'M OFF WORK A BIT EARLY, TOO.
I COULD COME OVER TO YOUR PLACE♡
...MEET ME AT THE SWEET LIP HOTEL.
22:13
通話時間 3分48秒
PIP
CALL TIME: 3 MIN. 48 SEC.
ANOTHER BIG DIFFERENCE...
MASAHIRO ALWAYS SEEMS TO KNOW WHEN I NEED IT, AND CALLS ME.
22:15
忠則
090XXXXXXXX
発信
184+発信
DIALING: TADANORI...
I AM CURRENTLY UNAVAILABLE TO TAKE YOUR CALL.
AFTER THE TONE, PLEASE LEA --
TADANORI...
DOESN'T LIKE BEING TIED DOWN TO ANYONE.
HE NEVER CALLS ME BACK...
NO MATTER HOW MANY MESSAGES I LEAVE HIM.
BEEEP
TADANORI... I'M SORRY, BUT...
I CAN'T SEE YOU ANYMORE.

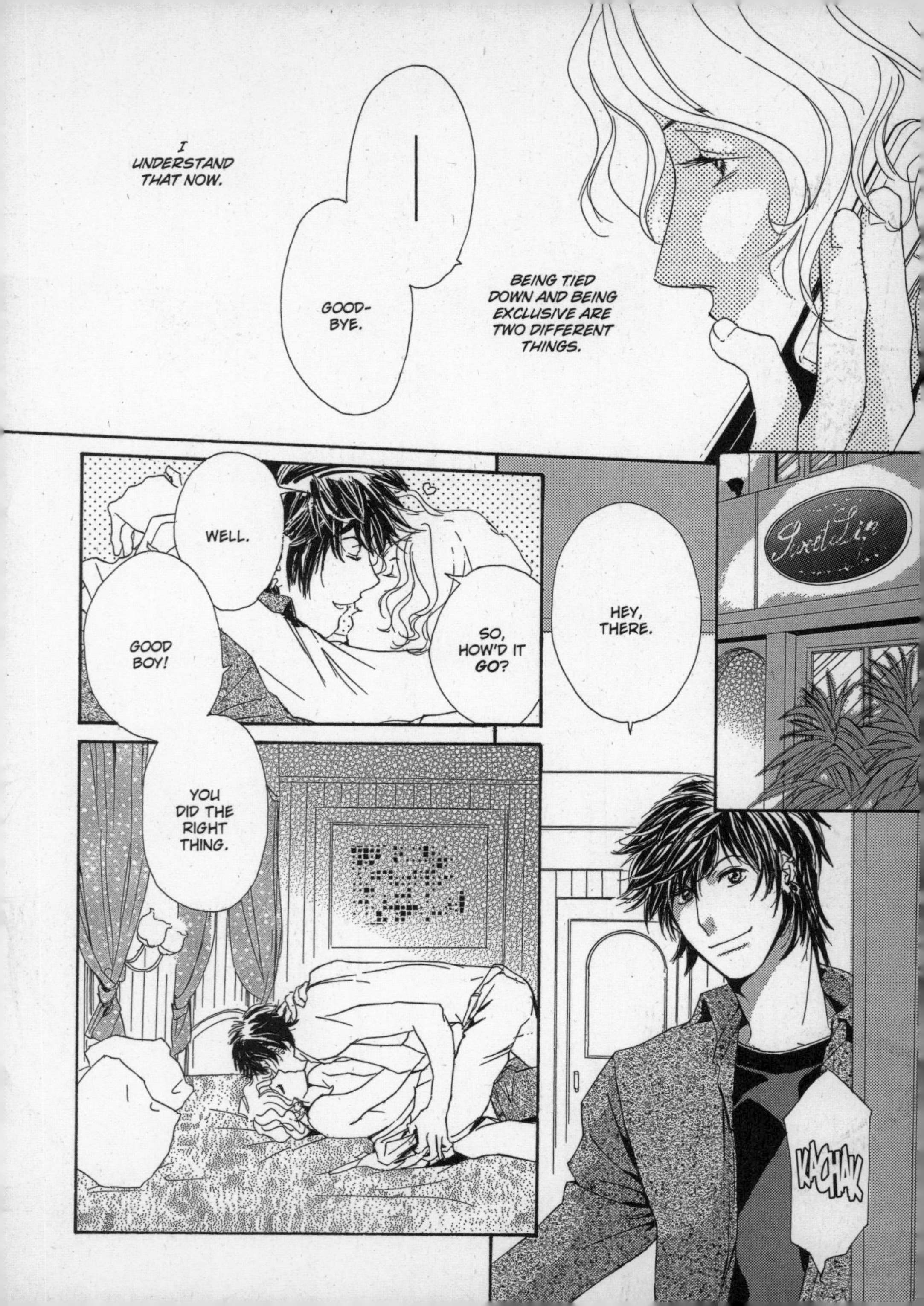
BEING TIED DOWN AND BEING EXCLUSIVE ARE TWO DIFFERENT THINGS.
—
GOOD-BYE.
I UNDERSTAND THAT NOW.
HEY, THERE.
SO, HOW'D IT GO?
KACHAK
WELL.
GOOD BOY!
YOU DID THE RIGHT THING.

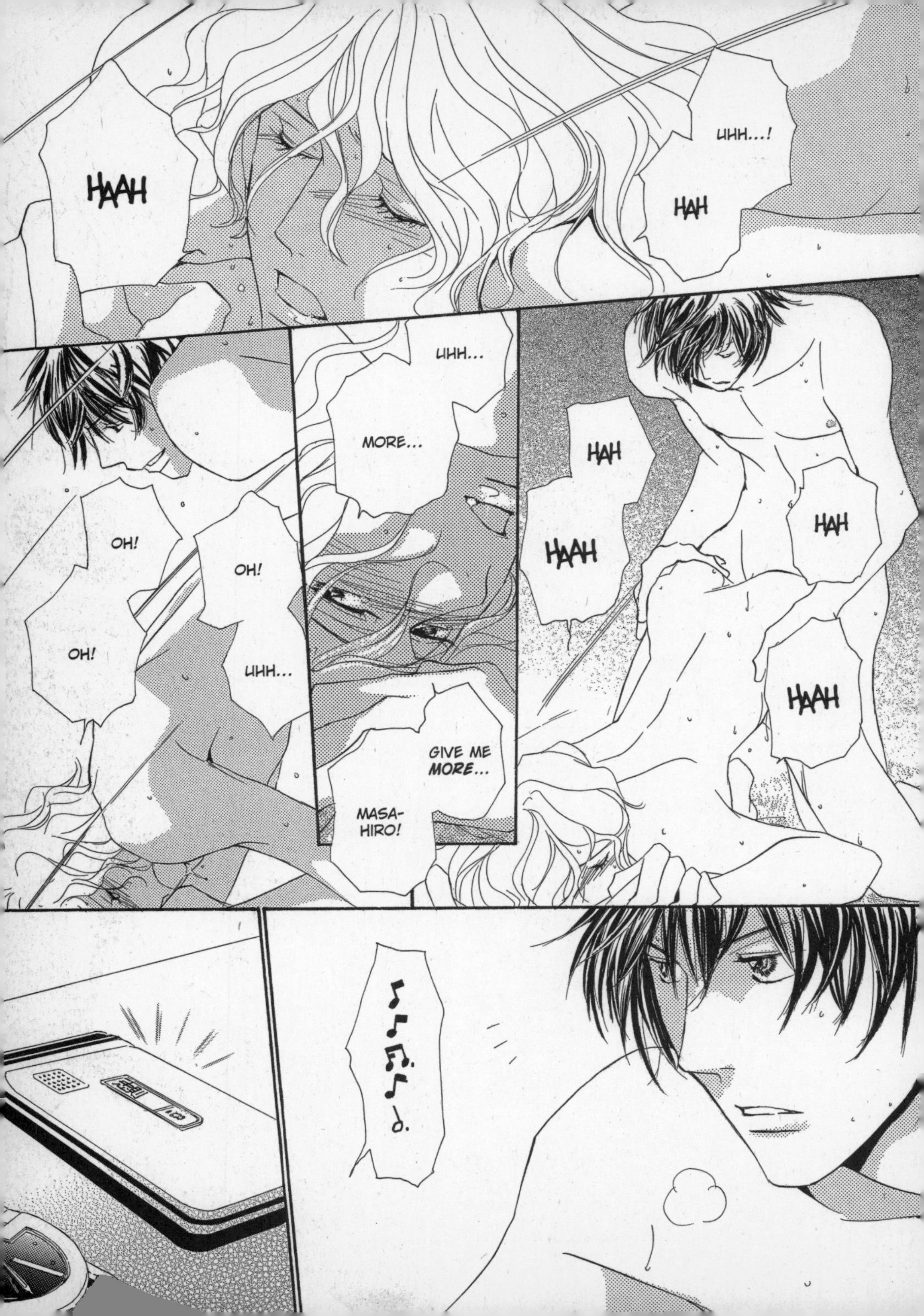
UHH...!
HAH
HAAH
HAH
HAH
HAAH
HAAH
UHH...
MORE...
GIVE ME MORE...
MASA-HIRO!
OH!
OH!
UHH...
OH!

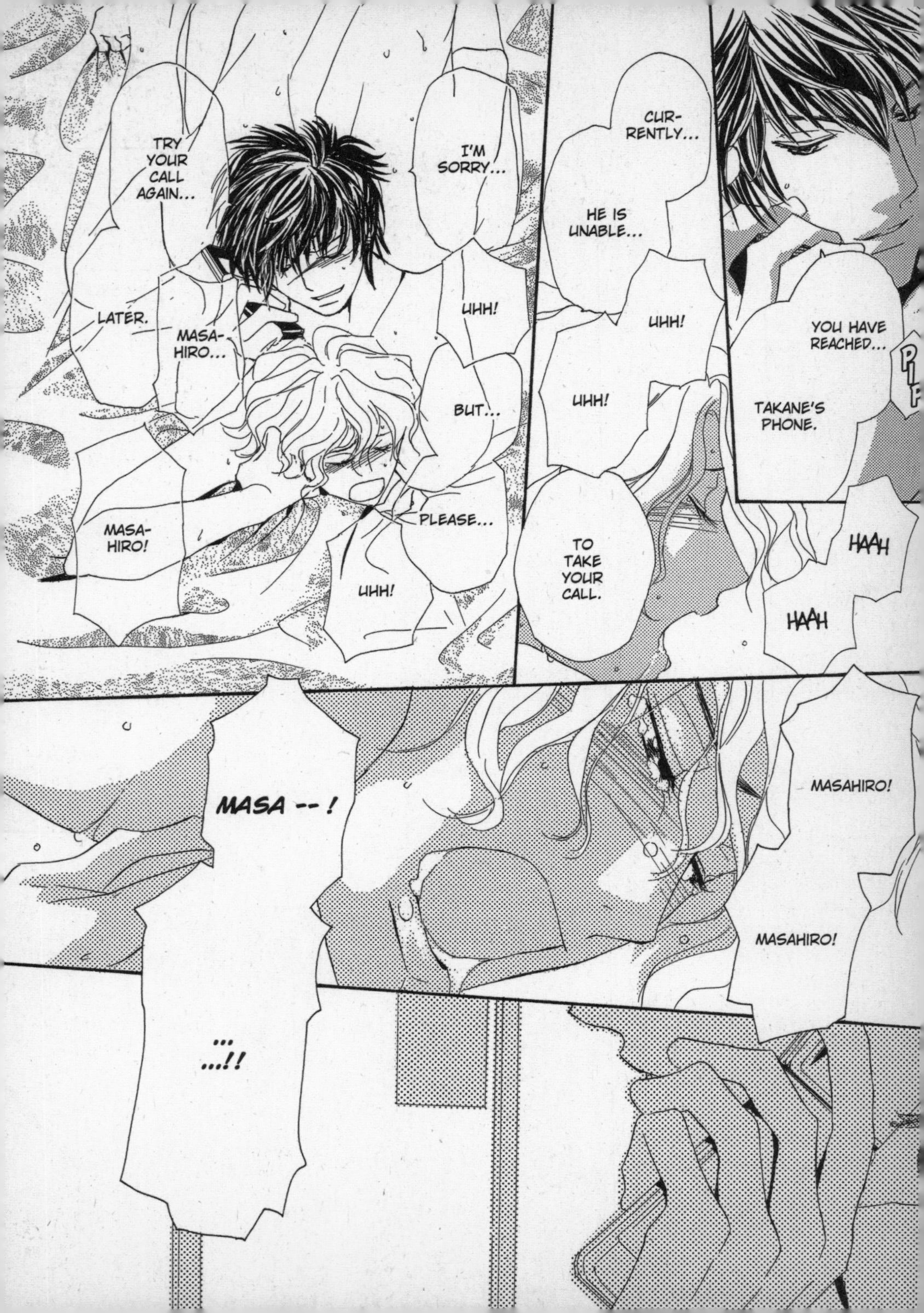
PIP
YOU HAVE REACHED...
TAKANE'S PHONE.
CUR-RENTLY...
HE IS UNABLE...
UHH!
UHH!
TO TAKE YOUR CALL.
HAAH
HAAH
I'M SORRY...
UHH!
BUT...
PLEASE...
UHH!
TRY YOUR CALL AGAIN...
LATER.
MASA-HIRO...
MASA-HIRO!
MASAHIRO!
MASAHIRO!
MASA -- !
... ...!!

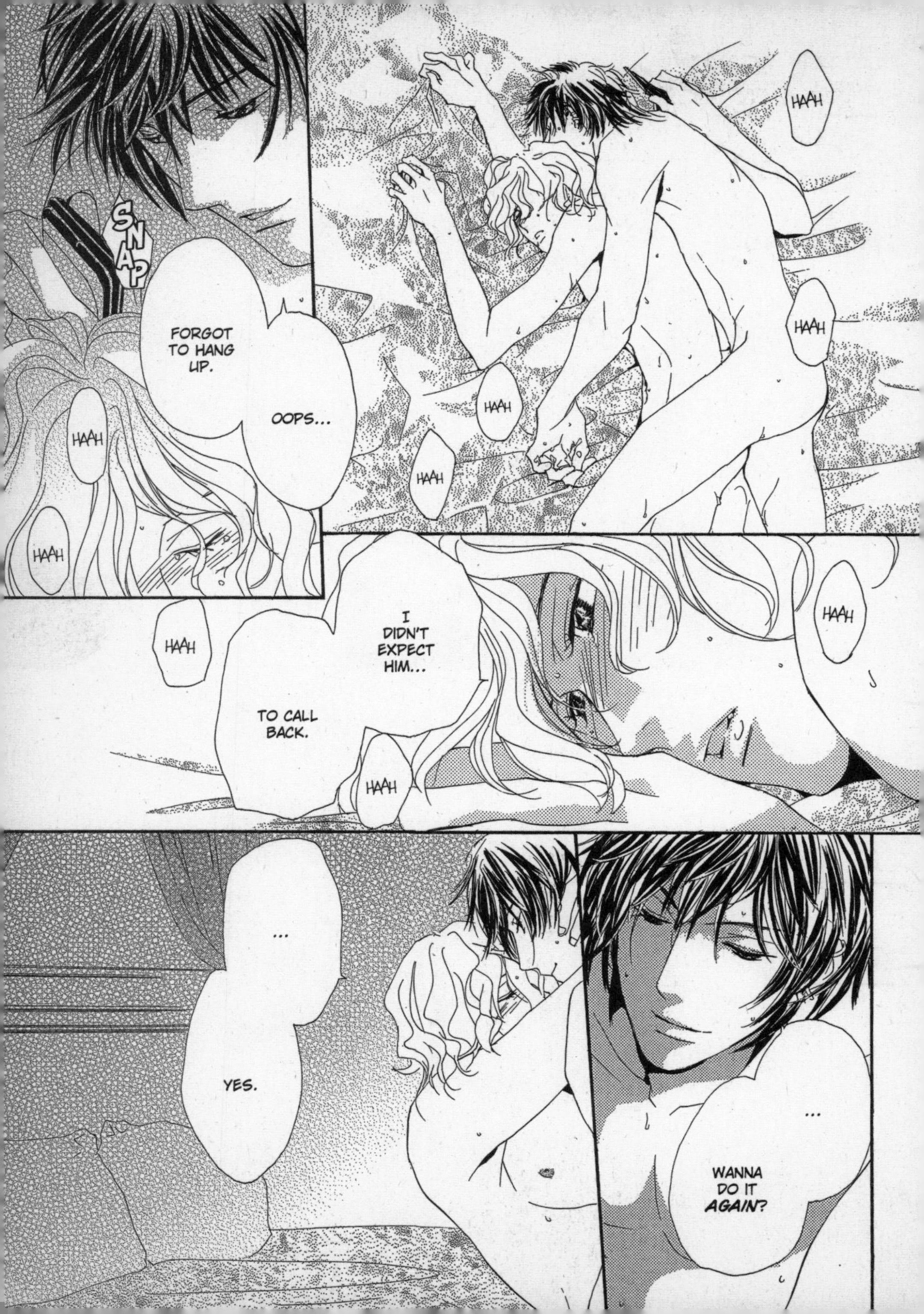
HAAH
HAAH
HAAH
HAAH
SNAP
FORGOT TO HANG UP.
OOPS...
HAAH
HAAH
HAAH
I DIDN'T EXPECT HIM...
HAAH
TO CALL BACK.
HAAH
...
WANNA DO IT *AGAIN*?
...
YES.

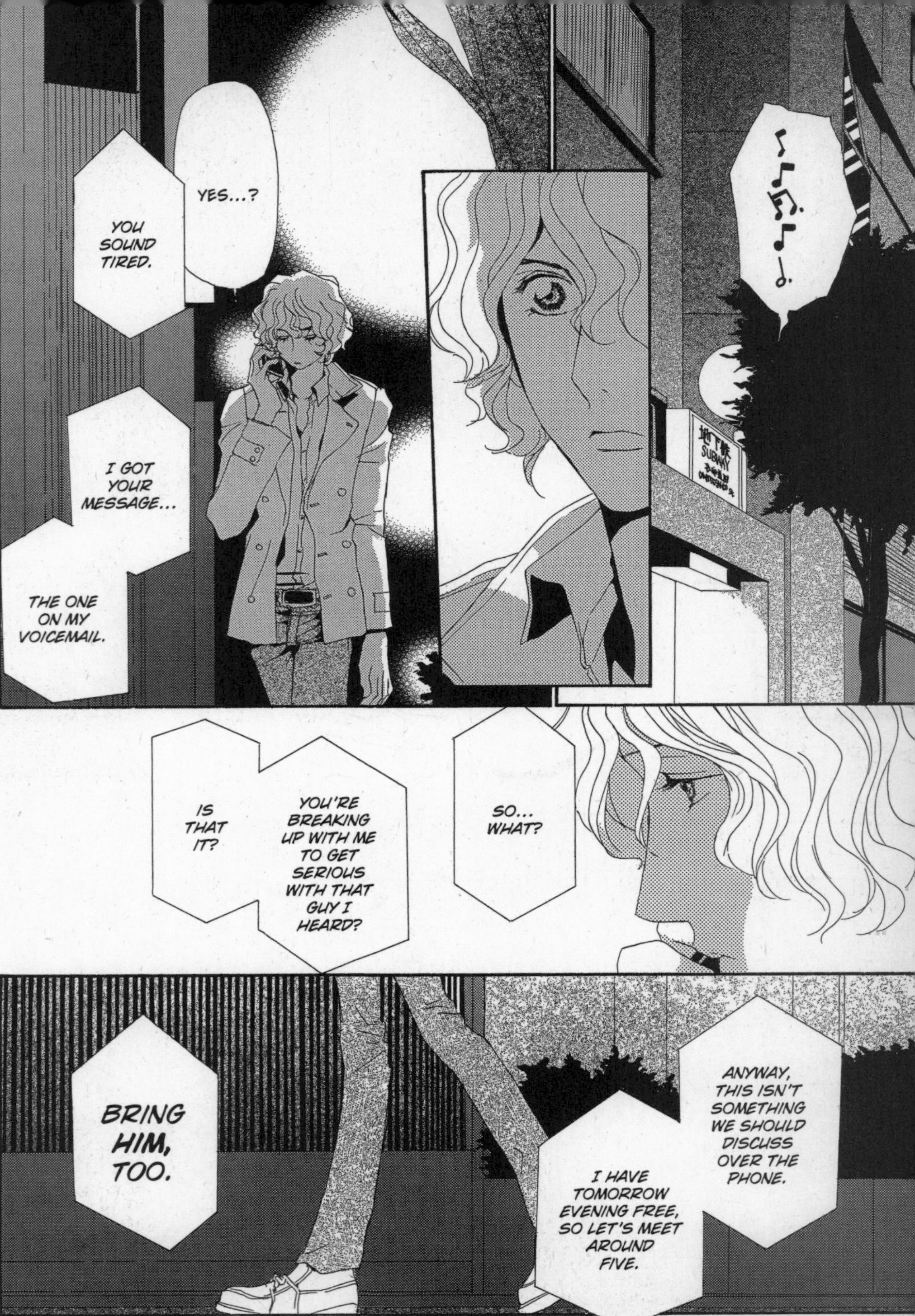
SUBWAY
YES...?
YOU SOUND TIRED.
I GOT YOUR MESSAGE...
THE ONE ON MY VOICEMAIL.
SO... WHAT?
YOU'RE BREAKING UP WITH ME TO GET SERIOUS WITH THAT GUY I HEARD?
IS THAT IT?
ANYWAY, THIS ISN'T SOMETHING WE SHOULD DISCUSS OVER THE PHONE.
I HAVE TOMORROW EVENING FREE, SO LET'S MEET AROUND FIVE.
BRING HIM, TOO.

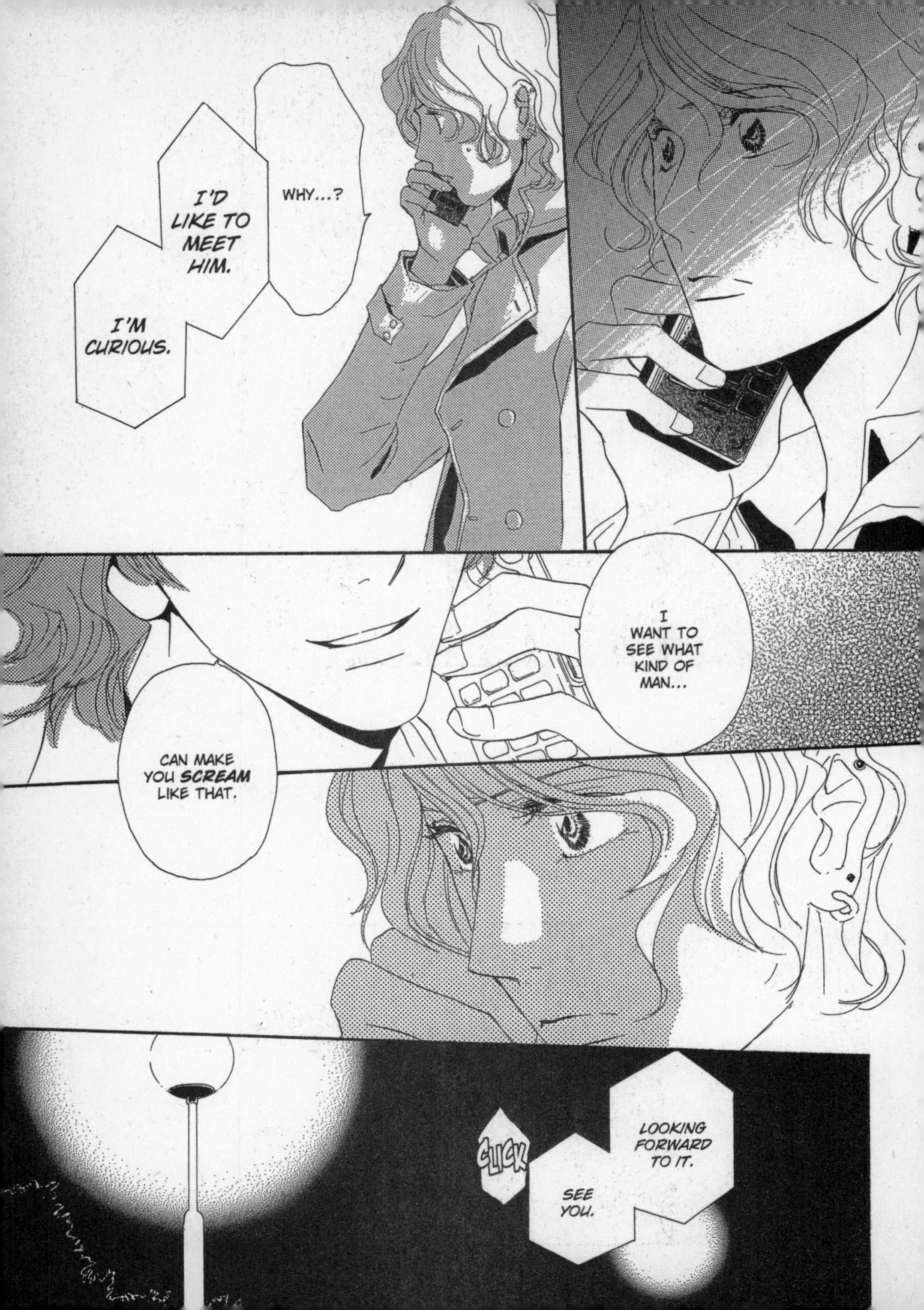
WHY...?
I'D LIKE TO MEET HIM.
I'M CURIOUS.
I WANT TO SEE WHAT KIND OF MAN...
CAN MAKE YOU **SCREAM** LIKE THAT.
LOOKING FORWARD TO IT.
CLICK
SEE YOU.

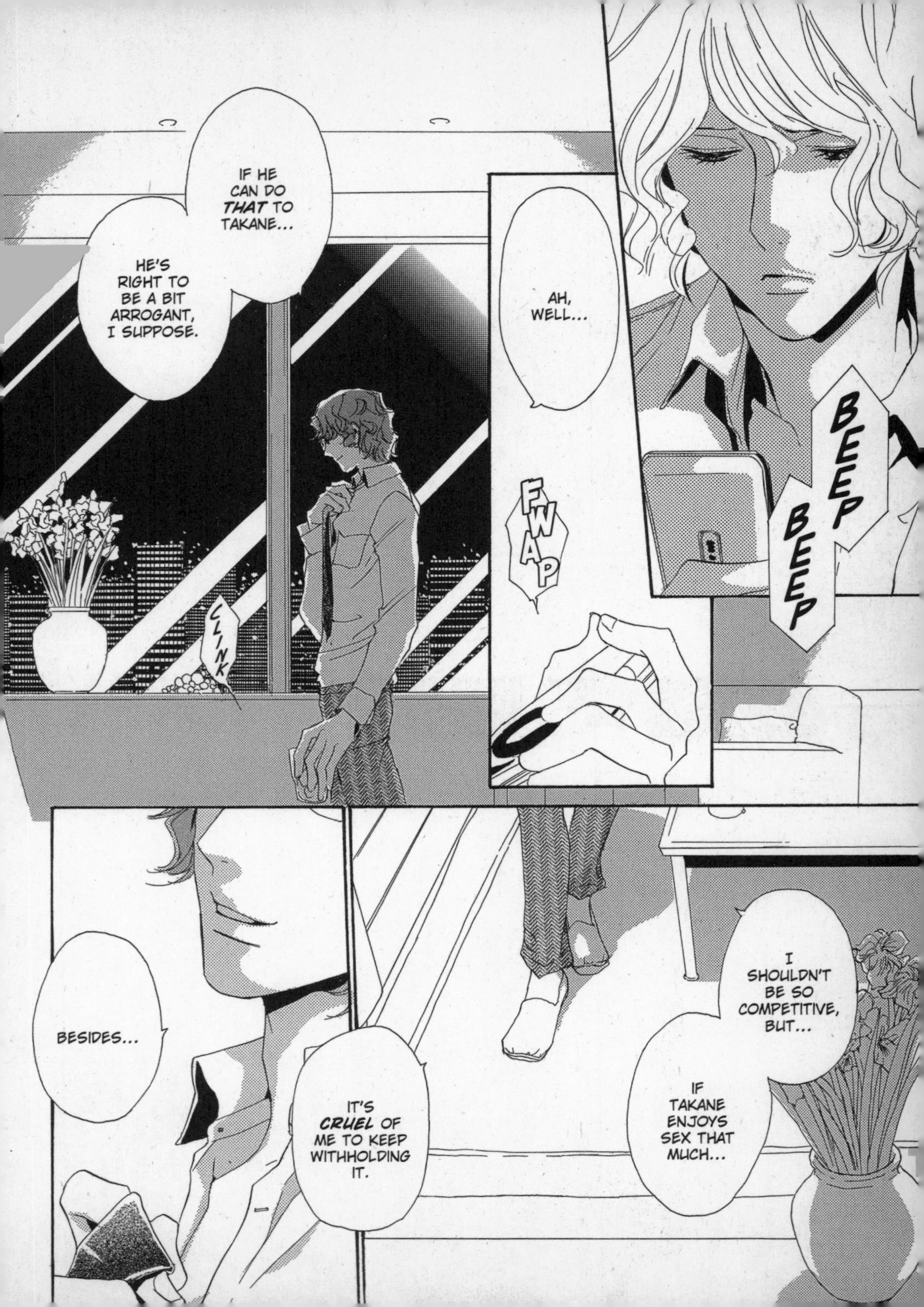
BEEP
BEEP
AH, WELL...
FWAP
IF HE CAN DO *THAT* TO TAKANE...
HE'S RIGHT TO BE A BIT ARROGANT, I SUPPOSE.
CLINK
I SHOULDN'T BE SO COMPETITIVE, BUT...
IF TAKANE ENJOYS SEX THAT MUCH...
BESIDES...
IT'S *CRUEL* OF ME TO KEEP WITHHOLDING IT.

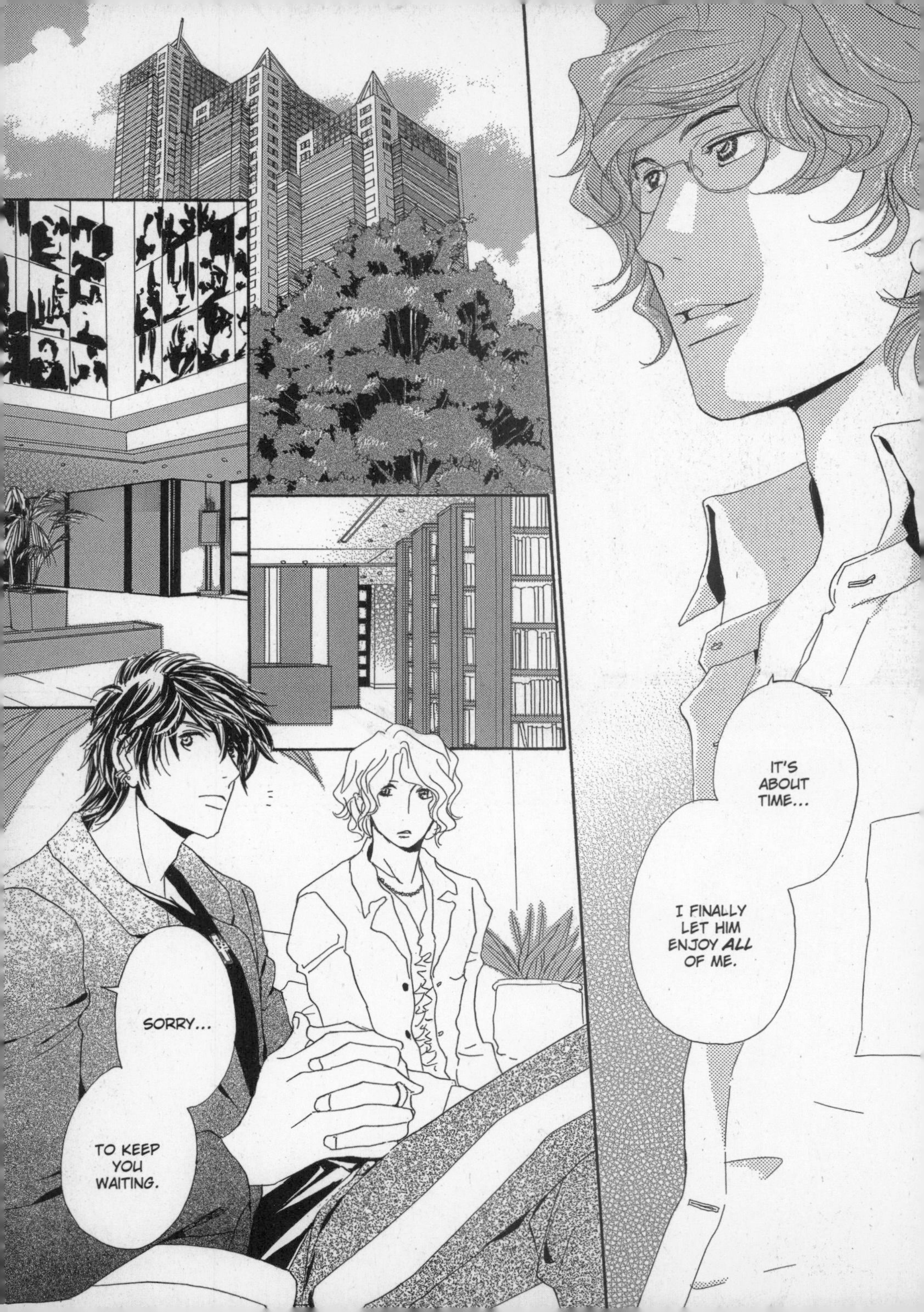
IT'S ABOUT TIME...
I FINALLY LET HIM ENJOY *ALL* OF ME.
SORRY...
TO KEEP YOU WAITING.

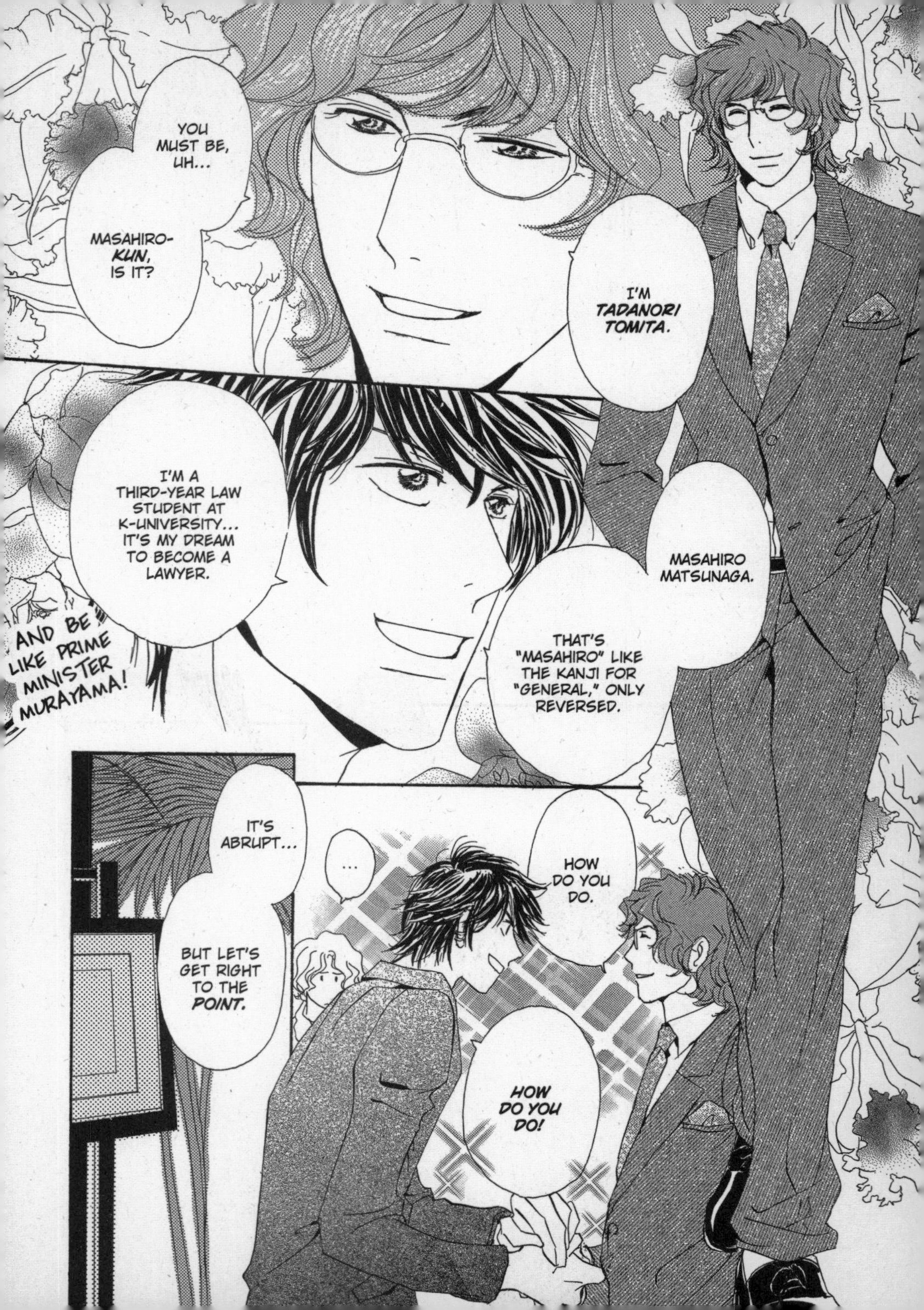
I'M *TADANORI TOMITA*.
YOU MUST BE, UH...
MASAHIRO-*KUN*, IS IT?
MASAHIRO MATSUNAGA.
THAT'S "MASAHIRO" LIKE THE KANJI FOR "GENERAL," ONLY REVERSED.
I'M A THIRD-YEAR LAW STUDENT AT K-UNIVERSITY... IT'S MY DREAM TO BECOME A LAWYER.
AND BE LIKE PRIME MINISTER MURAYAMA!
HOW DO YOU DO.
HOW DO YOU DO!
...
IT'S ABRUPT...
BUT LET'S GET RIGHT TO THE *POINT*.

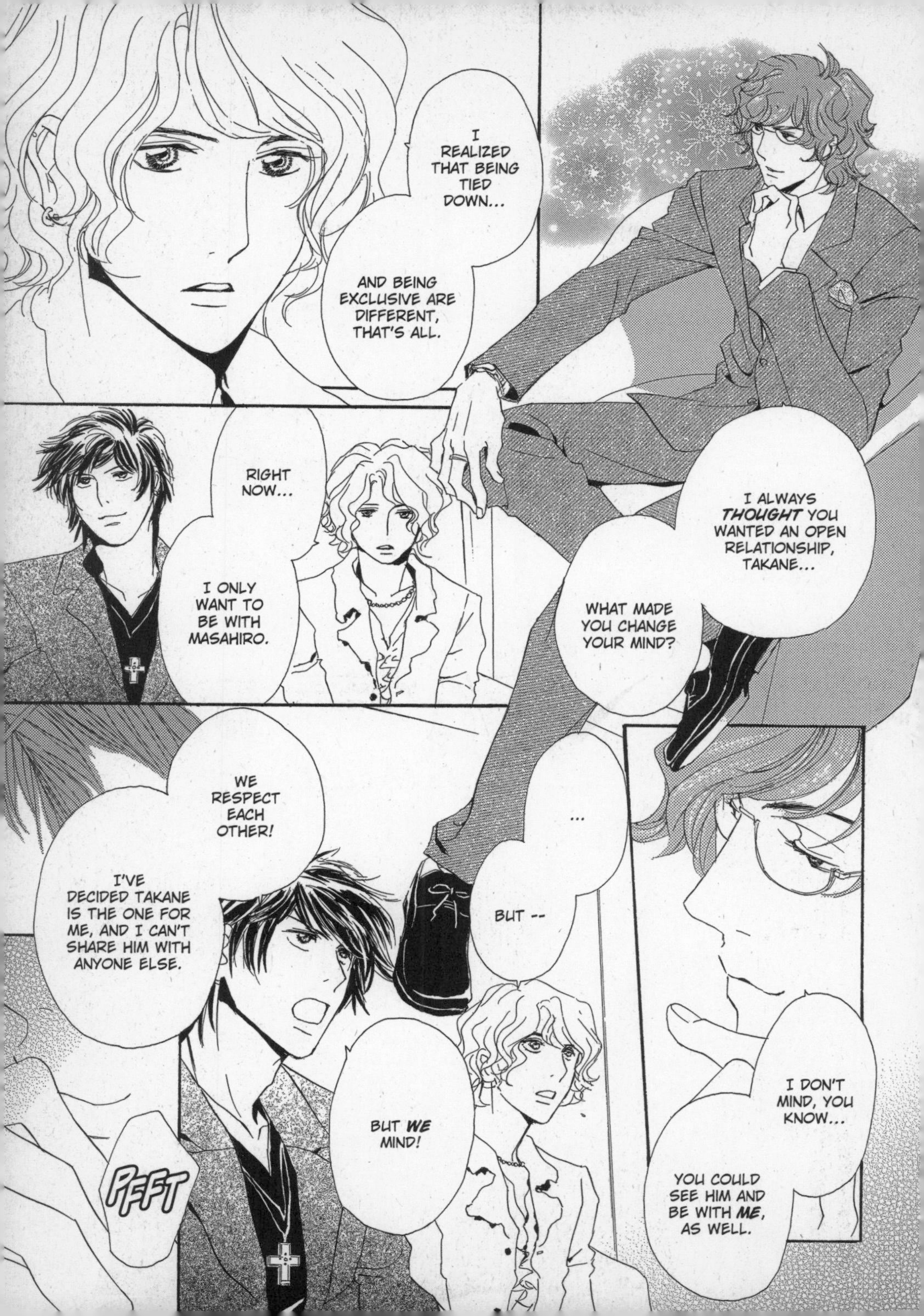
I ALWAYS *THOUGHT* YOU WANTED AN OPEN RELATIONSHIP, TAKANE...
WHAT MADE YOU CHANGE YOUR MIND?
I REALIZED THAT BEING TIED DOWN...
AND BEING EXCLUSIVE ARE DIFFERENT, THAT'S ALL.
RIGHT NOW...
I ONLY WANT TO BE WITH MASAHIRO.
...
BUT --
I DON'T MIND, YOU KNOW...
YOU COULD SEE HIM AND BE WITH *ME*, AS WELL.
WE RESPECT EACH OTHER!
I'VE DECIDED TAKANE IS THE ONE FOR ME, AND I CAN'T SHARE HIM WITH ANYONE ELSE.
BUT *WE* MIND!
PFFT

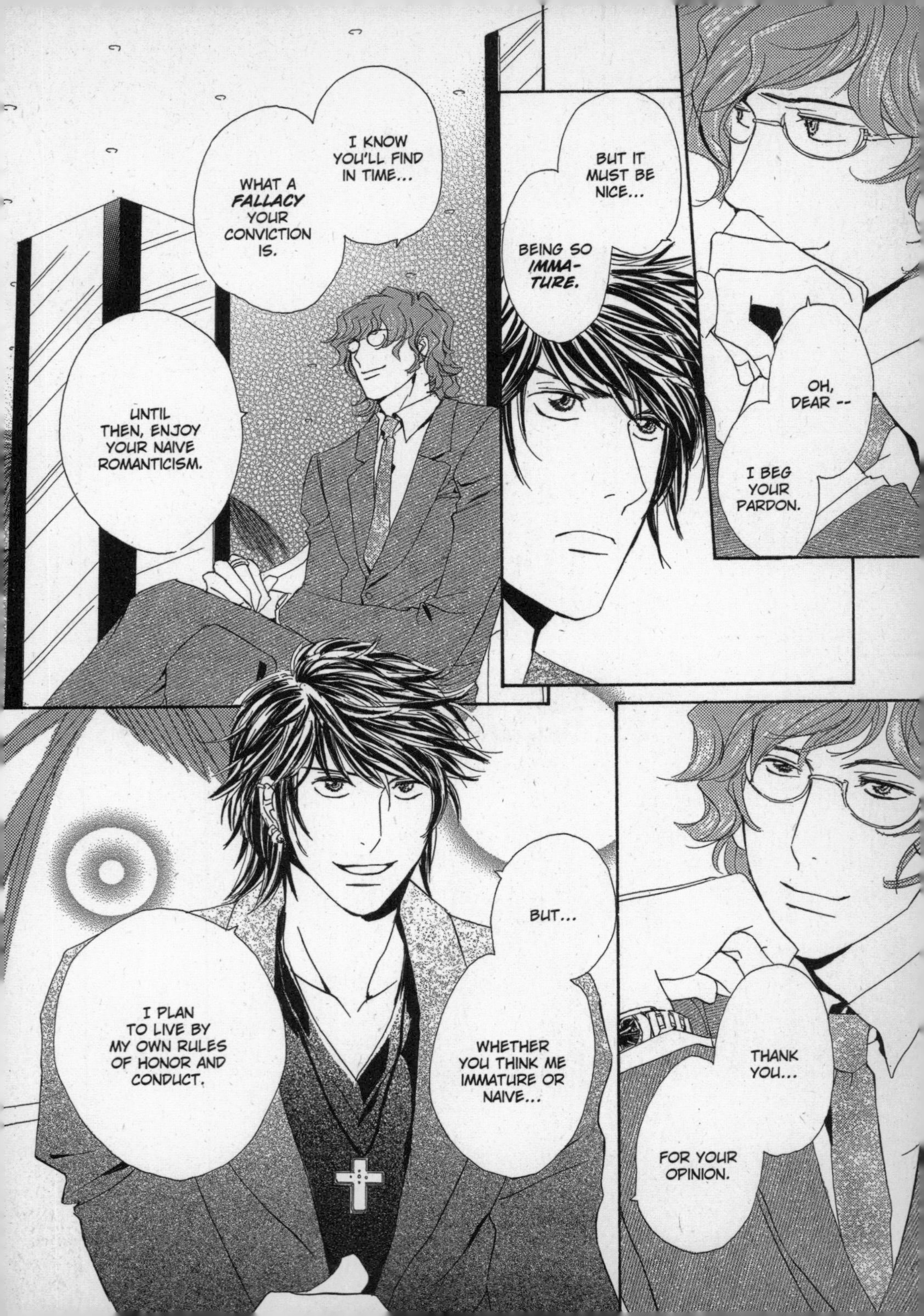
OH, DEAR --
I BEG YOUR PARDON.
BUT IT MUST BE NICE...
BEING SO *IMMATURE.*
I KNOW YOU'LL FIND IN TIME...
WHAT A *FALLACY* YOUR CONVICTION IS.
UNTIL THEN, ENJOY YOUR NAIVE ROMANTICISM.
THANK YOU...
FOR YOUR OPINION.
BUT...
WHETHER YOU THINK ME IMMATURE OR NAIVE...
I PLAN TO LIVE BY MY OWN RULES OF HONOR AND CONDUCT.

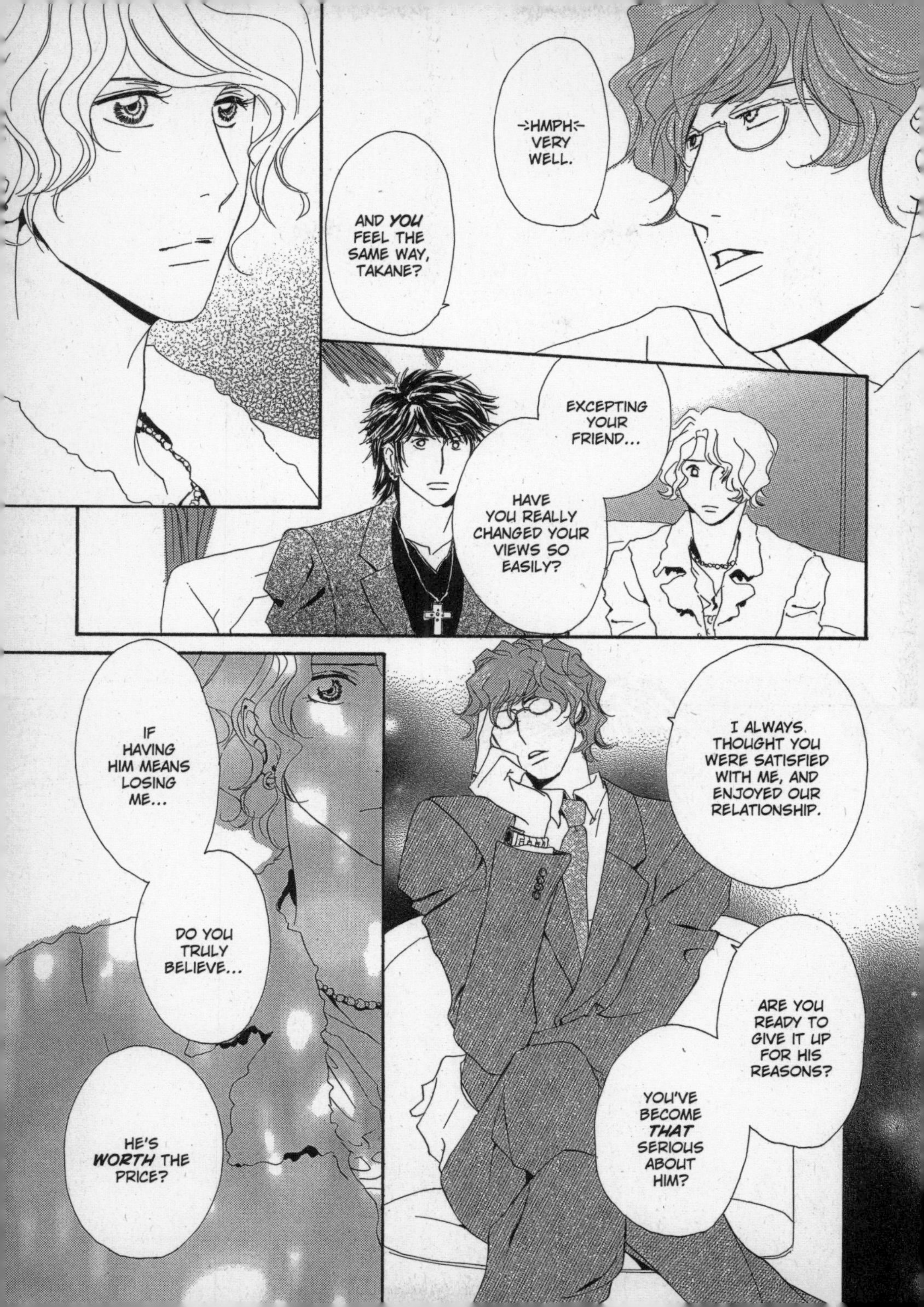
—HMPH— VERY WELL.
AND *YOU* FEEL THE SAME WAY, TAKANE?
EXCEPTING YOUR FRIEND...
HAVE YOU REALLY CHANGED YOUR VIEWS SO EASILY?
I ALWAYS THOUGHT YOU WERE SATISFIED WITH ME, AND ENJOYED OUR RELATIONSHIP.
ARE YOU READY TO GIVE IT UP FOR HIS REASONS?
YOU'VE BECOME *THAT* SERIOUS ABOUT HIM?
IF HAVING HIM MEANS LOSING ME...
DO YOU TRULY BELIEVE...
HE'S *WORTH* THE PRICE?

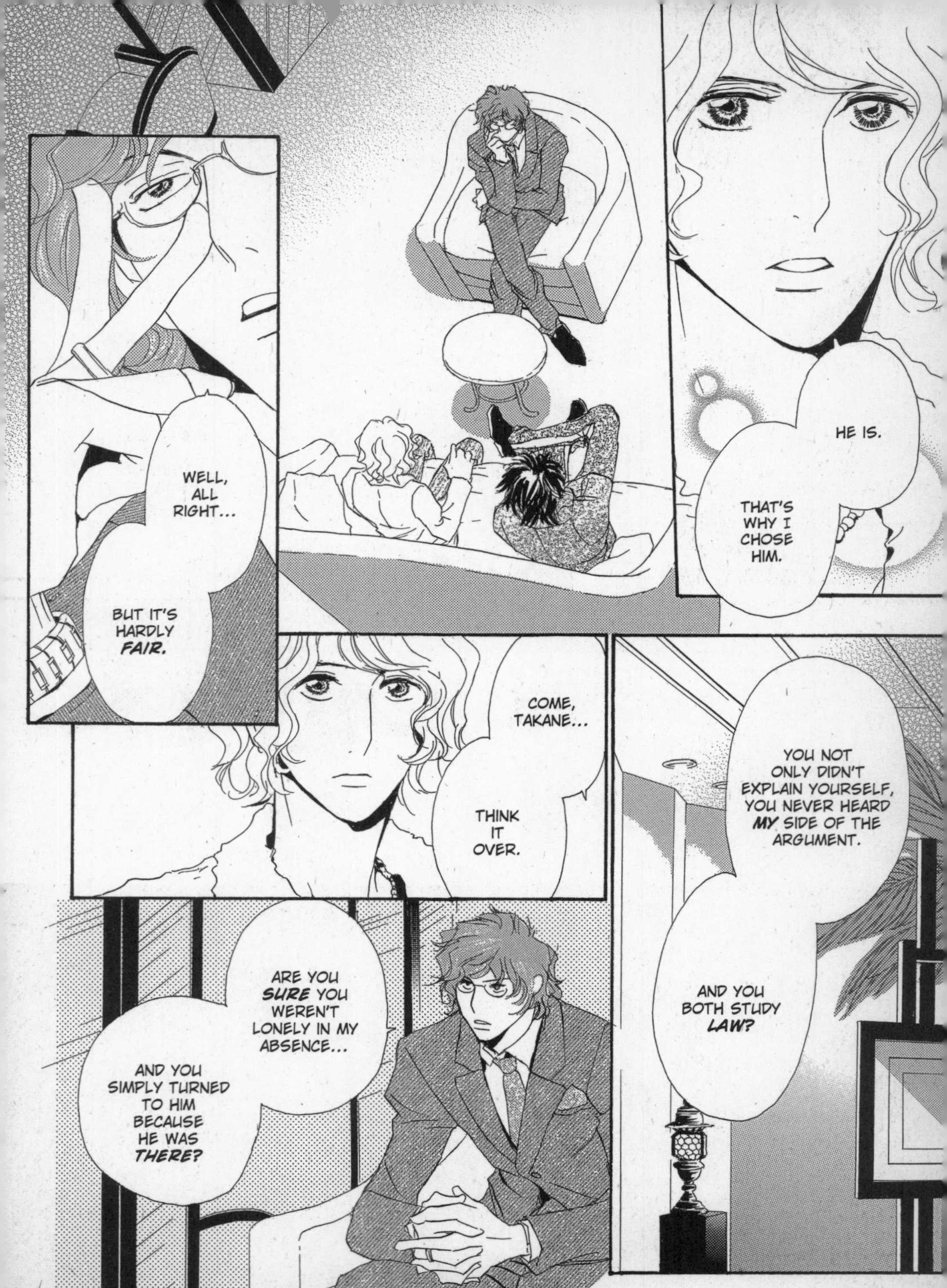
HE IS.
THAT'S WHY I CHOSE HIM.
WELL, ALL RIGHT...
BUT IT'S HARDLY **FAIR.**
YOU NOT ONLY DIDN'T EXPLAIN YOURSELF, YOU NEVER HEARD **MY** SIDE OF THE ARGUMENT.
AND YOU BOTH STUDY **LAW?**
COME, TAKANE...
THINK IT OVER.
ARE YOU **SURE** YOU WEREN'T LONELY IN MY ABSENCE...
AND YOU SIMPLY TURNED TO HIM BECAUSE HE WAS **THERE?**

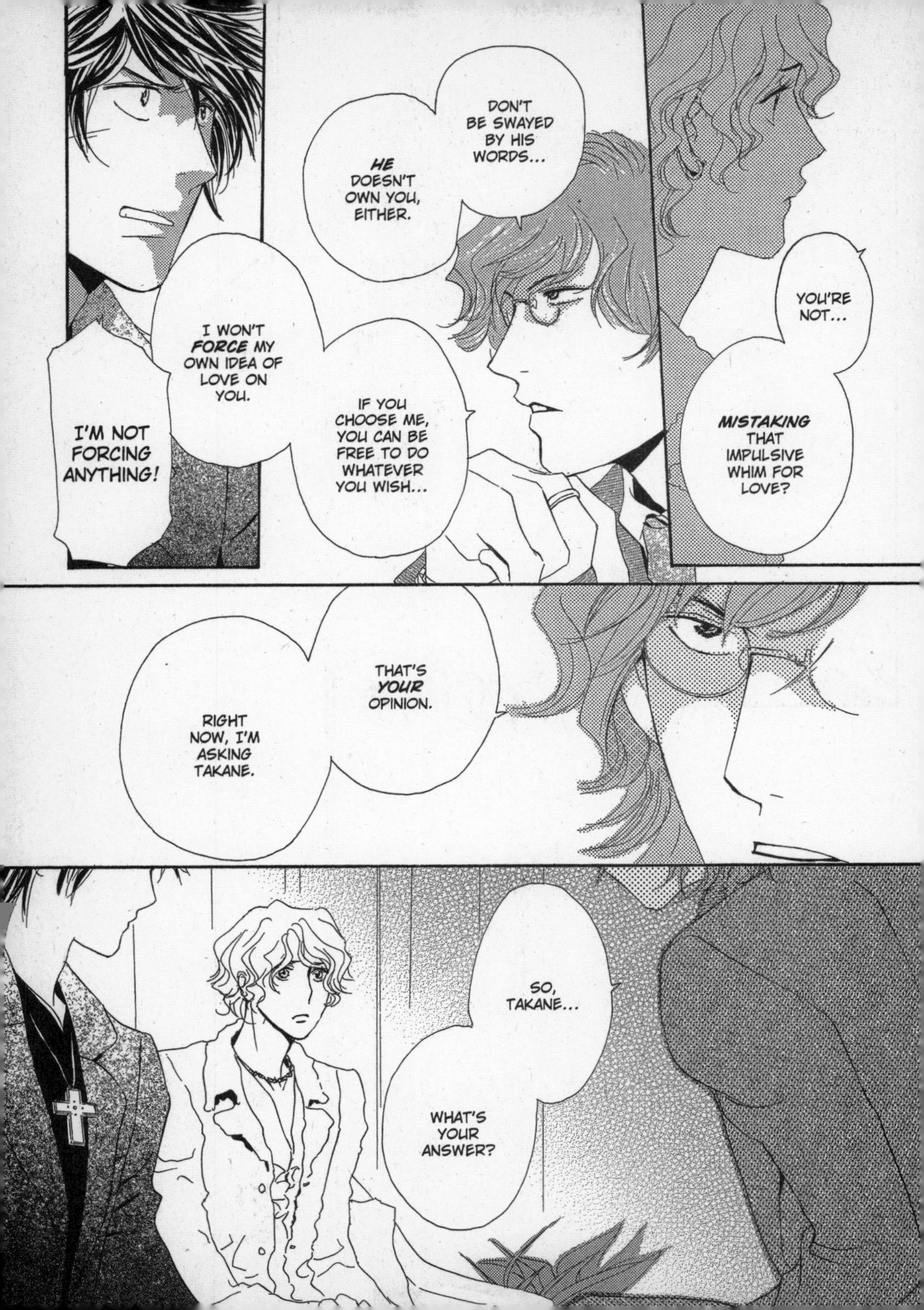

YOU'RE NOT...
MISTAKING THAT IMPULSIVE WHIM FOR LOVE?
DON'T BE SWAYED BY HIS WORDS...
HE DOESN'T OWN YOU, EITHER.
I WON'T *FORCE* MY OWN IDEA OF LOVE ON YOU.
IF YOU CHOOSE ME, YOU CAN BE FREE TO DO WHATEVER YOU WISH...
I'M NOT FORCING ANYTHING!
THAT'S *YOUR* OPINION.
RIGHT NOW, I'M ASKING TAKANE.
SO, TAKANE...
WHAT'S YOUR ANSWER?

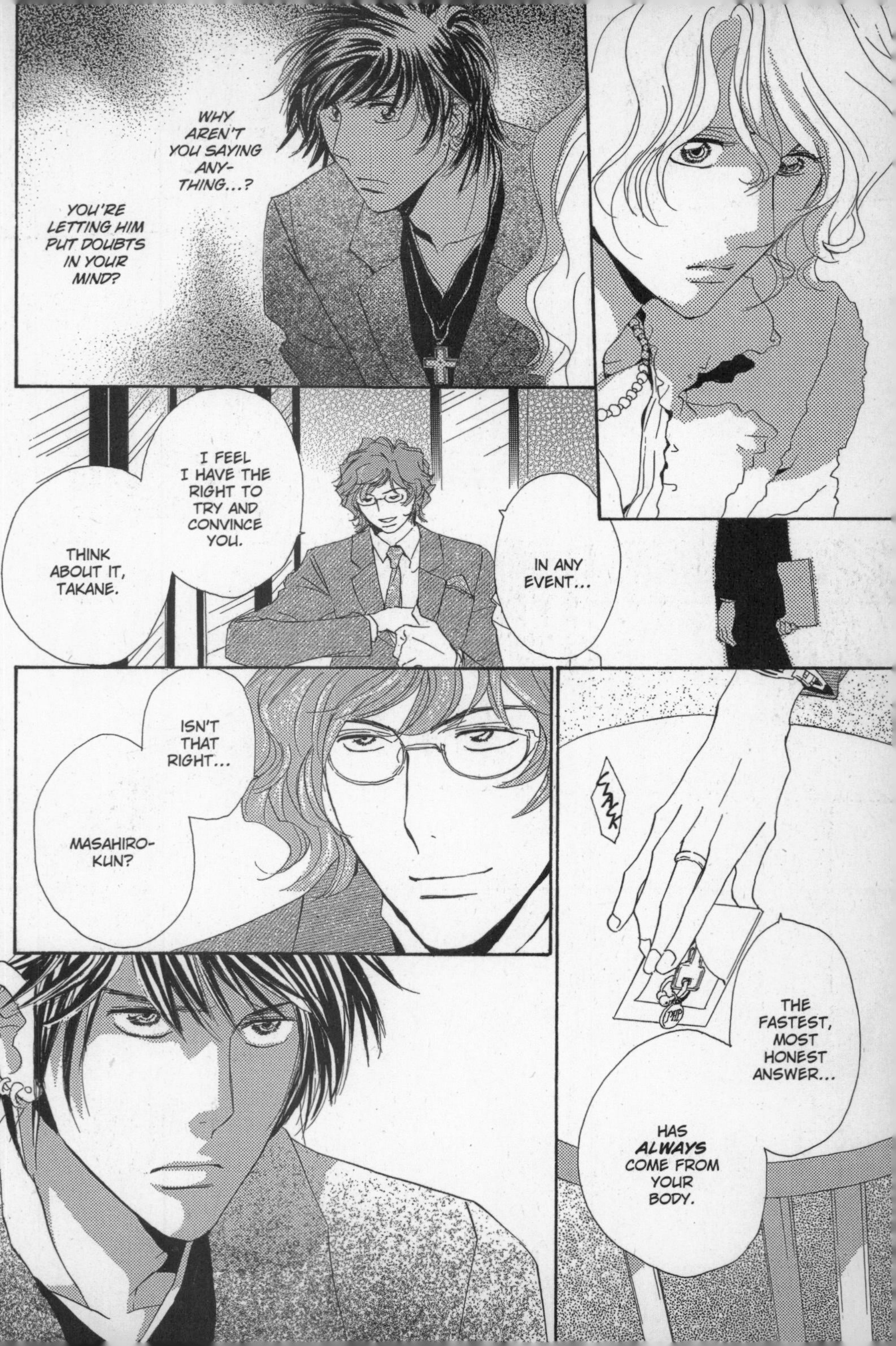
WHY AREN'T YOU SAYING ANY-THING...?
YOU'RE LETTING HIM PUT DOUBTS IN YOUR MIND?
IN ANY EVENT...
I FEEL I HAVE THE RIGHT TO TRY AND CONVINCE YOU.
THINK ABOUT IT, TAKANE.
CLACK
THE FASTEST, MOST HONEST ANSWER...
HAS ***ALWAYS*** COME FROM YOUR BODY.
ISN'T THAT RIGHT...
MASAHIRO-KUN?

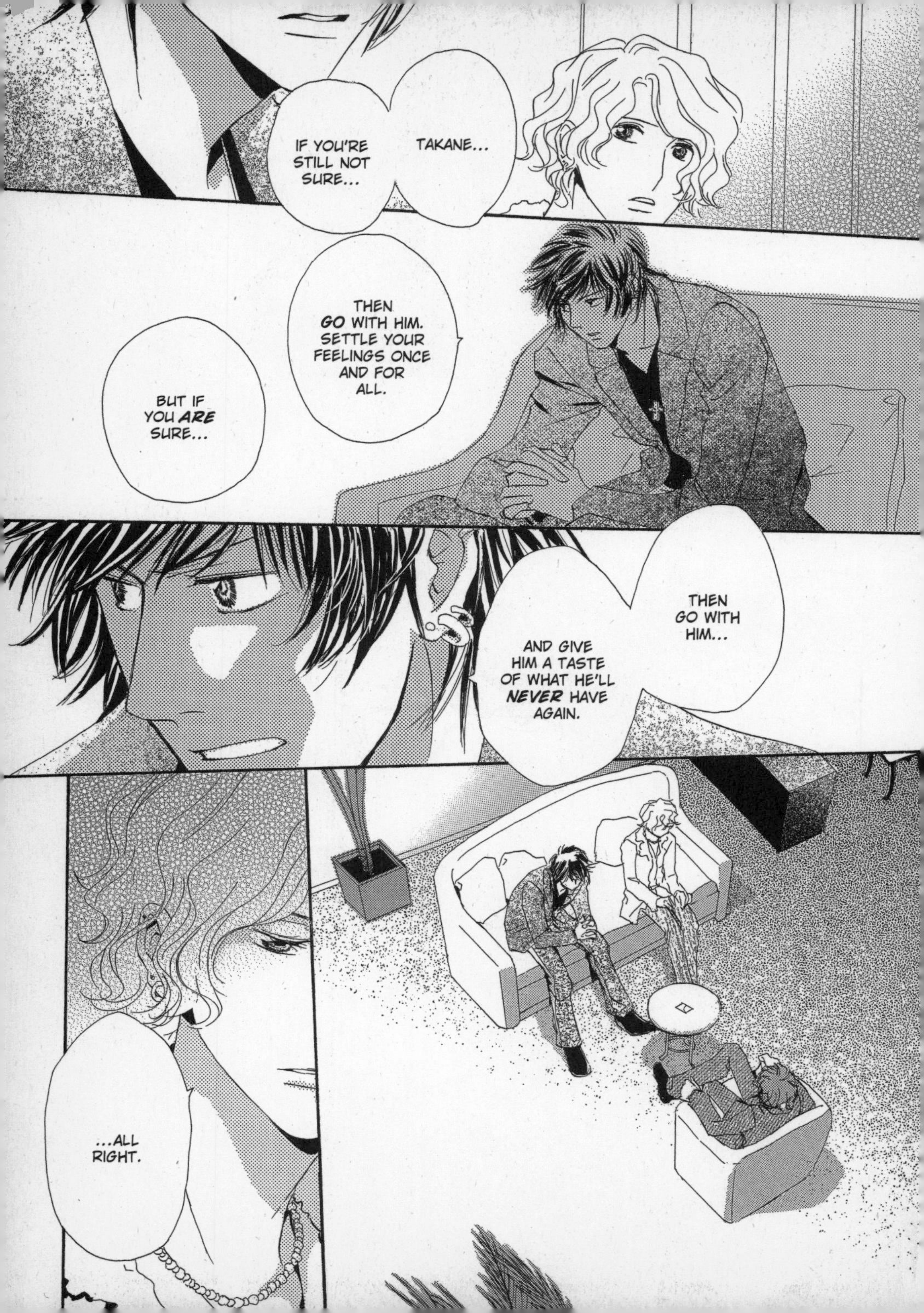
TAKANE...
IF YOU'RE STILL NOT SURE...
THEN GO WITH HIM. SETTLE YOUR FEELINGS ONCE AND FOR ALL.
BUT IF YOU ARE SURE...
THEN GO WITH HIM...
AND GIVE HIM A TASTE OF WHAT HE'LL NEVER HAVE AGAIN.
...ALL RIGHT.

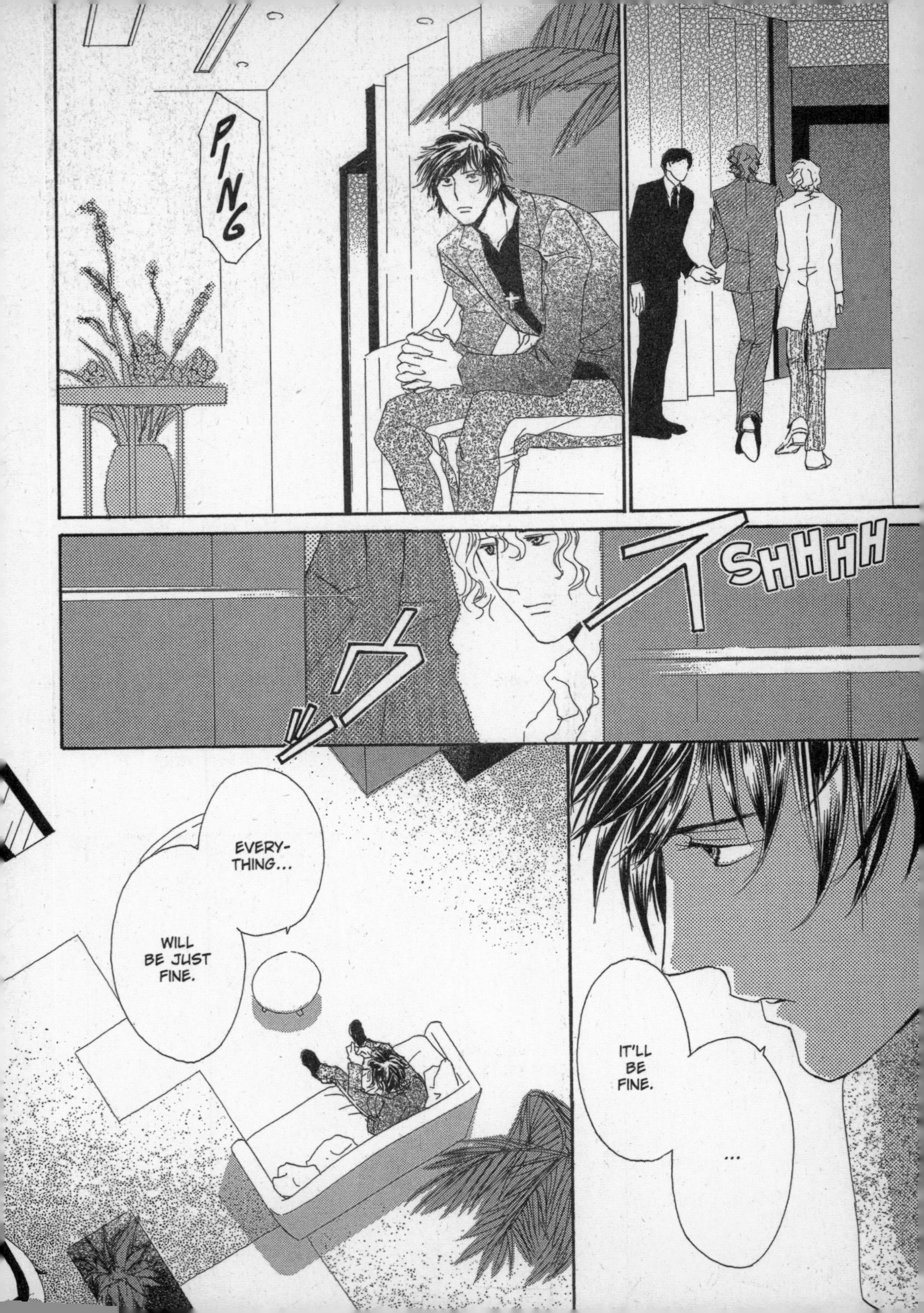
PING
SHHHH
IT'LL BE FINE.
...
EVERY-THING...
WILL BE JUST FINE.

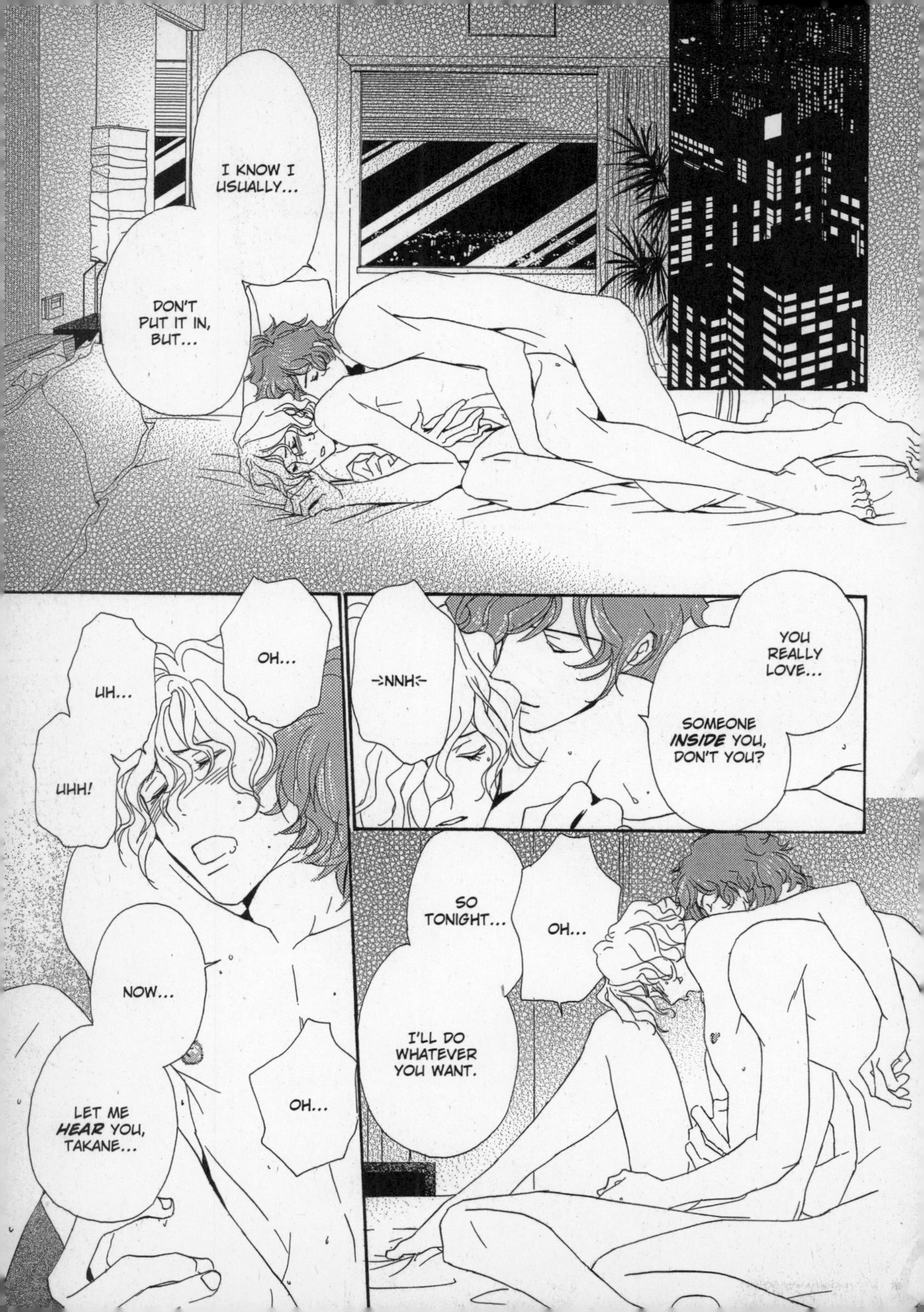
I KNOW I USUALLY...
DON'T PUT IT IN, BUT...
YOU REALLY LOVE...
SOMEONE *INSIDE* YOU, DON'T YOU?
NNH
SO TONIGHT...
OH...
I'LL DO WHATEVER YOU WANT.
OH...
UH...
UHH!
NOW...
OH...
LET ME *HEAR* YOU, TAKANE...

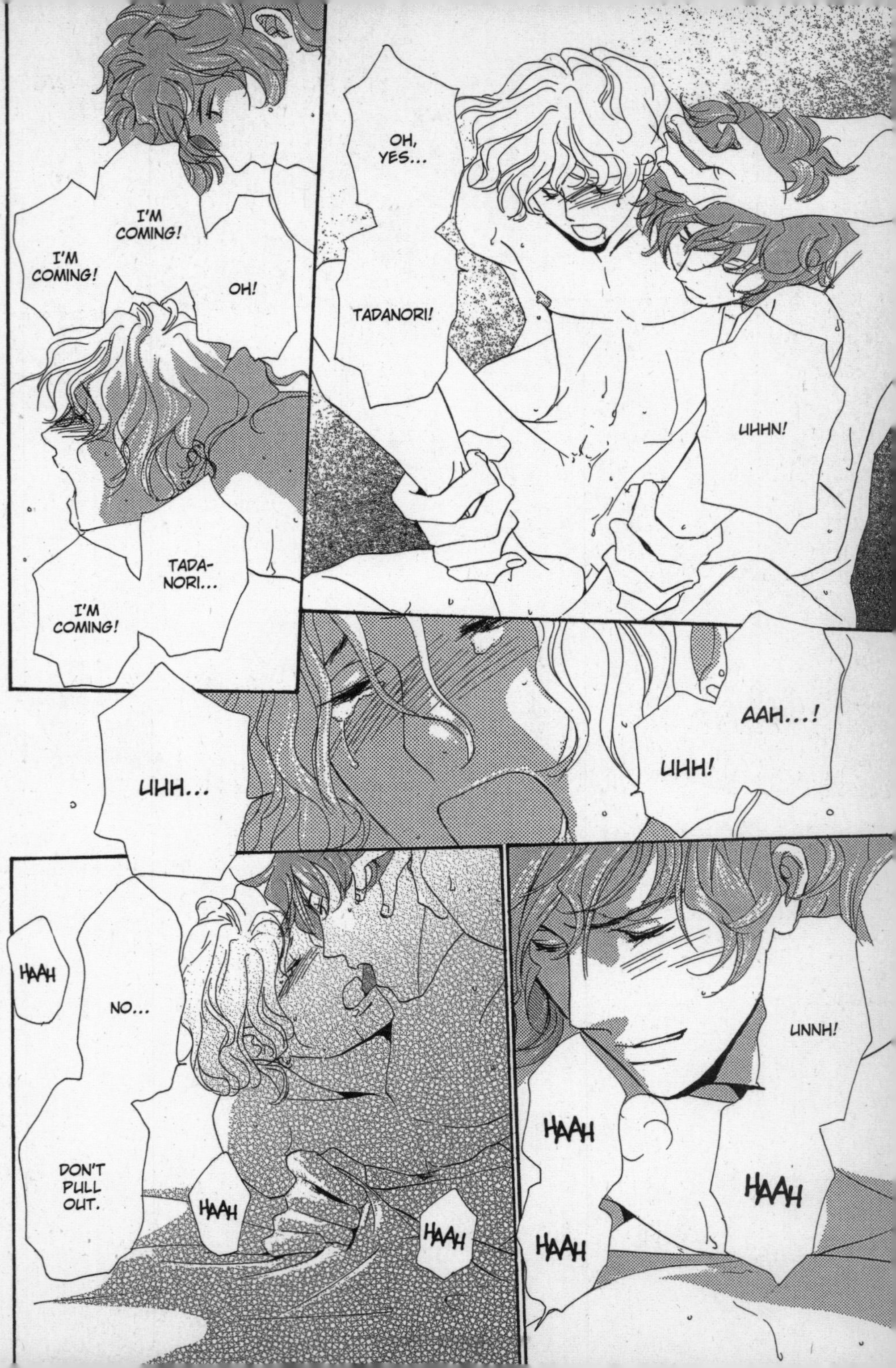

OH, YES...
TADANORI!
UHHN!
I'M COMING!
I'M COMING!
OH!
TADA-NORI...
I'M COMING!
AAH...!
UHH!
UHH...
UNNH!
HAAH
HAAH
HAAH
HAAH
NO...
DON'T PULL OUT.
HAAH
HAAH

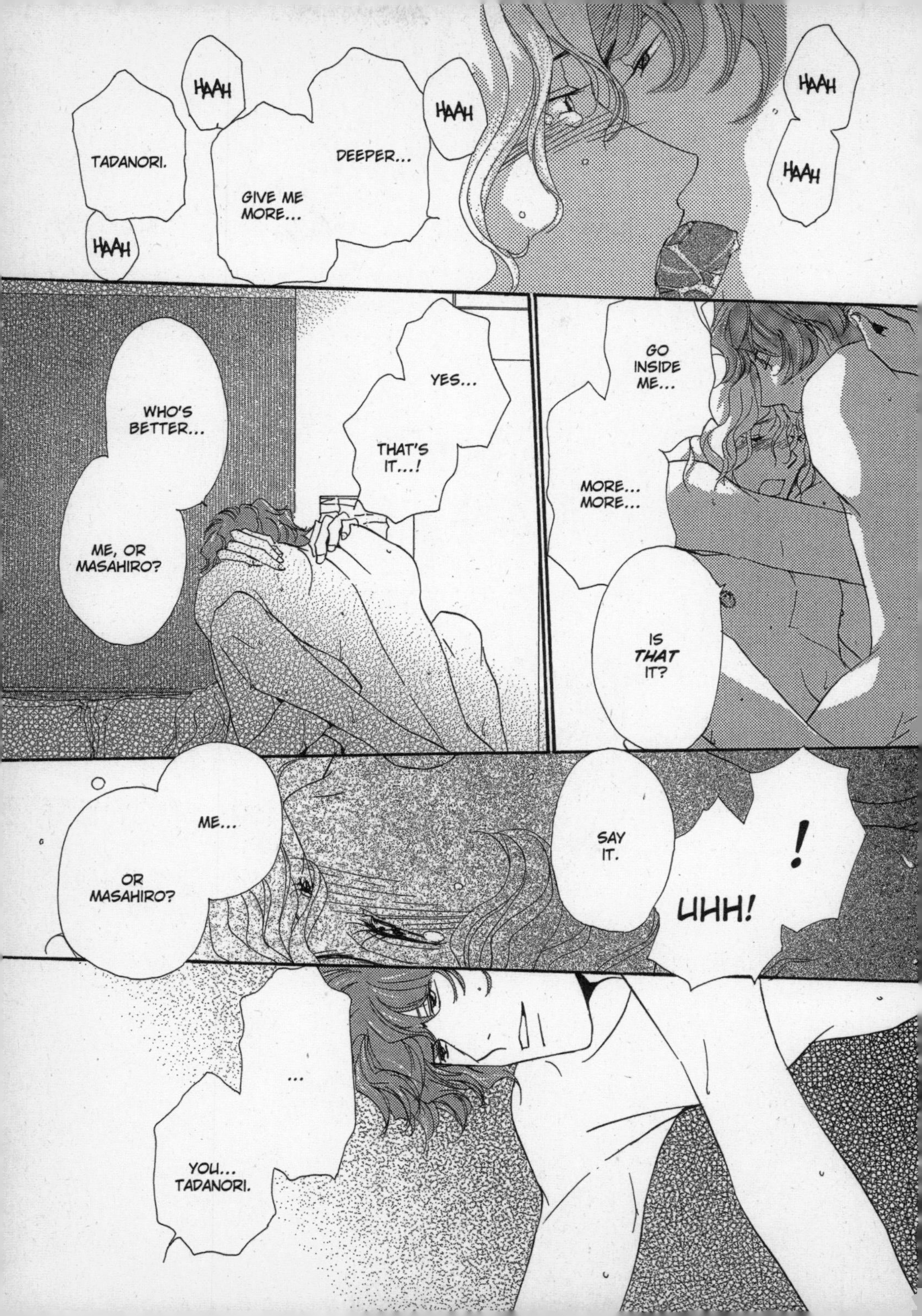

HAAH
HAAH
HAAH
DEEPER... GIVE ME MORE...
HAAH
TADANORI.
HAAH
GO INSIDE ME...
MORE... MORE...
IS *THAT* IT?
YES...
THAT'S IT...!
WHO'S BETTER...
ME, OR MASAHIRO?
!
UHH!
SAY IT.
ME...
OR MASAHIRO?
...
YOU... TADANORI.

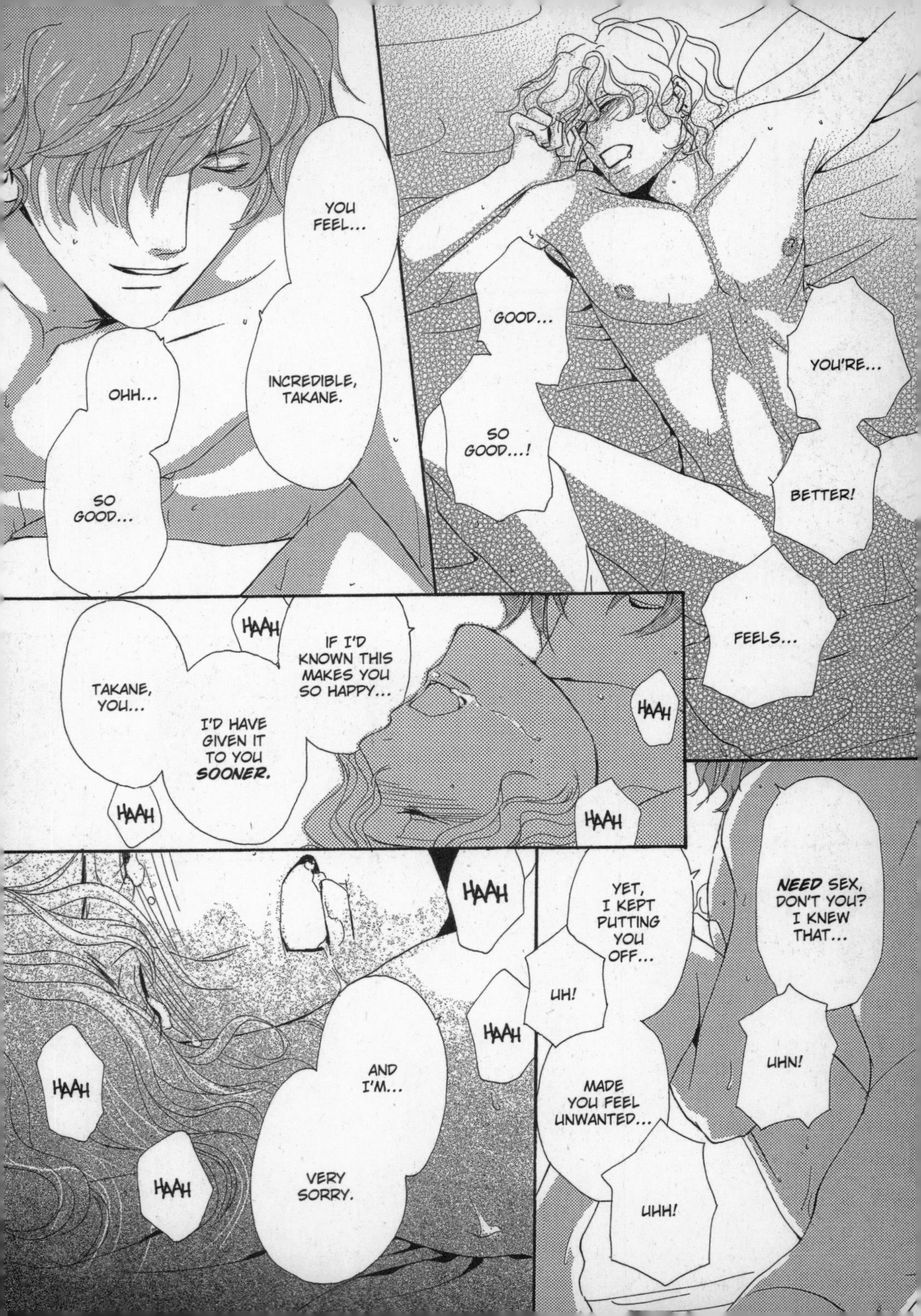

YOU'RE...
BETTER!
FEELS...
GOOD...
SO GOOD...!
YOU FEEL...
INCREDIBLE, TAKANE.
OHH...
SO GOOD...
HAAH
HAAH
IF I'D KNOWN THIS MAKES YOU SO HAPPY...
I'D HAVE GIVEN IT TO YOU ***SOONER.***
TAKANE, YOU...
HAAH
HAAH
NEED SEX, DON'T YOU? I KNEW THAT...
UHN!
YET, I KEPT PUTTING YOU OFF...
UH!
MADE YOU FEEL UNWANTED...
UHH!
HAAH
HAAH
AND I'M...
VERY SORRY.
HAAH
HAAH

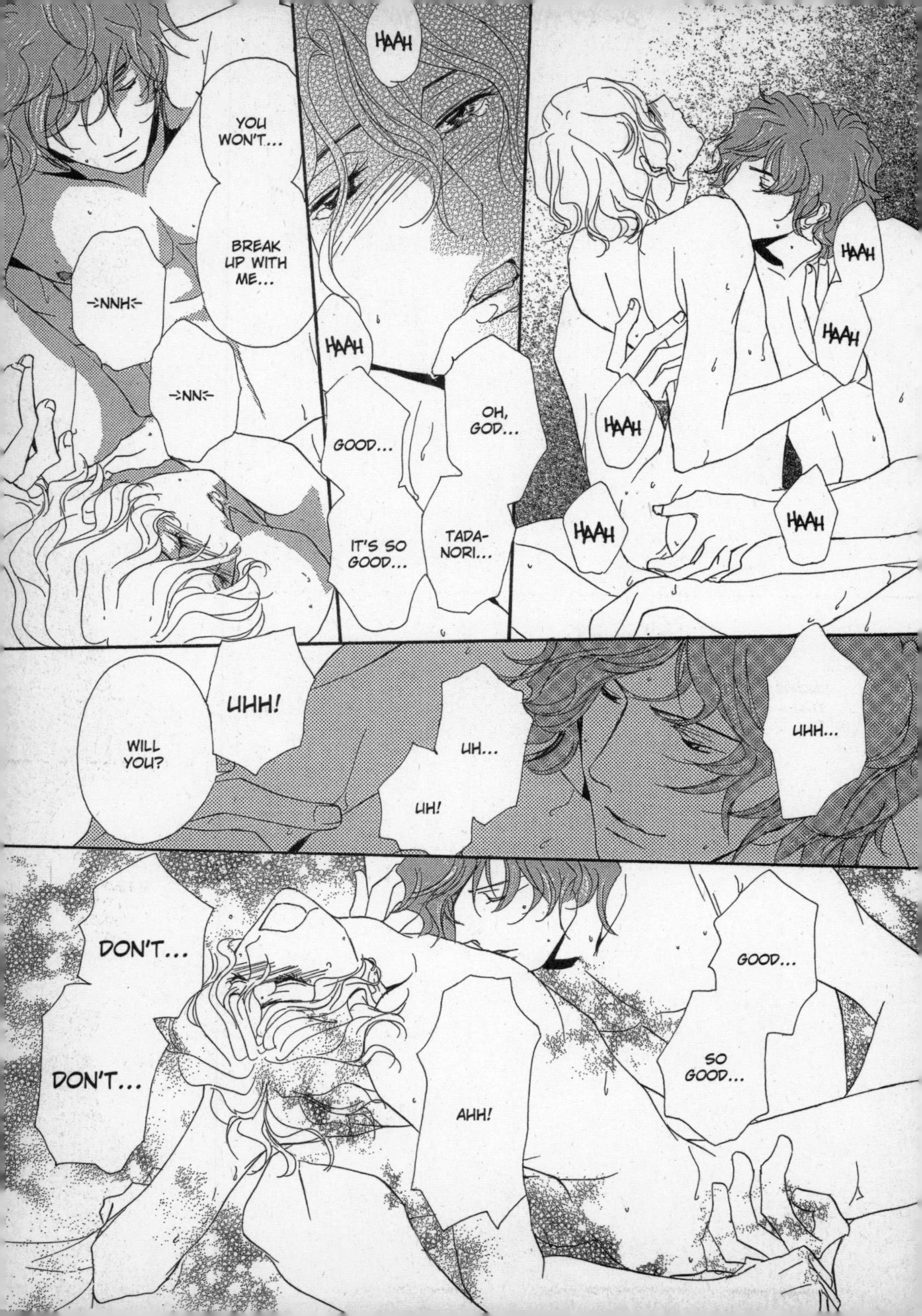
HAAH
HAAH
HAAH
HAAH
HAAH
HAAH
HAAH
OH, GOD...
GOOD...
TADA-NORI...
IT'S SO GOOD...
YOU WON'T...
BREAK UP WITH ME...
-NNH-
-NN-
UHH...
UH...
UH!
UHH!
WILL YOU?
GOOD...
SO GOOD...
AHH!
DON'T...
DON'T...

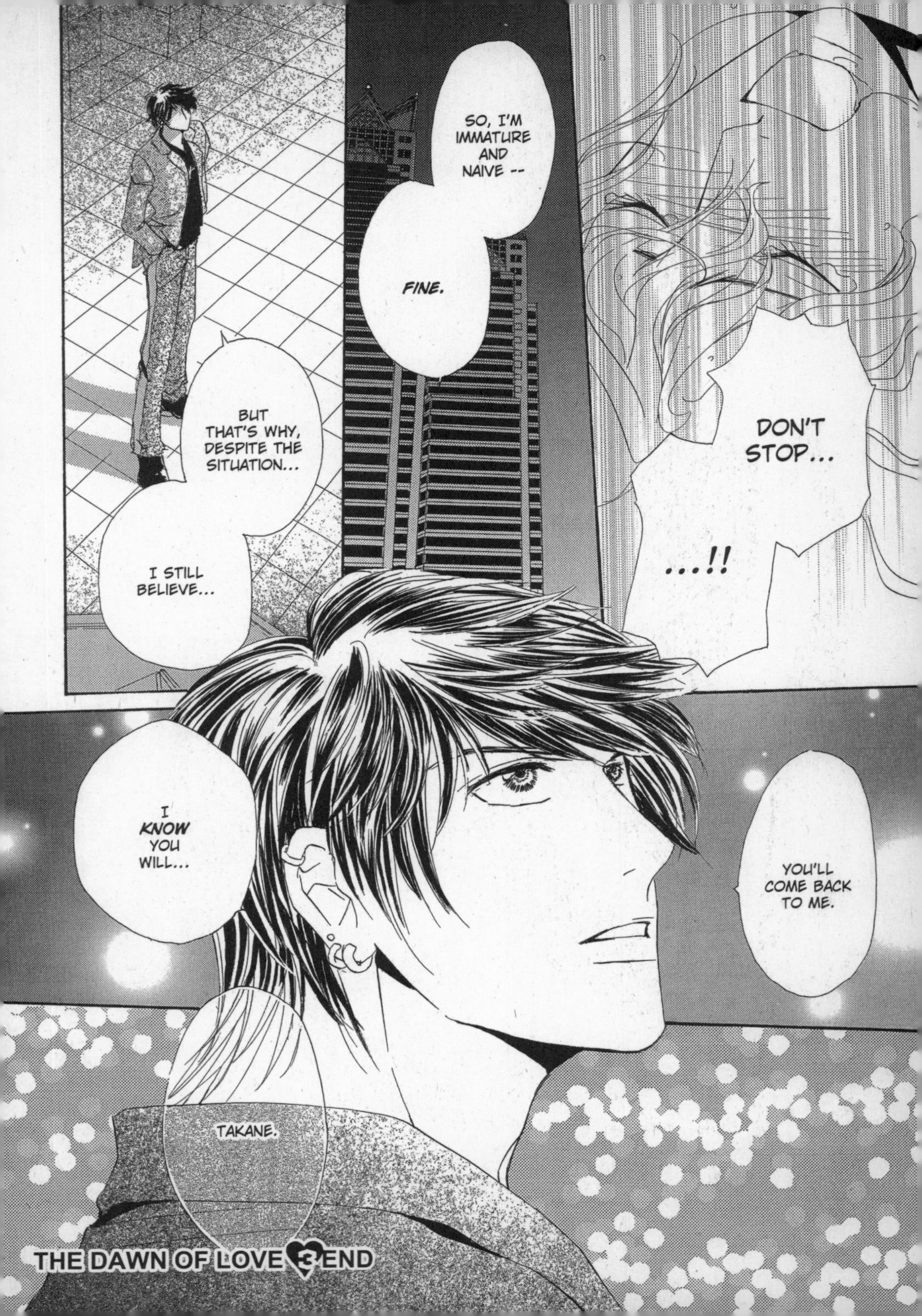
DON'T STOP...
...!!
SO, I'M IMMATURE AND NAIVE --
FINE.
BUT THAT'S WHY, DESPITE THE SITUATION...
I STILL BELIEVE...
YOU'LL COME BACK TO ME.
I KNOW YOU WILL...
TAKANE.
THE DAWN OF LOVE 3 END

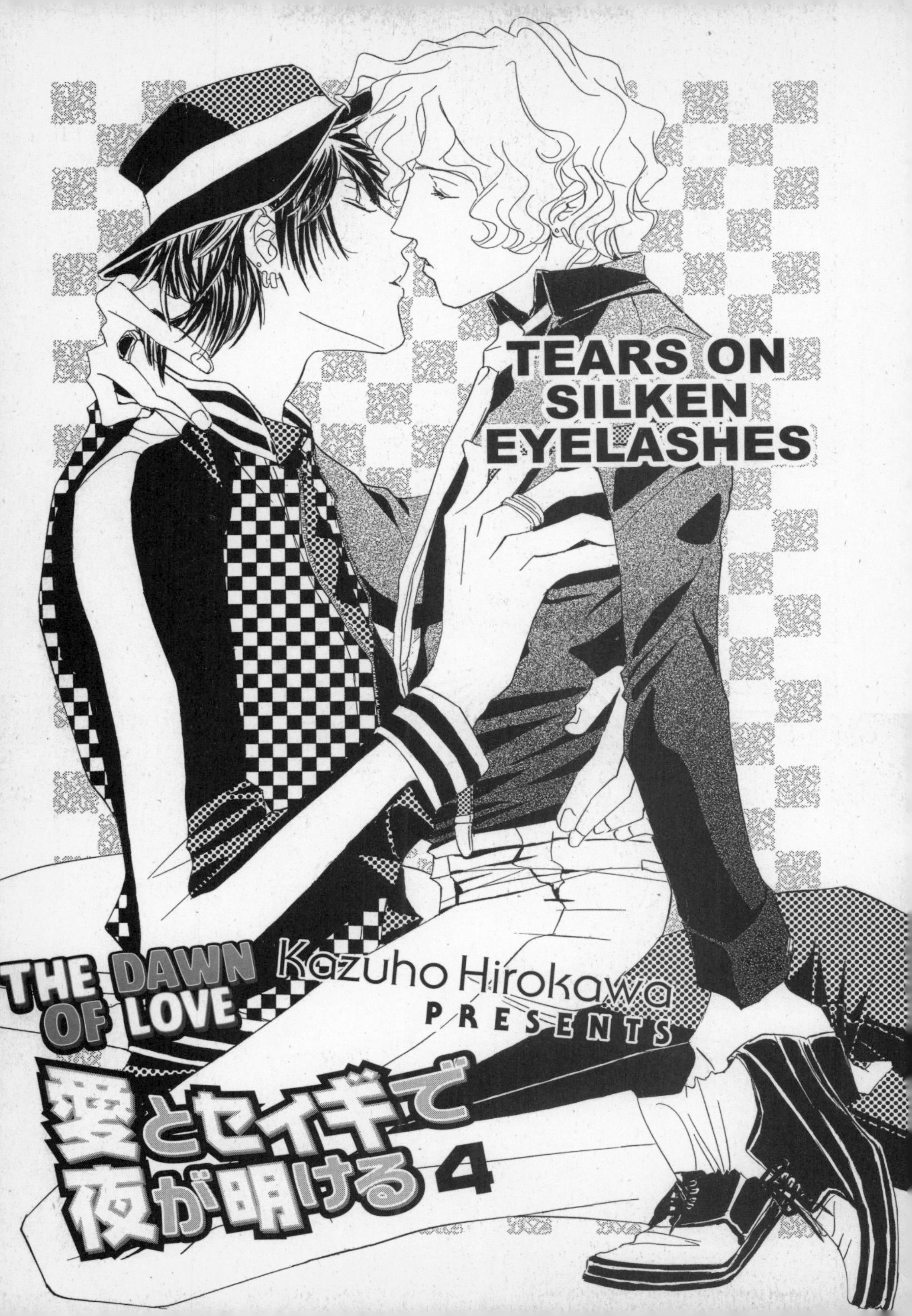
TEARS ON SILKEN EYELASHES
THE DAWN OF LOVE
Kazuho Hirokawa
PRESENTS
愛とセイギで夜が明ける 4

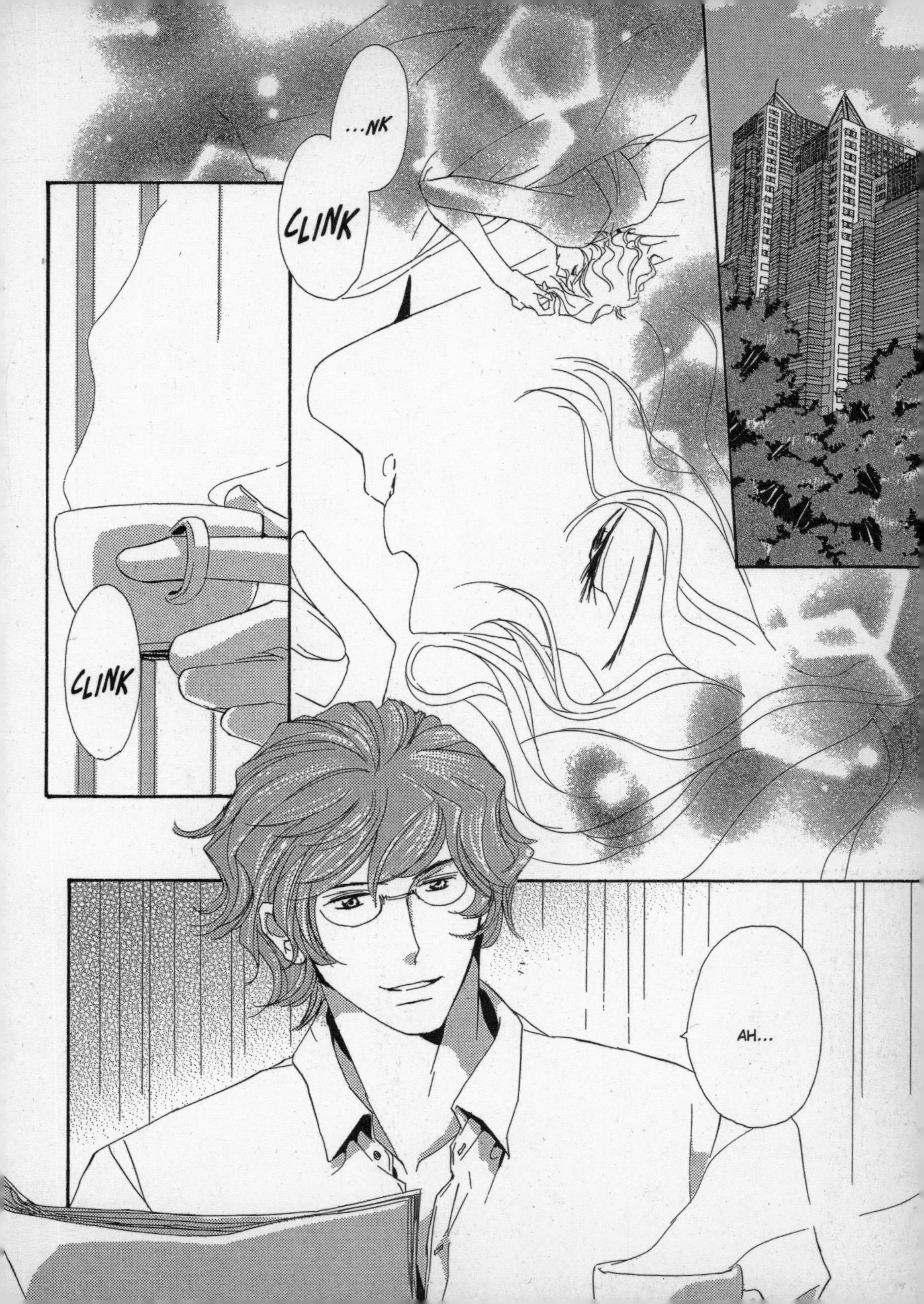
...NK
CLINK
CLINK
AH...

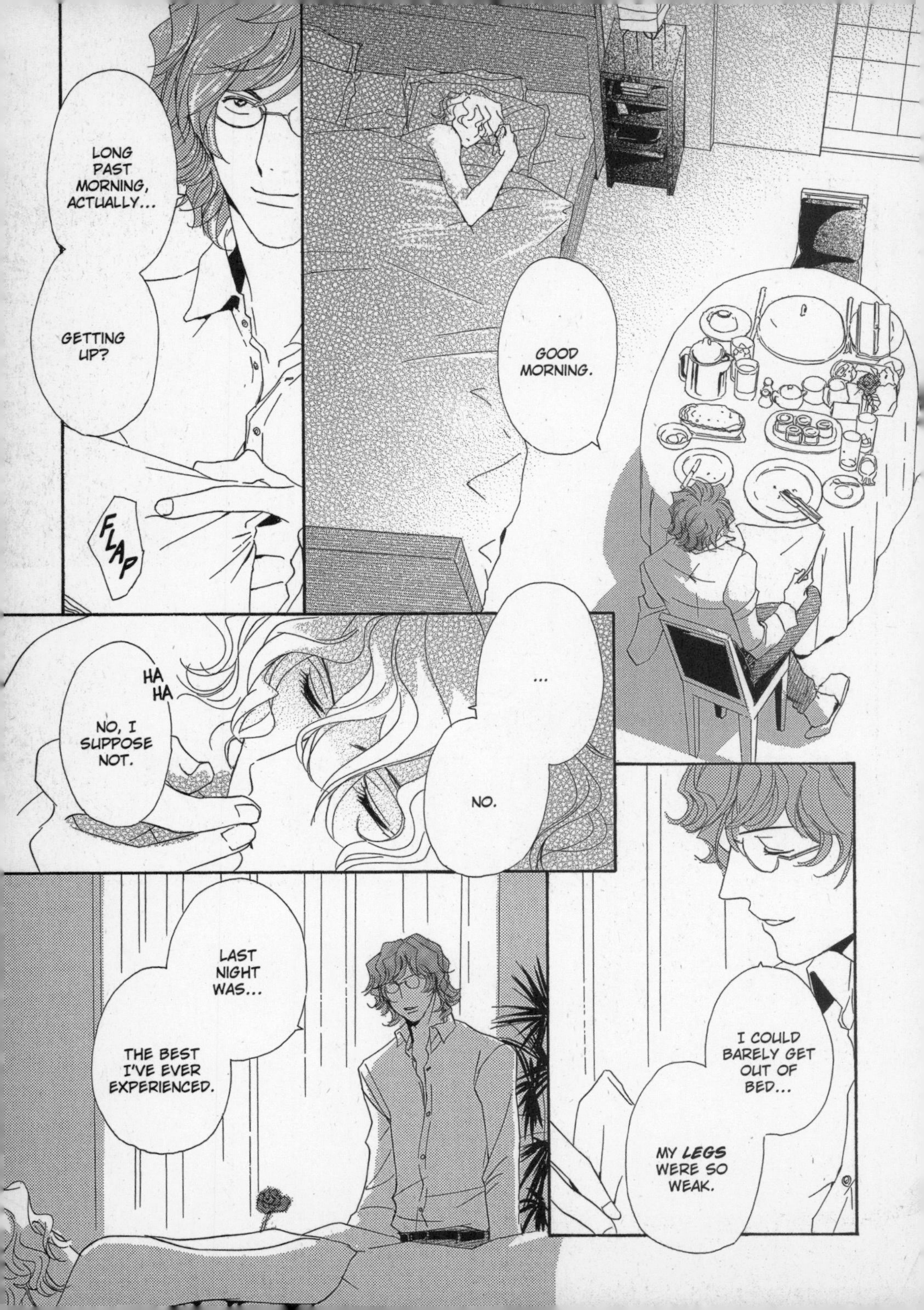
GOOD MORNING.
LONG PAST MORNING, ACTUALLY...
GETTING UP?
FLAP
...
NO.
HA HA
NO, I SUPPOSE NOT.
I COULD BARELY GET OUT OF BED...
MY LEGS WERE SO WEAK.
LAST NIGHT WAS...
THE BEST I'VE EVER EXPERIENCED.

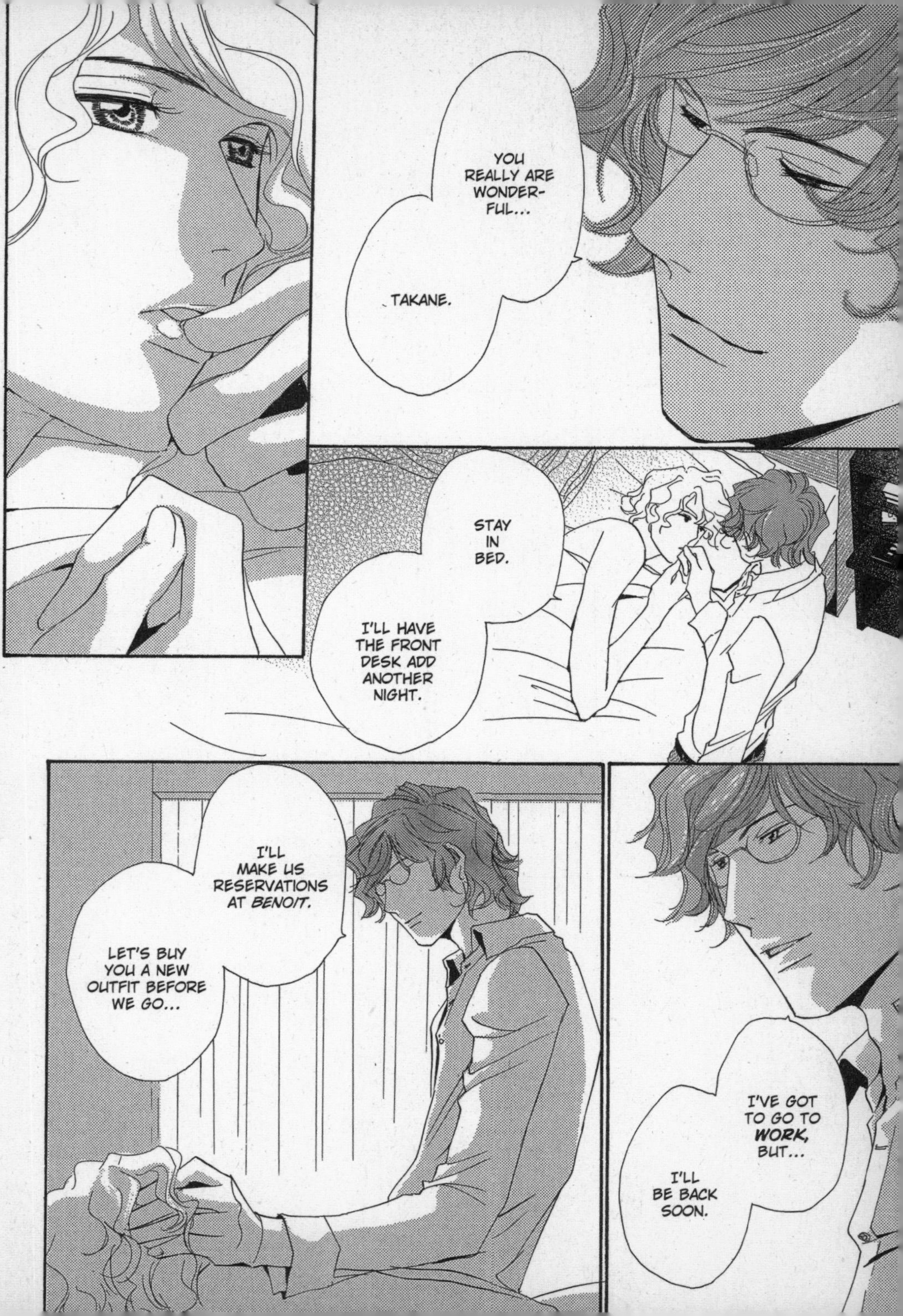
YOU REALLY ARE WONDERFUL...
TAKANE.
STAY IN BED.
I'LL HAVE THE FRONT DESK ADD ANOTHER NIGHT.
I'VE GOT TO GO TO *WORK,* BUT...
I'LL BE BACK SOON.
I'LL MAKE US RESERVATIONS AT *BENOIT.*
LET'S BUY YOU A NEW OUTFIT BEFORE WE GO...

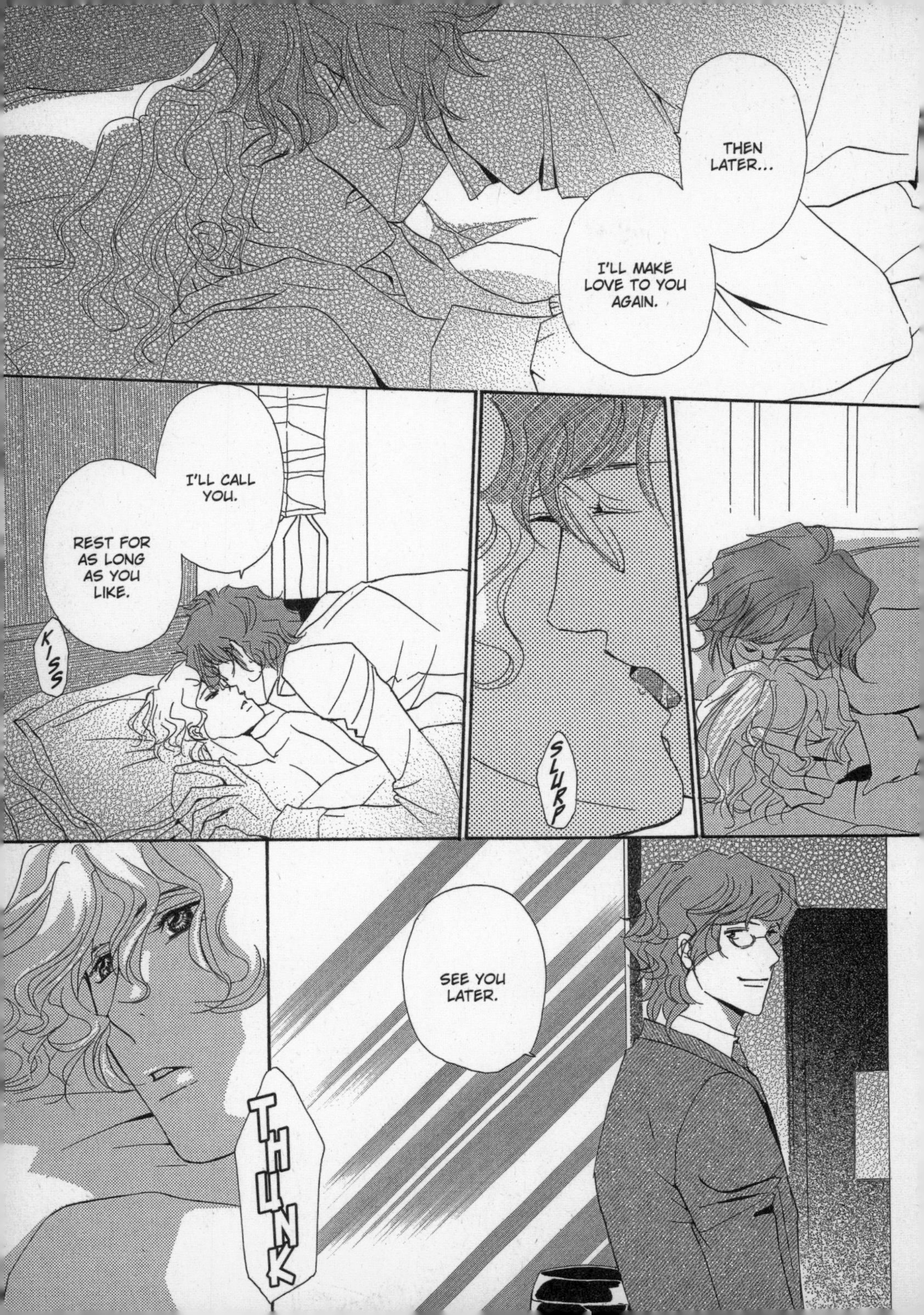
THEN LATER...
I'LL MAKE LOVE TO YOU AGAIN.
SLURP
I'LL CALL YOU.
REST FOR AS LONG AS YOU LIKE.
KISS
SEE YOU LATER.
THUNK

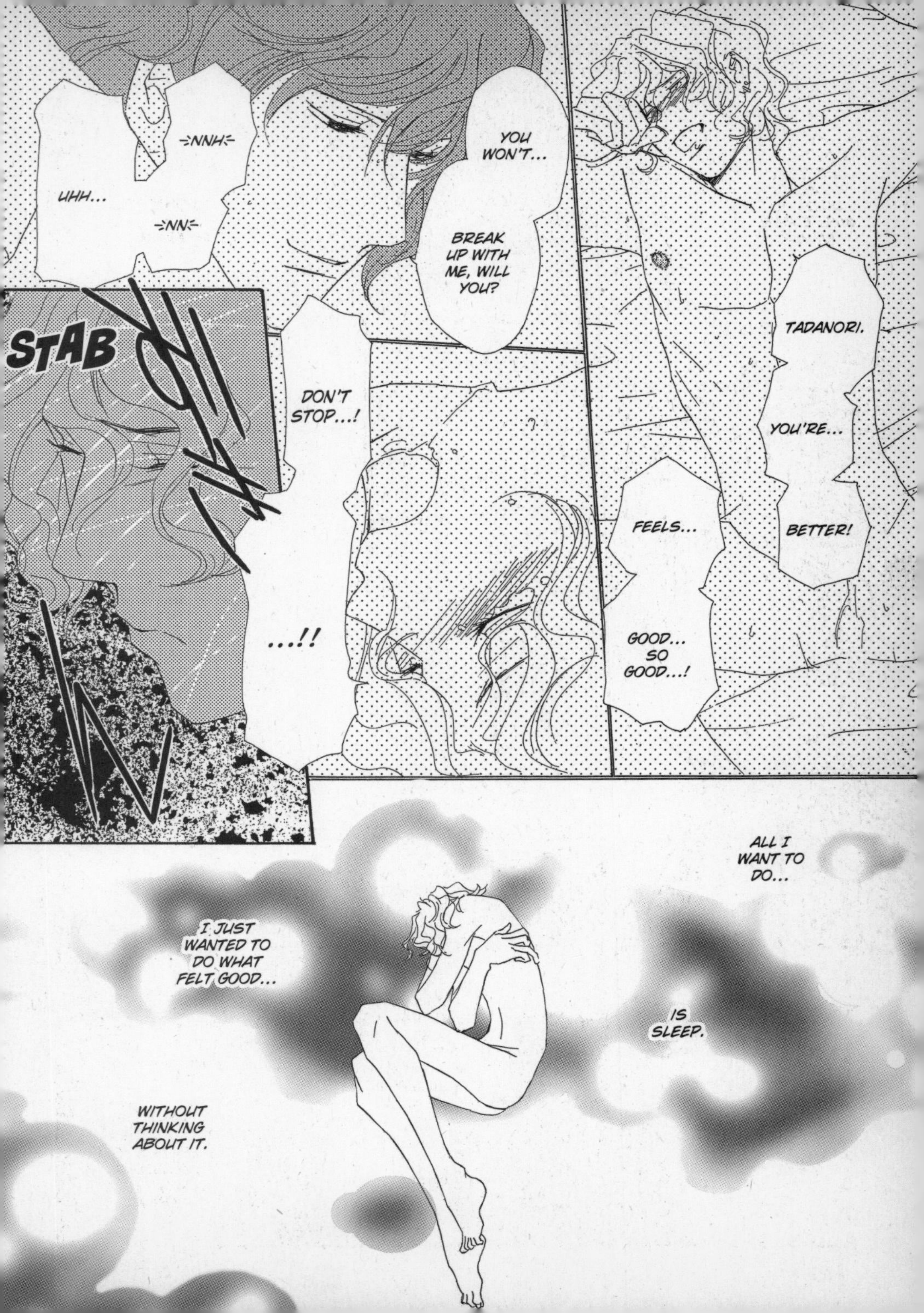
TADANORI.
YOU'RE...
BETTER!
FEELS...
GOOD... SO GOOD...!
YOU WON'T...
BREAK UP WITH ME, WILL YOU?
NNH
UHH...
NN
DON'T STOP...!
STAB
...!!
ALL I WANT TO DO...
IS SLEEP.
I JUST WANTED TO DO WHAT FELT GOOD...
WITHOUT THINKING ABOUT IT.

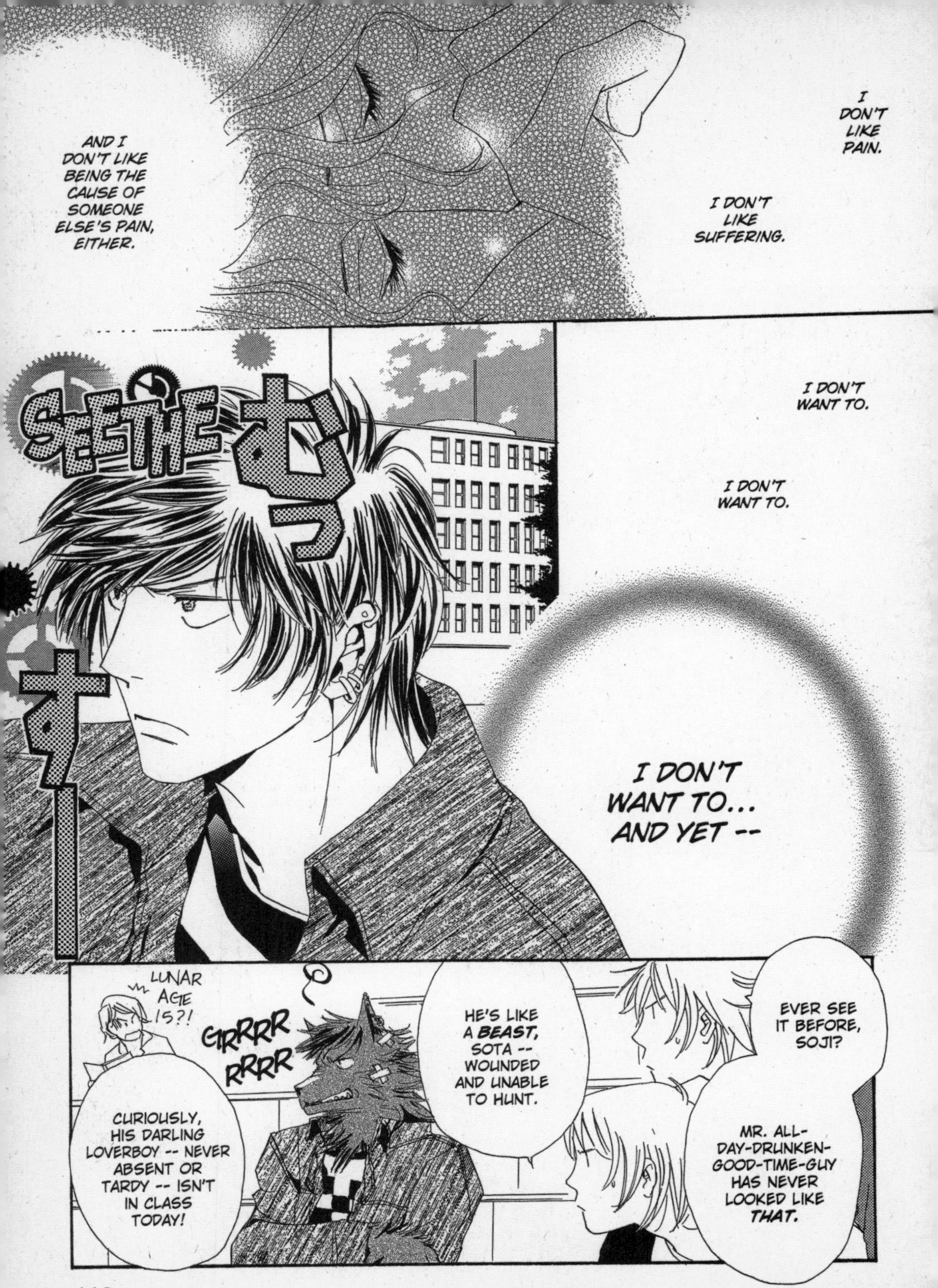
I DON'T LIKE PAIN.
I DON'T LIKE SUFFERING.
AND I DON'T LIKE BEING THE CAUSE OF SOMEONE ELSE'S PAIN, EITHER.
I DON'T WANT TO.
I DON'T WANT TO.
SEETHE
I DON'T WANT TO... AND YET --
EVER SEE IT BEFORE, SOJI?
MR. ALL-DAY-DRUNKEN-GOOD-TIME-GUY HAS NEVER LOOKED LIKE *THAT*.
HE'S LIKE A *BEAST*, SOTA -- WOUNDED AND UNABLE TO HUNT.
GRRRR RRRR
LUNAR AGE 15?!
CURIOUSLY, HIS DARLING LOVERBOY -- NEVER ABSENT OR TARDY -- ISN'T IN CLASS TODAY!

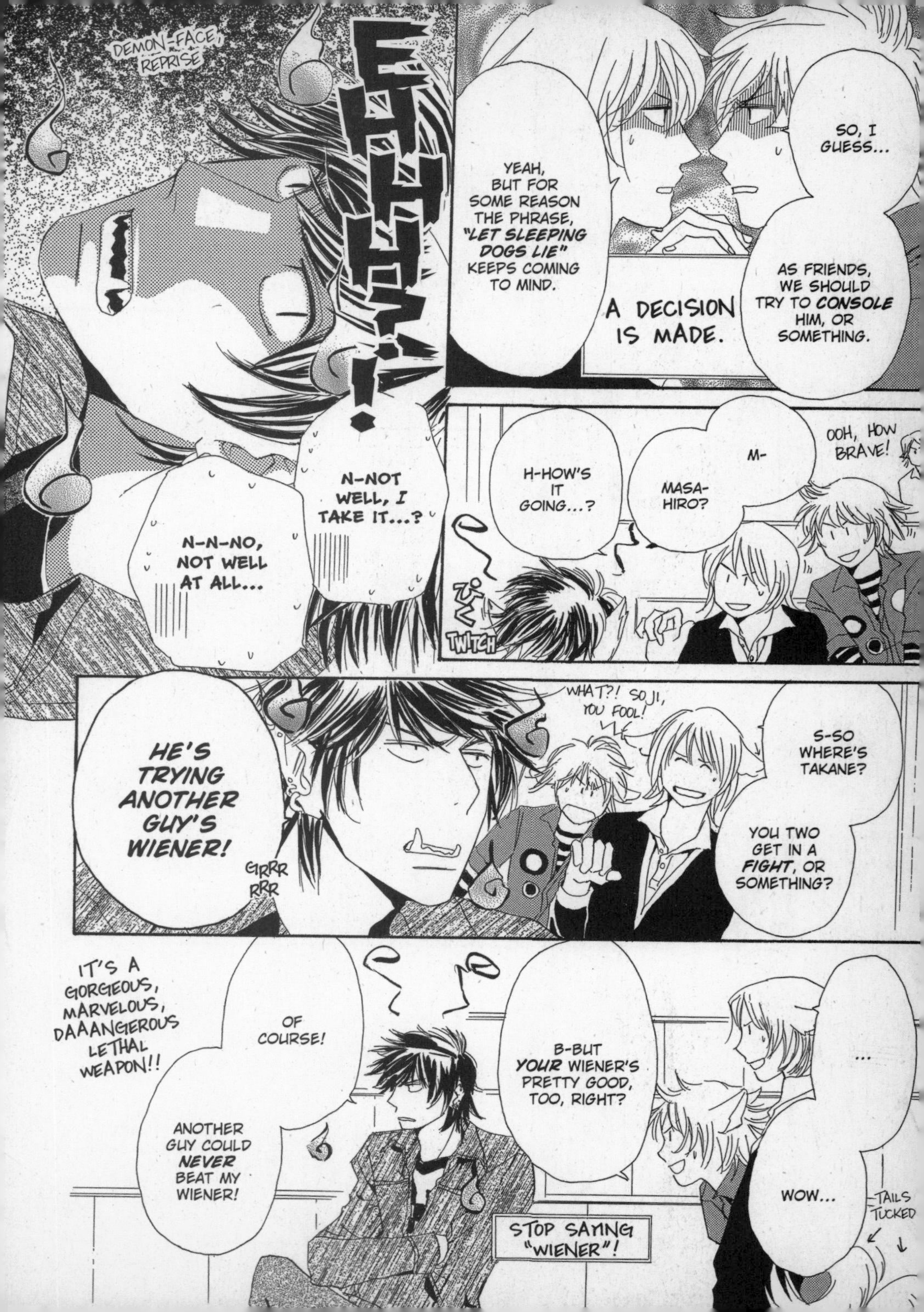
SO, I GUESS...
AS FRIENDS, WE SHOULD TRY TO CONSOLE HIM, OR SOMETHING.
YEAH, BUT FOR SOME REASON THE PHRASE, "LET SLEEPING DOGS LIE" KEEPS COMING TO MIND.
A DECISION IS MADE.
OOH, HOW BRAVE!
M-
MASA-HIRO?
H-HOW'S IT GOING...?
TWITCH
DEMON-FACE, REPRISE
EHHHH!?!
N-NOT WELL, I TAKE IT...?
N-N-NO, NOT WELL AT ALL...
S-SO WHERE'S TAKANE?
YOU TWO GET IN A FIGHT, OR SOMETHING?
WHAT?! SOJI, YOU FOOL!
HE'S TRYING ANOTHER GUY'S WIENER!
GRRR RRR
...
WOW...
TAILS TUCKED
B-BUT YOUR WIENER'S PRETTY GOOD, TOO, RIGHT?
STOP SAYING "WIENER"!
OF COURSE!
ANOTHER GUY COULD NEVER BEAT MY WIENER!
IT'S A GORGEOUS, MARVELOUS, DAAANGEROUS LETHAL WEAPON!!

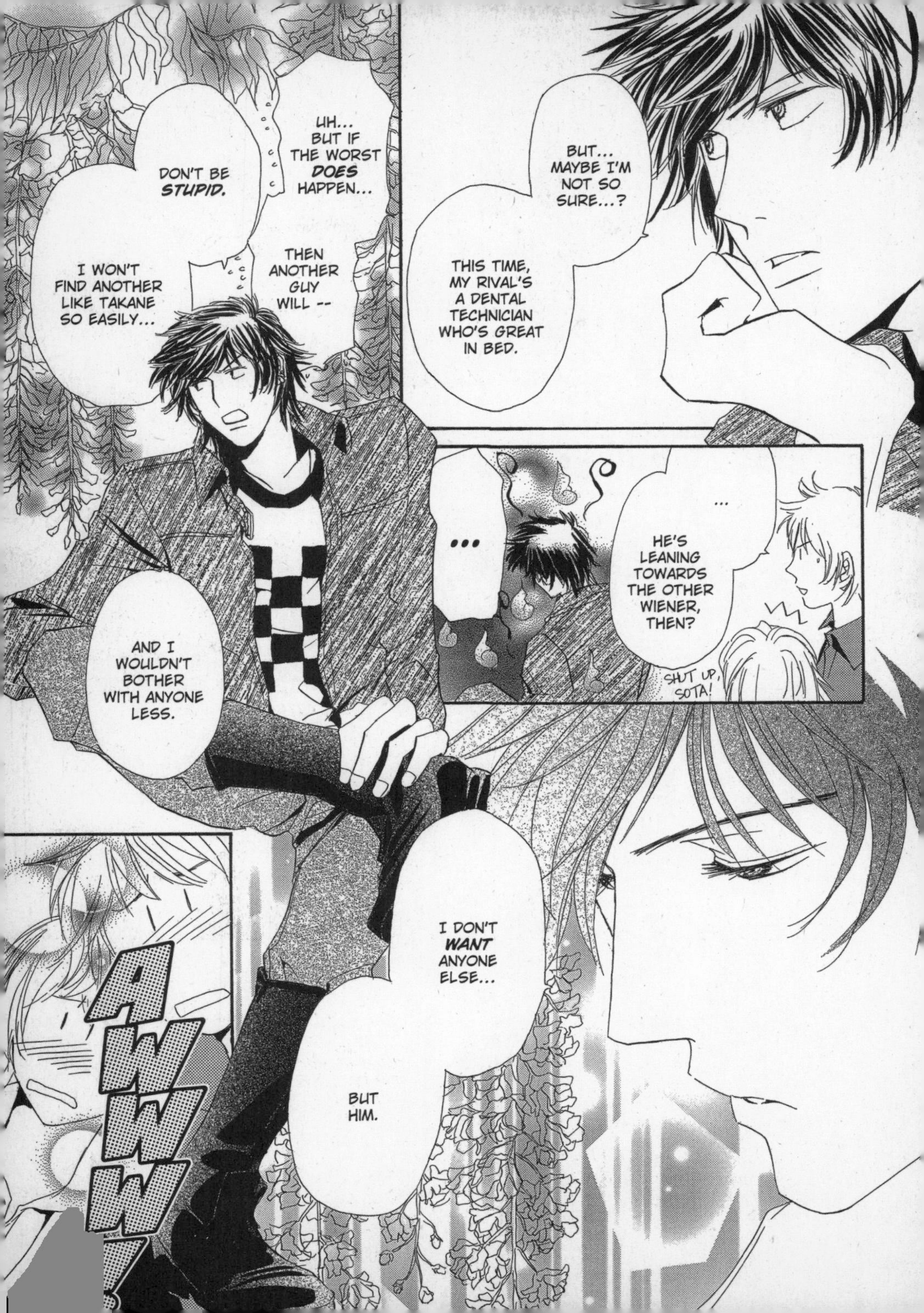
BUT... MAYBE I'M NOT SO SURE...?
THIS TIME, MY RIVAL'S A DENTAL TECHNICIAN WHO'S GREAT IN BED.
UH... BUT IF THE WORST **DOES** HAPPEN...
THEN ANOTHER GUY WILL --
DON'T BE **STUPID.**
I WON'T FIND ANOTHER LIKE TAKANE SO EASILY...
...
HE'S LEANING TOWARDS THE OTHER WIENER, THEN?
SHUT UP, SOTA!
...
AND I WOULDN'T BOTHER WITH ANYONE LESS.
I DON'T **WANT** ANYONE ELSE...
BUT HIM.
AWWW

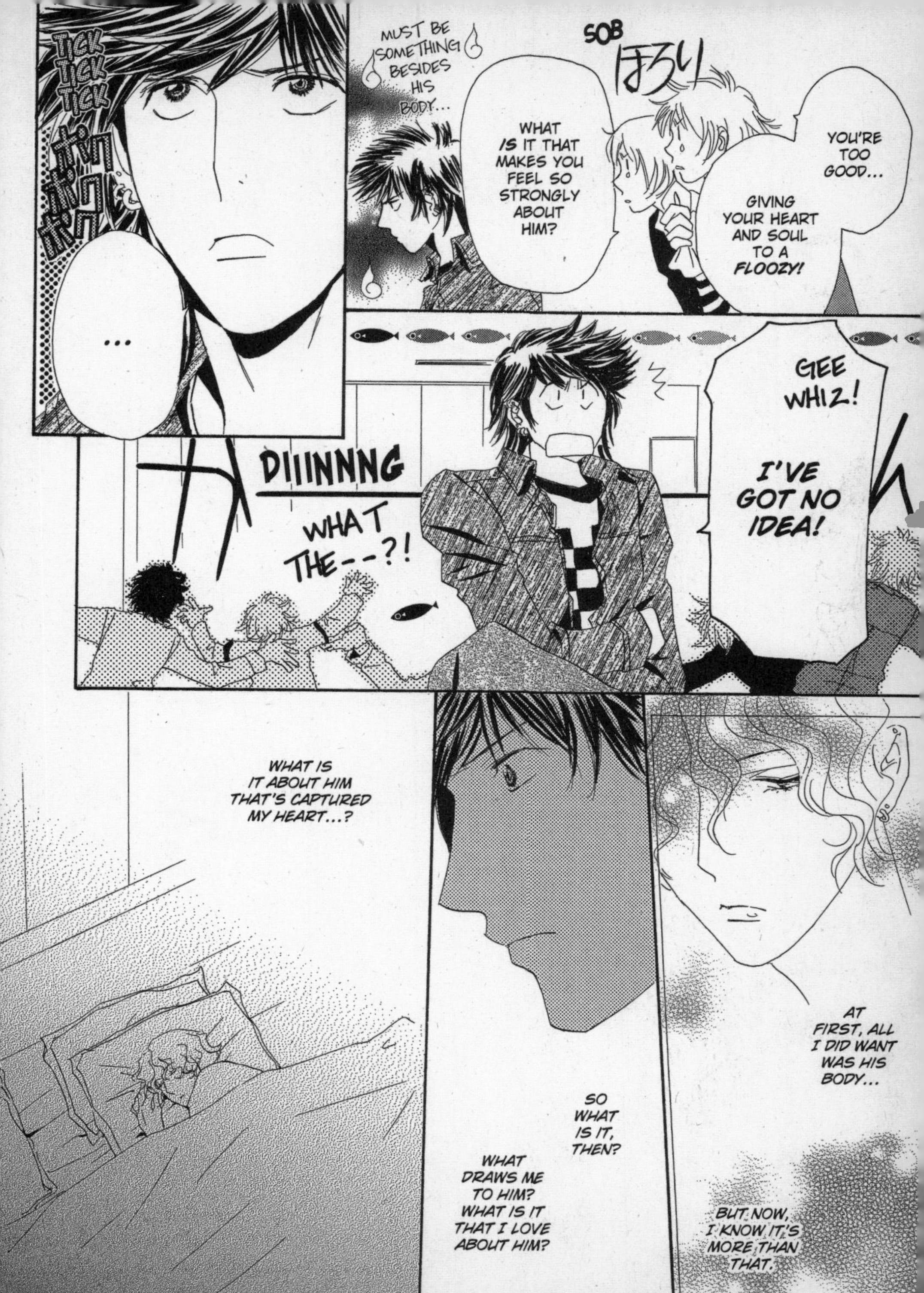
YOU'RE TOO GOOD...
GIVING YOUR HEART AND SOUL TO A *FLOOZY!*
SOB
ほろり
WHAT *IS* IT THAT MAKES YOU FEEL SO STRONGLY ABOUT HIM?
MUST BE SOMETHING BESIDES HIS BODY...
TICK TICK TICK
ポクポクポク
...
GEE WHIZ!
I'VE GOT NO IDEA!
DIIINNNG
WHAT THE--?!
AT FIRST, ALL I DID WANT WAS HIS BODY...
BUT NOW, I KNOW IT'S MORE THAN THAT.
SO WHAT IS IT, THEN?
WHAT DRAWS ME TO HIM? WHAT IS IT THAT I LOVE ABOUT HIM?
WHAT IS IT ABOUT HIM THAT'S CAPTURED MY HEART...?

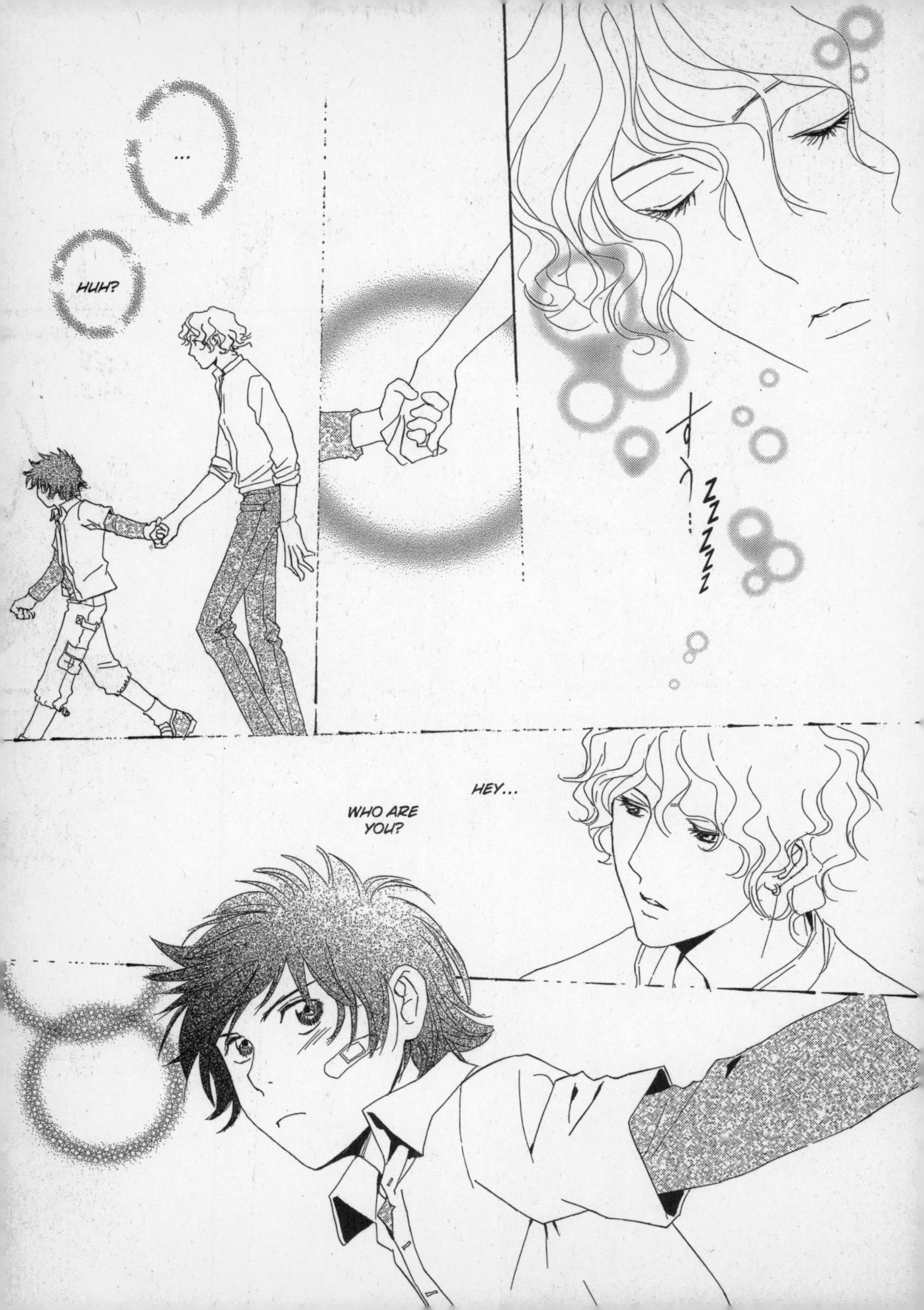
すー…
ZZZZZ
...
HUH?
HEY...
WHO ARE YOU?

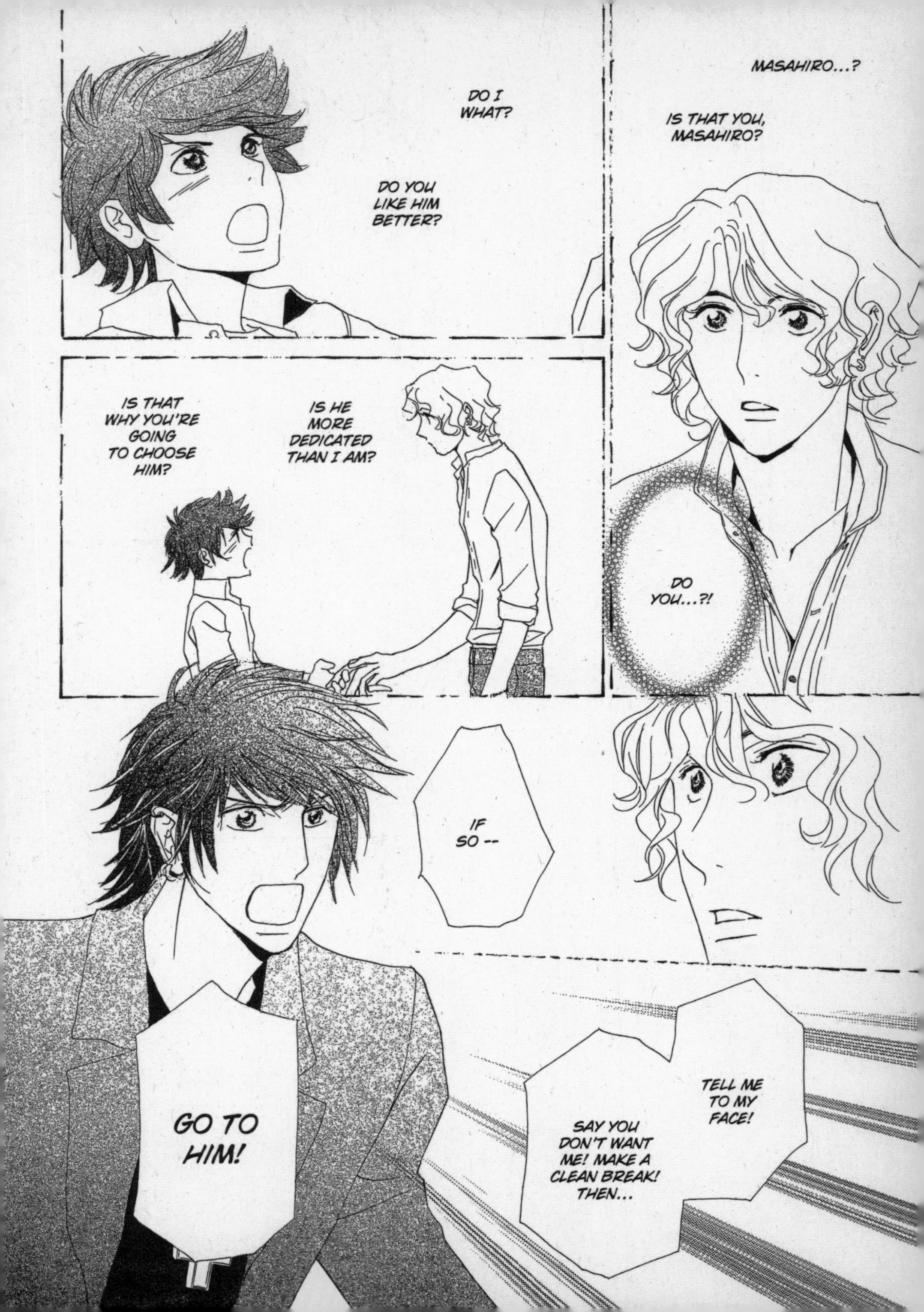
MASAHIRO...?
IS THAT YOU, MASAHIRO?
DO YOU...?!
DO I WHAT?
DO YOU LIKE HIM BETTER?
IS HE MORE DEDICATED THAN I AM?
IS THAT WHY YOU'RE GOING TO CHOOSE HIM?
IF SO --
TELL ME TO MY FACE!
SAY YOU DON'T WANT ME! MAKE A CLEAN BREAK! THEN...
GO TO HIM!

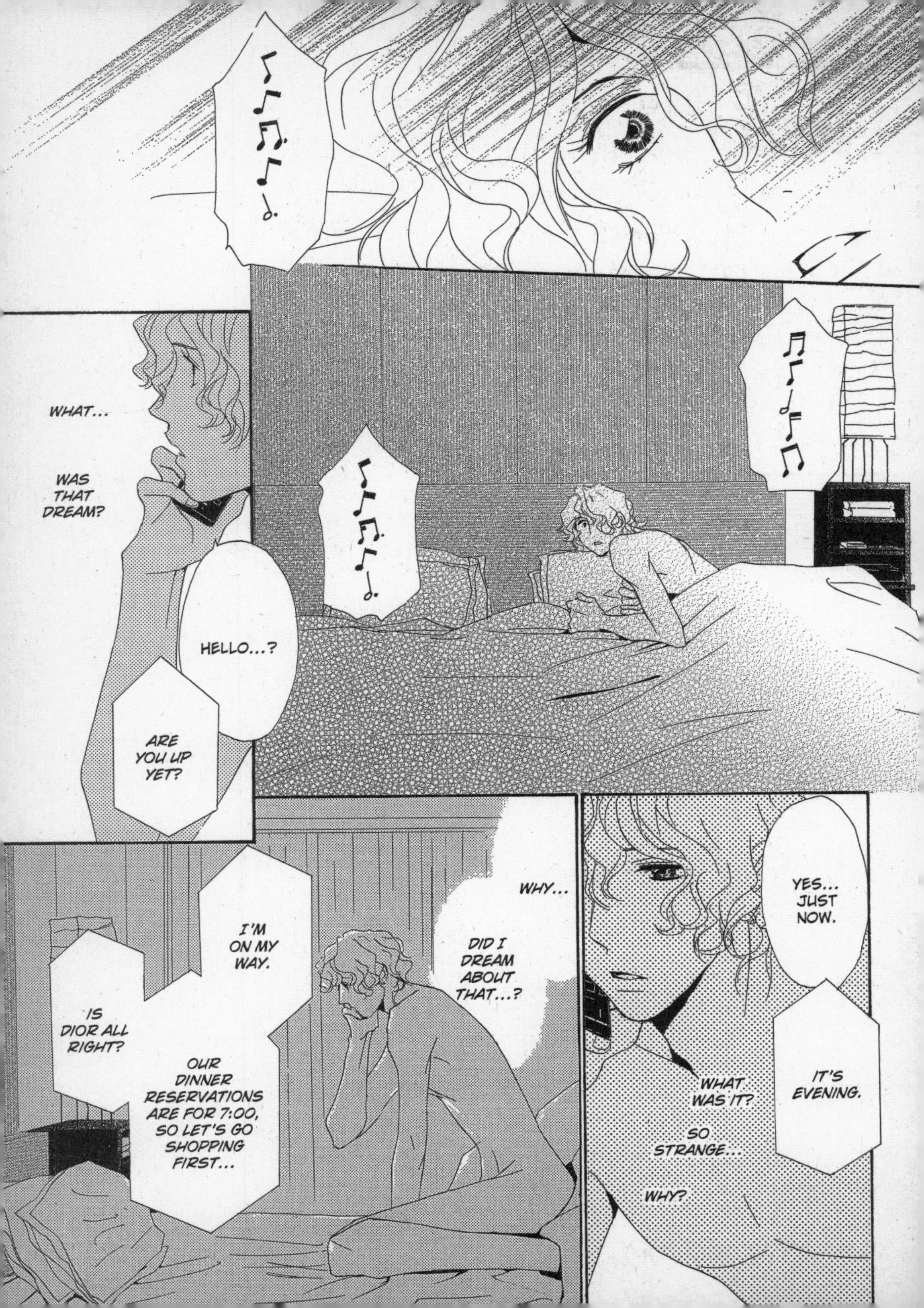
WHAT...
WAS THAT DREAM?
HELLO...?
ARE YOU UP YET?
YES... JUST NOW.
IT'S EVENING.
WHAT WAS IT?
SO STRANGE...
WHY?
WHY...
DID I DREAM ABOUT THAT...?
I'M ON MY WAY.
IS DIOR ALL RIGHT?
OUR DINNER RESERVATIONS ARE FOR 7:00, SO LET'S GO SHOPPING FIRST...

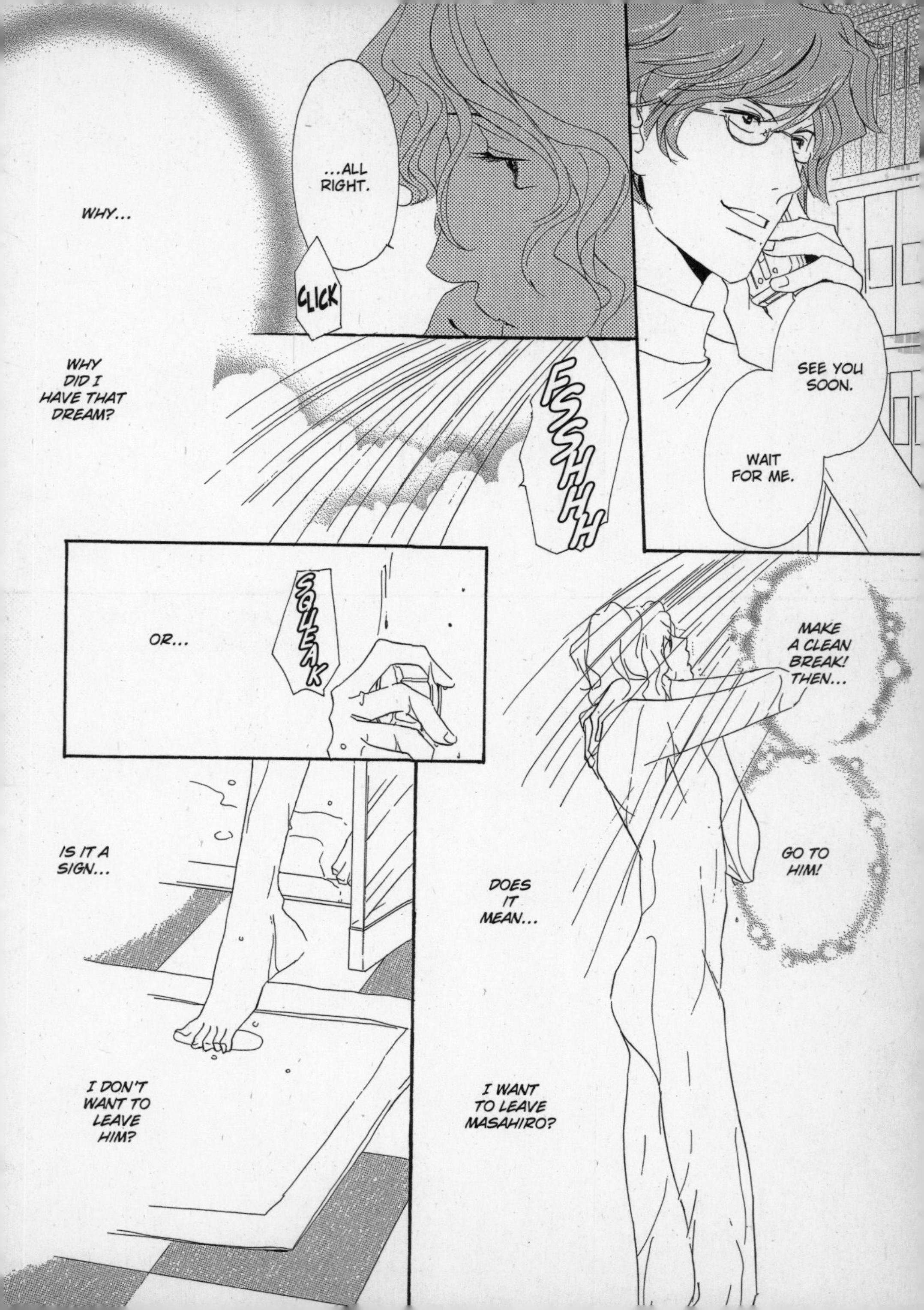

SEE YOU SOON.
WAIT FOR ME.
...ALL RIGHT.
CLICK
WHY...
WHY DID I HAVE THAT DREAM?
FSHHH
MAKE A CLEAN BREAK! THEN...
GO TO HIM!
DOES IT MEAN...
I WANT TO LEAVE MASAHIRO?
OR...
SQUEAK
IS IT A SIGN...
I DON'T WANT TO LEAVE HIM?

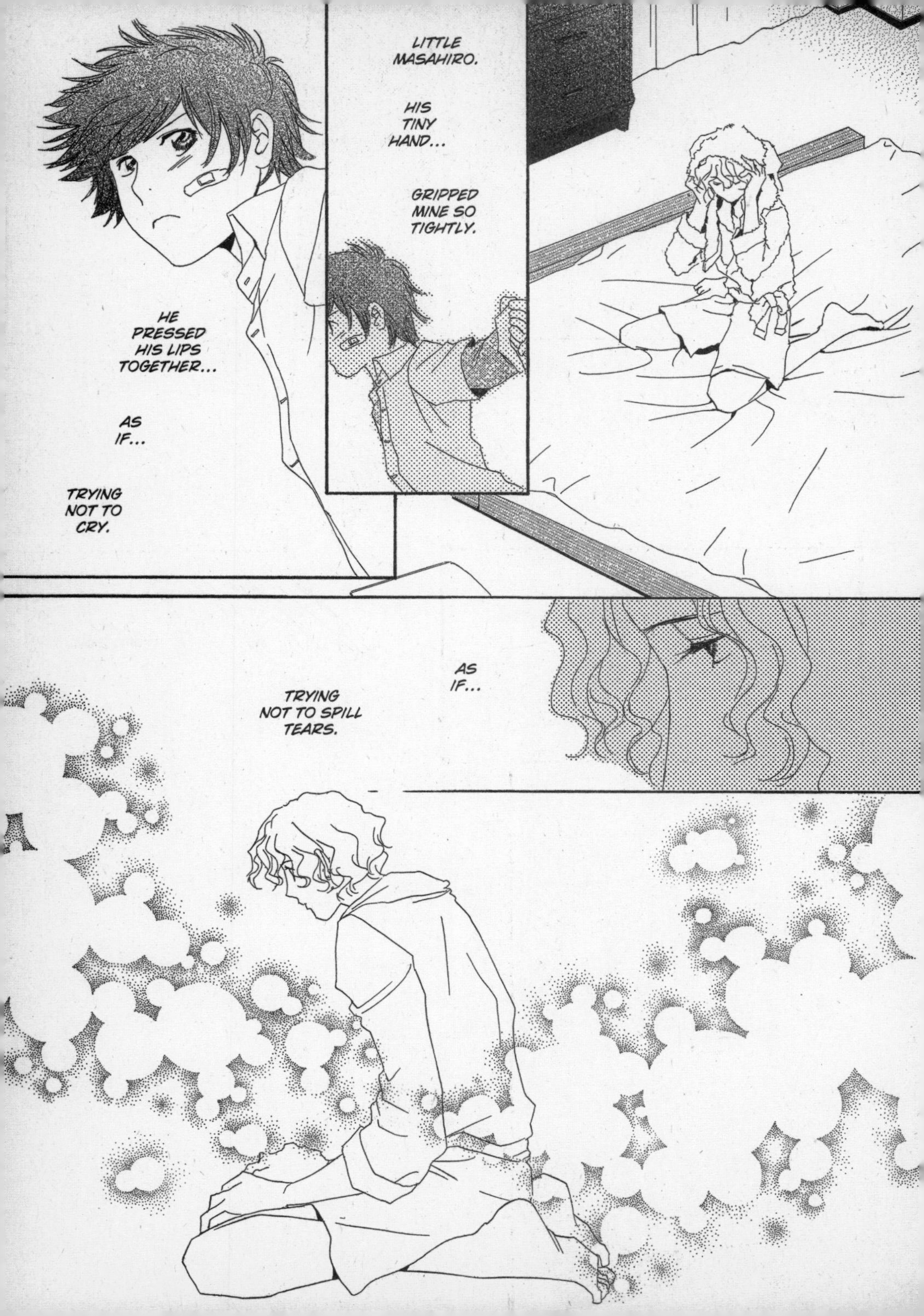
LITTLE MASAHIRO.
HIS TINY HAND...
GRIPPED MINE SO TIGHTLY.
HE PRESSED HIS LIPS TOGETHER...
AS IF...
TRYING NOT TO CRY.
AS IF...
TRYING NOT TO SPILL TEARS.

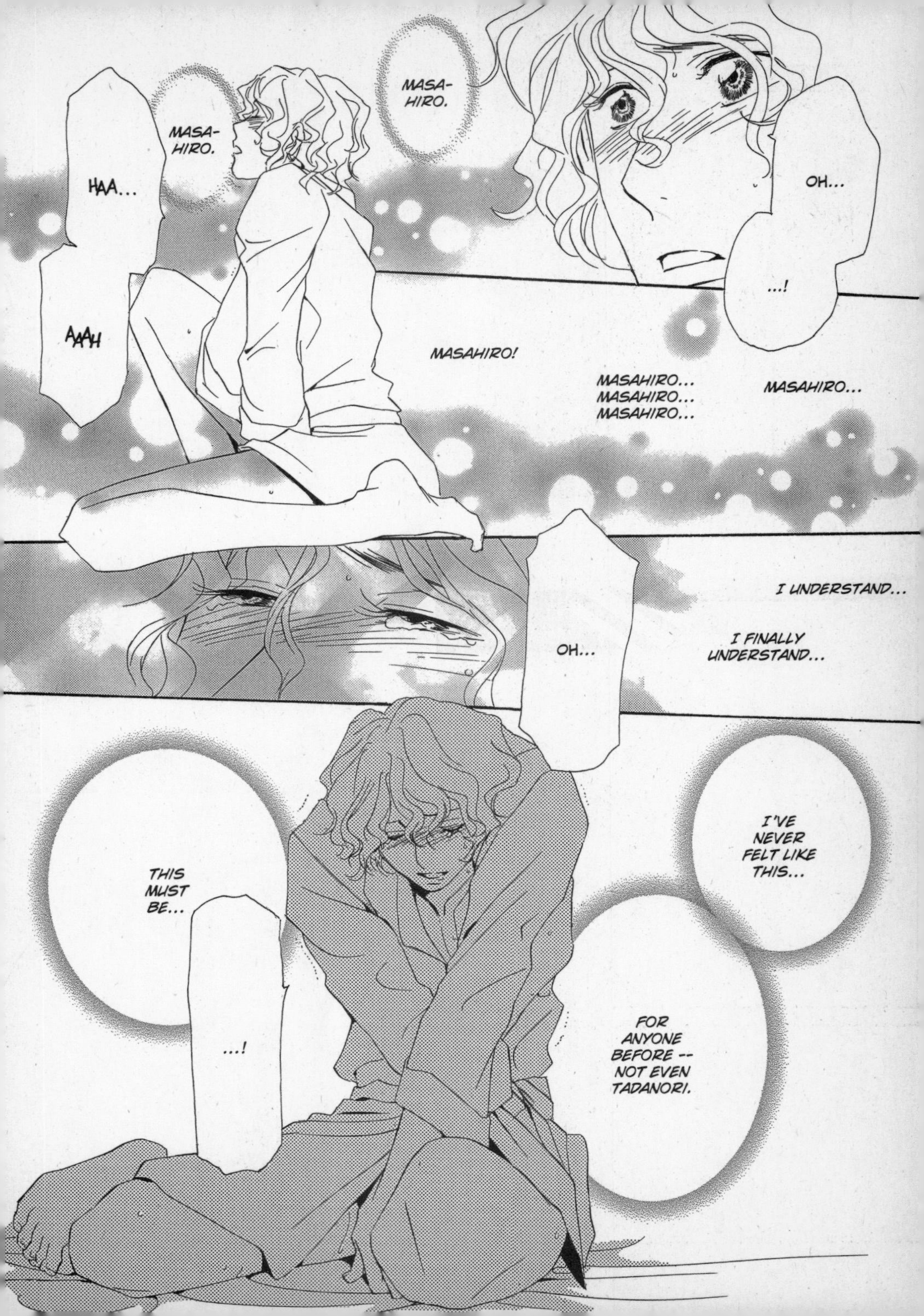
MASA-HIRO.
OH...
...!
MASA-HIRO.
HAA...
AAAH
MASAHIRO...
MASAHIRO... MASAHIRO... MASAHIRO...
MASAHIRO!
I UNDERSTAND...
I FINALLY UNDERSTAND...
OH...
I'VE NEVER FELT LIKE THIS...
FOR ANYONE BEFORE -- NOT EVEN TADANORI.
THIS MUST BE...
...!

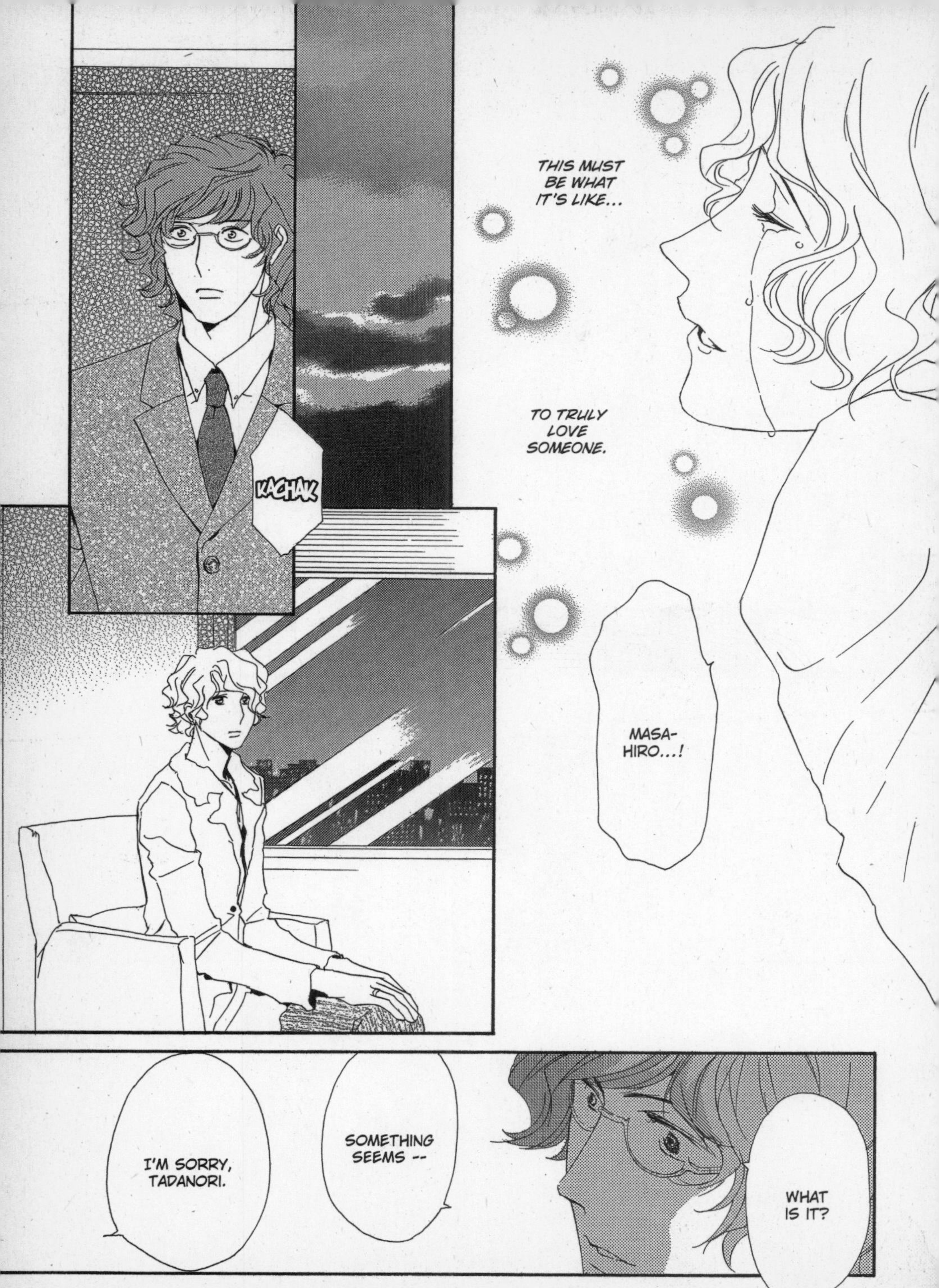
THIS MUST BE WHAT IT'S LIKE...
TO TRULY LOVE SOMEONE.
MASA-HIRO...!
KACHAK
WHAT IS IT?
SOMETHING SEEMS --
I'M SORRY, TADANORI.

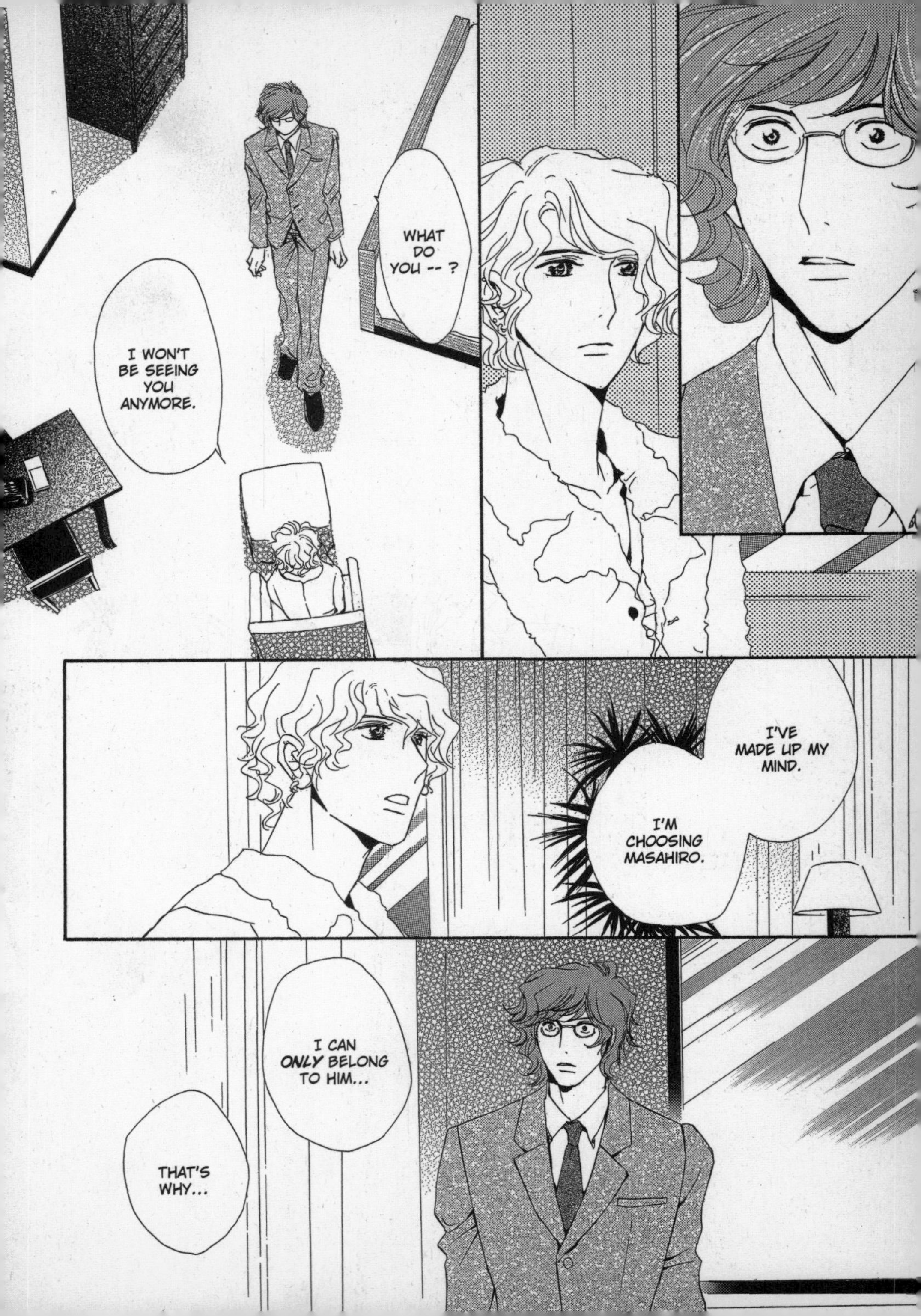
WHAT DO YOU -- ?
I WON'T BE SEEING YOU ANYMORE.
I'VE MADE UP MY MIND.
I'M CHOOSING MASAHIRO.
I CAN *ONLY* BELONG TO HIM...
THAT'S WHY...

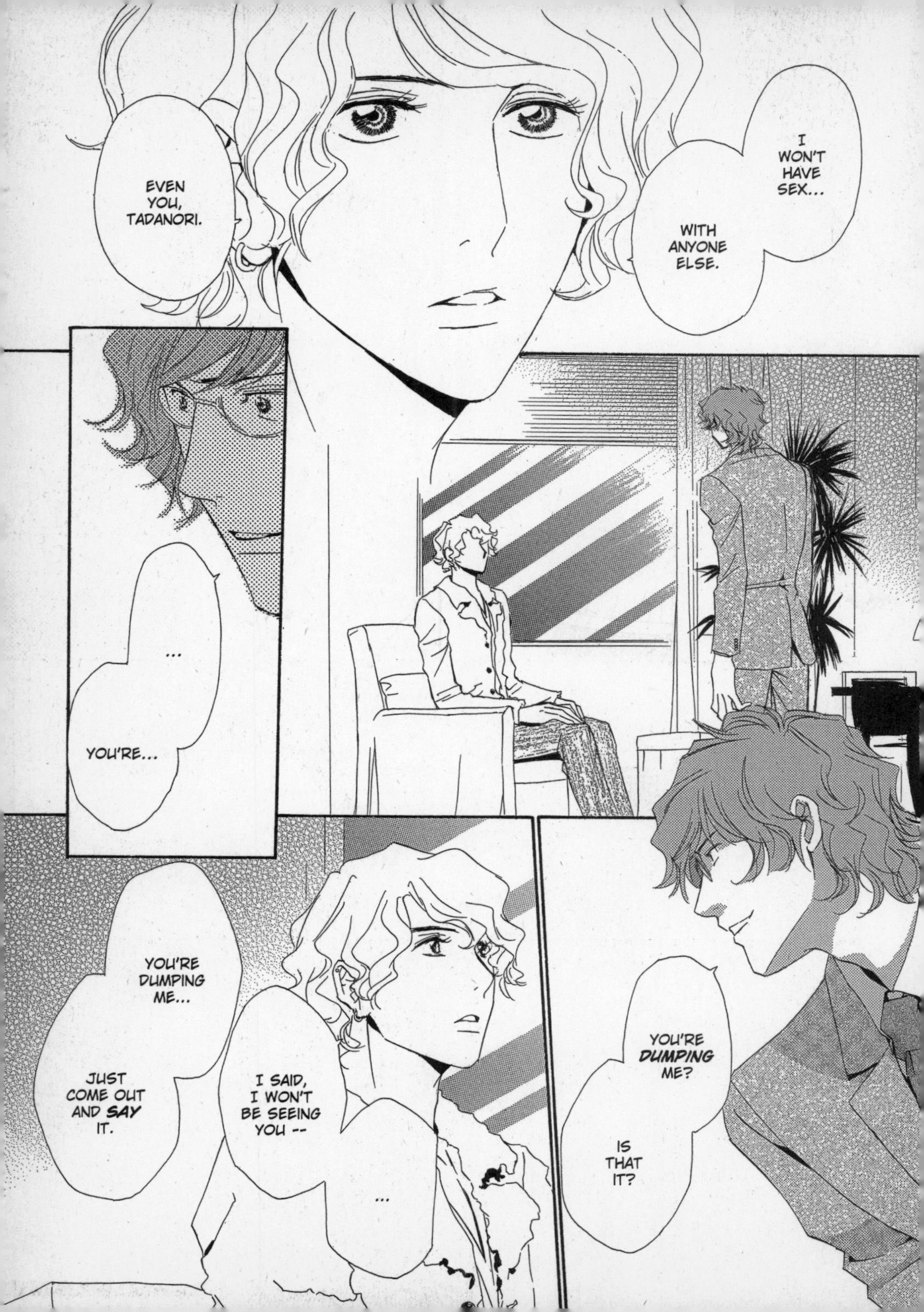
I WON'T HAVE SEX...
WITH ANYONE ELSE.
EVEN YOU, TADANORI.
...
YOU'RE...
YOU'RE *DUMPING* ME?
IS THAT IT?
I SAID, I WON'T BE SEEING YOU --
YOU'RE DUMPING ME...
JUST COME OUT AND *SAY* IT.
...

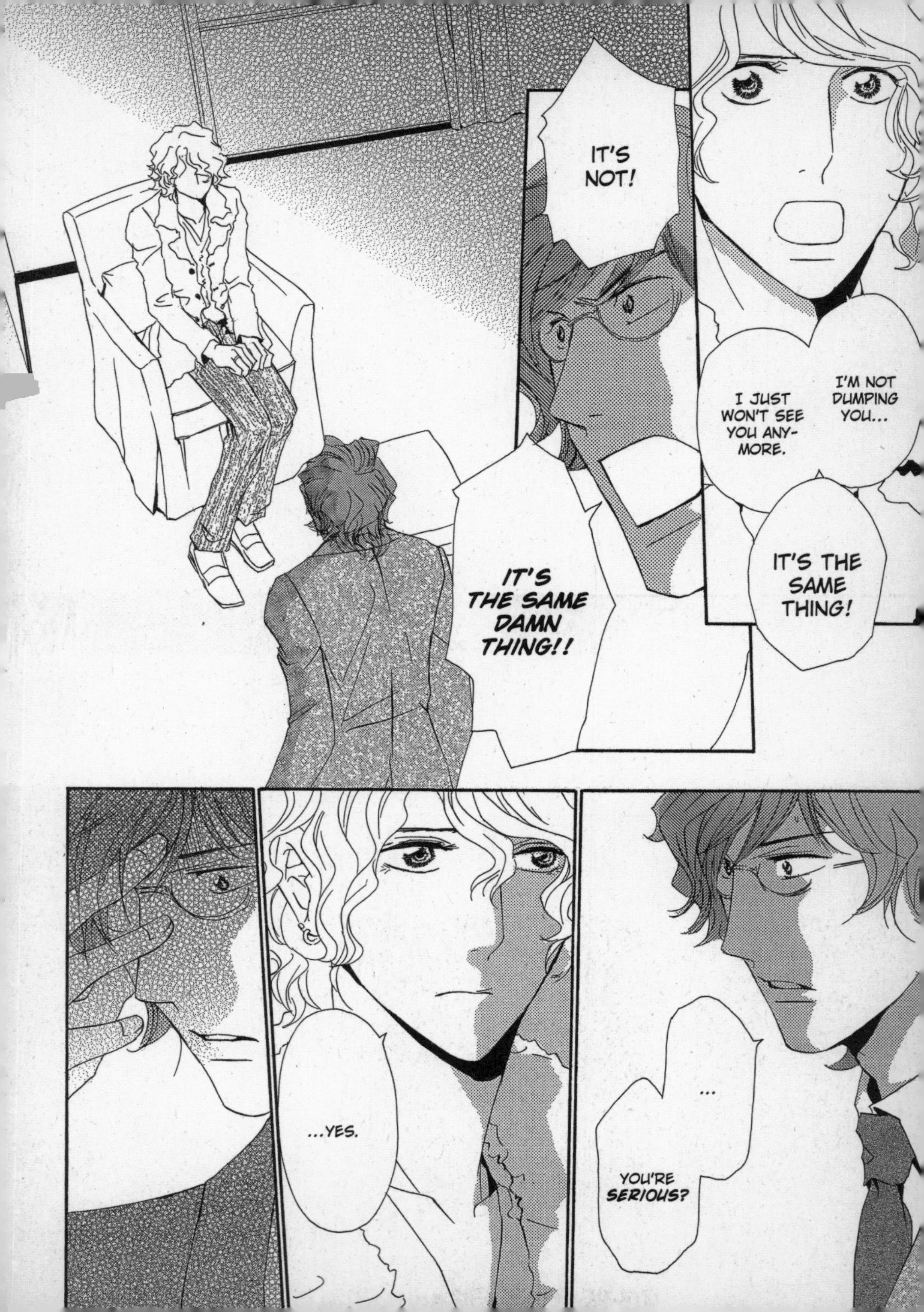
IT'S NOT!
I'M NOT DUMPING YOU...
I JUST WON'T SEE YOU ANY-MORE.
IT'S THE SAME THING!
IT'S THE SAME DAMN THING!!
...
YOU'RE SERIOUS?
...YES.

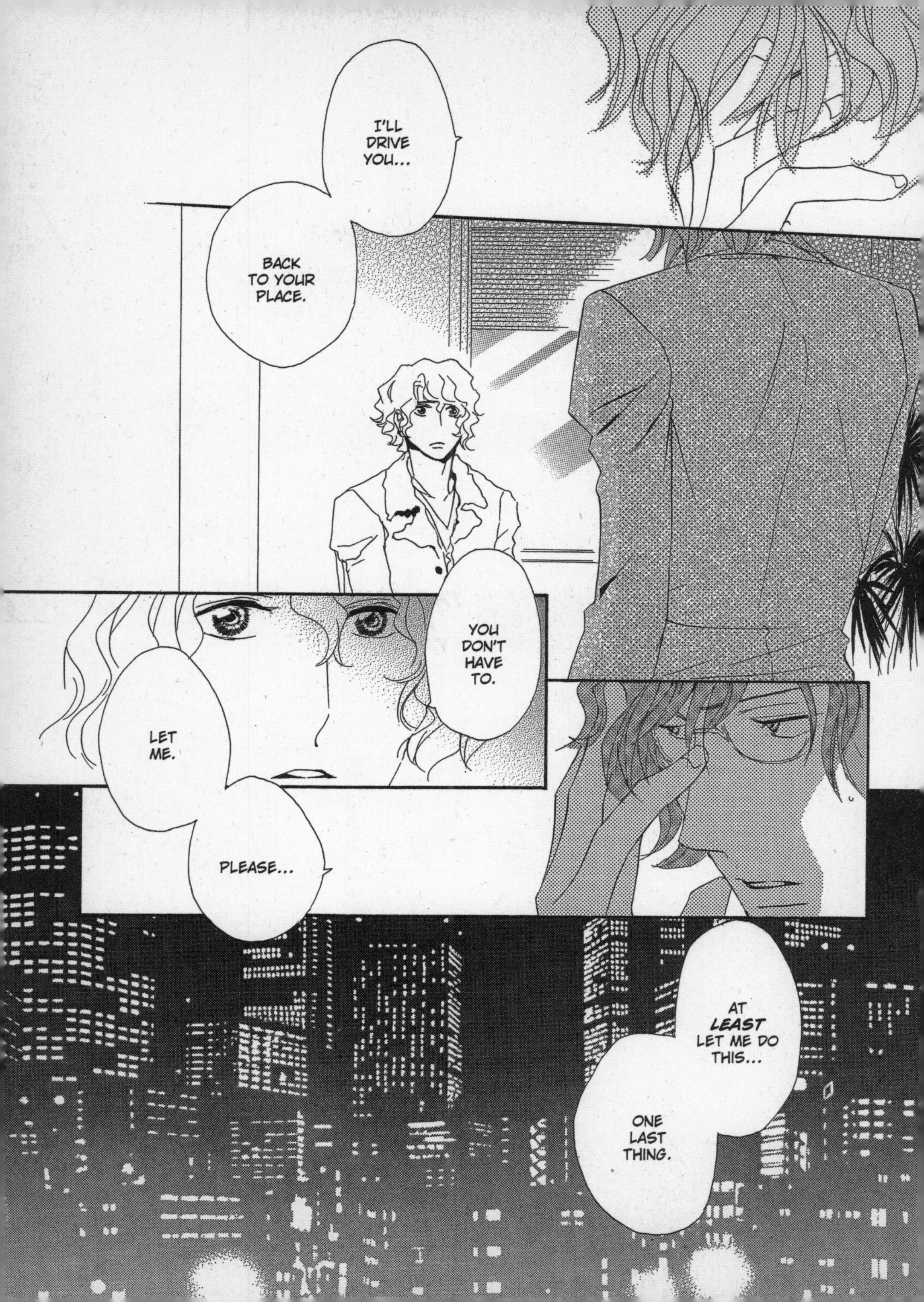

I'LL DRIVE YOU...
BACK TO YOUR PLACE.
YOU DON'T HAVE TO.
LET ME.
PLEASE...
AT *LEAST* LET ME DO THIS...
ONE LAST THING.

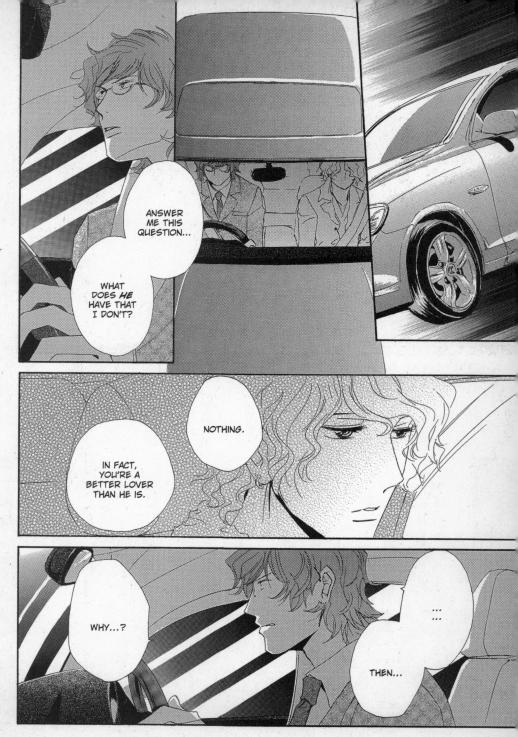

ANSWER ME THIS QUESTION...

WHAT DOES *HE* HAVE THAT I DON'T?

NOTHING.

IN FACT, YOU'RE A BETTER LOVER THAN HE IS.

WHY...?

...
...

THEN...

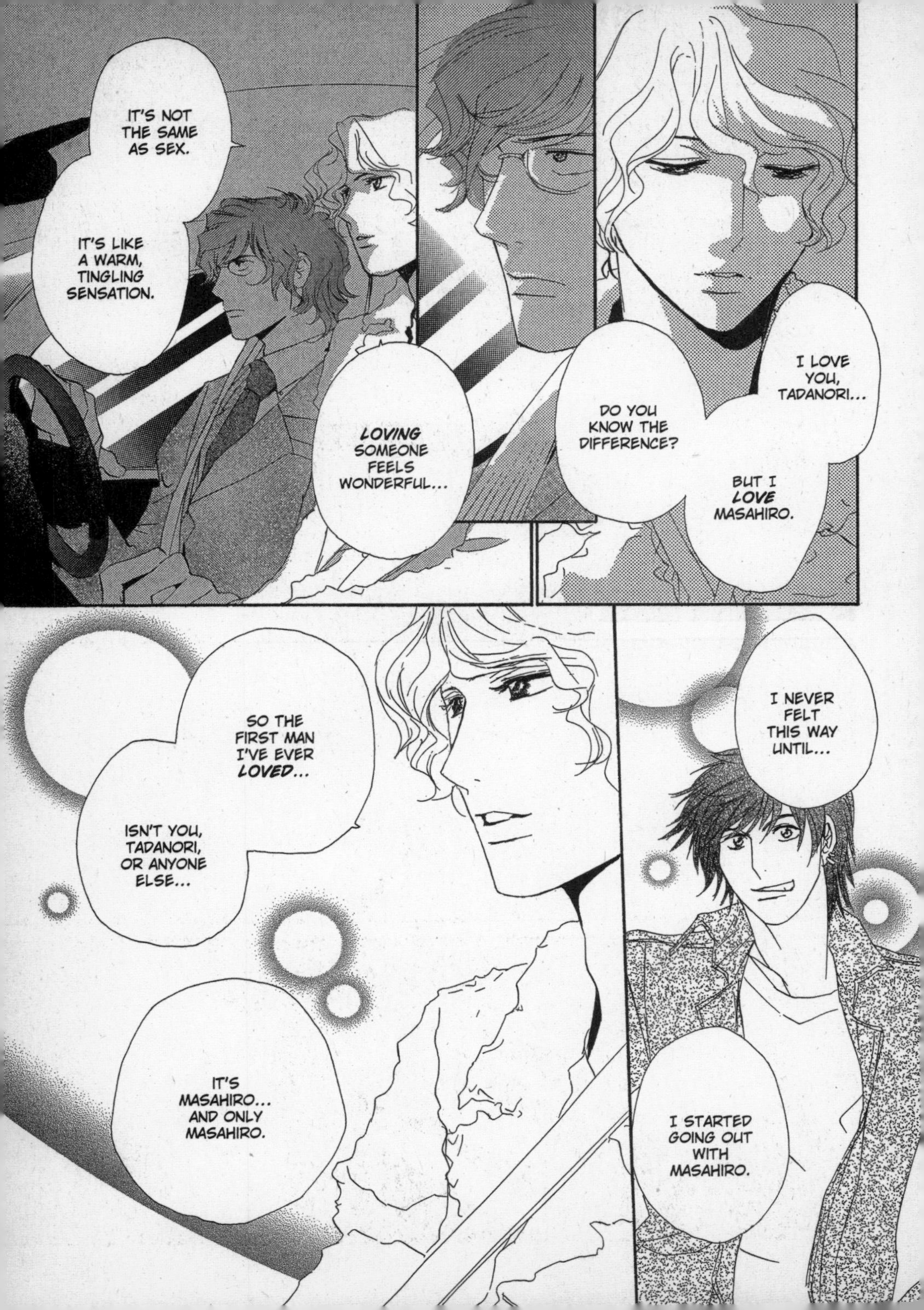
I LOVE YOU, TADANORI...
BUT I *LOVE* MASAHIRO.
DO YOU KNOW THE DIFFERENCE?
LOVING SOMEONE FEELS WONDERFUL...
IT'S NOT THE SAME AS SEX.
IT'S LIKE A WARM, TINGLING SENSATION.
I NEVER FELT THIS WAY UNTIL...
I STARTED GOING OUT WITH MASAHIRO.
SO THE FIRST MAN I'VE EVER *LOVED*...
ISN'T YOU, TADANORI, OR ANYONE ELSE...
IT'S MASAHIRO... AND ONLY MASAHIRO.

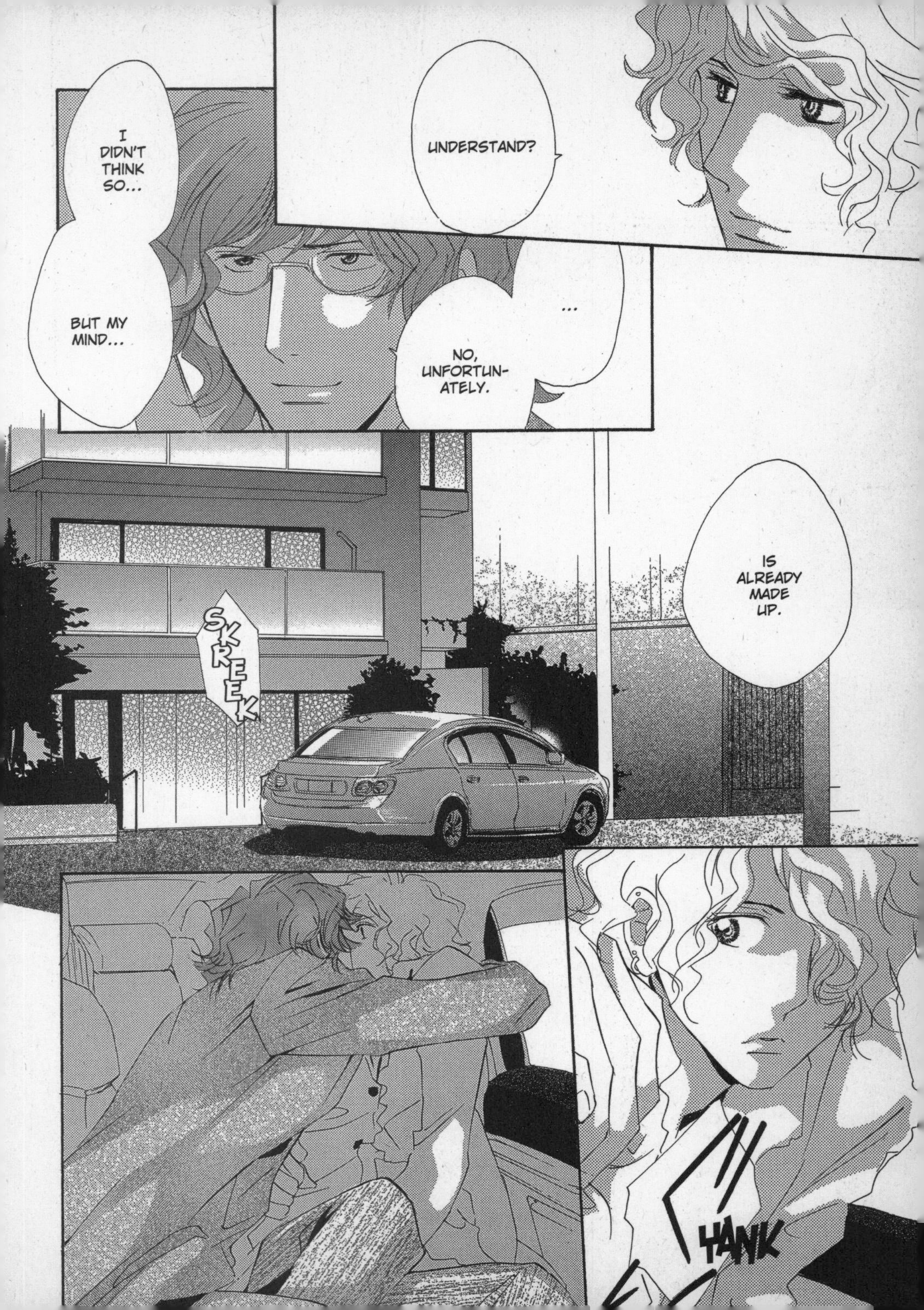
UNDERSTAND?
...
NO, UNFORTUNATELY.
I DIDN'T THINK SO...
BUT MY MIND...
IS ALREADY MADE UP.
SKREEK
YANK

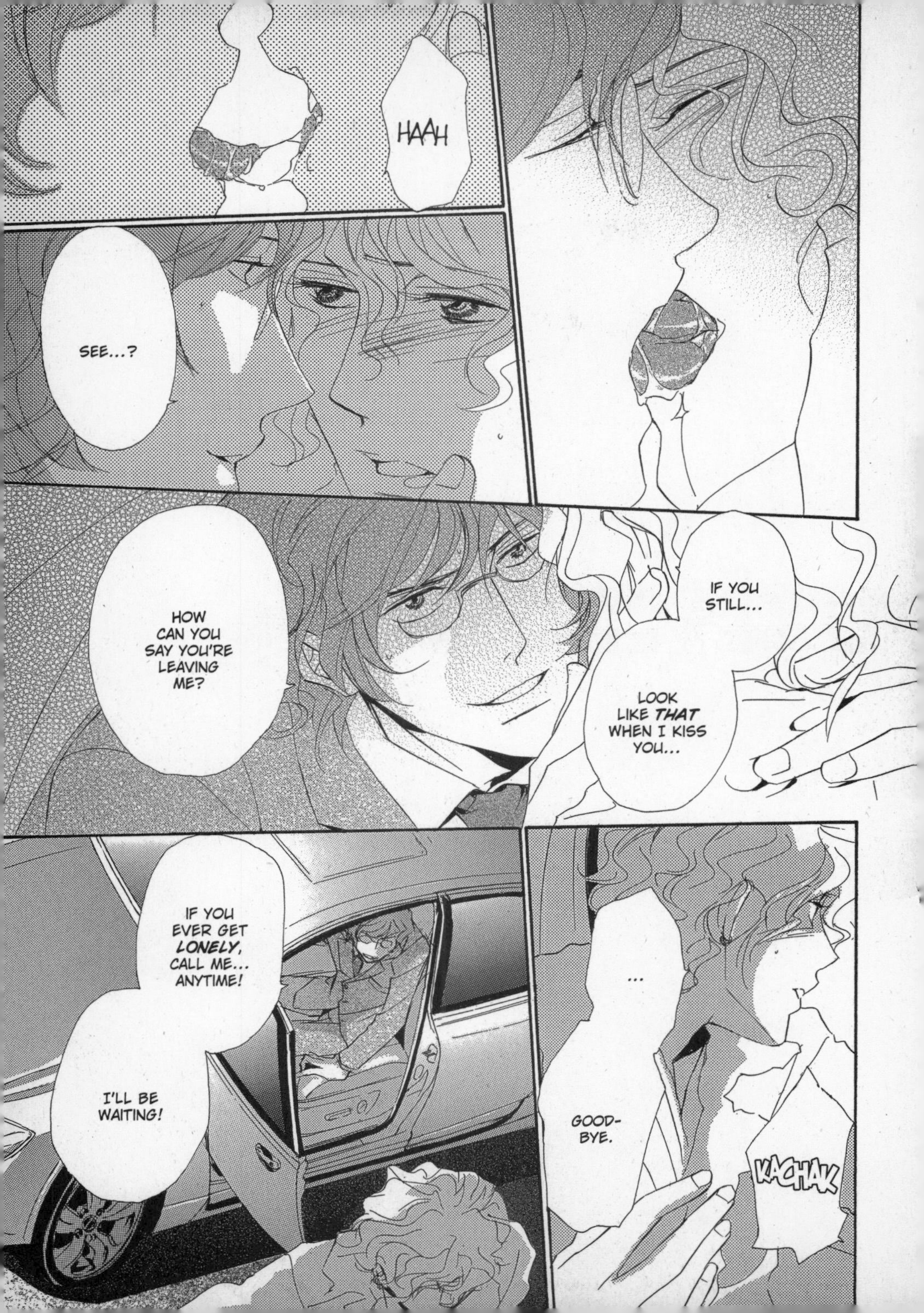
HAAH
SEE...?
IF YOU STILL...
LOOK LIKE *THAT* WHEN I KISS YOU...
HOW CAN YOU SAY YOU'RE LEAVING ME?
...
GOOD-BYE.
KACHAK
IF YOU EVER GET *LONELY*, CALL ME... ANYTIME!
I'LL BE WAITING!

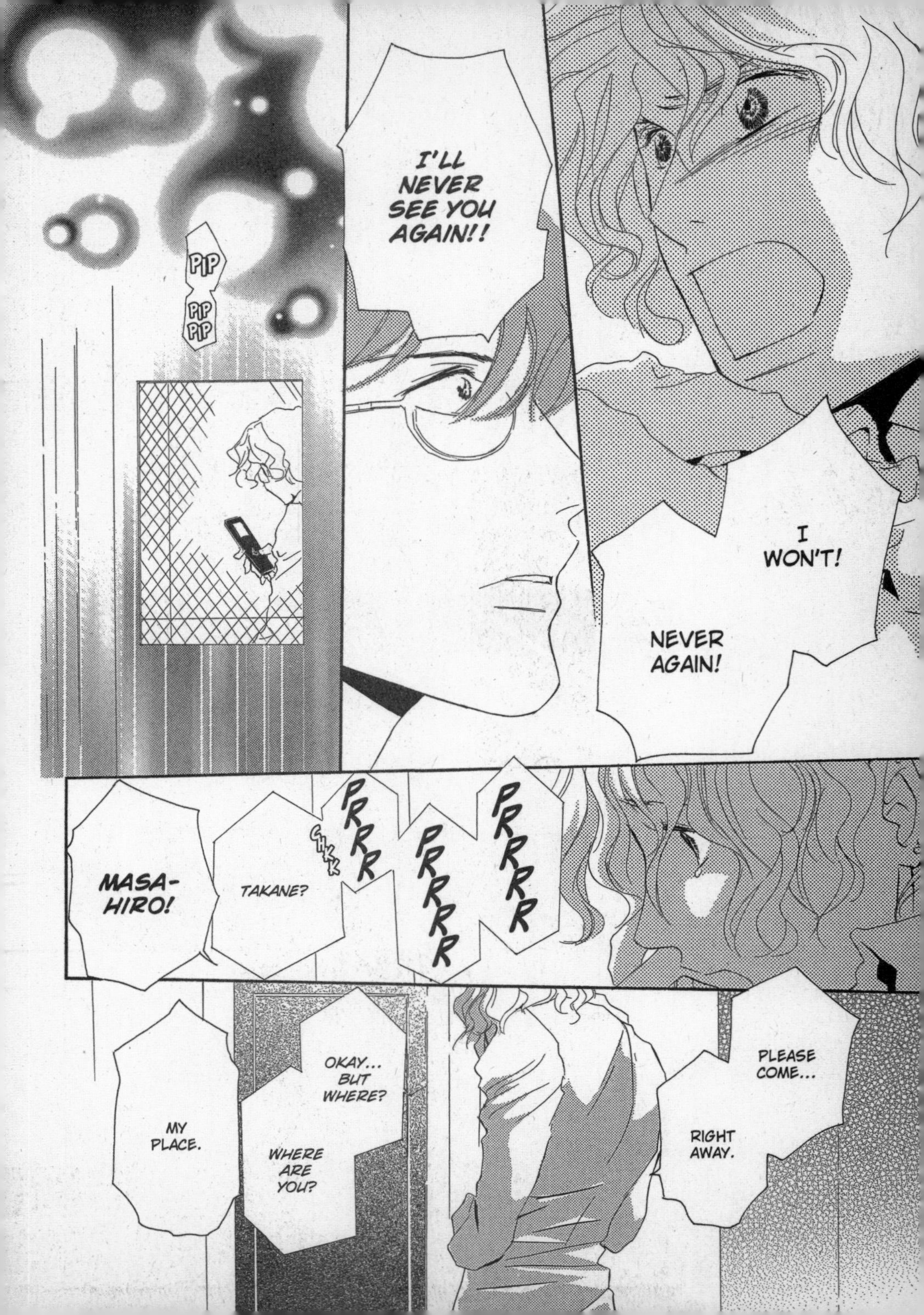
I WON'T!
NEVER AGAIN!
I'LL NEVER SEE YOU AGAIN!!
PIP
PIP PIP
PRRRR
PRRRR
PRRR
CHKK
TAKANE?
MASA-HIRO!
PLEASE COME...
RIGHT AWAY.
OKAY... BUT WHERE?
WHERE ARE YOU?
MY PLACE.

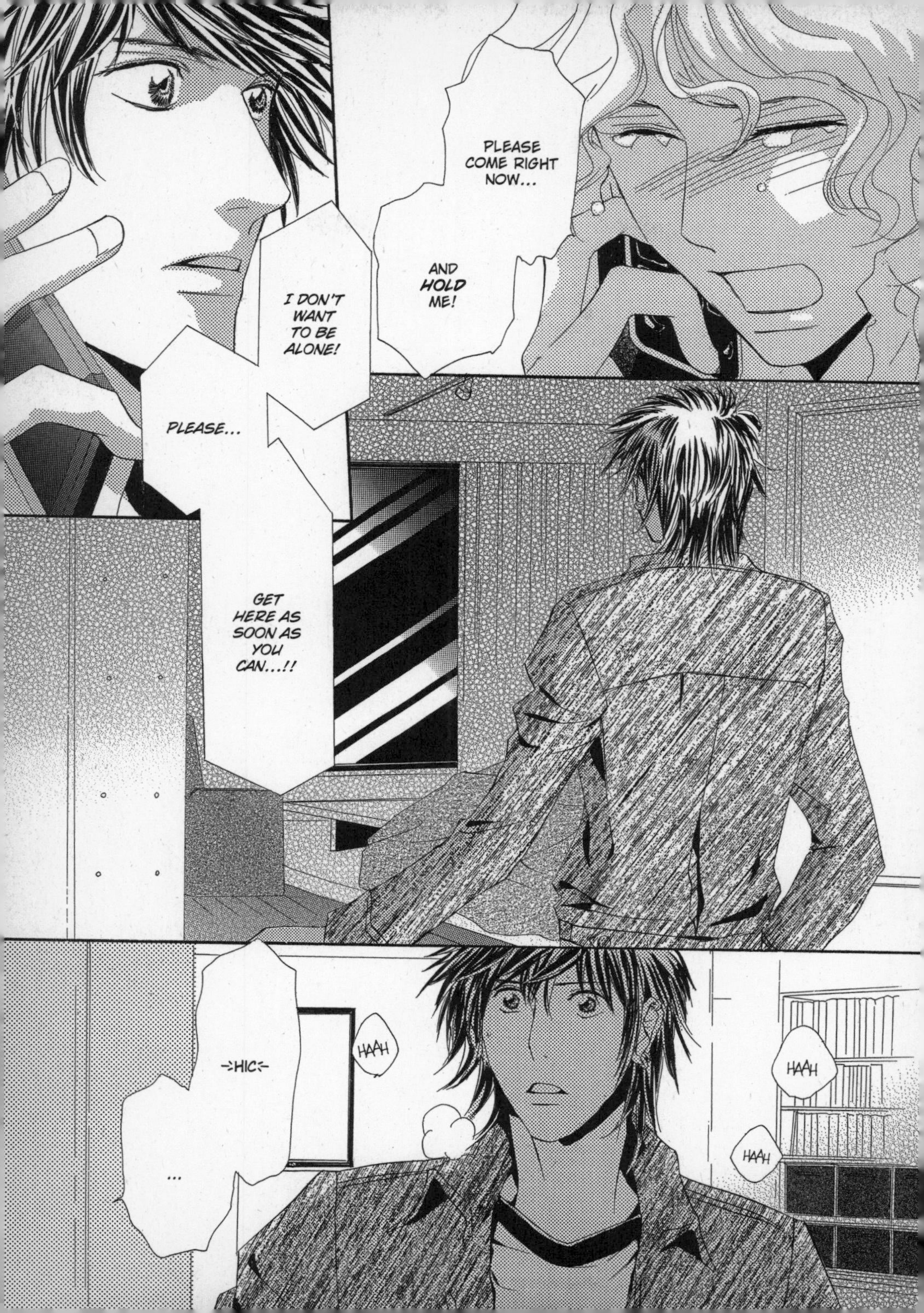
PLEASE COME RIGHT NOW...
AND HOLD ME!
I DON'T WANT TO BE ALONE!
PLEASE...
GET HERE AS SOON AS YOU CAN...!!
HAAH
HAAH
HAAH
-HIC-
...

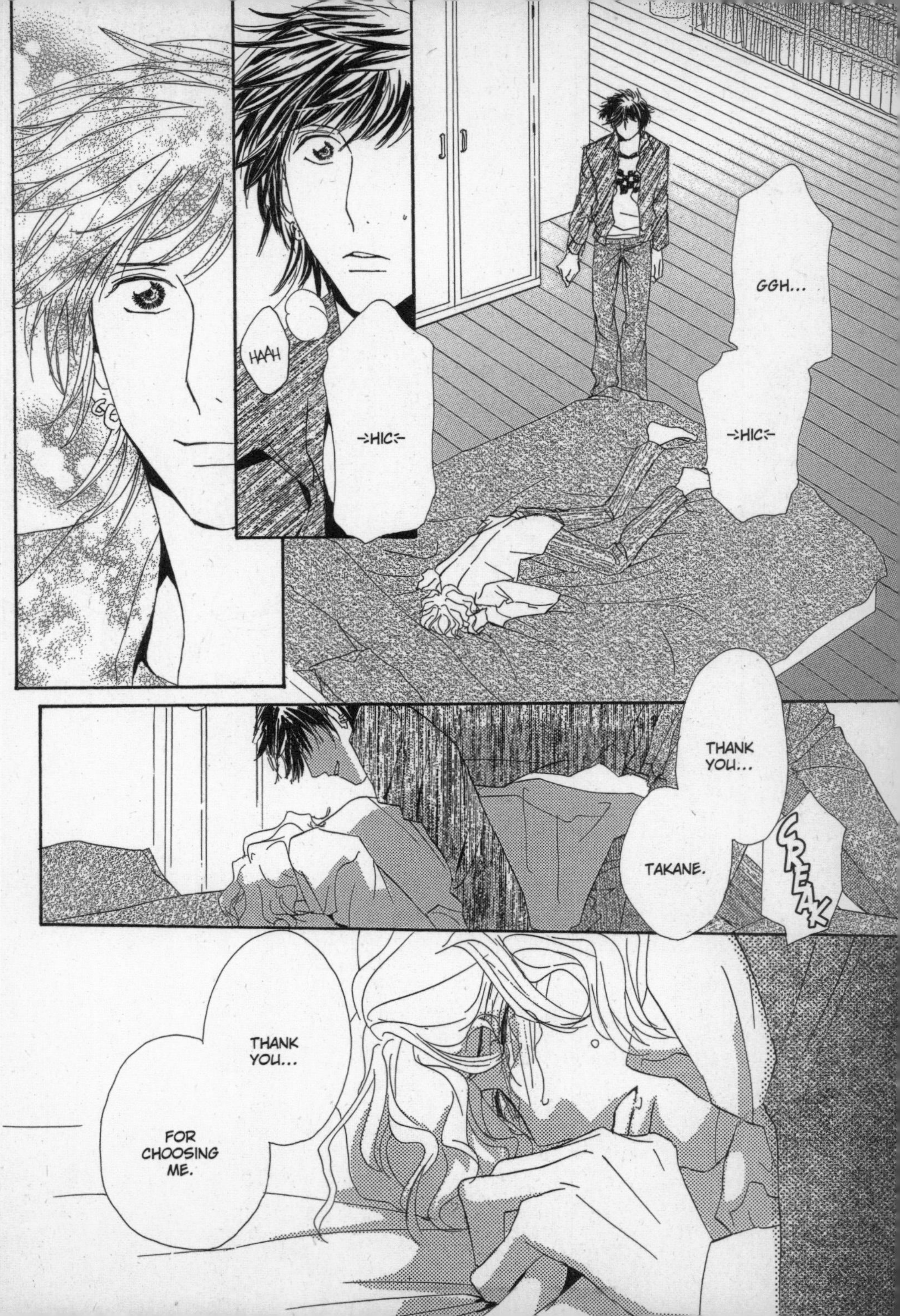
GGH...
HIC
HAAH
HIC
THANK YOU...
TAKANE.
CREAK
THANK YOU...
FOR CHOOSING ME.

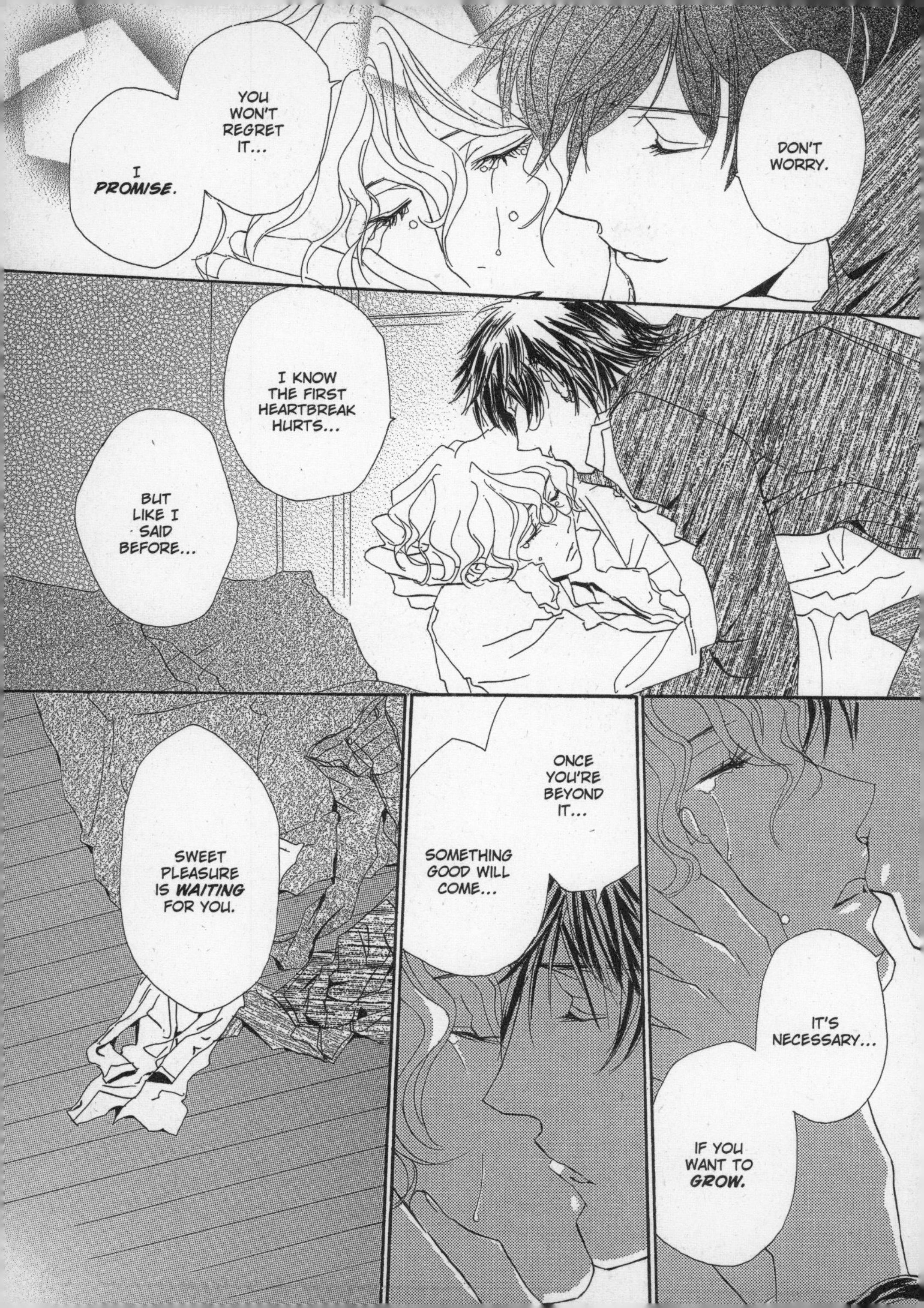
DON'T WORRY.
YOU WON'T REGRET IT...
I **PROMISE**.
I KNOW THE FIRST HEARTBREAK HURTS...
BUT LIKE I SAID BEFORE...
IT'S NECESSARY...
IF YOU WANT TO **GROW**.
ONCE YOU'RE BEYOND IT...
SOMETHING GOOD WILL COME...
SWEET PLEASURE IS **WAITING** FOR YOU.

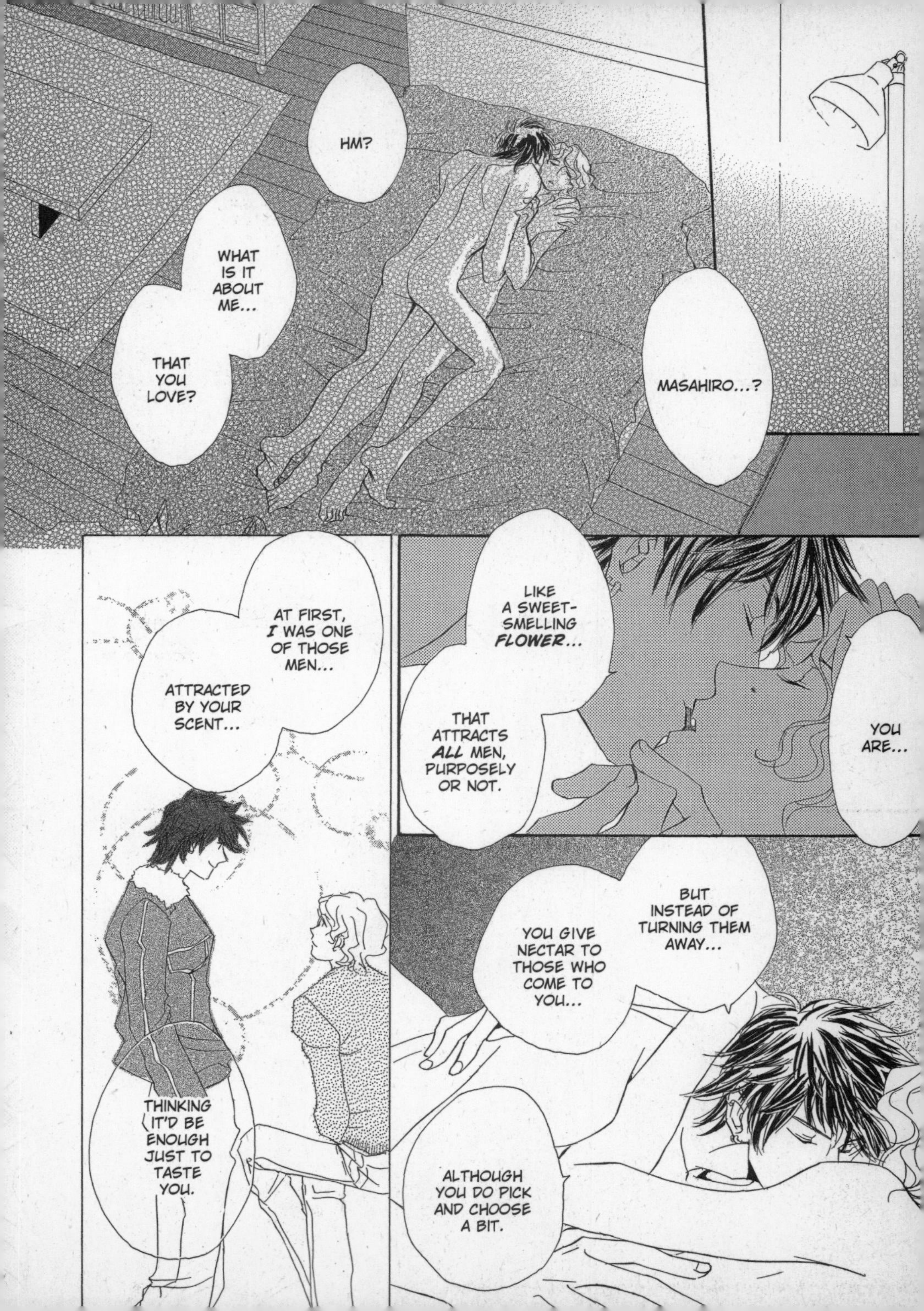
MASAHIRO...?
HM?
WHAT IS IT ABOUT ME...
THAT YOU LOVE?
YOU ARE...
LIKE A SWEET-SMELLING *FLOWER*...
THAT ATTRACTS *ALL* MEN, PURPOSELY OR NOT.
BUT INSTEAD OF TURNING THEM AWAY...
YOU GIVE NECTAR TO THOSE WHO COME TO YOU...
ALTHOUGH YOU DO PICK AND CHOOSE A BIT.
AT FIRST, *I* WAS ONE OF THOSE MEN...
ATTRACTED BY YOUR SCENT...
THINKING IT'D BE ENOUGH JUST TO TASTE YOU.

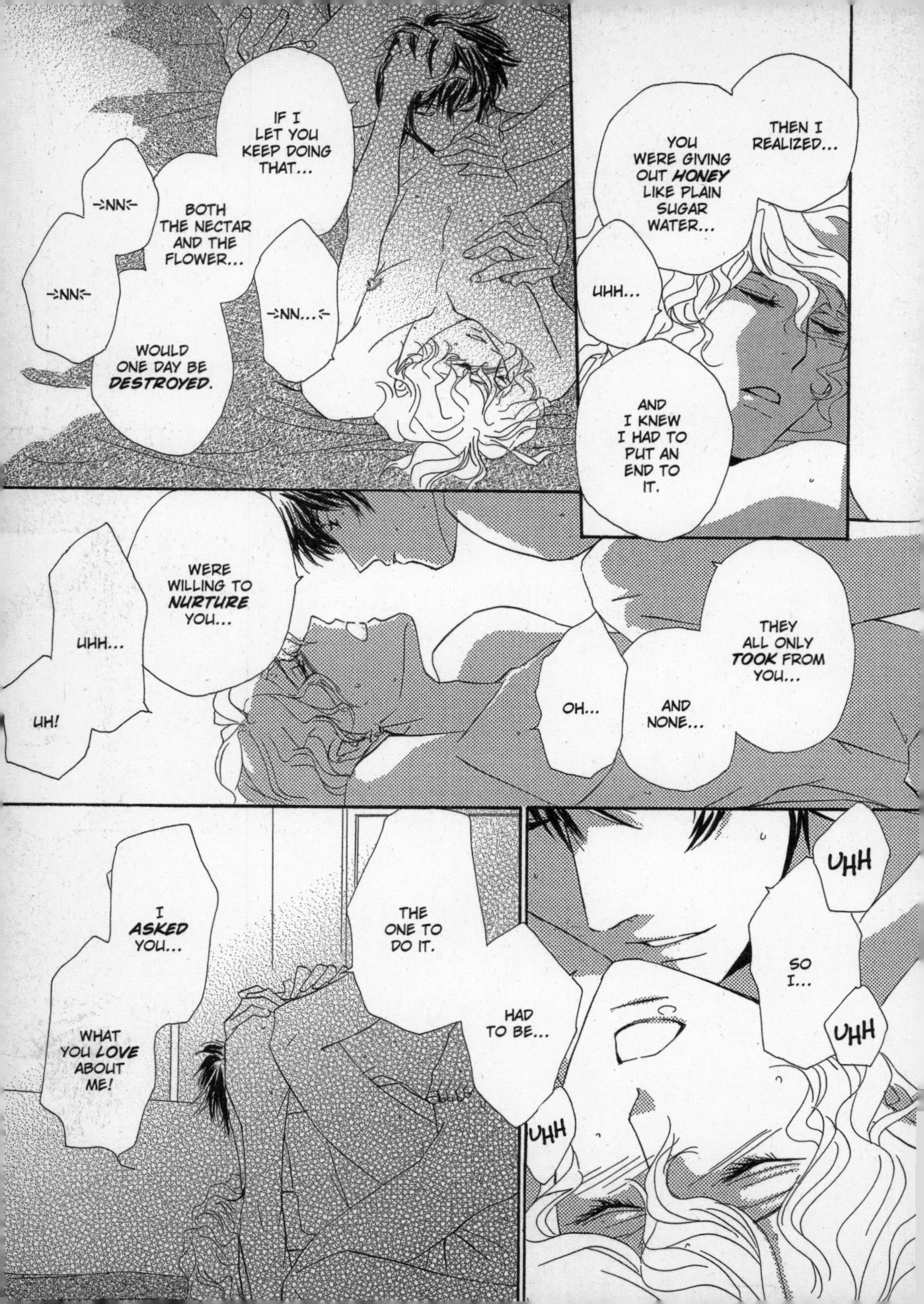

THEN I REALIZED...
YOU WERE GIVING OUT **HONEY** LIKE PLAIN SUGAR WATER...
UHH...
AND I KNEW I HAD TO PUT AN END TO IT.
IF I LET YOU KEEP DOING THAT...
~NN...~
BOTH THE NECTAR AND THE FLOWER...
~NN~
~NN~
WOULD ONE DAY BE **DESTROYED**.
THEY ALL ONLY **TOOK** FROM YOU...
AND NONE...
OH...
WERE WILLING TO **NURTURE** YOU...
UHH...
UH!
UHH
SO I...
UHH
UHH
HAD TO BE...
THE ONE TO DO IT.
I **ASKED** YOU...
WHAT YOU **LOVE** ABOUT ME!

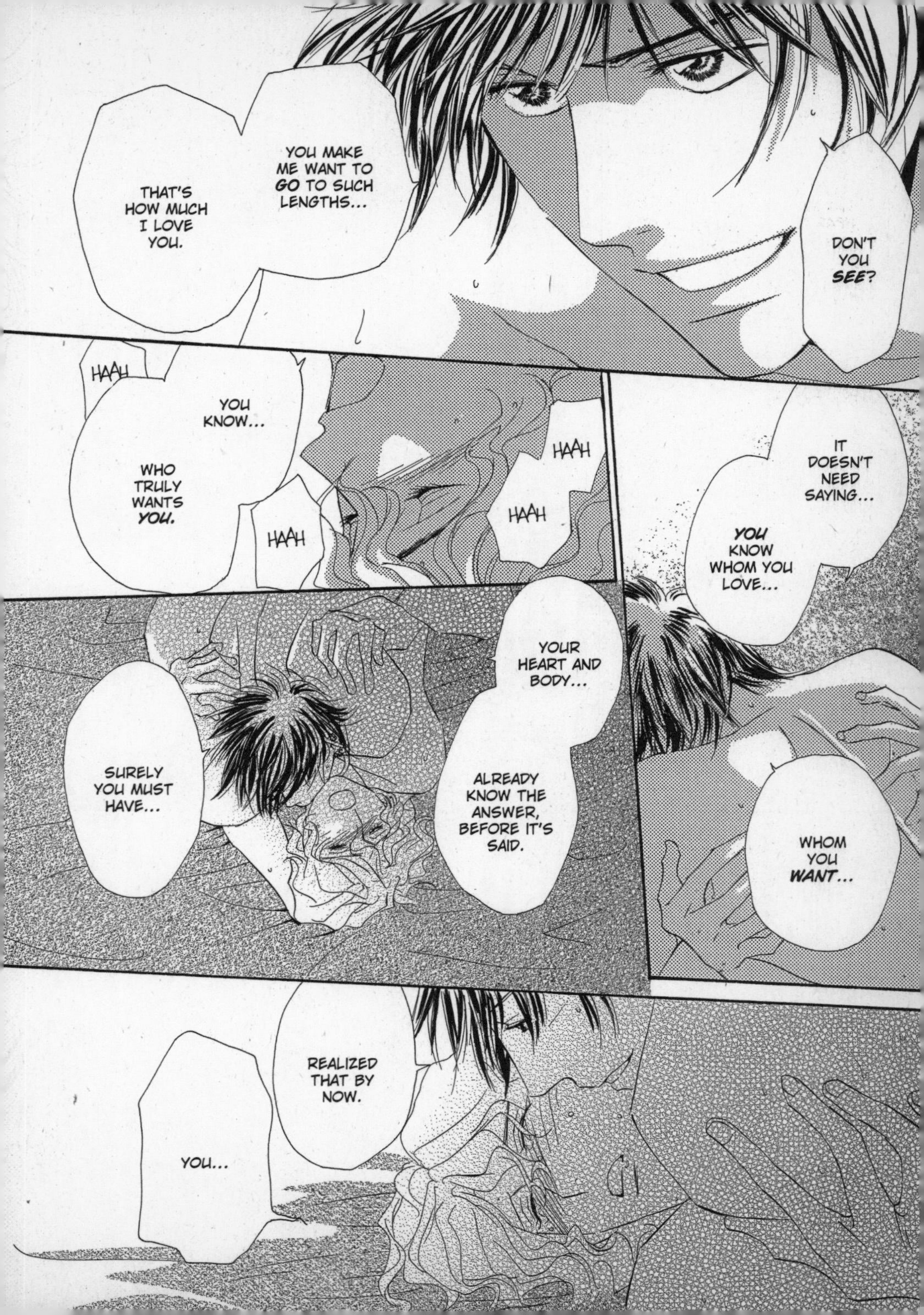
DON'T YOU SEE?
YOU MAKE ME WANT TO GO TO SUCH LENGTHS...
THAT'S HOW MUCH I LOVE YOU.
IT DOESN'T NEED SAYING...
YOU KNOW WHOM YOU LOVE...
WHOM YOU WANT...
HAAH
HAAH
YOU KNOW...
WHO TRULY WANTS YOU.
HAAH
HAAH
YOUR HEART AND BODY...
ALREADY KNOW THE ANSWER, BEFORE IT'S SAID.
SURELY YOU MUST HAVE...
REALIZED THAT BY NOW.
YOU...

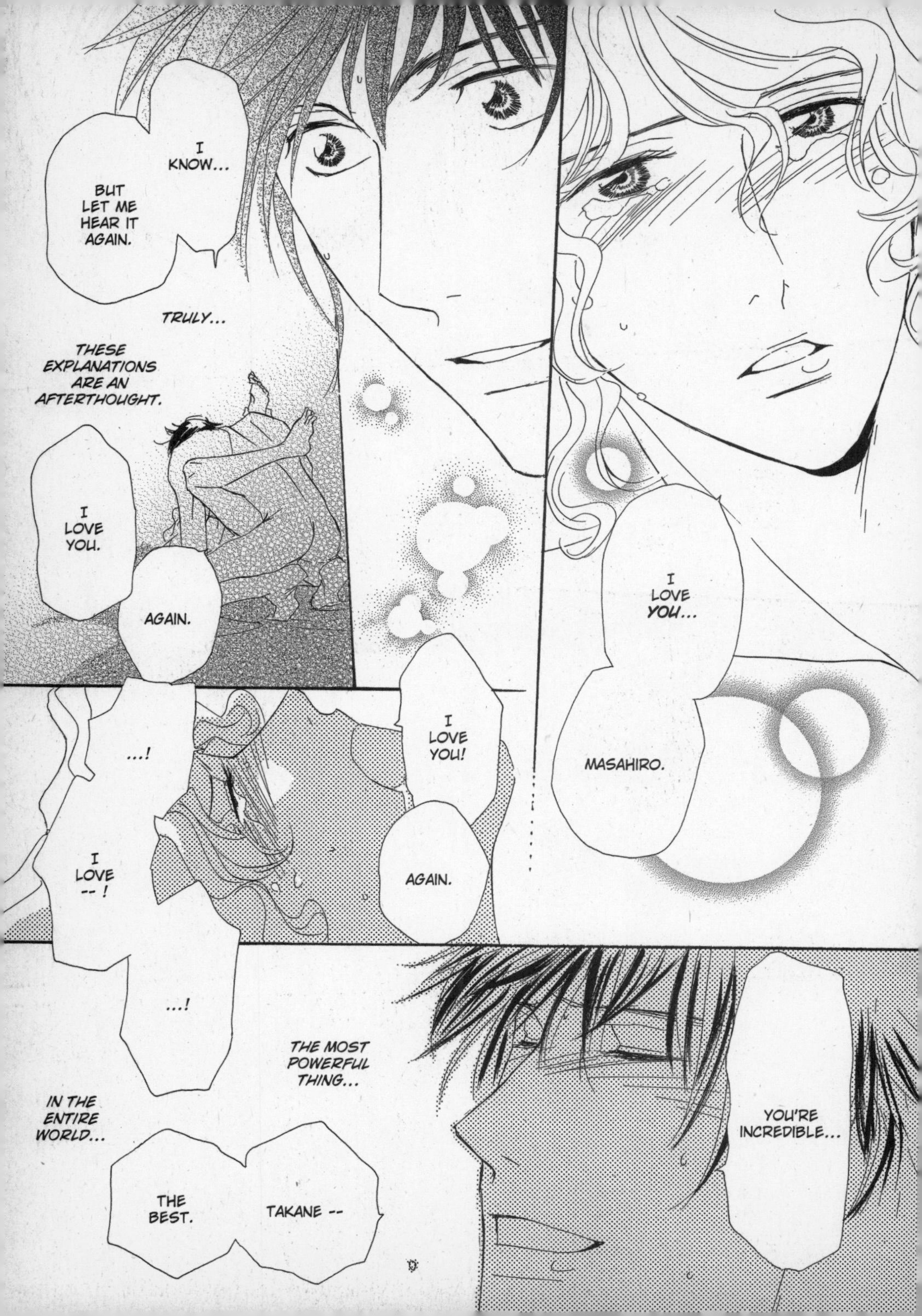
I LOVE YOU...
MASAHIRO.
I KNOW...
BUT LET ME HEAR IT AGAIN.
TRULY...
THESE EXPLANATIONS ARE AN AFTERTHOUGHT.
I LOVE YOU.
AGAIN.
I LOVE YOU!
AGAIN.
...!
I LOVE --!
YOU'RE INCREDIBLE...
TAKANE --
THE BEST.
...!
THE MOST POWERFUL THING...
IN THE ENTIRE WORLD...

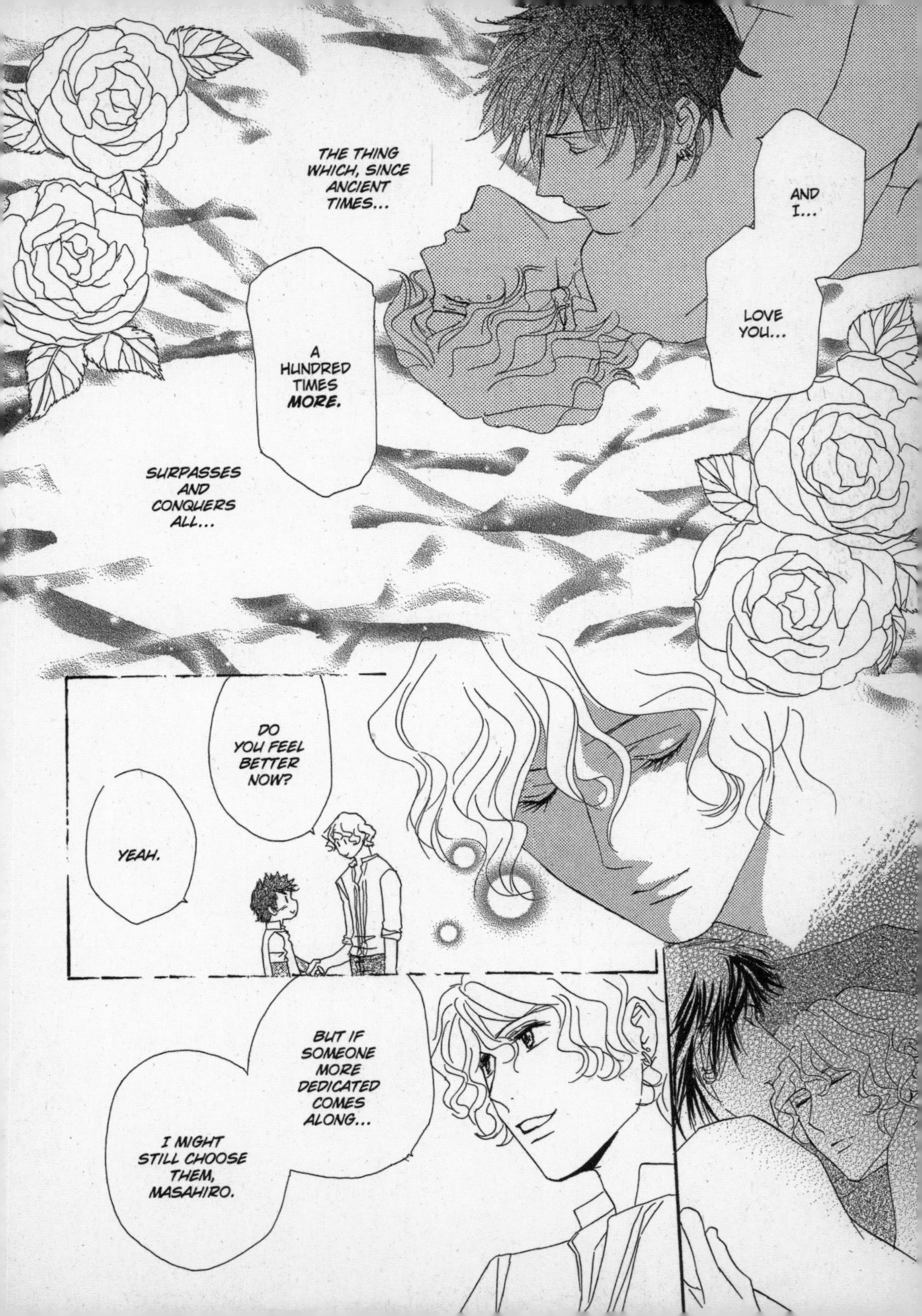

AND I...
LOVE YOU...
THE THING WHICH, SINCE ANCIENT TIMES...
A HUNDRED TIMES MORE.
SURPASSES AND CONQUERS ALL...
DO YOU FEEL BETTER NOW?
YEAH.
BUT IF SOMEONE MORE DEDICATED COMES ALONG...
I MIGHT STILL CHOOSE THEM, MASAHIRO.

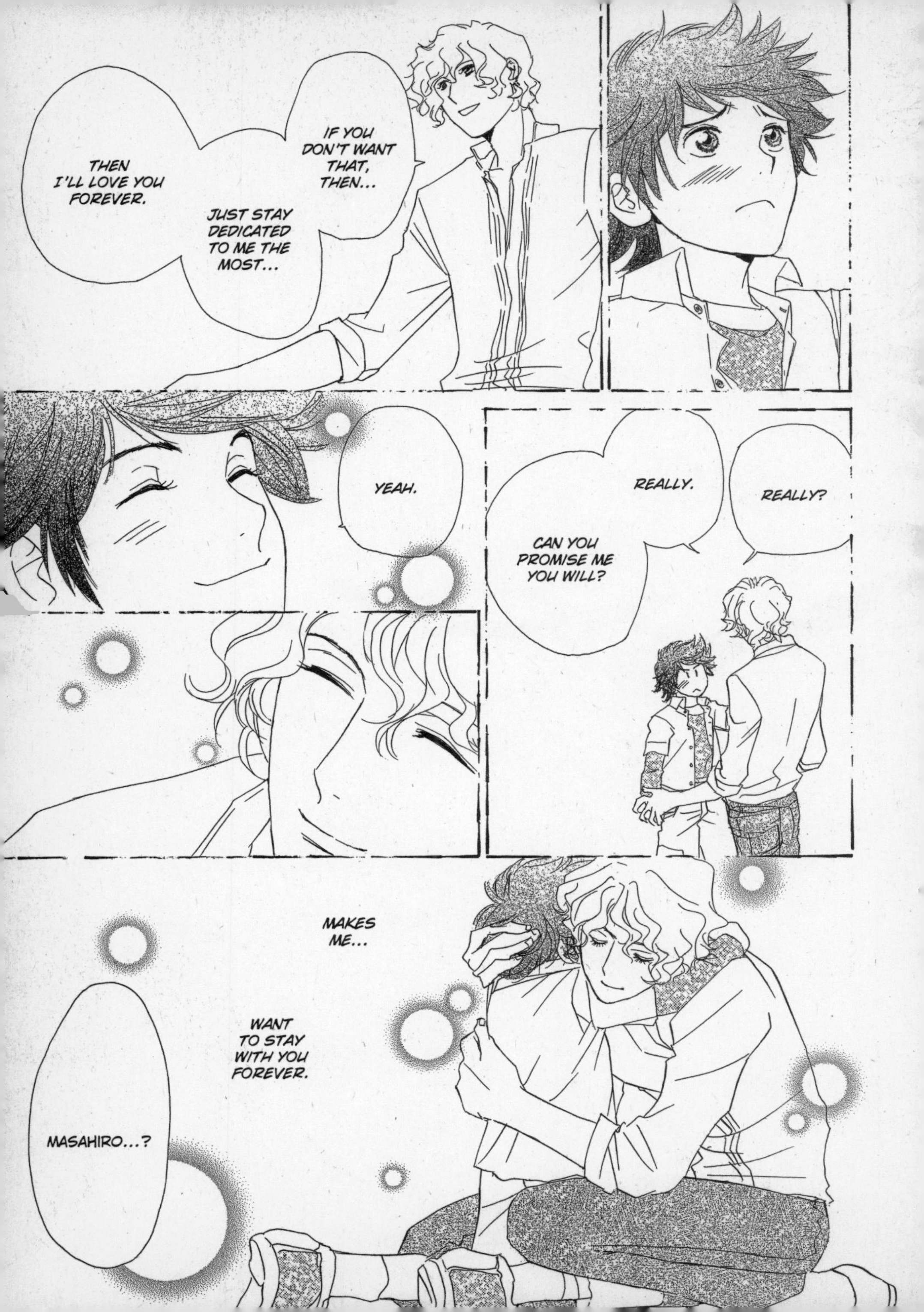
IF YOU DON'T WANT THAT, THEN...
JUST STAY DEDICATED TO ME THE MOST...
THEN I'LL LOVE YOU FOREVER.
REALLY?
REALLY.
CAN YOU PROMISE ME YOU WILL?
YEAH.
MAKES ME...
WANT TO STAY WITH YOU FOREVER.
MASAHIRO...?

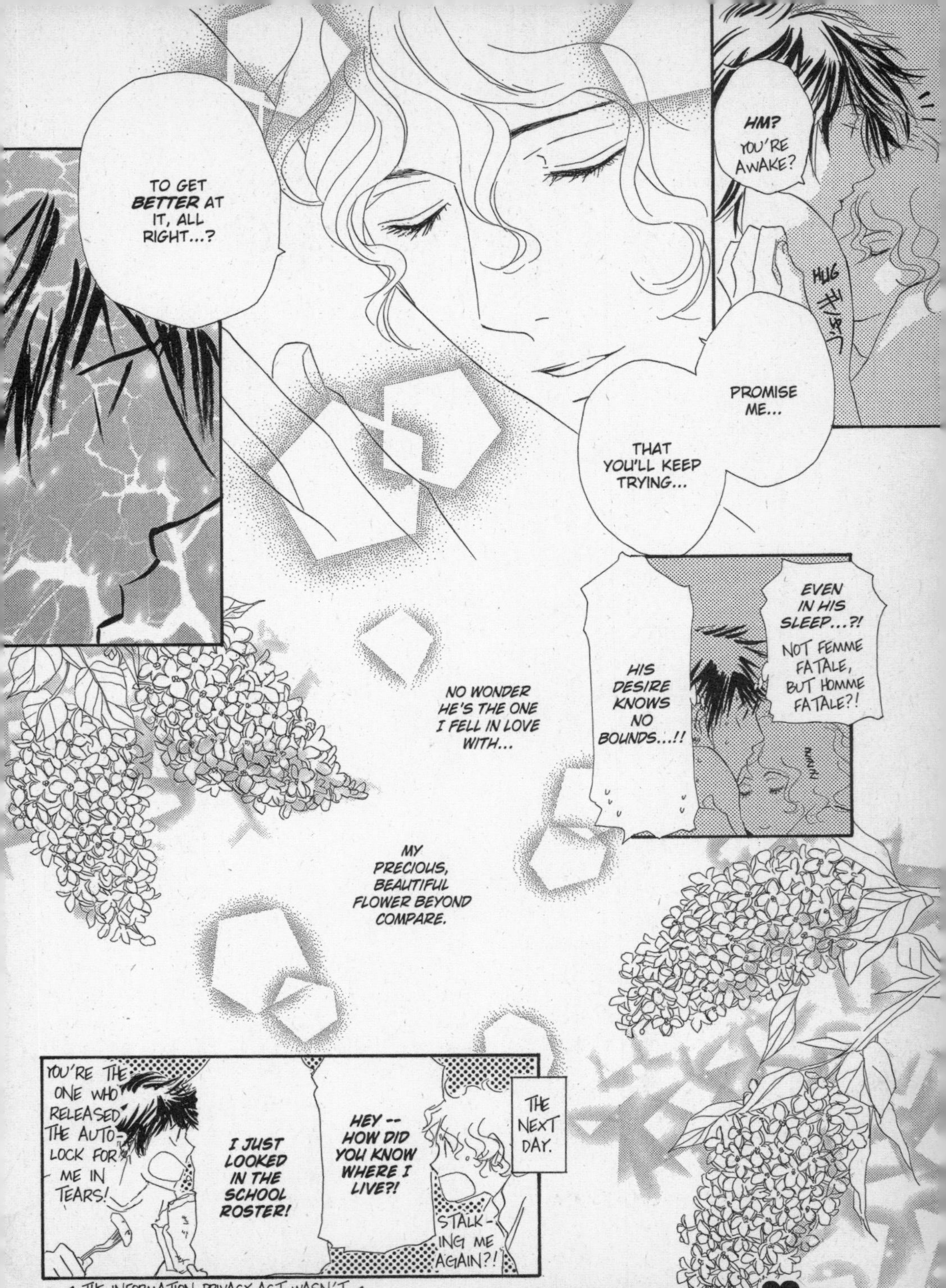
HM?
YOU'RE AWAKE?
HUG
PROMISE ME...
THAT YOU'LL KEEP TRYING...
TO GET BETTER AT IT, ALL RIGHT...?
EVEN IN HIS SLEEP...?!
NOT FEMME FATALE, BUT HOMME FATALE?!
HIS DESIRE KNOWS NO BOUNDS...!!
NO WONDER HE'S THE ONE I FELL IN LOVE WITH...
MY PRECIOUS, BEAUTIFUL FLOWER BEYOND COMPARE.
THE NEXT DAY.
HEY -- HOW DID YOU KNOW WHERE I LIVE?!
STALKING ME AGAIN?!
I JUST LOOKED IN THE SCHOOL ROSTER!
YOU'RE THE ONE WHO RELEASED THE AUTO-LOCK FOR ME IN TEARS!

☆ THE INFORMATION PRIVACY ACT WASN'T ENFORCED YET WHEN THEY WERE ENROLLED ☆

THE DAWN OF LOVE 4 END

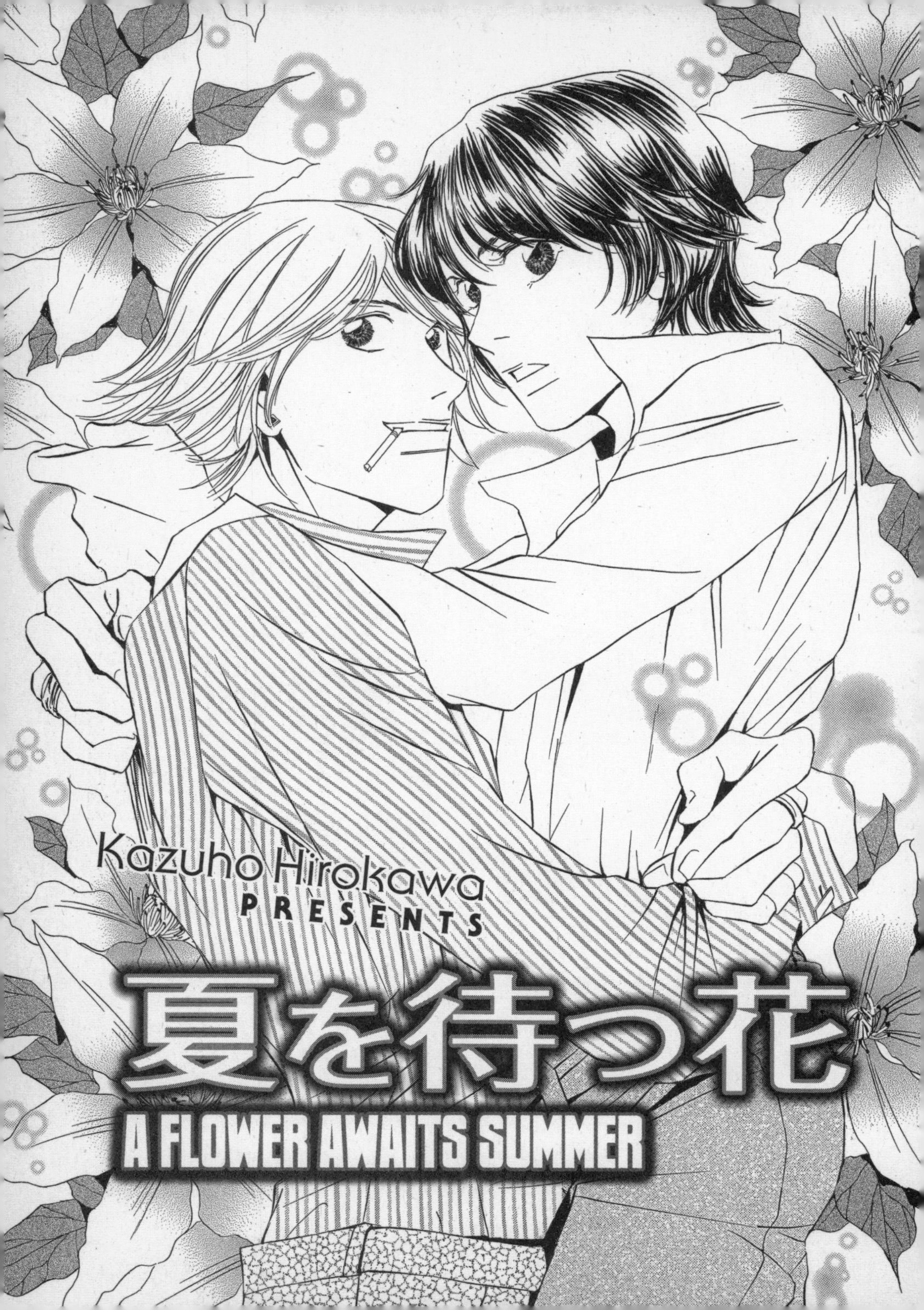
Kazuho Hirokawa
PRESENTS
夏を待つ花
A FLOWER AWAITS SUMMER

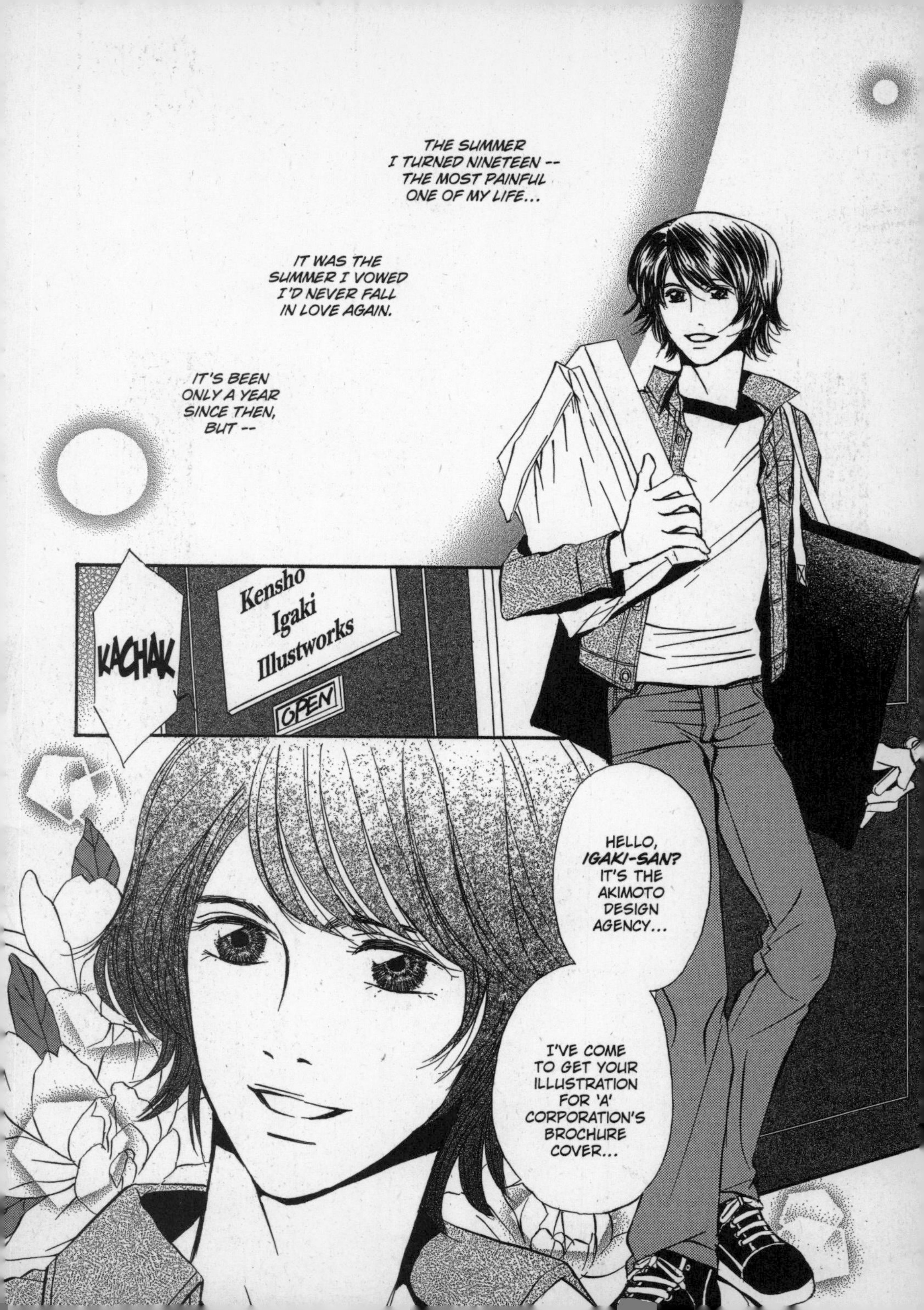
THE SUMMER I TURNED NINETEEN -- THE MOST PAINFUL ONE OF MY LIFE...
IT WAS THE SUMMER I VOWED I'D NEVER FALL IN LOVE AGAIN.
IT'S BEEN ONLY A YEAR SINCE THEN, BUT --
Kensho Igaki Illustworks
OPEN
KACHAK
HELLO, IGAKI-SAN? IT'S THE AKIMOTO DESIGN AGENCY...
I'VE COME TO GET YOUR ILLUSTRATION FOR 'A' CORPORATION'S BROCHURE COVER...

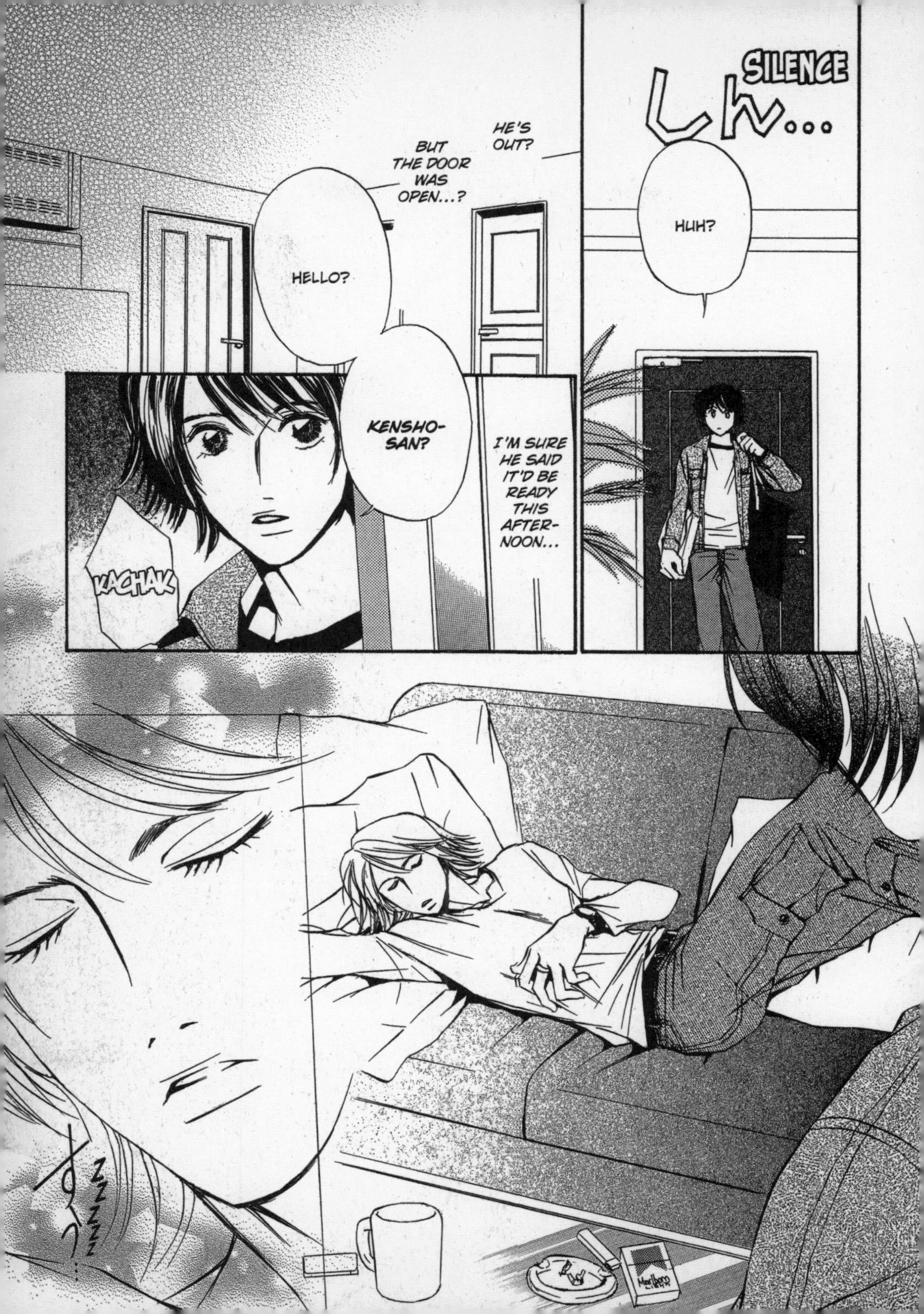
SILENCE
しん...
HUH?
HE'S OUT?
BUT THE DOOR WAS OPEN...?
HELLO?
KENSHO-SAN?
I'M SURE HE SAID IT'D BE READY THIS AFTERNOON...
KACHAK
ZZZZZ...

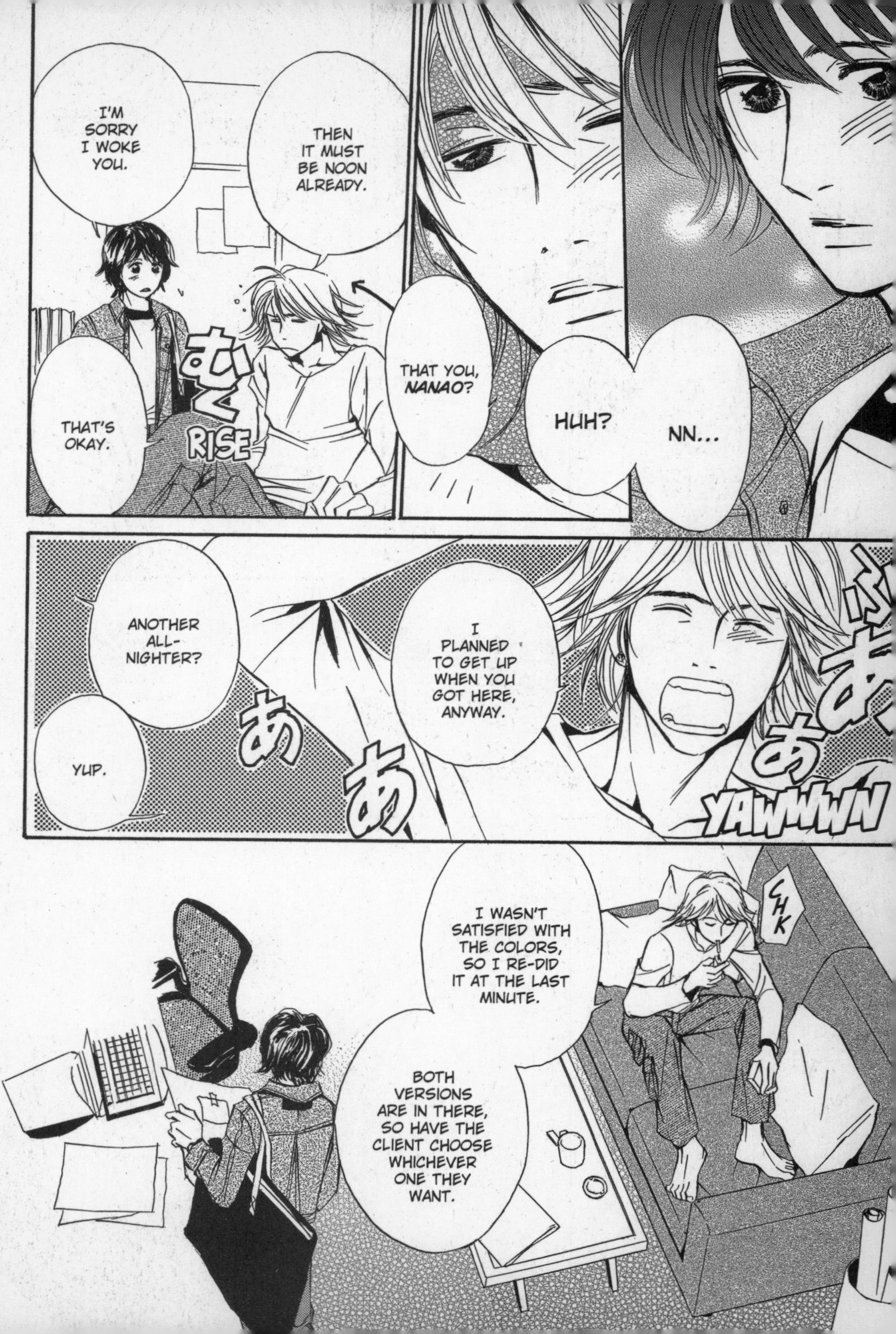
NN...
HUH?
THAT YOU, NANAO?
THEN IT MUST BE NOON ALREADY.
I'M SORRY I WOKE YOU.
むく
RISE
THAT'S OKAY.
ふああ
YAWWWN
I PLANNED TO GET UP WHEN YOU GOT HERE, ANYWAY.
ああ
ANOTHER ALL-NIGHTER?
YUP.
CHK
I WASN'T SATISFIED WITH THE COLORS, SO I RE-DID IT AT THE LAST MINUTE.
BOTH VERSIONS ARE IN THERE, SO HAVE THE CLIENT CHOOSE WHICHEVER ONE THEY WANT.

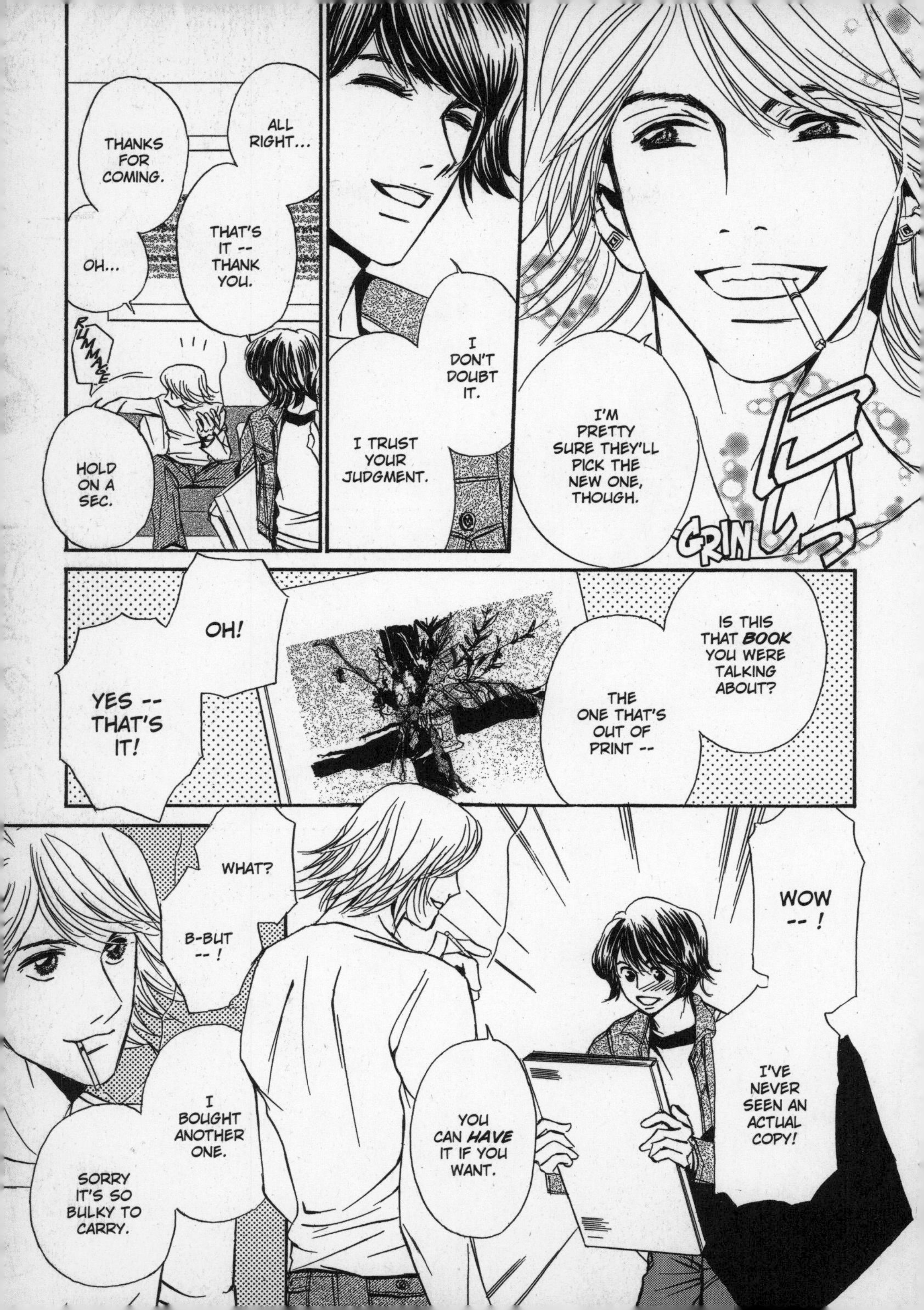
I'M PRETTY SURE THEY'LL PICK THE NEW ONE, THOUGH.
GRIN
I DON'T DOUBT IT.
I TRUST YOUR JUDGMENT.
ALL RIGHT...
THANKS FOR COMING.
THAT'S IT -- THANK YOU.
OH...
RUMMAGE
HOLD ON A SEC.
IS THIS THAT BOOK YOU WERE TALKING ABOUT?
THE ONE THAT'S OUT OF PRINT --
OH!
YES -- THAT'S IT!
WOW -- !
I'VE NEVER SEEN AN ACTUAL COPY!
YOU CAN HAVE IT IF YOU WANT.
WHAT?
B-BUT -- !
I BOUGHT ANOTHER ONE.
SORRY IT'S SO BULKY TO CARRY.

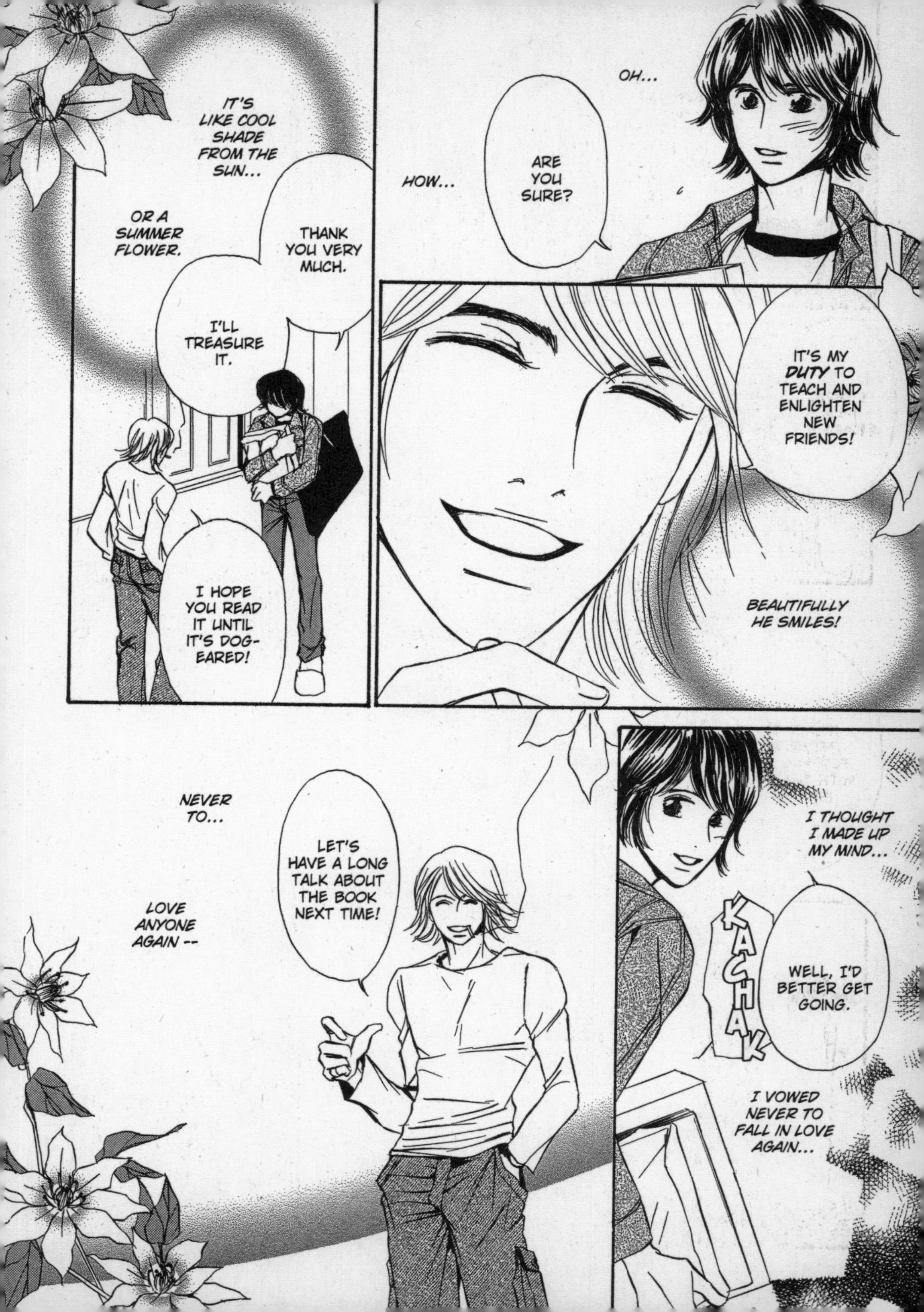
OH...
ARE YOU SURE?
HOW...
IT'S MY DUTY TO TEACH AND ENLIGHTEN NEW FRIENDS!
BEAUTIFULLY HE SMILES!
IT'S LIKE COOL SHADE FROM THE SUN...
THANK YOU VERY MUCH.
OR A SUMMER FLOWER.
I'LL TREASURE IT.
I HOPE YOU READ IT UNTIL IT'S DOG-EARED!
I THOUGHT I MADE UP MY MIND...
KACHAK
WELL, I'D BETTER GET GOING.
I VOWED NEVER TO FALL IN LOVE AGAIN...
LET'S HAVE A LONG TALK ABOUT THE BOOK NEXT TIME!
NEVER TO...
LOVE ANYONE AGAIN --

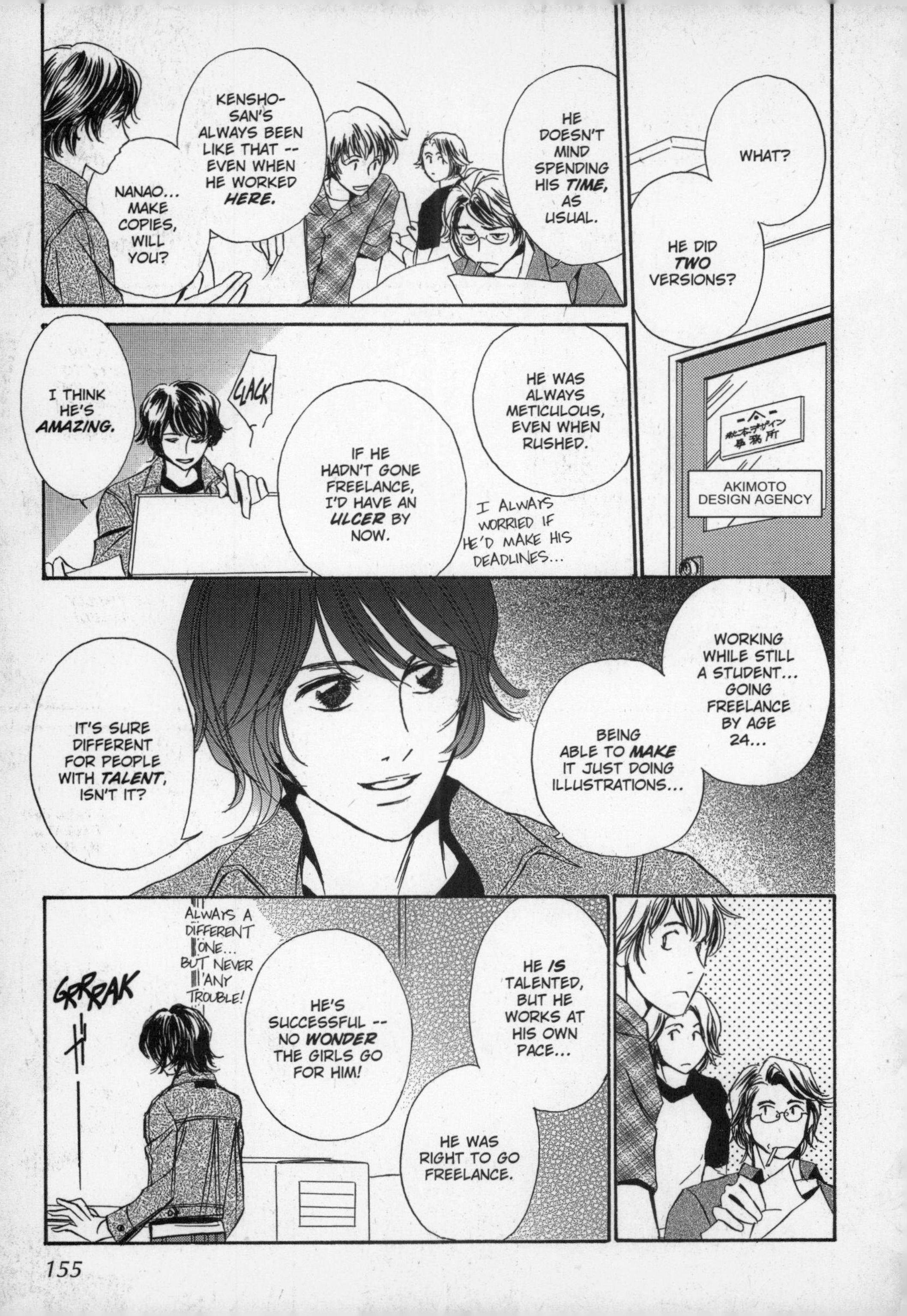
WHAT?
HE DID *TWO* VERSIONS?
HE DOESN'T MIND SPENDING HIS *TIME,* AS USUAL.
KENSHO-SAN'S ALWAYS BEEN LIKE THAT -- EVEN WHEN HE WORKED *HERE.*
NANAO... MAKE COPIES, WILL YOU?
AKIMOTO DESIGN AGENCY
HE WAS ALWAYS METICULOUS, EVEN WHEN RUSHED.
IF HE HADN'T GONE FREELANCE, I'D HAVE AN *ULCER* BY NOW.
I ALWAYS WORRIED IF HE'D MAKE HIS DEADLINES...
CLACK
I THINK HE'S *AMAZING.*
WORKING WHILE STILL A STUDENT... GOING FREELANCE BY AGE 24...
BEING ABLE TO *MAKE* IT JUST DOING ILLUSTRATIONS...
IT'S SURE DIFFERENT FOR PEOPLE WITH *TALENT*, ISN'T IT?
HE *IS* TALENTED, BUT HE WORKS AT HIS OWN PACE...
HE WAS RIGHT TO GO FREELANCE.
HE'S SUCCESSFUL -- NO *WONDER* THE GIRLS GO FOR HIM!
ALWAYS A DIFFERENT ONE... BUT NEVER ANY TROUBLE!
GRRRAK

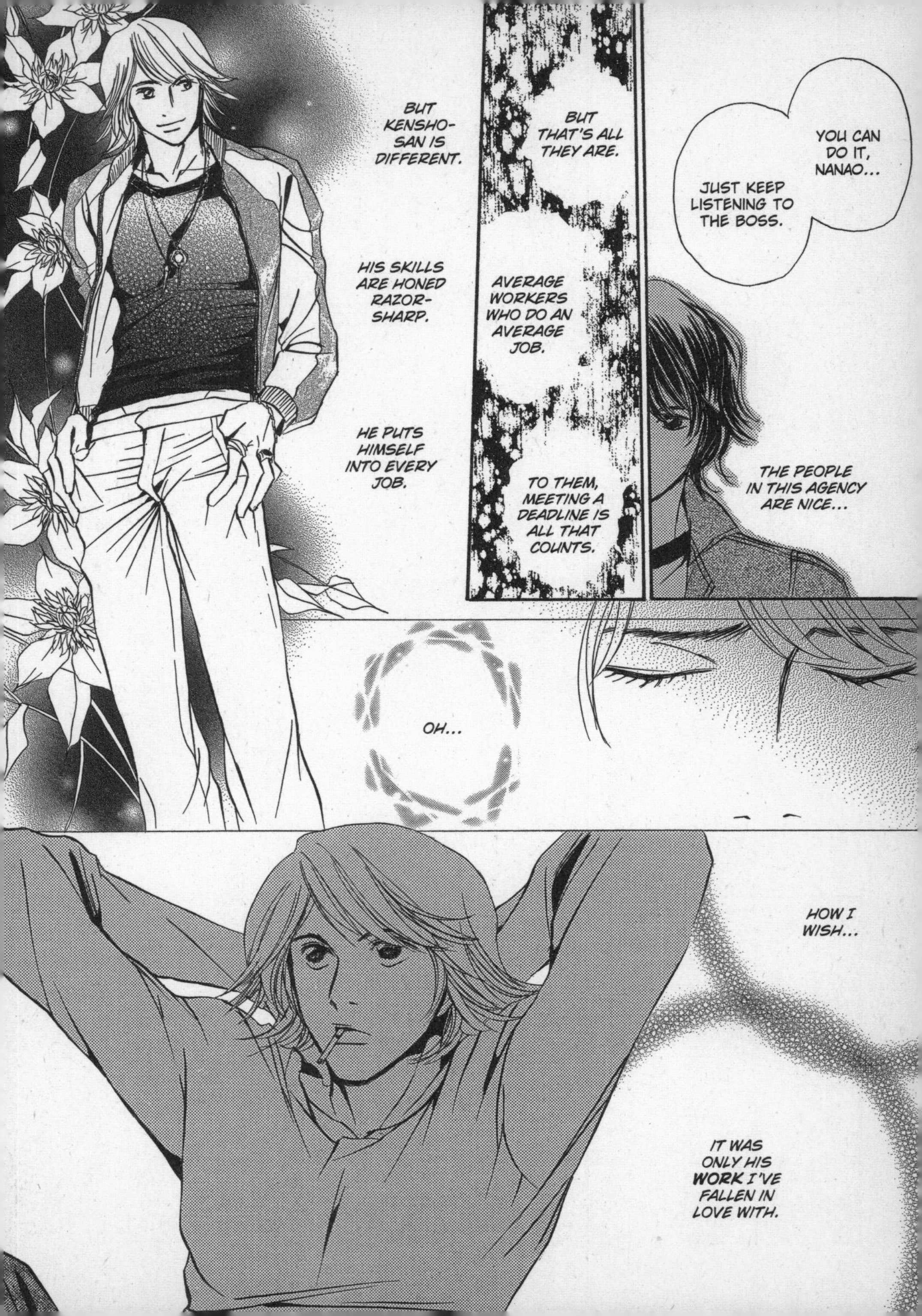
YOU CAN DO IT, NANAO...
JUST KEEP LISTENING TO THE BOSS.
THE PEOPLE IN THIS AGENCY ARE NICE...
BUT THAT'S ALL THEY ARE.
AVERAGE WORKERS WHO DO AN AVERAGE JOB.
TO THEM, MEETING A DEADLINE IS ALL THAT COUNTS.
OH...
BUT KENSHO-SAN IS DIFFERENT.
HIS SKILLS ARE HONED RAZOR-SHARP.
HE PUTS HIMSELF INTO EVERY JOB.
HOW I WISH...
IT WAS ONLY HIS **WORK** I'VE FALLEN IN LOVE WITH.

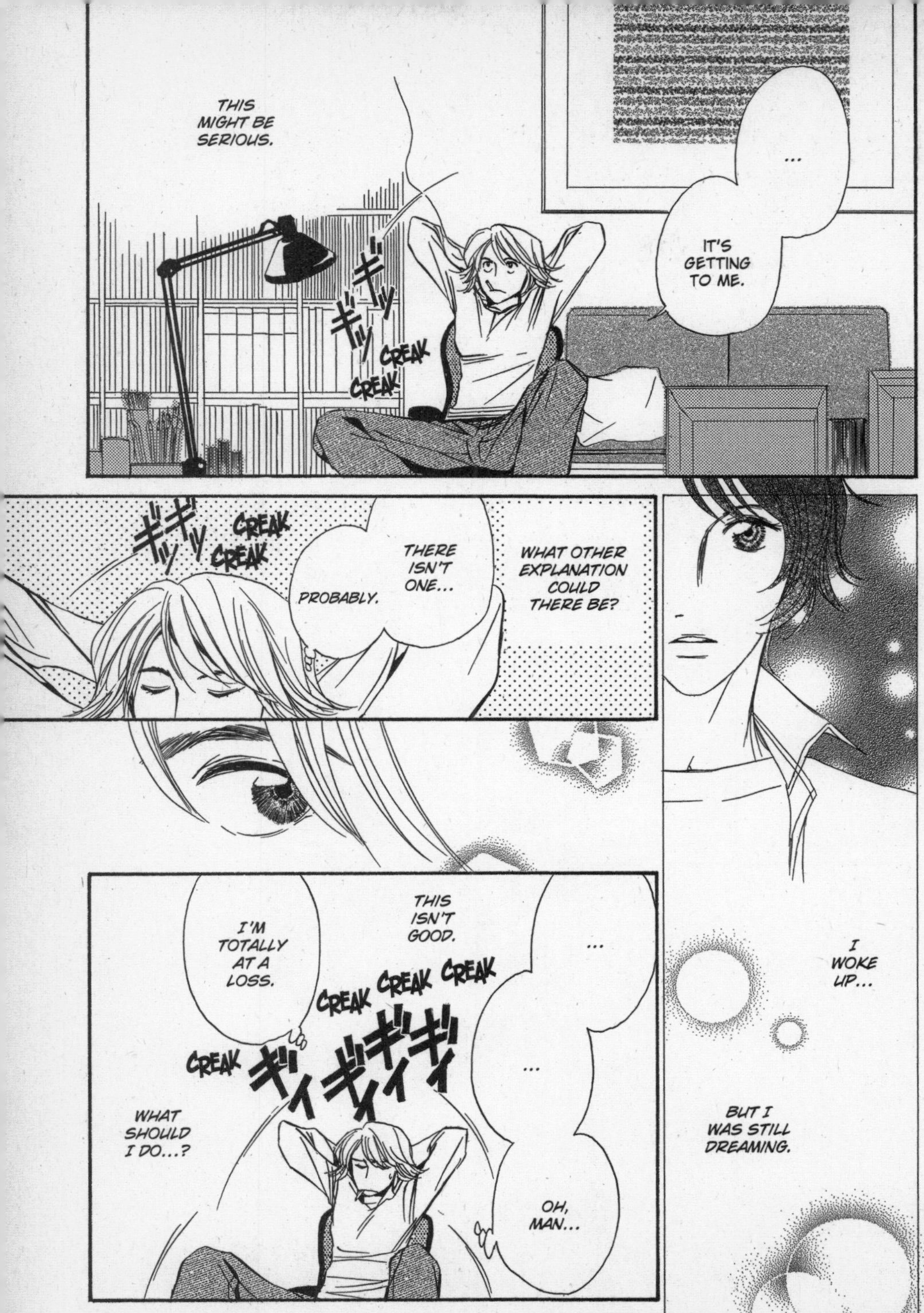
...
IT'S GETTING TO ME.
ギッ ギッ
CREAK
CREAK
THIS MIGHT BE SERIOUS.
I WOKE UP...
BUT I WAS STILL DREAMING.
WHAT OTHER EXPLANATION COULD THERE BE?
THERE ISN'T ONE...
PROBABLY.
CREAK
CREAK
ギッ ギッ
...
...
OH, MAN...
THIS ISN'T GOOD.
I'M TOTALLY AT A LOSS.
CREAK CREAK CREAK
CREAK
WHAT SHOULD I DO...?

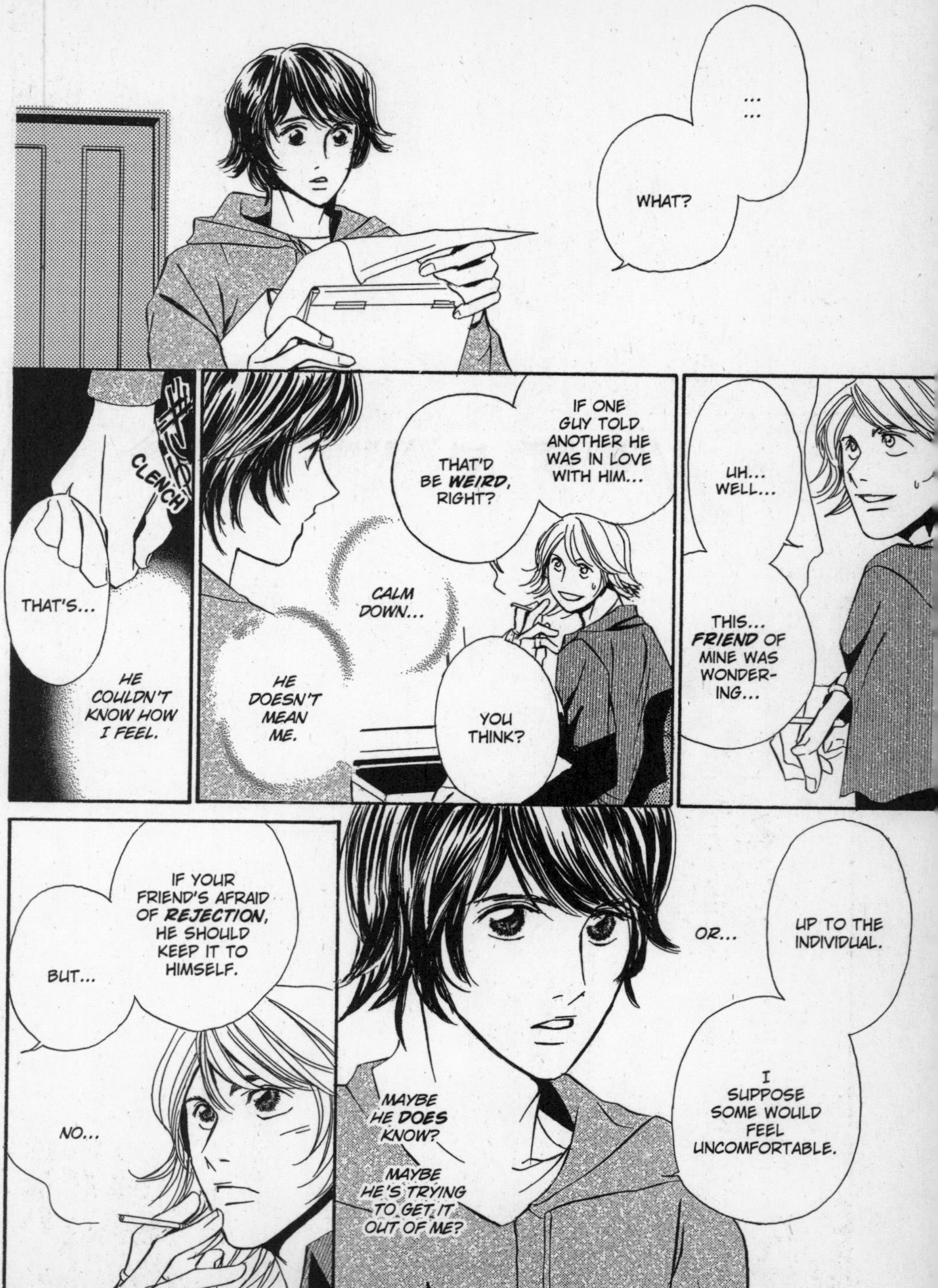
...
...
WHAT?
UH... WELL...
THIS... *FRIEND* OF MINE WAS WONDER-ING...
IF ONE GUY TOLD ANOTHER HE WAS IN LOVE WITH HIM...
THAT'D BE *WEIRD*, RIGHT?
CALM DOWN...
HE DOESN'T MEAN ME.
YOU THINK?
CLENCH
THAT'S...
HE COULDN'T KNOW HOW I FEEL.
I SUPPOSE SOME WOULD FEEL UNCOMFORTABLE.
OR...
UP TO THE INDIVIDUAL.
MAYBE HE *DOES* KNOW?
MAYBE HE'S TRYING TO GET IT OUT OF ME?
IF YOUR FRIEND'S AFRAID OF *REJECTION*, HE SHOULD KEEP IT TO HIMSELF.
BUT...
NO...

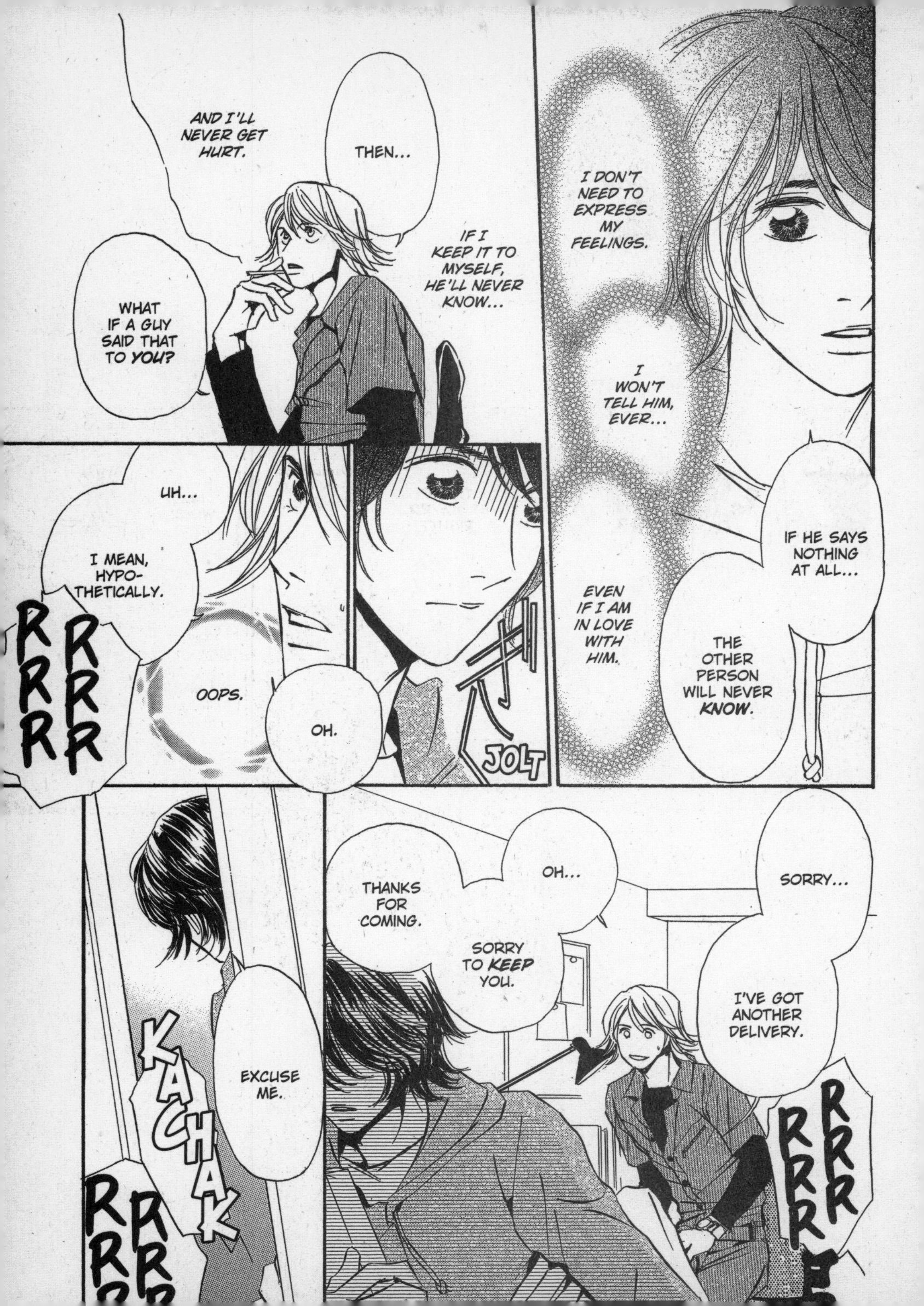
I DON'T NEED TO EXPRESS MY FEELINGS.
I WON'T TELL HIM, EVER...
IF HE SAYS NOTHING AT ALL...
THE OTHER PERSON WILL NEVER KNOW.
EVEN IF I AM IN LOVE WITH HIM.
THEN...
IF I KEEP IT TO MYSELF, HE'LL NEVER KNOW...
AND I'LL NEVER GET HURT.
WHAT IF A GUY SAID THAT TO YOU?
JOLT
UH...
I MEAN, HYPOTHETICALLY.
OH.
OOPS.
RRRR RRR
SORRY...
I'VE GOT ANOTHER DELIVERY.
OH...
THANKS FOR COMING.
SORRY TO KEEP YOU.
RRRRR RRR
EXCUSE ME.
KACHAK
RRRR

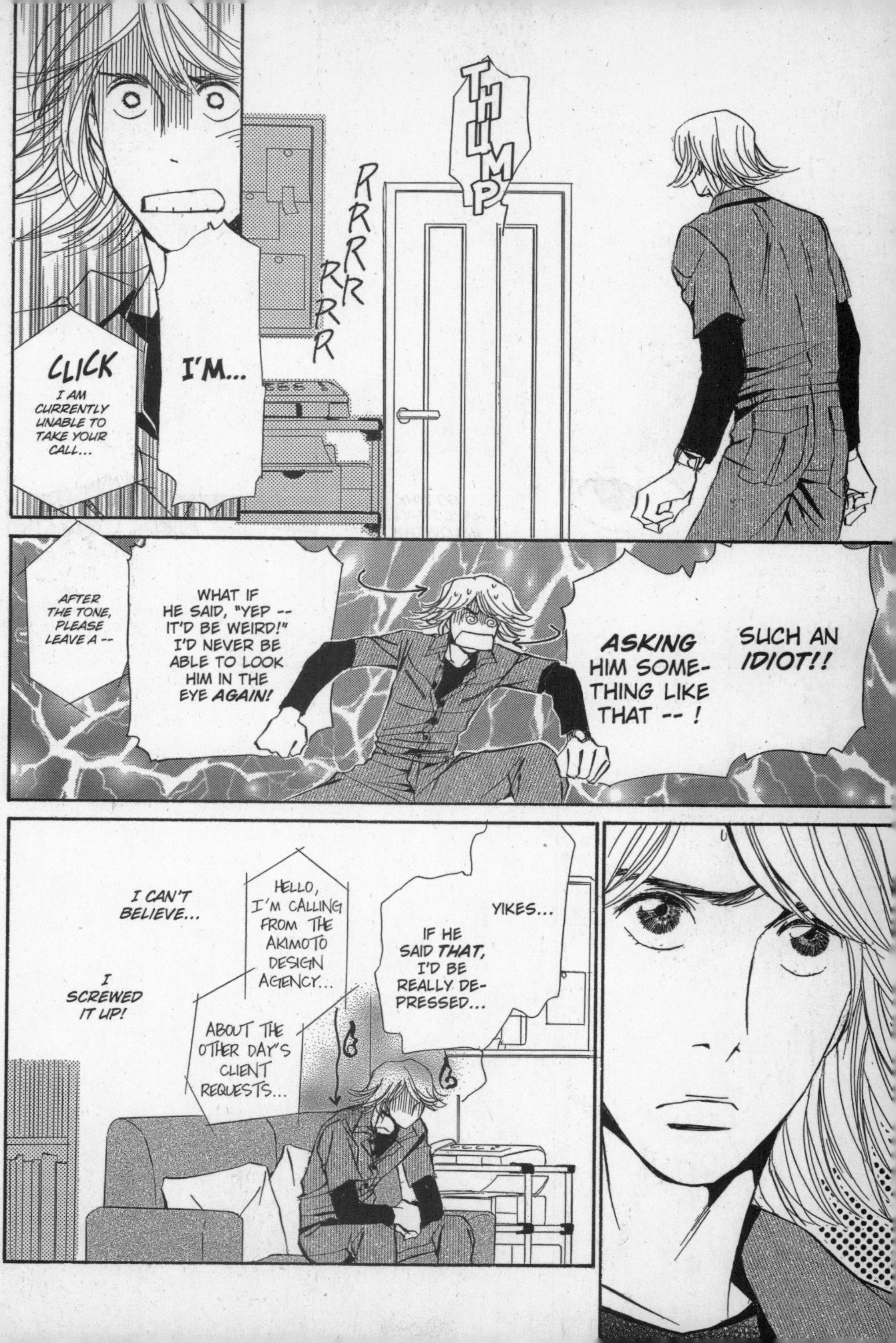
THUMP
RRRRRRR
I'M...
CLICK
I AM CURRENTLY UNABLE TO TAKE YOUR CALL...
SUCH AN IDIOT!!
ASKING HIM SOME-THING LIKE THAT -- !
WHAT IF HE SAID, "YEP -- IT'D BE WEIRD!" I'D NEVER BE ABLE TO LOOK HIM IN THE EYE AGAIN!
AFTER THE TONE, PLEASE LEAVE A --
YIKES...
IF HE SAID THAT, I'D BE REALLY DE-PRESSED...
HELLO, I'M CALLING FROM THE AKIMOTO DESIGN AGENCY...
I CAN'T BELIEVE...
ABOUT THE OTHER DAY'S CLIENT REQUESTS...
I SCREWED IT UP!

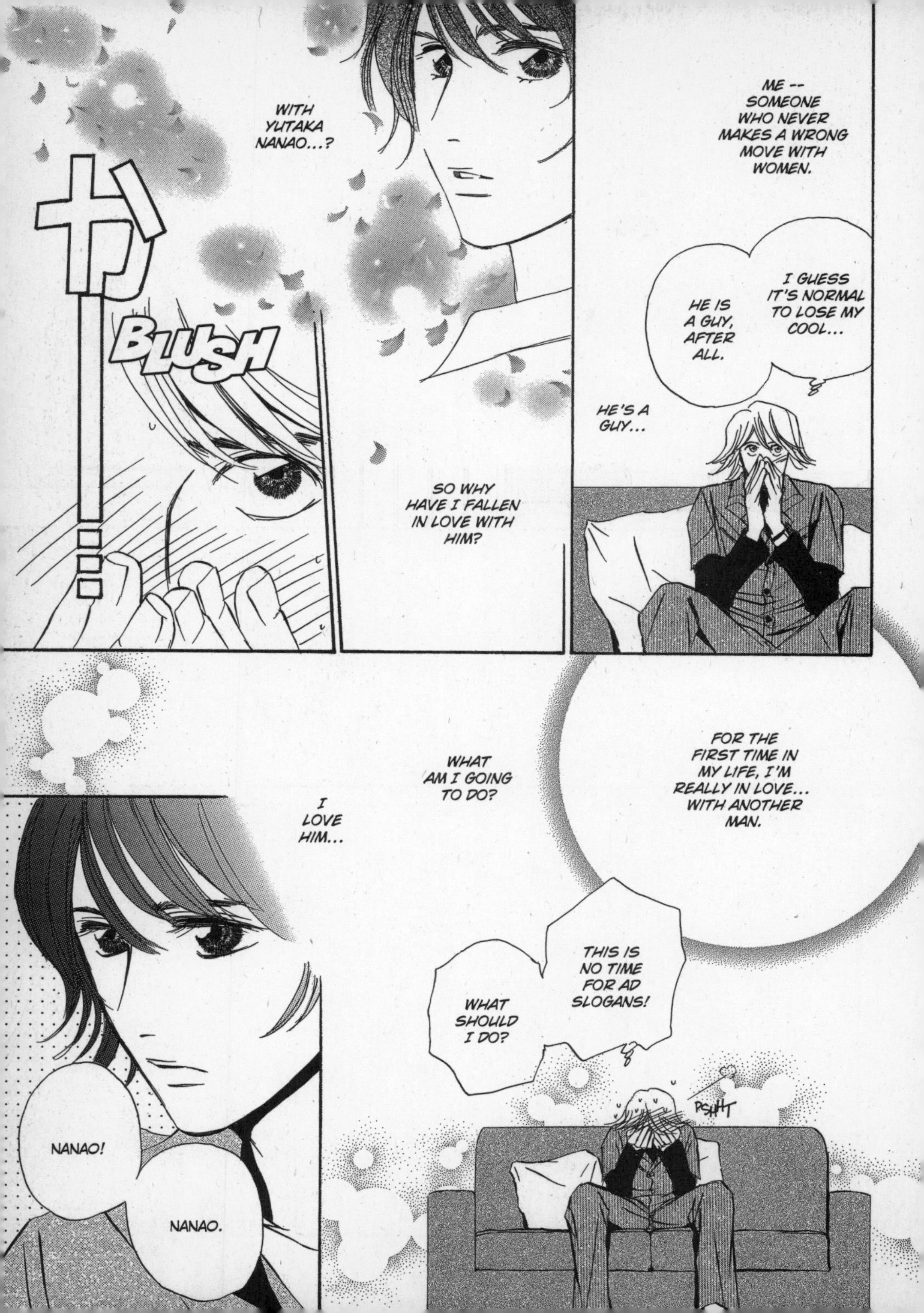
ME -- SOMEONE WHO NEVER MAKES A WRONG MOVE WITH WOMEN.
I GUESS IT'S NORMAL TO LOSE MY COOL...
HE IS A GUY, AFTER ALL.
HE'S A GUY...
SO WHY HAVE I FALLEN IN LOVE WITH HIM?
WITH YUTAKA NANAO...?
が
BLUSH
!...
FOR THE FIRST TIME IN MY LIFE, I'M REALLY IN LOVE... WITH ANOTHER MAN.
WHAT AM I GOING TO DO?
I LOVE HIM...
THIS IS NO TIME FOR AD SLOGANS!
WHAT SHOULD I DO?
PSHHT
NANAO!
NANAO.

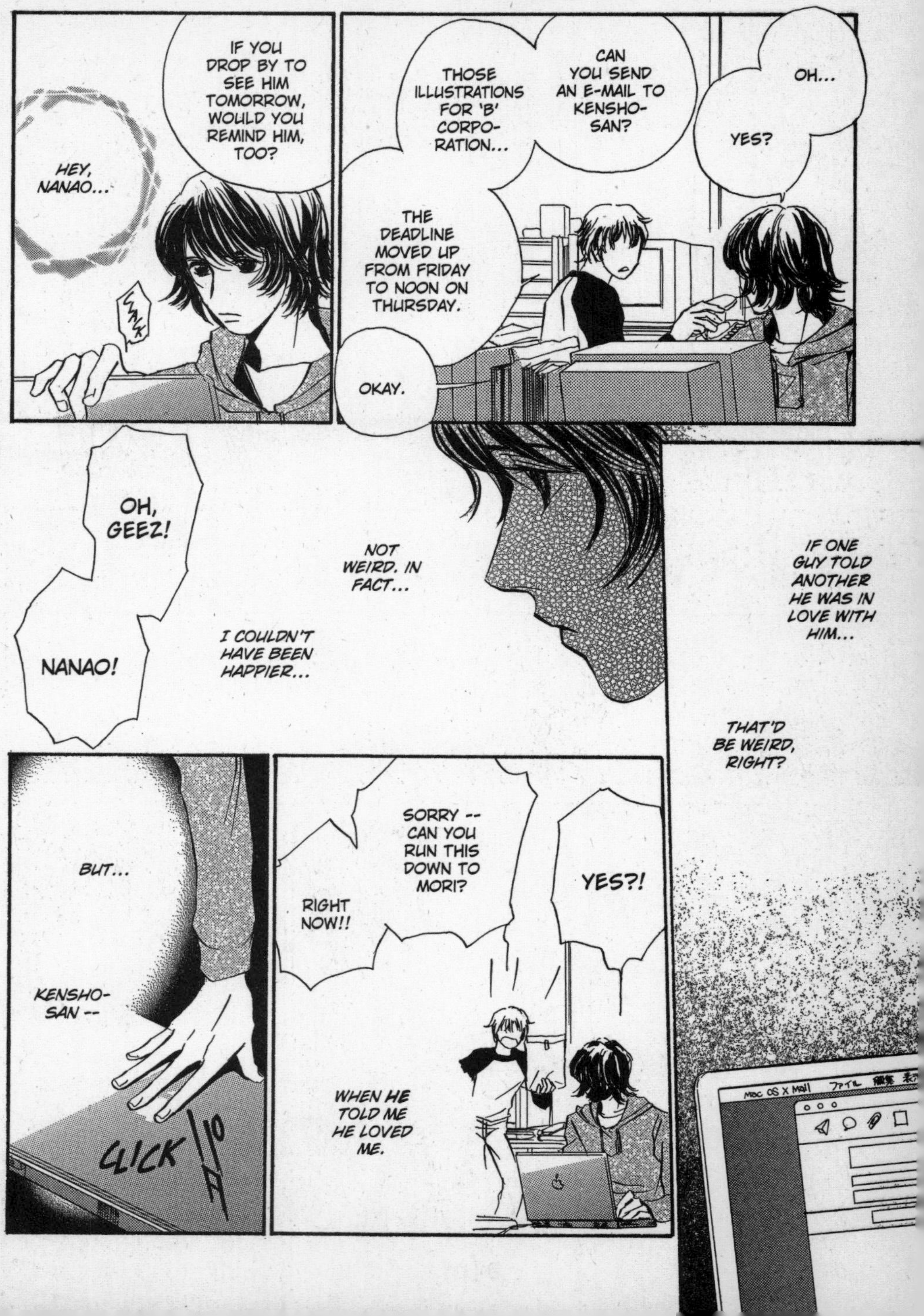
OH...
YES?
CAN YOU SEND AN E-MAIL TO KENSHO-SAN?
THOSE ILLUSTRATIONS FOR 'B' CORPORATION...
THE DEADLINE MOVED UP FROM FRIDAY TO NOON ON THURSDAY.
OKAY.
IF YOU DROP BY TO SEE HIM TOMORROW, WOULD YOU REMIND HIM, TOO?
HEY, NANAO...
IF ONE GUY TOLD ANOTHER HE WAS IN LOVE WITH HIM...
THAT'D BE WEIRD, RIGHT?
Mac OS X Mail ファイル 編集
NOT WEIRD. IN FACT...
I COULDN'T HAVE BEEN HAPPIER...
OH, GEEZ!
NANAO!
YES?!
SORRY -- CAN YOU RUN THIS DOWN TO MORI?
RIGHT NOW!!
WHEN HE TOLD ME HE LOVED ME.
BUT...
KENSHO-SAN --
CLICK

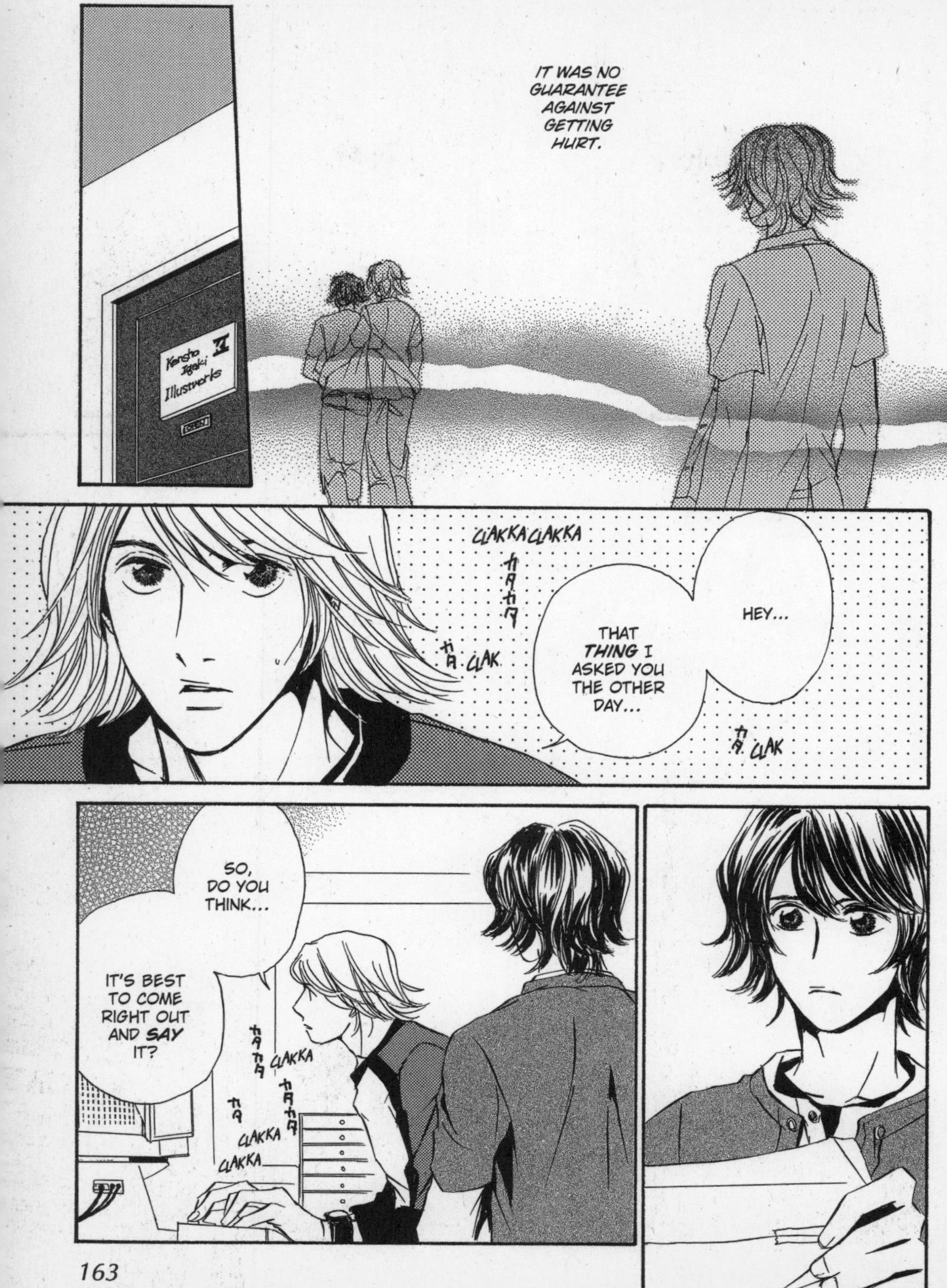
IT WAS NO GUARANTEE AGAINST GETTING HURT.
Illustworks
HEY...
THAT *THING* I ASKED YOU THE OTHER DAY...
CLAKKA CLAKKA
CLAK
CLAK
SO, DO YOU THINK...
IT'S BEST TO COME RIGHT OUT AND *SAY* IT?
CLAKKA
CLAKKA
CLAKKA

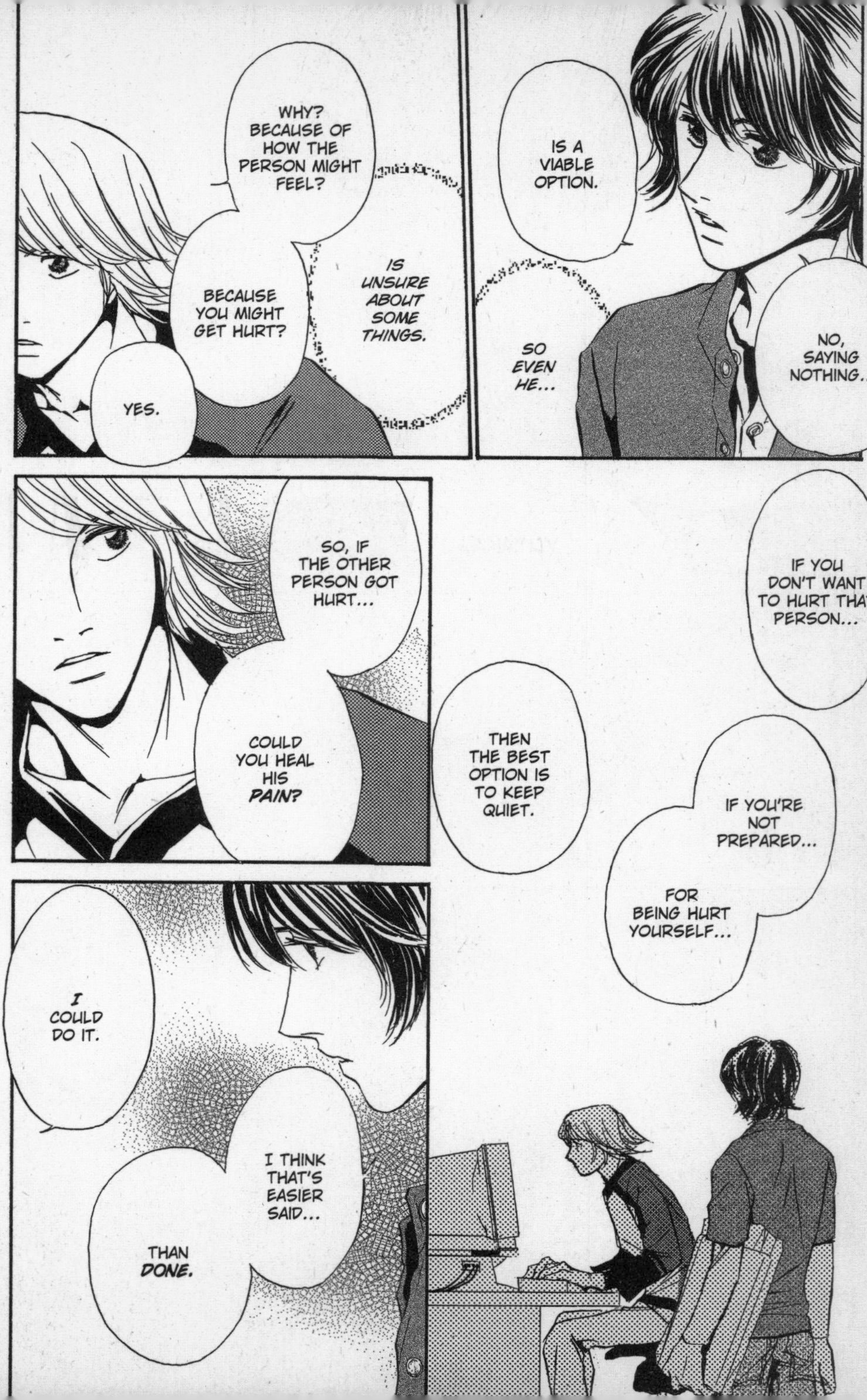
NO, SAYING NOTHING...
IS A VIABLE OPTION.
SO EVEN HE...
IS UNSURE ABOUT SOME THINGS.
WHY? BECAUSE OF HOW THE PERSON MIGHT FEEL?
BECAUSE YOU MIGHT GET HURT?
YES.
IF YOU DON'T WANT TO HURT THAT PERSON...
THEN THE BEST OPTION IS TO KEEP QUIET.
IF YOU'RE NOT PREPARED...
FOR BEING HURT YOURSELF...
SO, IF THE OTHER PERSON GOT HURT...
COULD YOU HEAL HIS *PAIN?*
I COULD DO IT.
I THINK THAT'S EASIER SAID...
THAN ***DONE.***

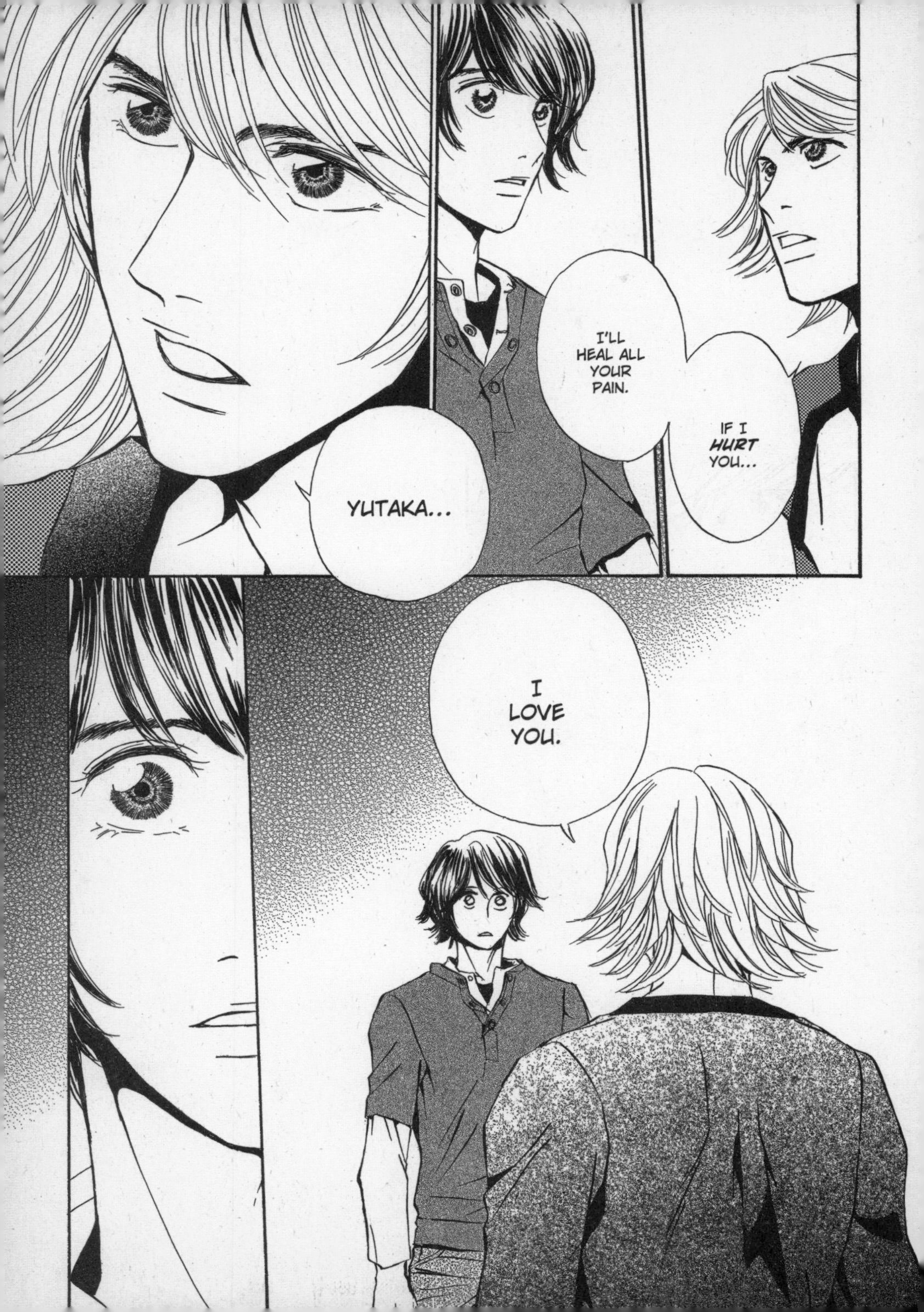
IF I HURT YOU...
I'LL HEAL ALL YOUR PAIN.
YUTAKA...
I LOVE YOU.

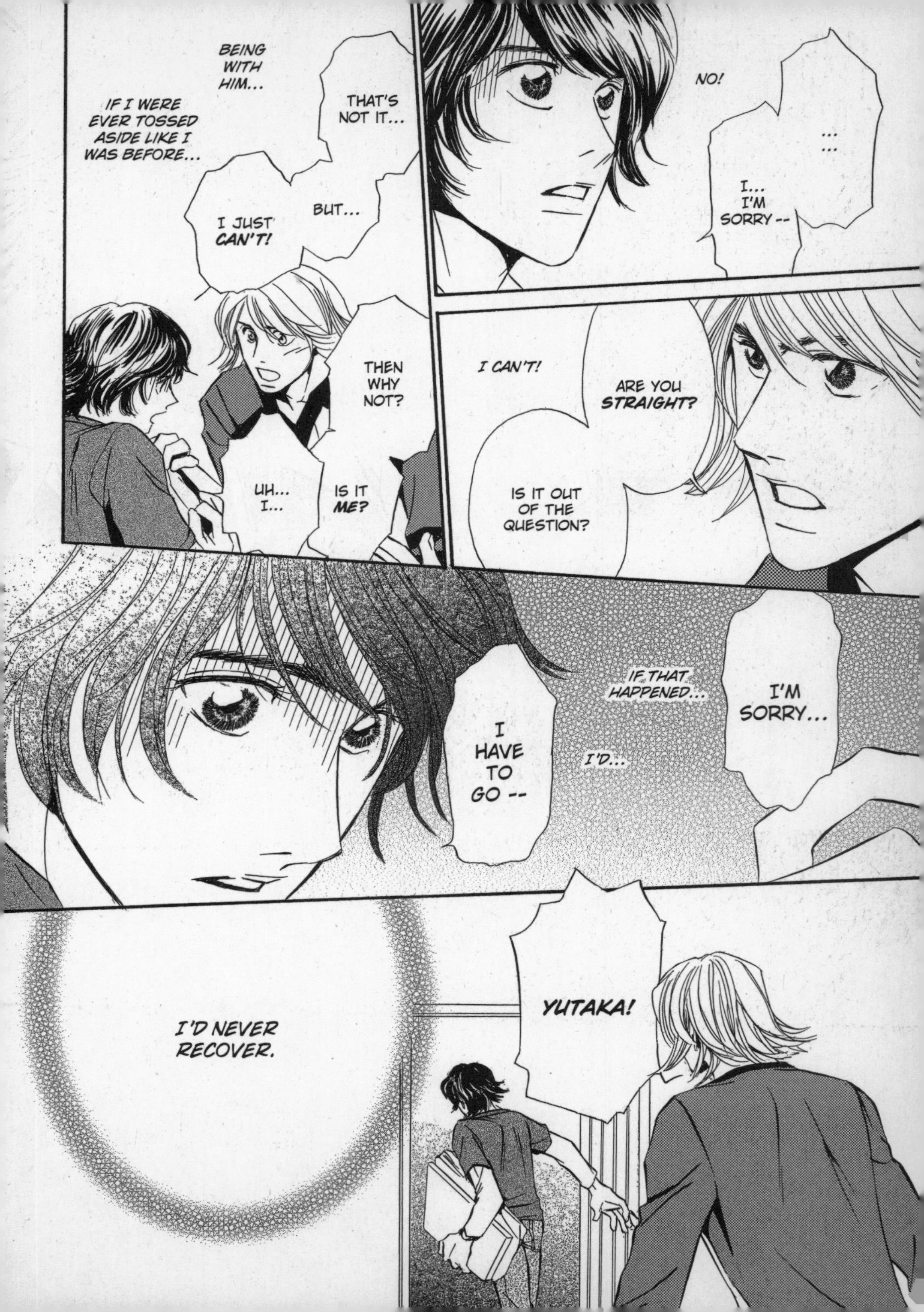
NO!
... ...
I... I'M SORRY --
ARE YOU STRAIGHT?
I CAN'T!
IS IT OUT OF THE QUESTION?
THAT'S NOT IT...
BEING WITH HIM...
IF I WERE EVER TOSSED ASIDE LIKE I WAS BEFORE...
BUT...
I JUST CAN'T!
THEN WHY NOT?
IS IT ME?
UH... I...
I'M SORRY...
IF THAT HAPPENED...
I'D...
I HAVE TO GO --
YUTAKA!
I'D NEVER RECOVER.

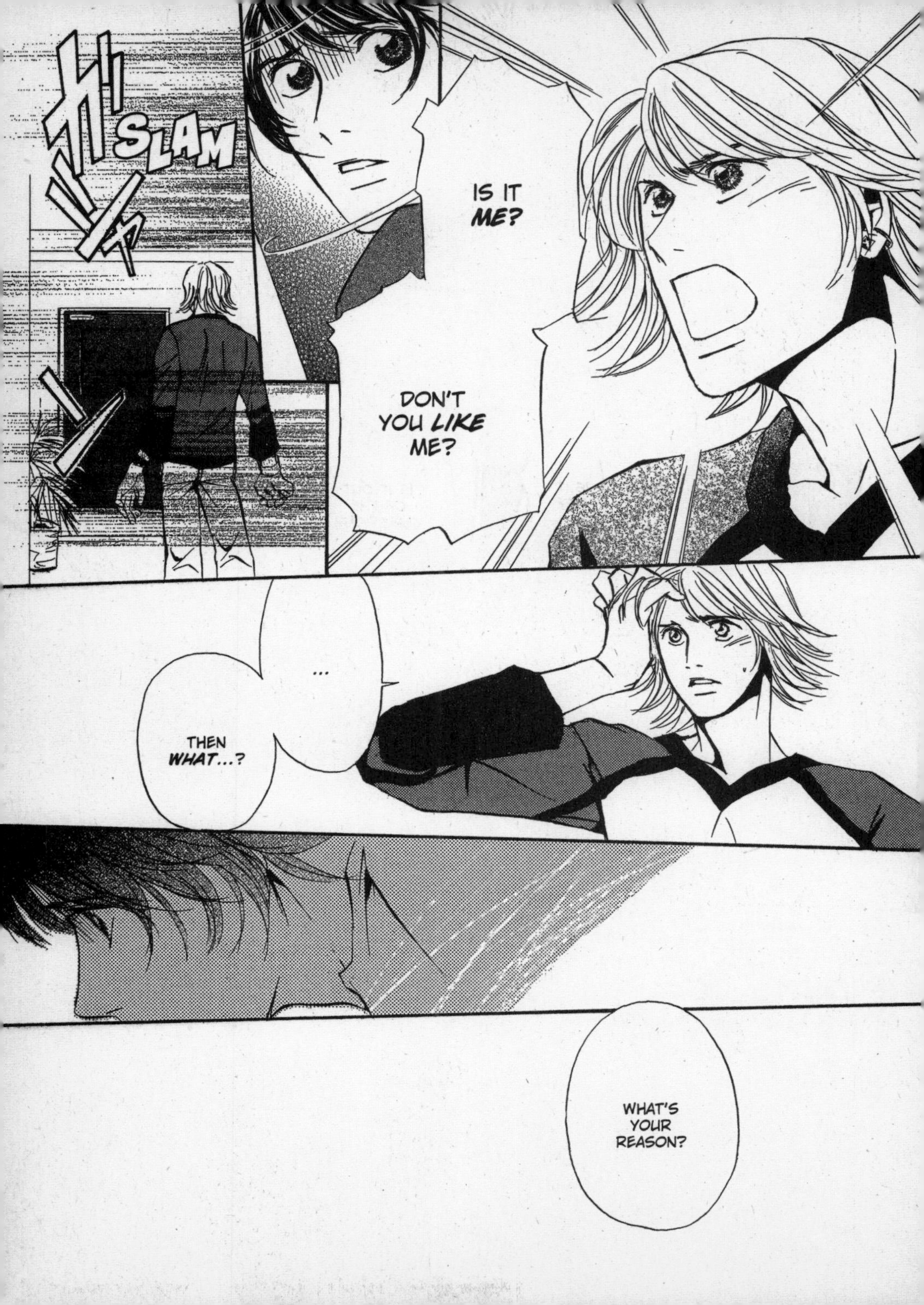
IS IT ME?
DON'T YOU LIKE ME?
SLAM
...
THEN WHAT...?
WHAT'S YOUR REASON?

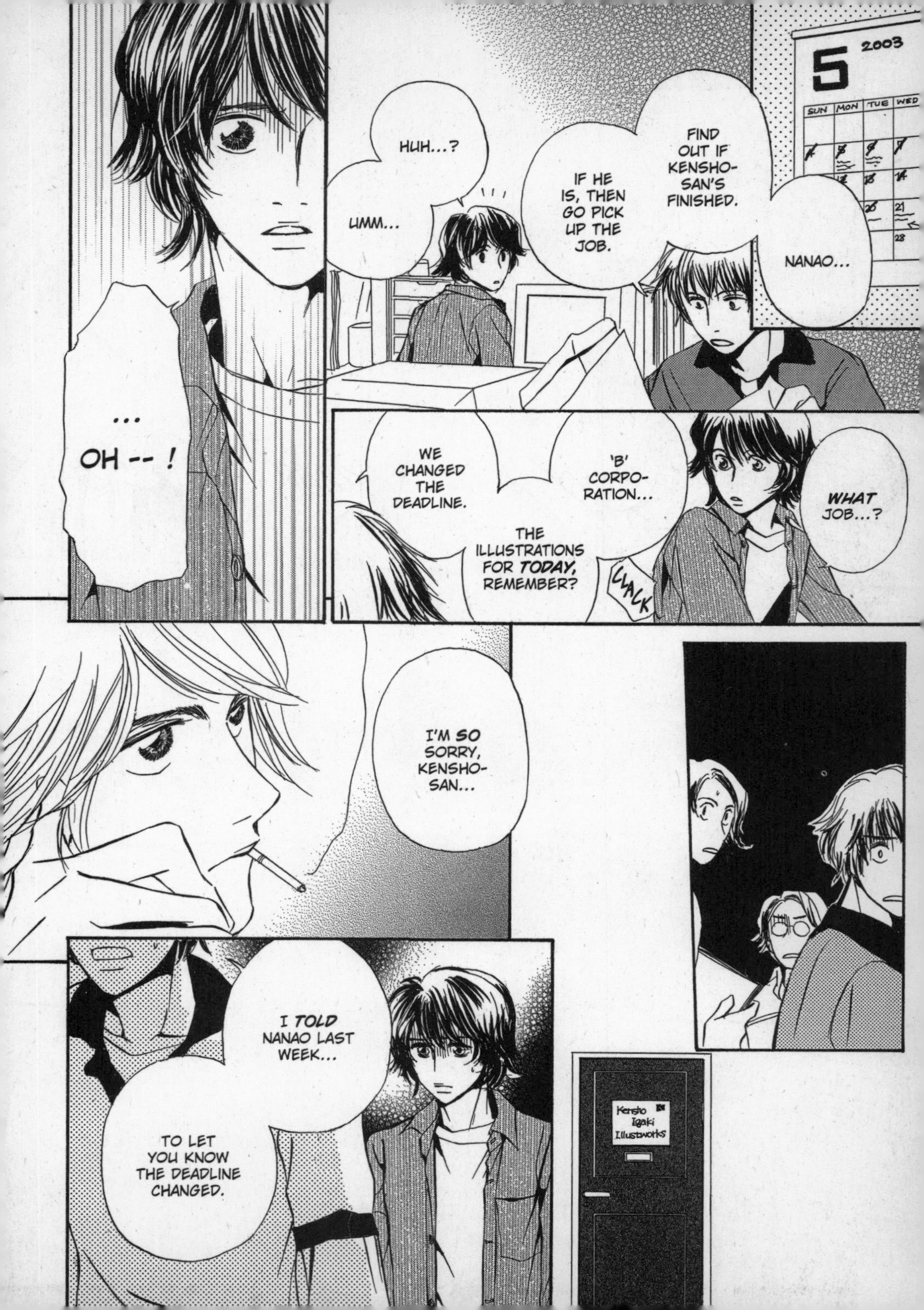
5
2003
SUN MON TUE WED
NANAO...
FIND OUT IF KENSHO-SAN'S FINISHED.
IF HE IS, THEN GO PICK UP THE JOB.
HUH...?
UMM...
WHAT JOB...?
'B' CORPORATION...
WE CHANGED THE DEADLINE.
THE ILLUSTRATIONS FOR TODAY, REMEMBER?
CLACK
... OH -- !
Kensho Igaki Illustworks
I'M SO SORRY, KENSHO-SAN...
I TOLD NANAO LAST WEEK...
TO LET YOU KNOW THE DEADLINE CHANGED.

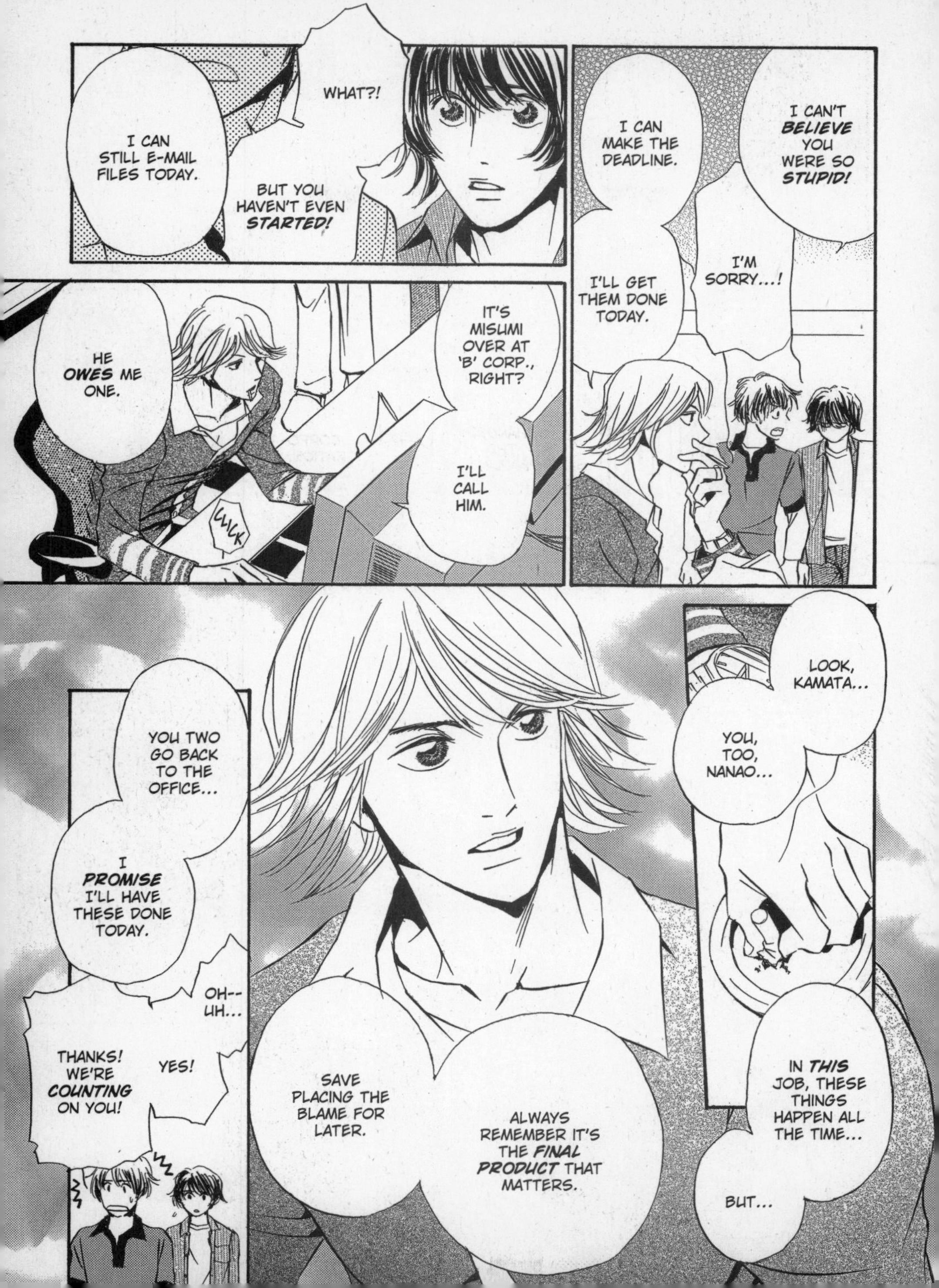
I CAN'T BELIEVE YOU WERE SO STUPID!
I CAN MAKE THE DEADLINE.
I'M SORRY...!
I'LL GET THEM DONE TODAY.
WHAT?!
BUT YOU HAVEN'T EVEN STARTED!
I CAN STILL E-MAIL FILES TODAY.
IT'S MISUMI OVER AT 'B' CORP., RIGHT?
I'LL CALL HIM.
HE OWES ME ONE.
CLICK
LOOK, KAMATA...
YOU, TOO, NANAO...
IN THIS JOB, THESE THINGS HAPPEN ALL THE TIME...
BUT...
ALWAYS REMEMBER IT'S THE FINAL PRODUCT THAT MATTERS.
SAVE PLACING THE BLAME FOR LATER.
YOU TWO GO BACK TO THE OFFICE...
I PROMISE I'LL HAVE THESE DONE TODAY.
OH-- UH...
YES!
THANKS! WE'RE COUNTING ON YOU!

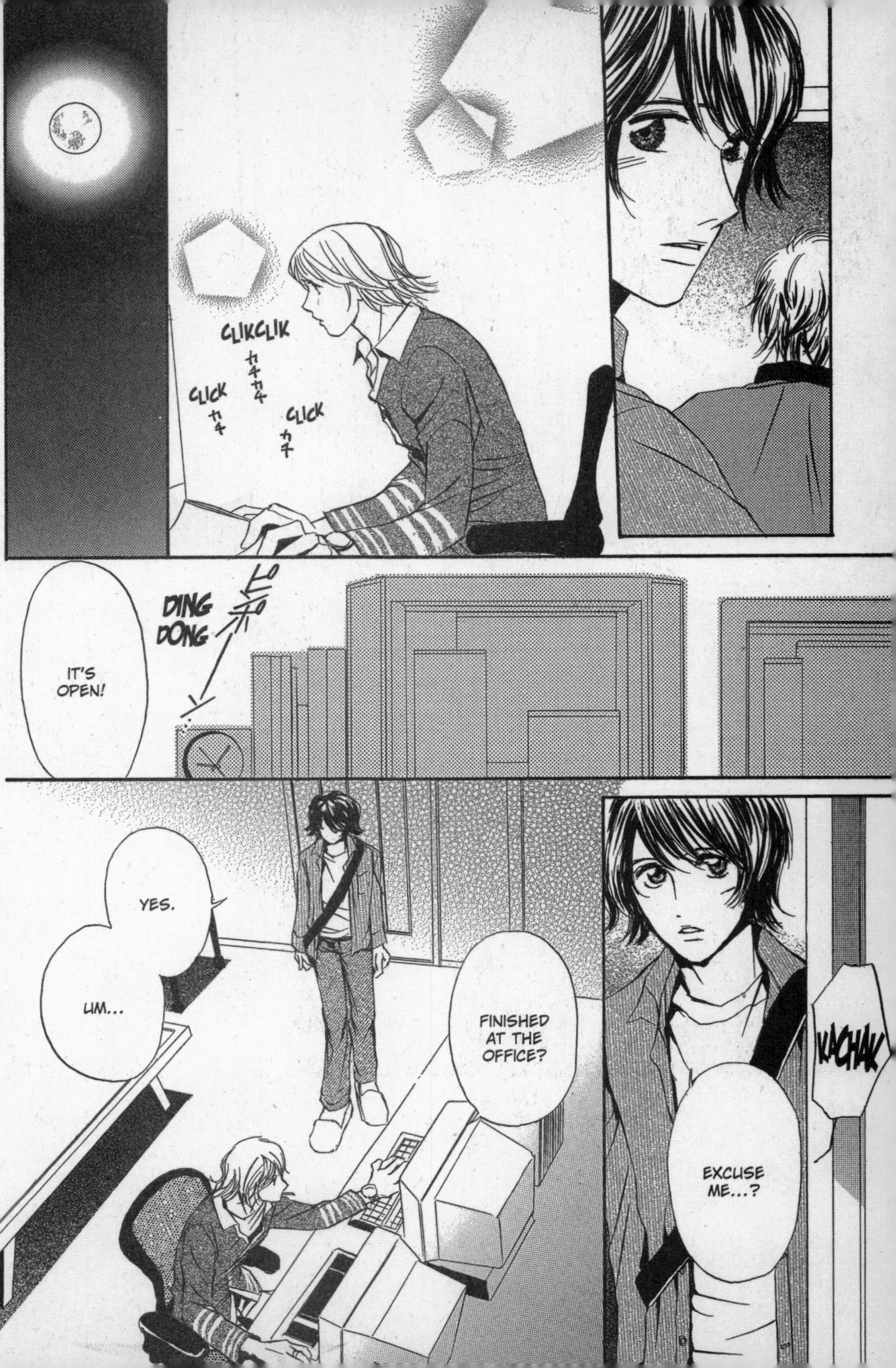
CLIKCLIK
カチカチ
CLICK
カチ
CLICK
カチ
DING DONG
ピンポン
IT'S OPEN!
KACHAK
EXCUSE ME...?
FINISHED AT THE OFFICE?
YES.
UM...

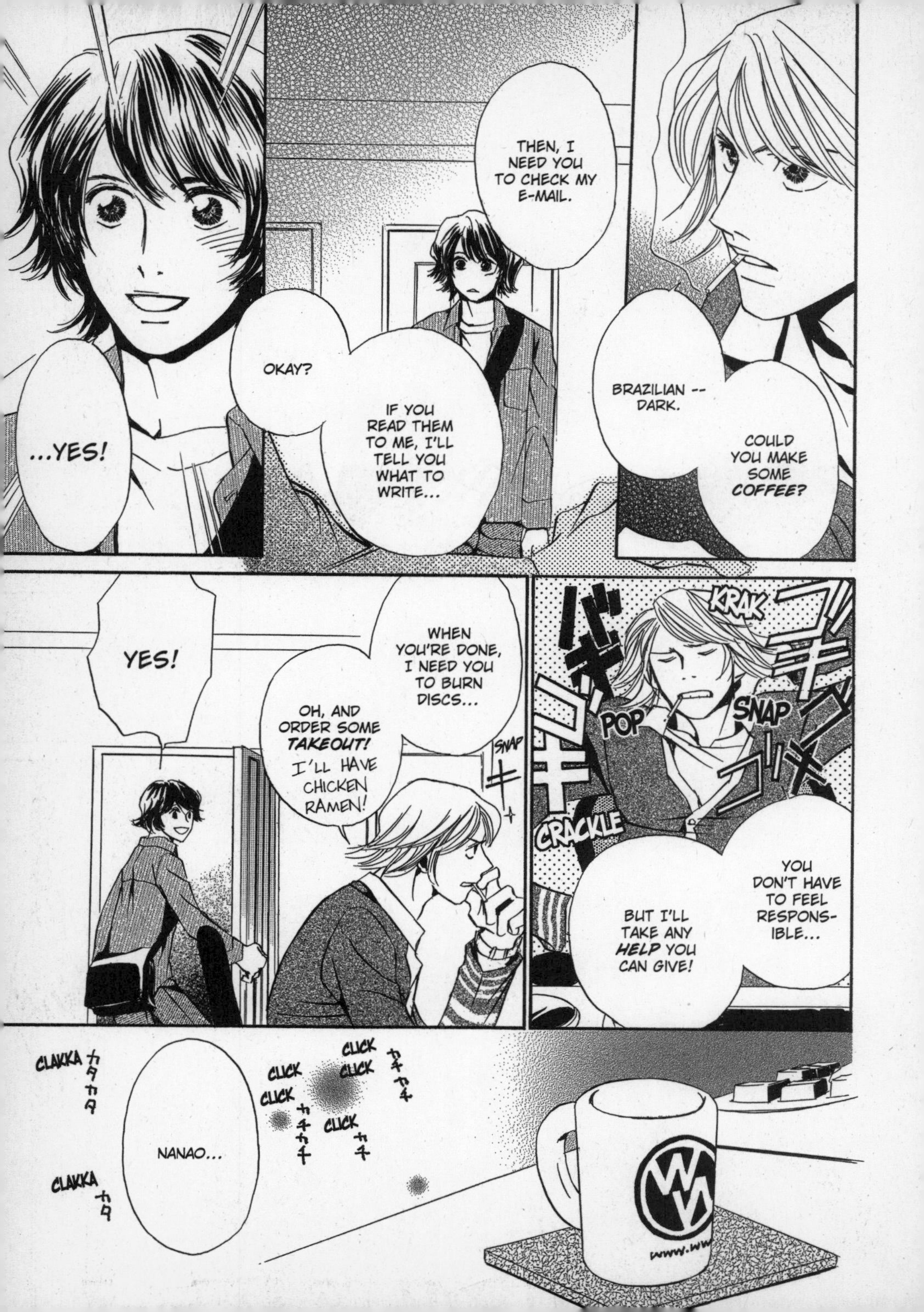
COULD YOU MAKE SOME COFFEE?
BRAZILIAN -- DARK.
THEN, I NEED YOU TO CHECK MY E-MAIL.
IF YOU READ THEM TO ME, I'LL TELL YOU WHAT TO WRITE...
OKAY?
...YES!
KRAK
SNAP
POP
CRACKLE
YOU DON'T HAVE TO FEEL RESPONSIBLE...
BUT I'LL TAKE ANY HELP YOU CAN GIVE!
WHEN YOU'RE DONE, I NEED YOU TO BURN DISCS...
OH, AND ORDER SOME TAKEOUT! I'LL HAVE CHICKEN RAMEN!
SNAP
YES!
CLICK
CLICK
CLICK
CLICK
CLICK
NANAO...
CLAKKA
CLAKKA
www.ww

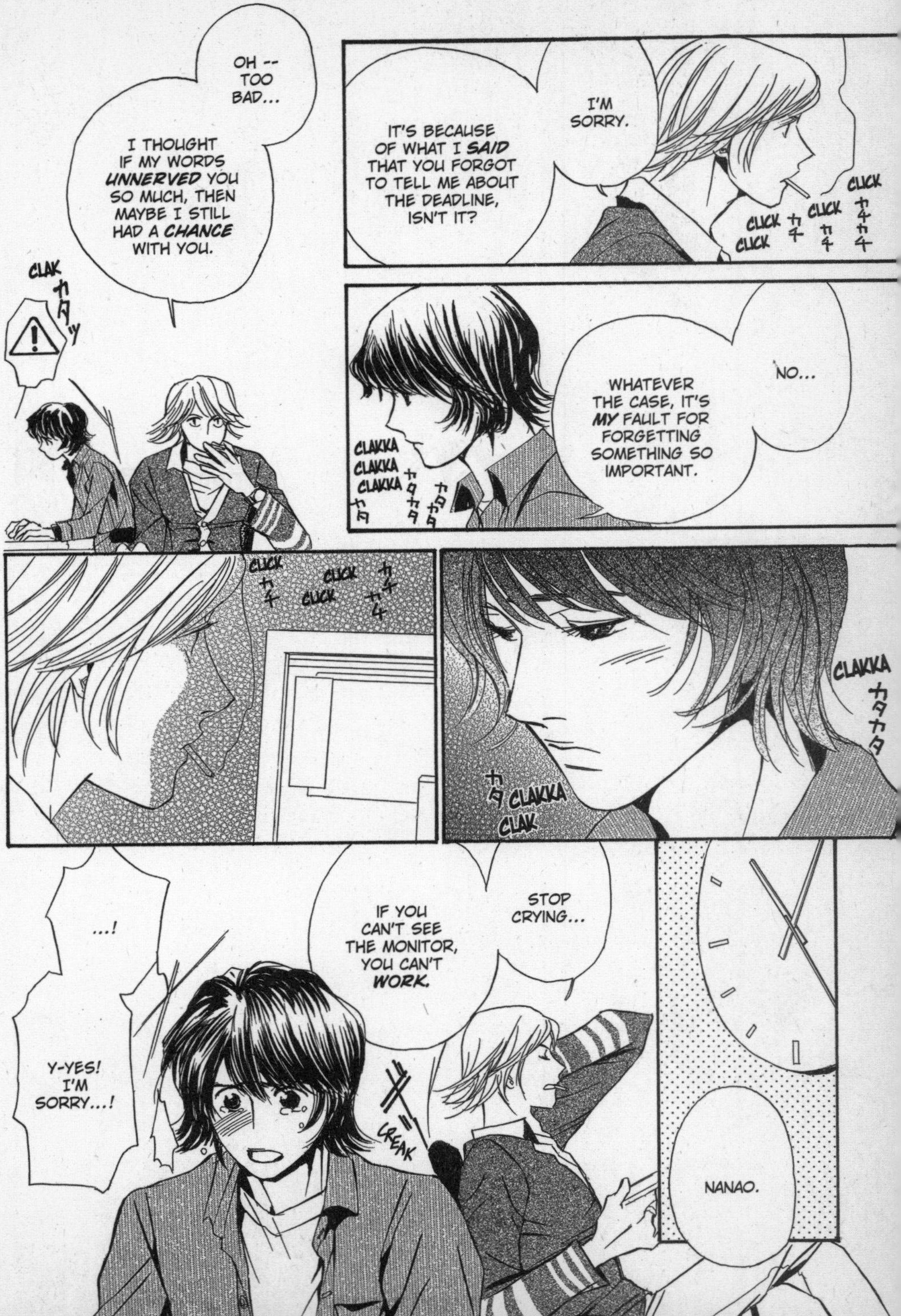

I'M SORRY.
IT'S BECAUSE OF WHAT I SAID THAT YOU FORGOT TO TELL ME ABOUT THE DEADLINE, ISN'T IT?
CLICK CLICK CLICK CLICK
NO...
WHATEVER THE CASE, IT'S MY FAULT FOR FORGETTING SOMETHING SO IMPORTANT.
CLAKKA CLAKKA CLAKKA
OH -- TOO BAD...
I THOUGHT IF MY WORDS UNNERVED YOU SO MUCH, THEN MAYBE I STILL HAD A CHANCE WITH YOU.
CLAK
CLAKKA
CLAKKA CLAK
CLICK CLICK CLICK
NANAO.
STOP CRYING...
IF YOU CAN'T SEE THE MONITOR, YOU CAN'T WORK.
CREAK
...!
Y-YES! I'M SORRY...!

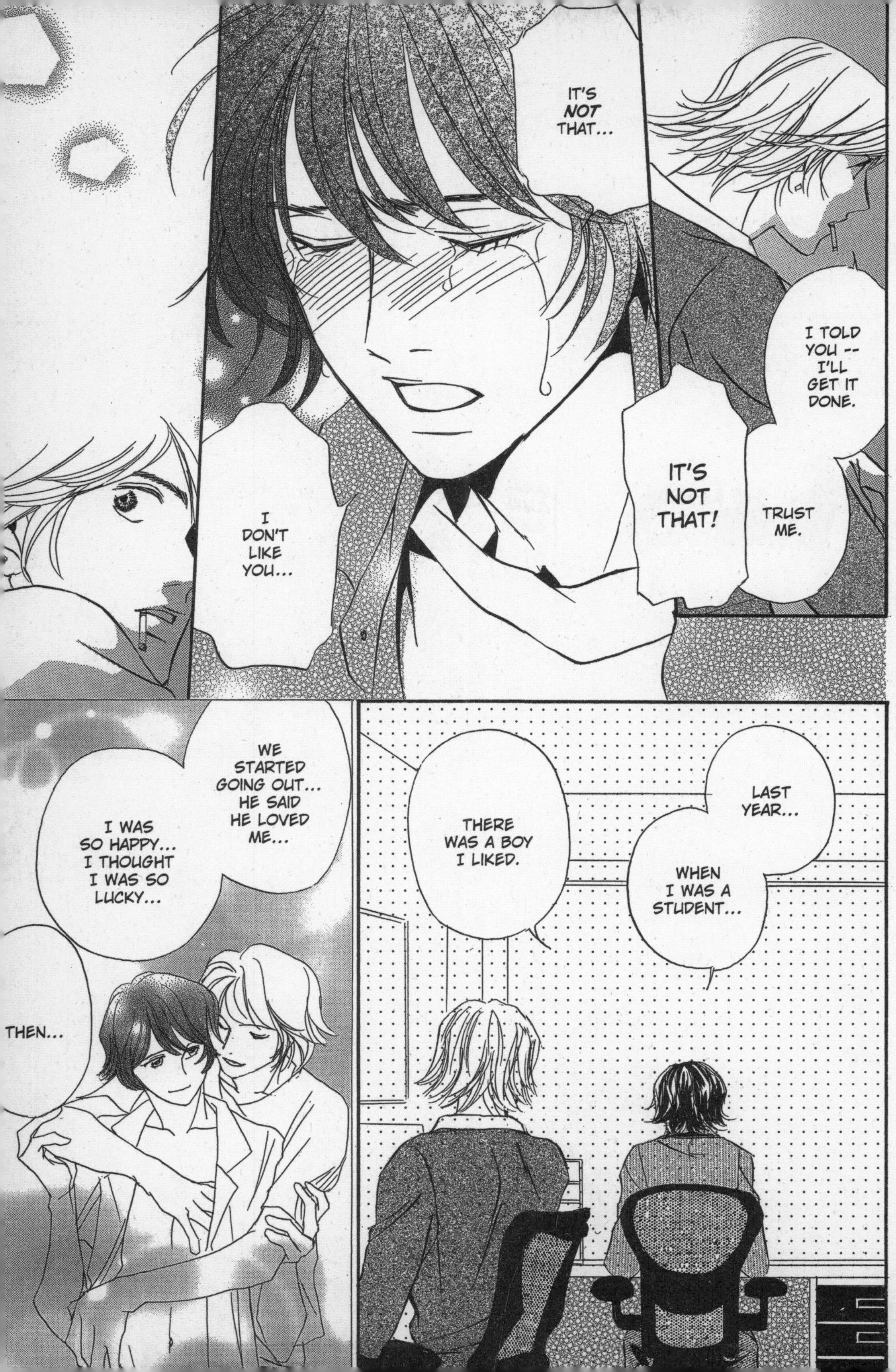
I TOLD YOU -- I'LL GET IT DONE.
TRUST ME.
IT'S *NOT* THAT...
IT'S NOT THAT!
I DON'T LIKE YOU...
LAST YEAR...
WHEN I WAS A STUDENT...
THERE WAS A BOY I LIKED.
WE STARTED GOING OUT... HE SAID HE LOVED ME...
I WAS SO HAPPY... I THOUGHT I WAS SO LUCKY...
THEN...

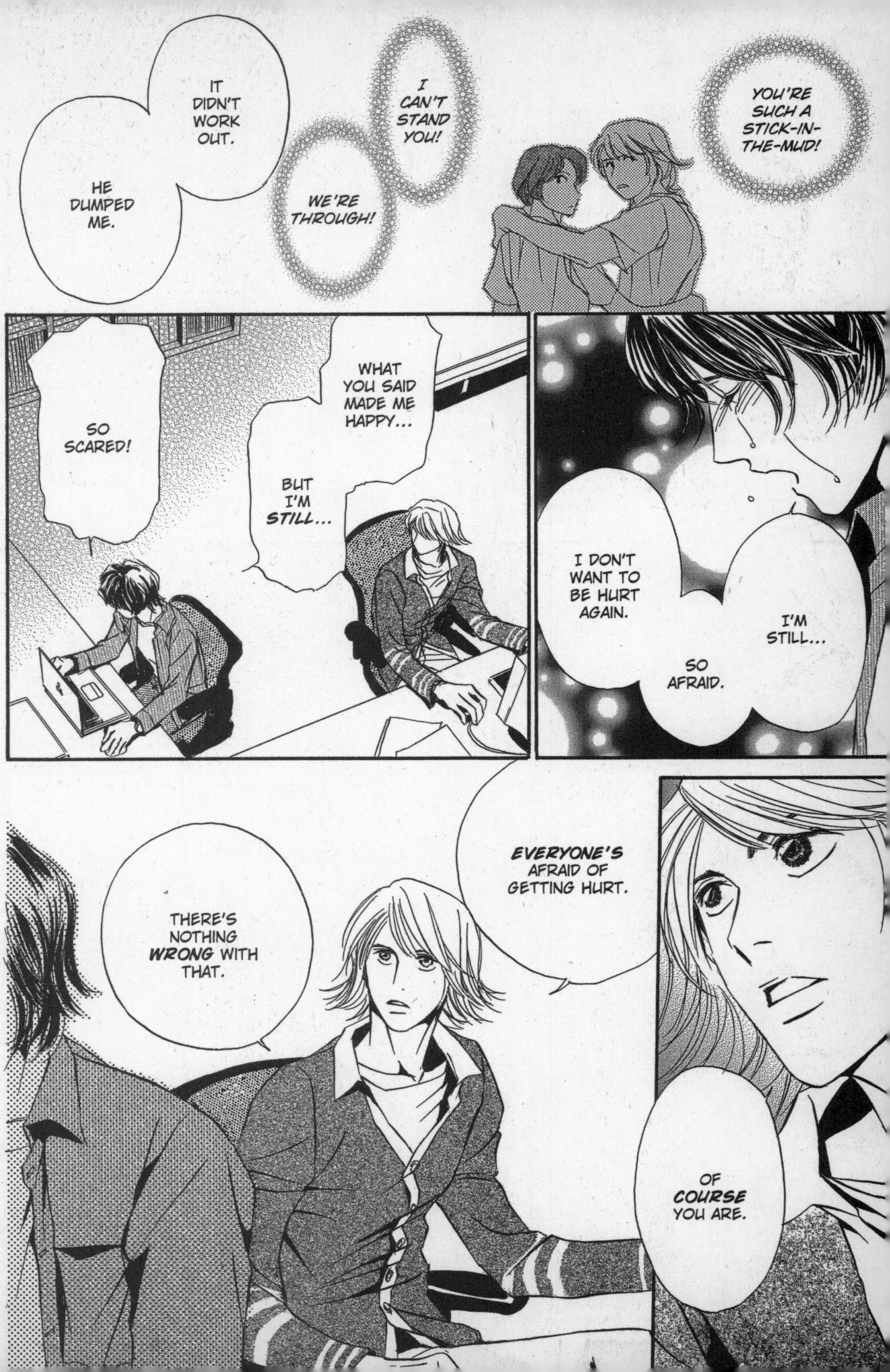
YOU'RE SUCH A STICK-IN-THE-MUD!
I CAN'T STAND YOU!
WE'RE THROUGH!
IT DIDN'T WORK OUT.
HE DUMPED ME.
I'M STILL...
SO AFRAID.
I DON'T WANT TO BE HURT AGAIN.
WHAT YOU SAID MADE ME HAPPY...
BUT I'M STILL...
SO SCARED!
OF COURSE YOU ARE.
EVERYONE'S AFRAID OF GETTING HURT.
THERE'S NOTHING WRONG WITH THAT.

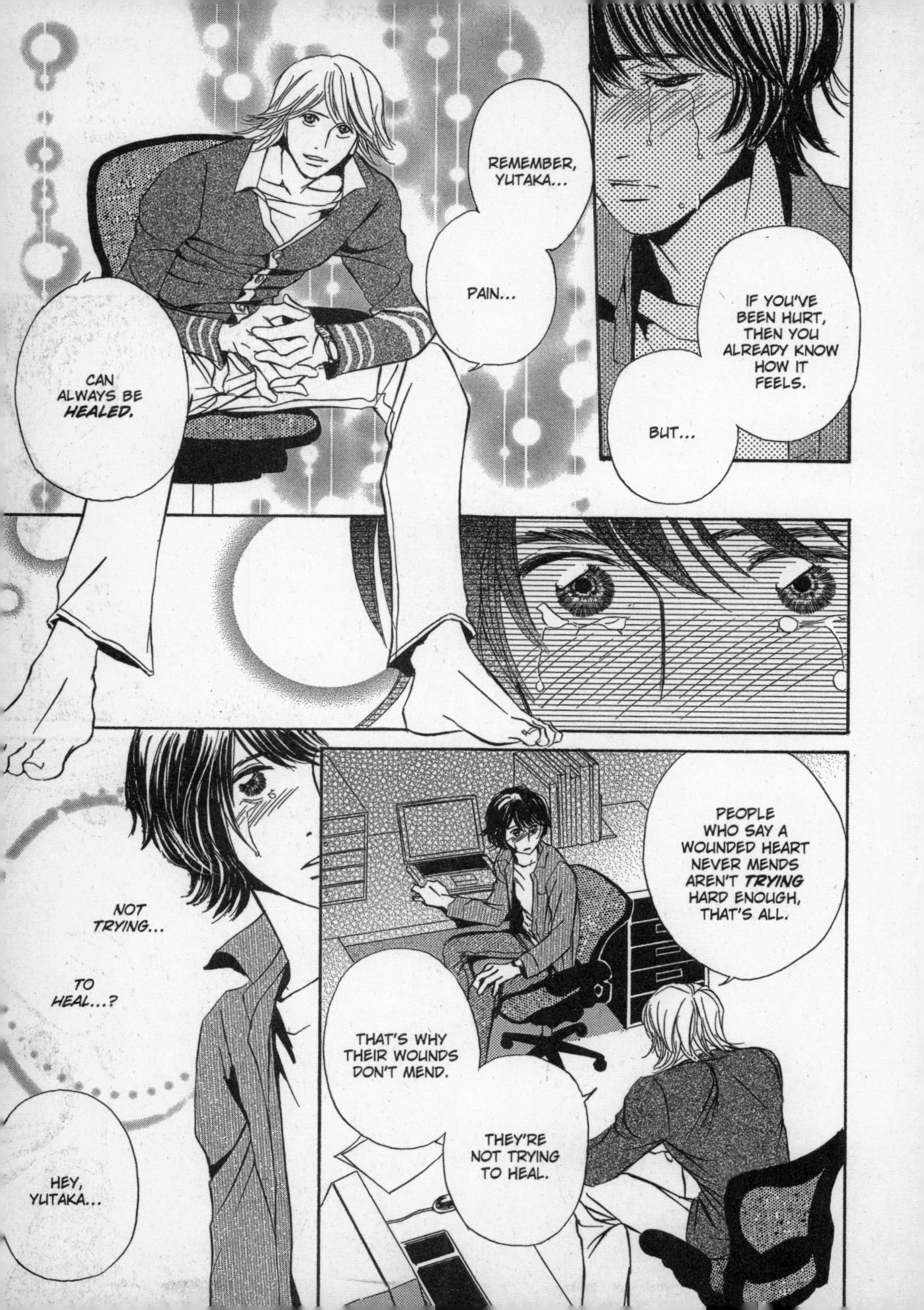
REMEMBER, YUTAKA...
IF YOU'VE BEEN HURT, THEN YOU ALREADY KNOW HOW IT FEELS.
BUT...
PAIN...
CAN ALWAYS BE *HEALED.*
PEOPLE WHO SAY A WOUNDED HEART NEVER MENDS AREN'T *TRYING* HARD ENOUGH, THAT'S ALL.
THAT'S WHY THEIR WOUNDS DON'T MEND.
THEY'RE NOT TRYING TO HEAL.
NOT TRYING...
TO HEAL...?
HEY, YUTAKA...

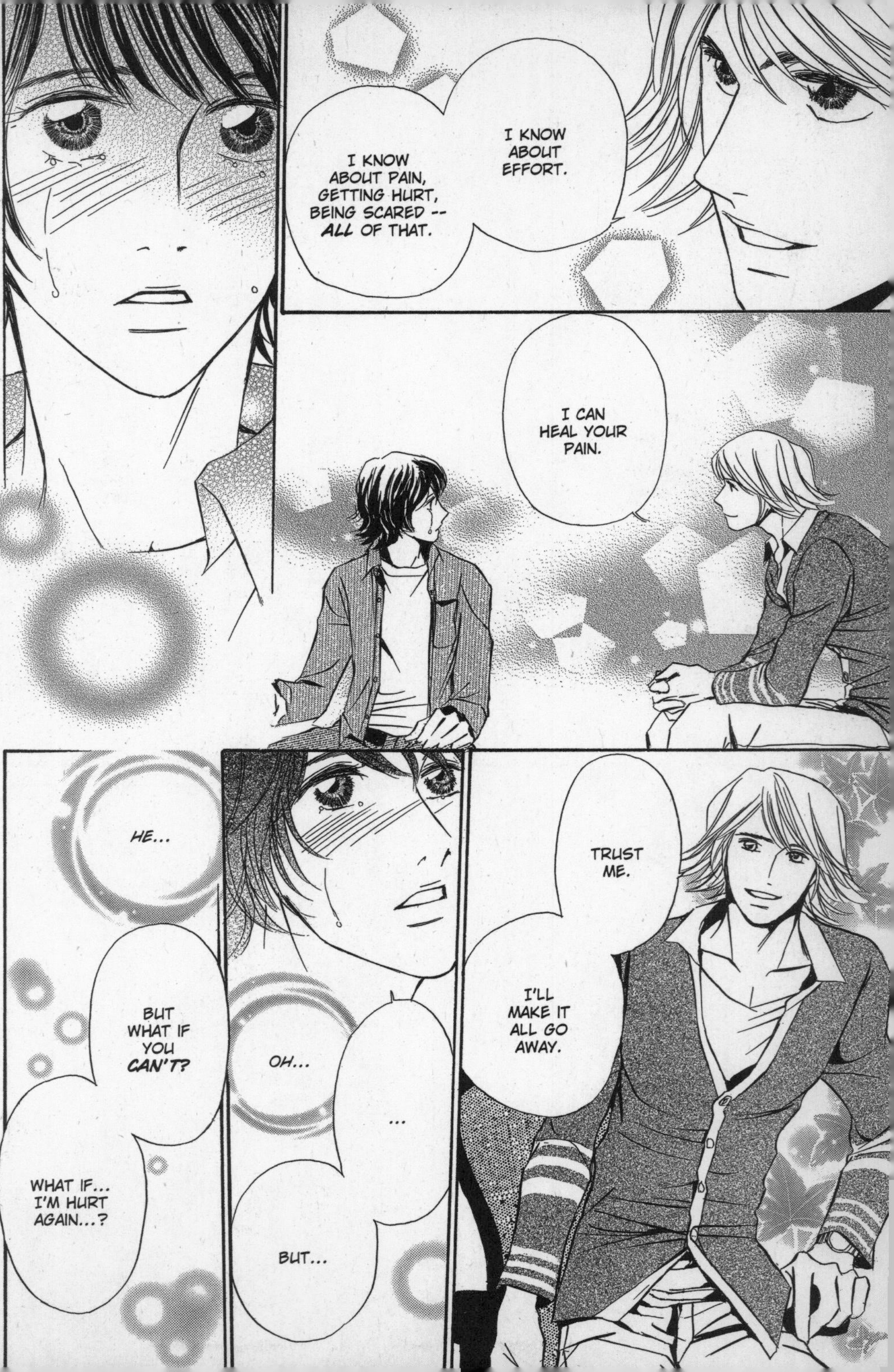
I KNOW ABOUT EFFORT.
I KNOW ABOUT PAIN, GETTING HURT, BEING SCARED -- *ALL* OF THAT.
I CAN HEAL YOUR PAIN.
TRUST ME.
I'LL MAKE IT ALL GO AWAY.
OH...
...
BUT...
HE...
BUT WHAT IF YOU *CAN'T?*
WHAT IF... I'M HURT AGAIN...?

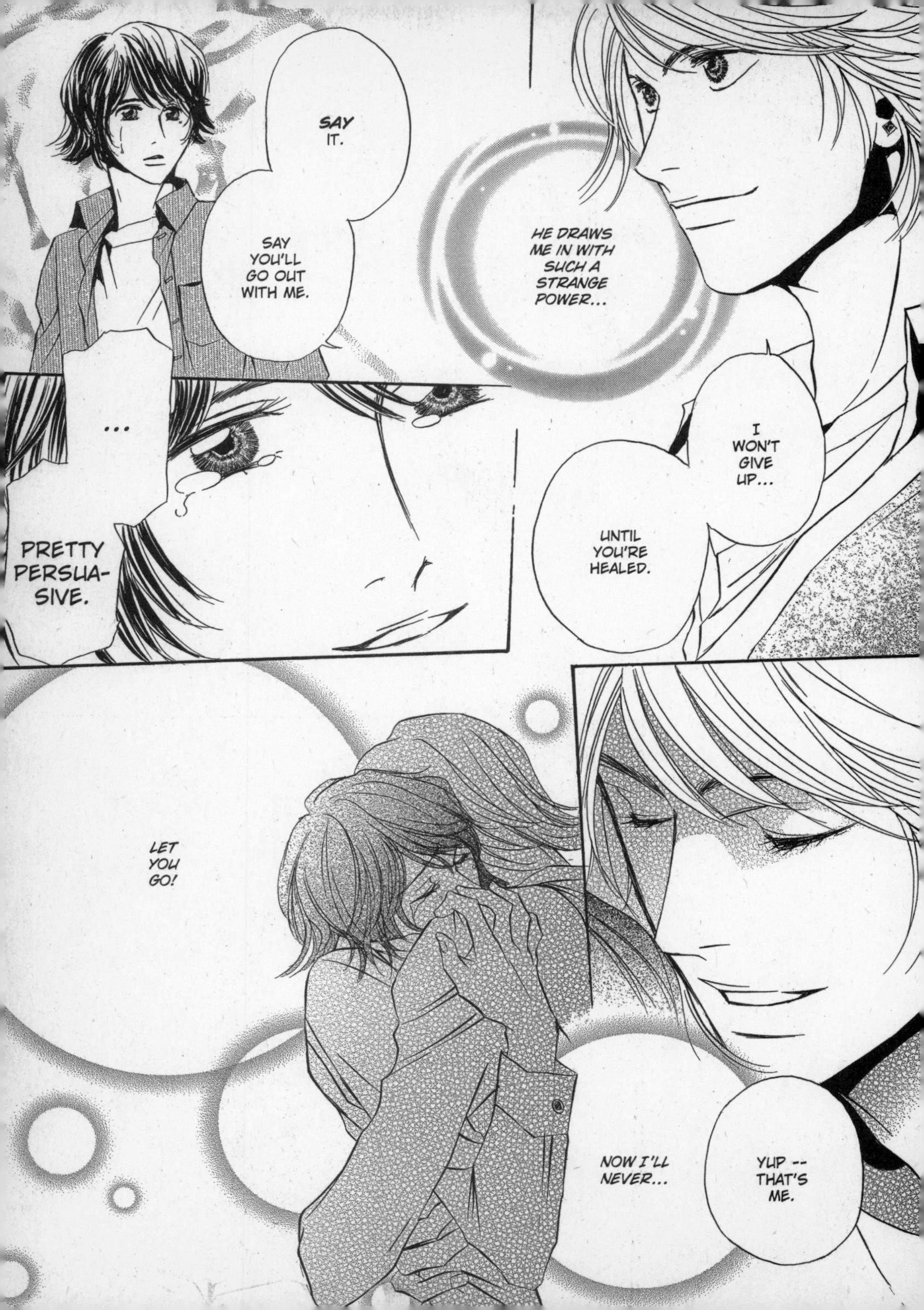
HE DRAWS ME IN WITH SUCH A STRANGE POWER...
SAY IT.
SAY YOU'LL GO OUT WITH ME.
I WON'T GIVE UP...
UNTIL YOU'RE HEALED.
...
PRETTY PERSUA-SIVE.
YUP -- THAT'S ME.
NOW I'LL NEVER...
LET YOU GO!

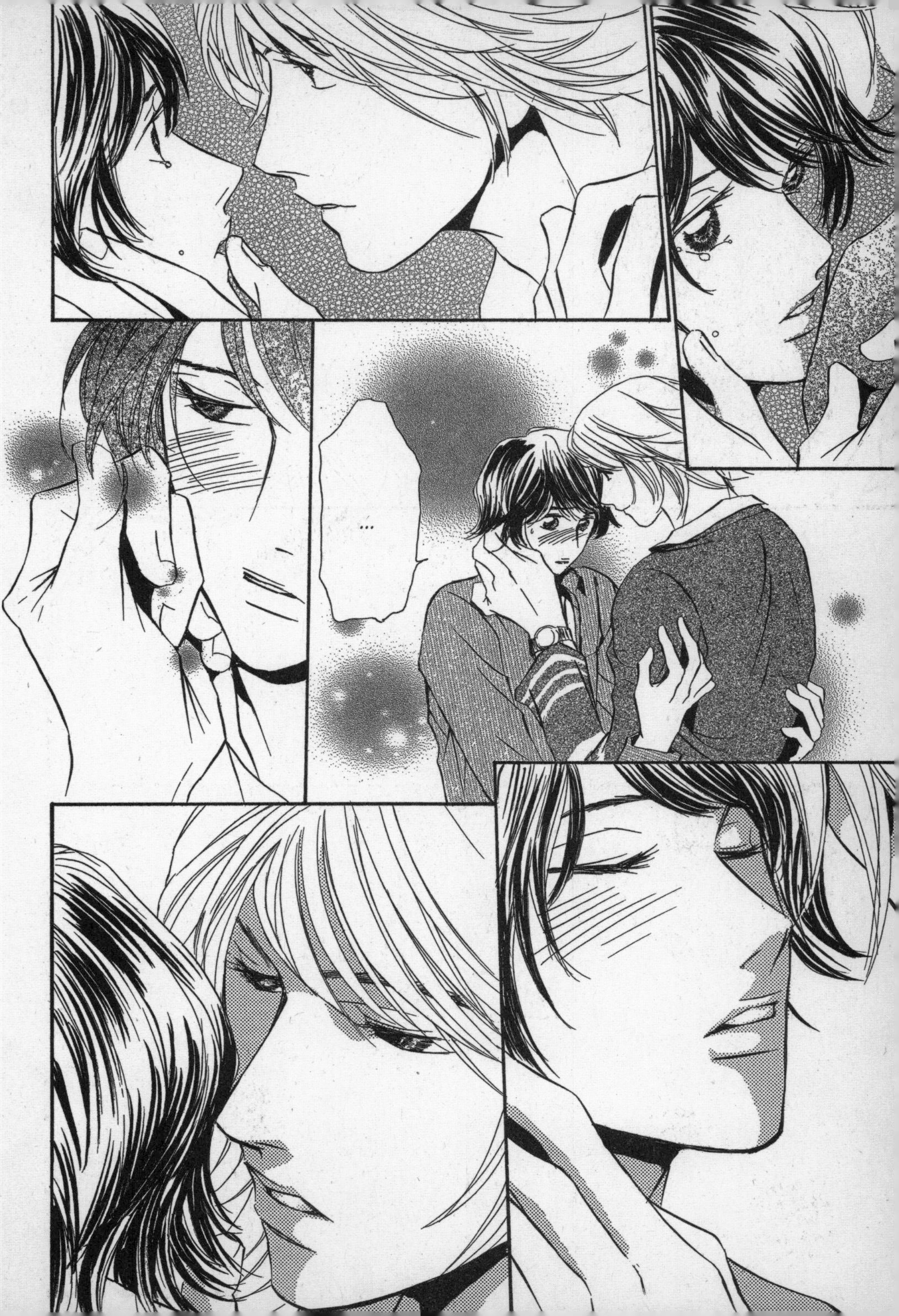
...

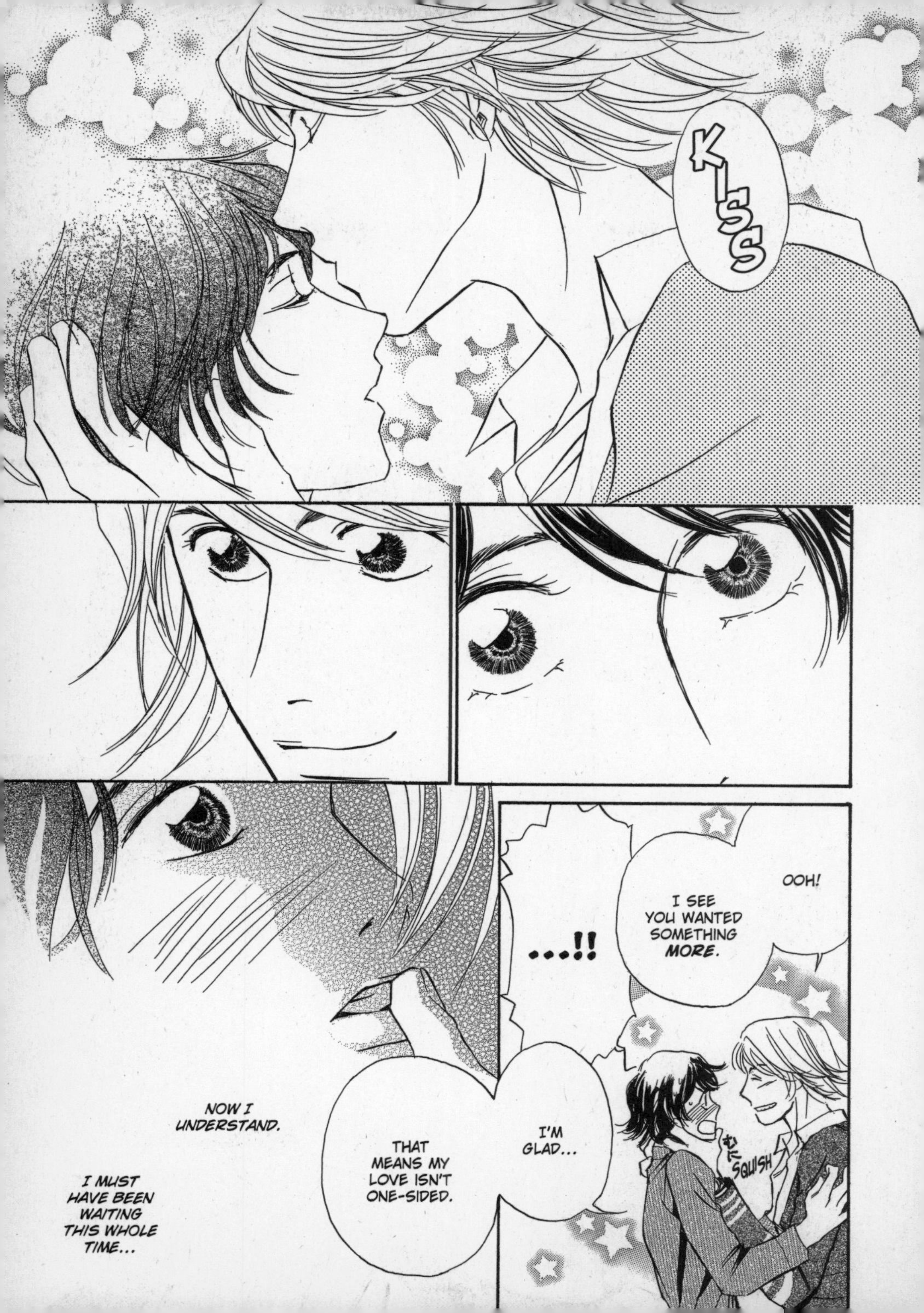
KISS
OOH!
I SEE YOU WANTED SOMETHING MORE.
...!!
SQUISH
I'M GLAD...
THAT MEANS MY LOVE ISN'T ONE-SIDED.
NOW I UNDERSTAND.
I MUST HAVE BEEN WAITING THIS WHOLE TIME...

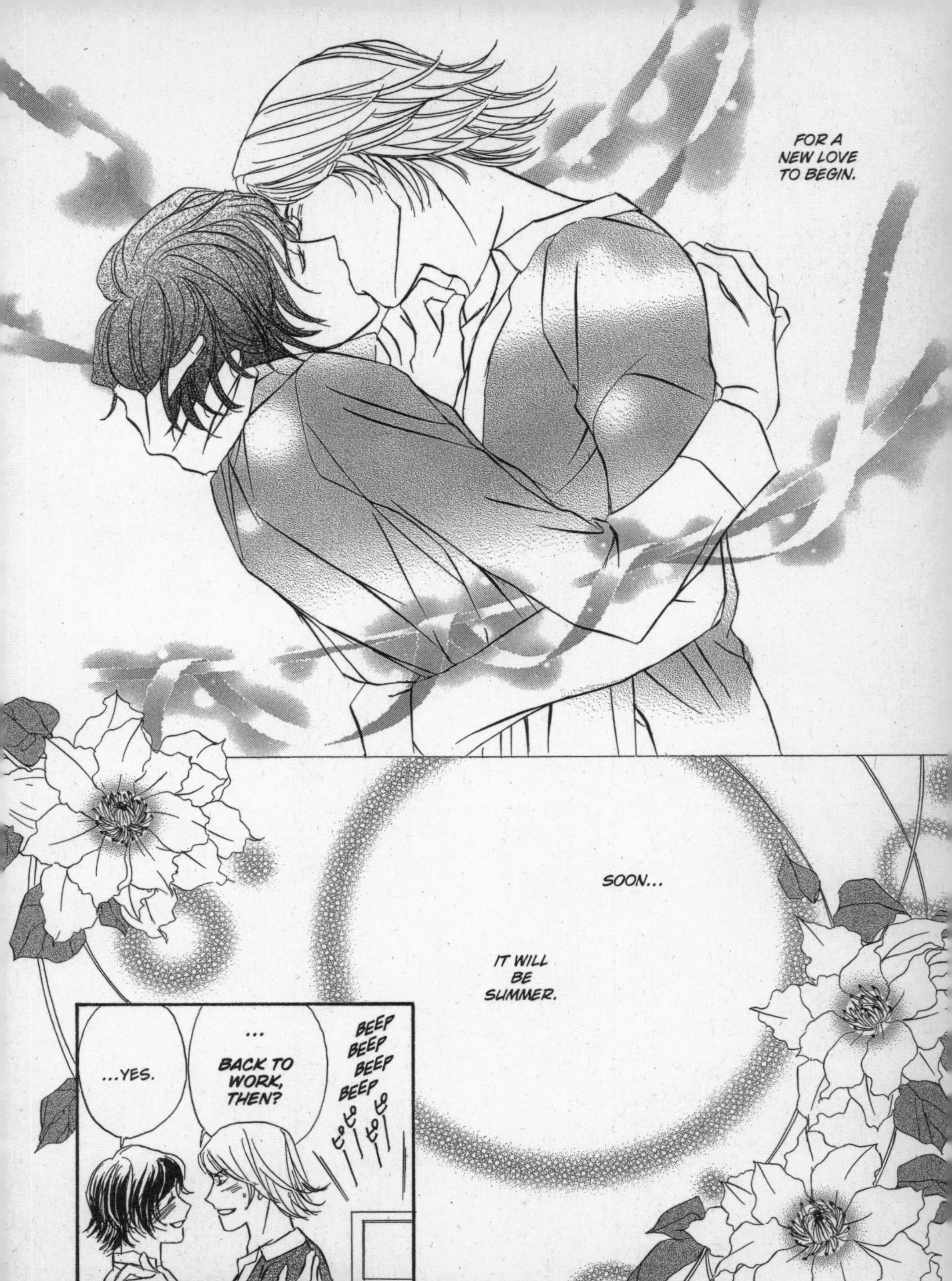
FOR A NEW LOVE TO BEGIN.
SOON...
IT WILL BE SUMMER.
BEEP BEEP BEEP BEEP
... BACK TO WORK, THEN?
...YES.

A FLOWER AWAITS SUMMER END

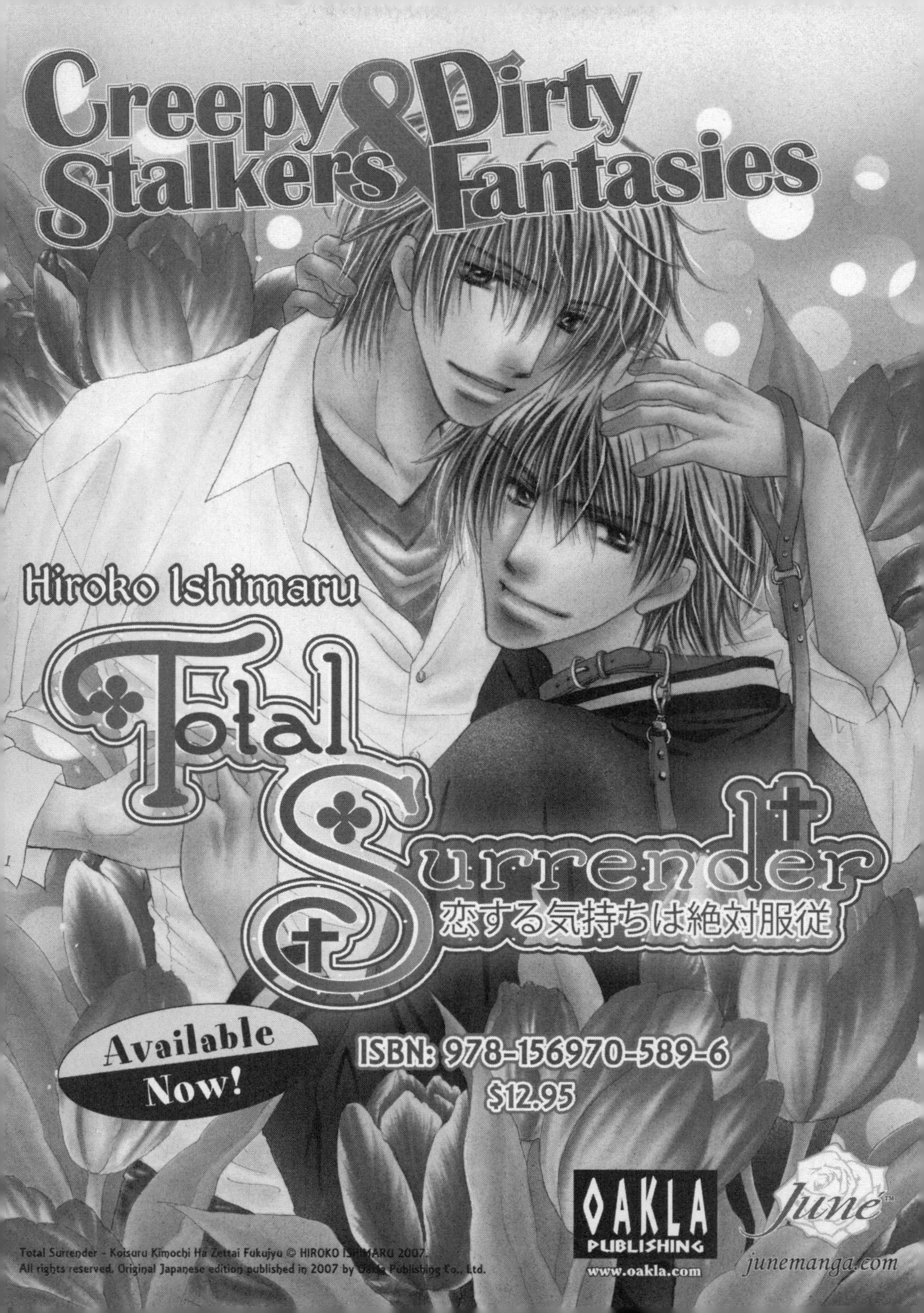

Creepy Stalkers & Dirty Fantasies
Hiroko Ishimaru
Total Surrender
恋する気持ちは絶対服従
Available Now!
ISBN: 978-156970-589-6
$12.95
OAKLA PUBLISHING
www.oakla.com
June™
junemanga.com
Total Surrender - Koisuru Kimochi Ha Zettai Fukujyu © HIROKO ISHIMARU 2007.
All rights reserved. Original Japanese edition published in 2007 by Oakla Publishing Co., Ltd.

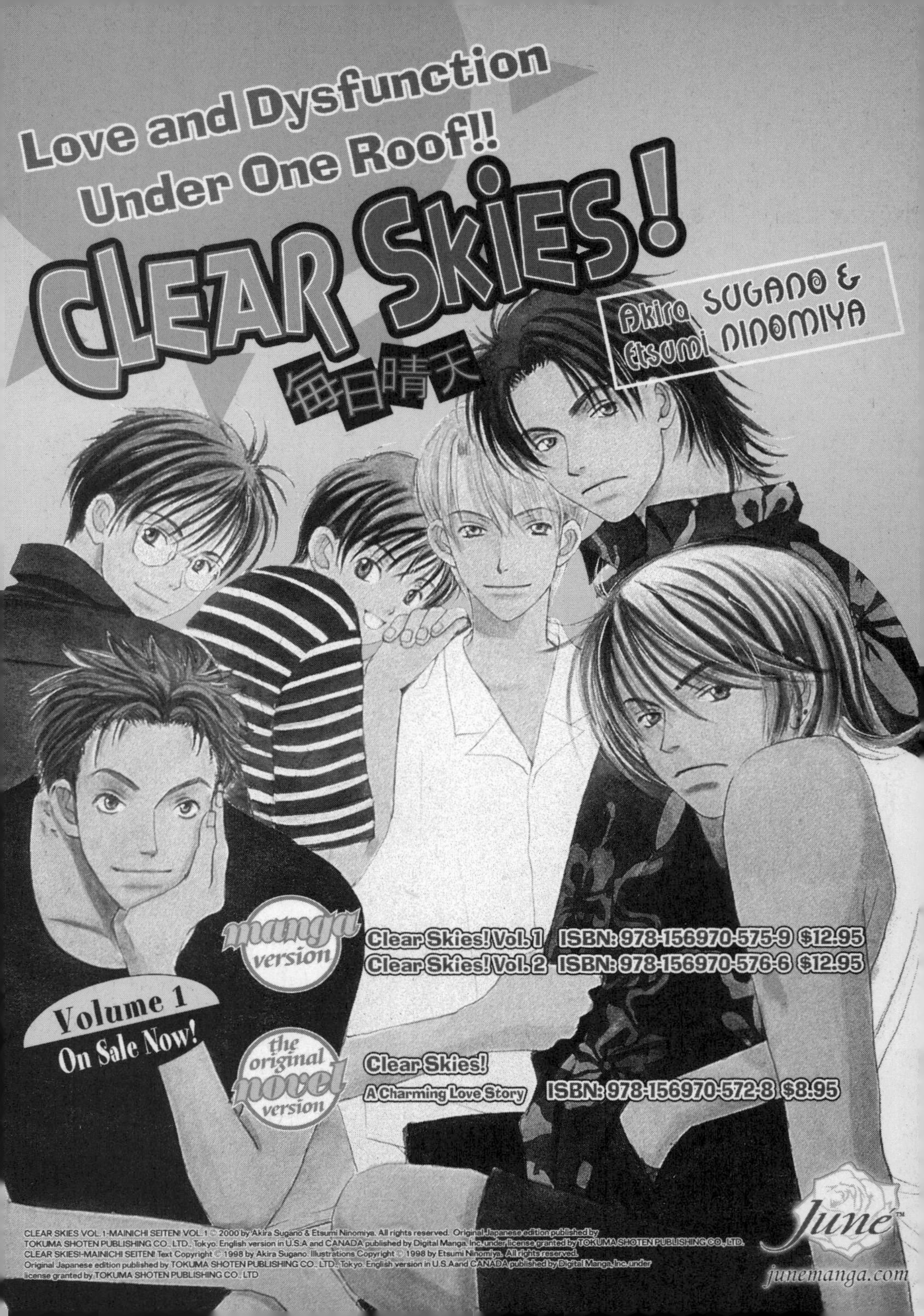
Love and Dysfunction
Under One Roof!!
CLEAR SKIES!
Akira SUGANO &
Etsumi NINOMIYA
毎日晴天
manga version
Clear Skies! Vol. 1 ISBN: 978-156970-575-9 $12.95
Clear Skies! Vol. 2 ISBN: 978-156970-576-6 $12.95
Volume 1
On Sale Now!
the original novel version
Clear Skies!
A Charming Love Story ISBN: 978-156970-572-8 $8.95
CLEAR SKIES VOL. 1-MAINICHI SEITEN! VOL. 1 © 2000 by Akira Sugano & Etsumi Ninomiya. All rights reserved. Original Japanese edition published by TOKUMA SHOTEN PUBLISHING CO., LTD., Tokyo. English version in U.S.A and CANADA published by Digital Manga, Inc. under license granted by TOKUMA SHOTEN PUBLISHING CO., LTD.
CLEAR SKIES!-MAINICHI SEITEN! Text Copyright © 1998 by Akira Sugano. Illustrations Copyright © 1998 by Etsumi Ninomiya. All rights reserved.
Original Japanese edition published by TOKUMA SHOTEN PUBLISHING CO., LTD., Tokyo. English version in U.S.Aand CANADA published by Digital Manga, Inc. under license granted by TOKUMA SHOTEN PUBLISHING CO., LTD
Juné™
junemanga.com

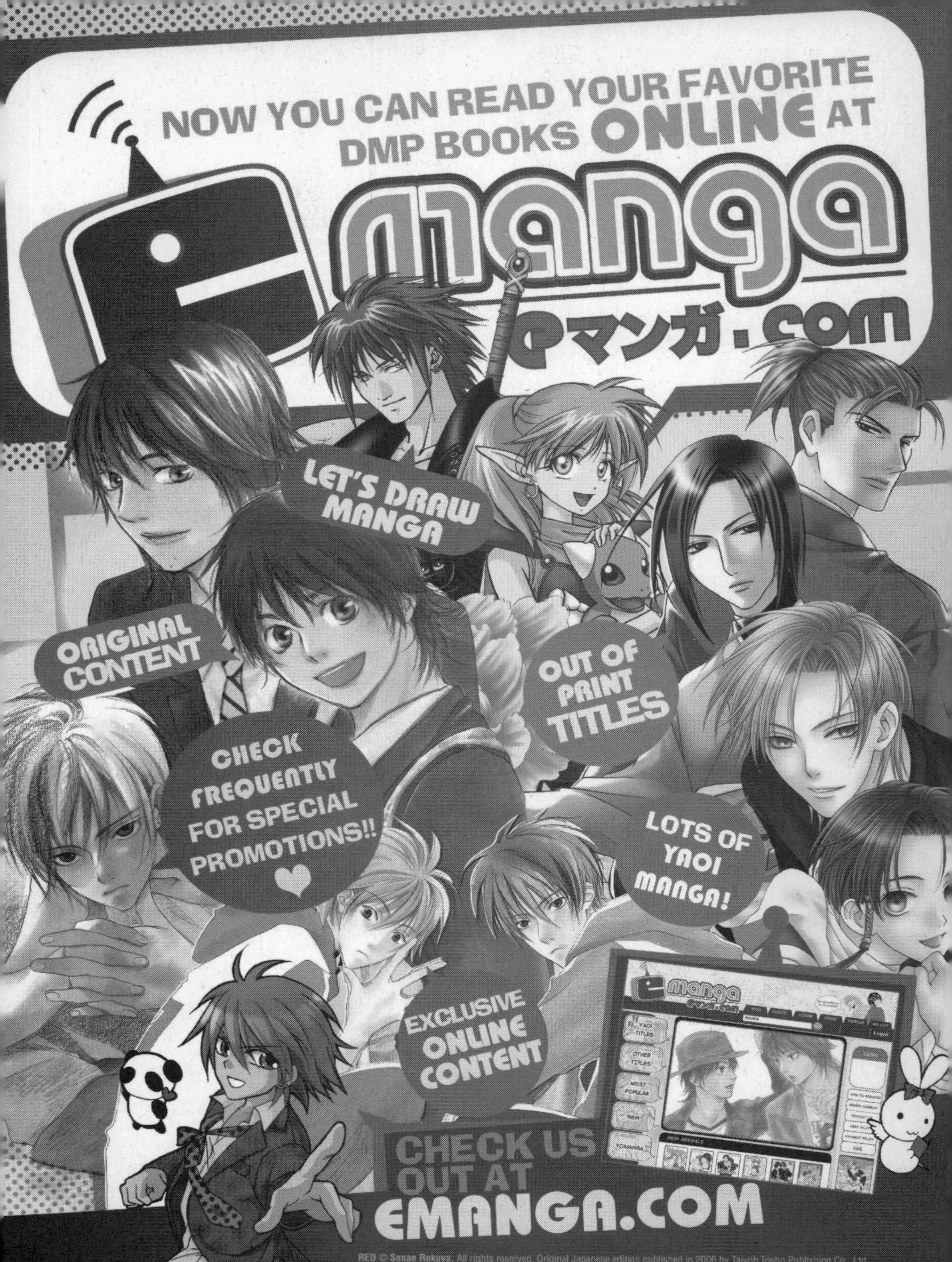
NOW YOU CAN READ YOUR FAVORITE
DMP BOOKS ONLINE AT
emanga
eマンガ.com
LET'S DRAW MANGA
ORIGINAL CONTENT
OUT OF PRINT TITLES
CHECK FREQUENTLY FOR SPECIAL PROMOTIONS!!
LOTS OF YAOI MANGA!
EXCLUSIVE ONLINE CONTENT
CHECK US OUT AT
EMANGA.COM

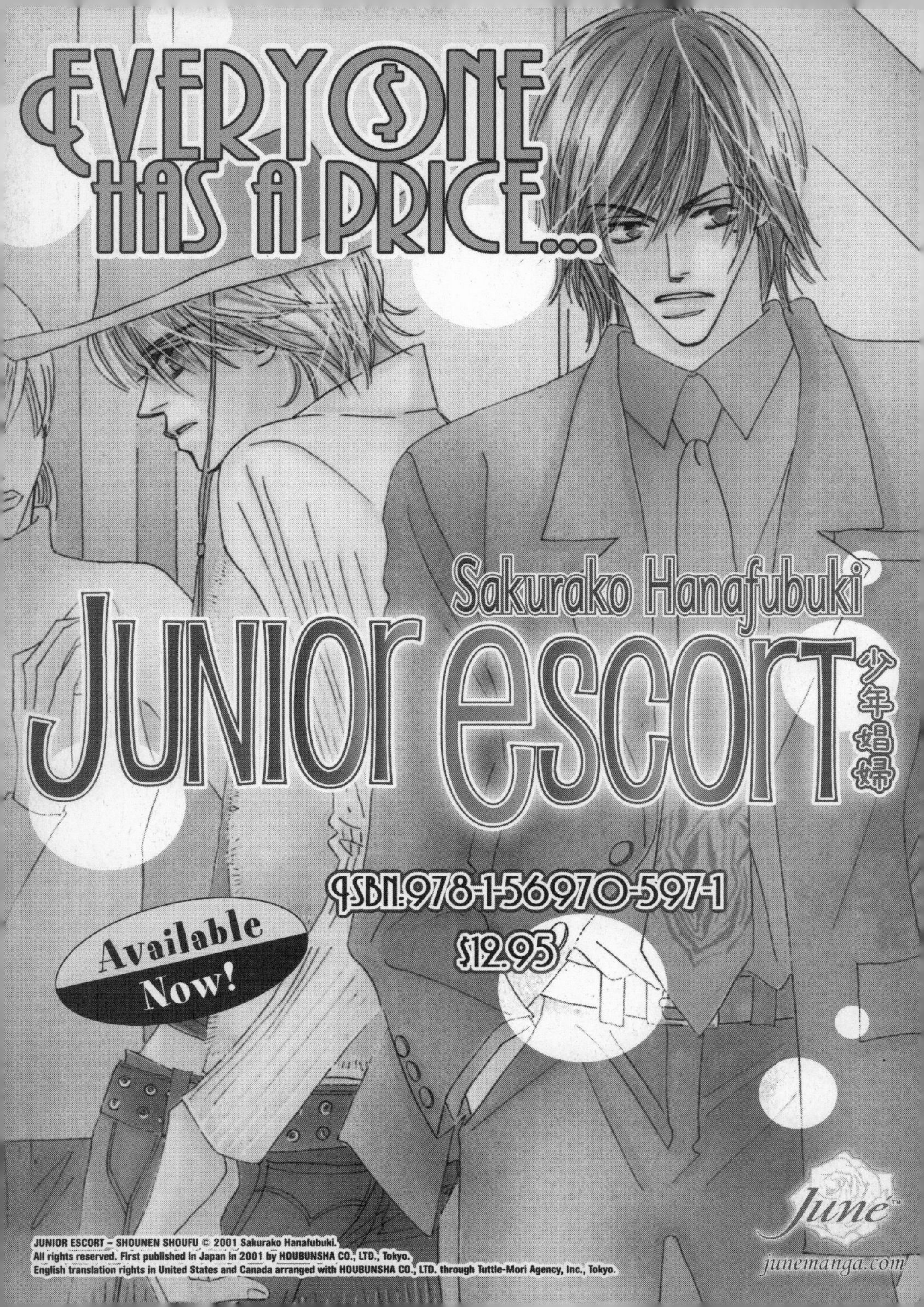
EVERYONE HAS A PRICE...
Sakurako Hanafubuki
JUNIOR escort
少年娼婦
ISBN: 978-1-56970-597-1
$12.95
Available Now!
June™
junemanga.com
JUNIOR ESCORT – SHOUNEN SHOUFU © 2001 Sakurako Hanafubuki.
All rights reserved. First published in Japan in 2001 by HOUBUNSHA CO., LTD., Tokyo.
English translation rights in United States and Canada arranged with HOUBUNSHA CO., LTD. through Tuttle-Mori Agency, Inc., Tokyo.

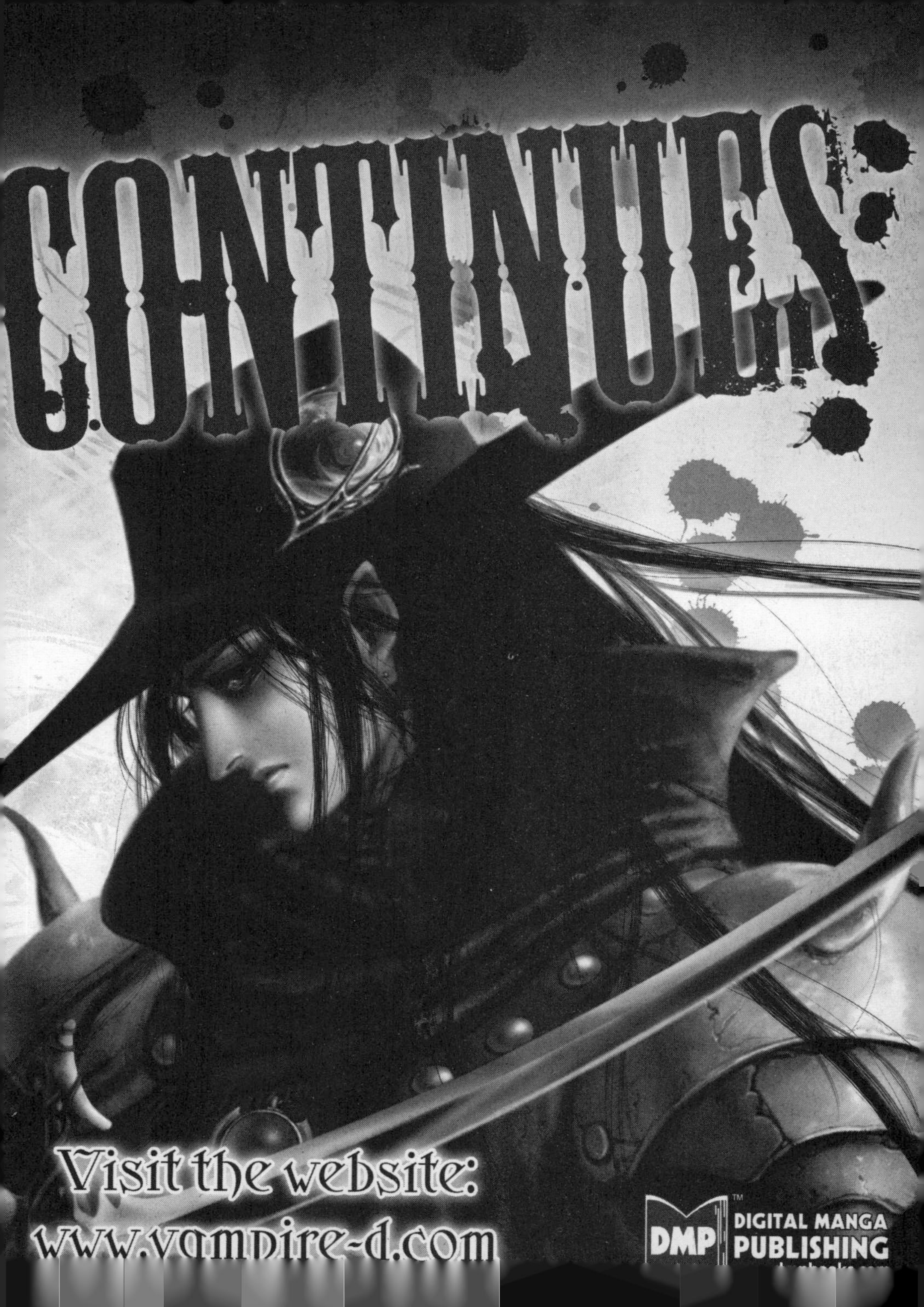
CONTINUES!
Visit the website:
www.vampire-d.com
DMP DIGITAL MANGA PUBLISHING

EVIL REMAINS
THE SAGA

HIDEYUKI KIKUCHI'S
Vampire Hunter D
2

**Volume 2
On Sale Now!**

Volume 1 ISBN: 978-1-56970-827-9 $12.95
Volume 2 ISBN: 978-1-56970-787-6 $12.95

STOP

This is the back of the book! Start from the other side.

NATIVE MANGA readers read manga from *right to left*.

1
2
1
3
2
3
5
4
4
6
5
8
7
6

If you run into our ***Native Manga*** *logo on any of our books... you'll know that this manga is published in it's true original native Japanese right to left reading format, as it was intended. Turn to the other side of the book and start reading from right to left, top to bottom.*

Follow the diagram to see how its done.
Surf's Up!

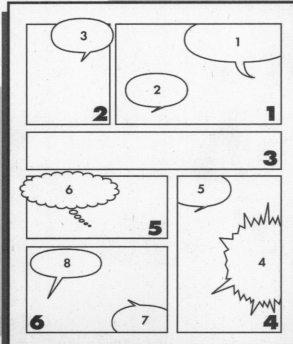

NATIVE MANGA
READ RIGHT TO LEFT